William S. Raikes Hodson, George H. Hodson

## Hodson of Hodson's Horse

Twelve years of a soldier's life in India

William S. Raikes Hodson, George H. Hodson

**Hodson of Hodson's Horse**
*Twelve years of a soldier's life in India*

ISBN/EAN: 9783337017675

Printed in Europe, USA, Canada, Australia, Japan

Cover: Foto ©ninafisch / pixelio.de

More available books at **www.hansebooks.com**

# HODSON OF HODSON'S HORSE

OR

## *TWELVE YEARS OF A SOLDIER'S LIFE IN INDIA*

BEING EXTRACTS FROM THE LETTERS OF THE LATE

### MAJOR W. S. R. HODSON, B.A.

TRINITY COLLEGE, CAMBRIDGE
FIRST BENGAL EUROPEAN FUSILIERS, COMMANDANT OF HODSON'S HORSE

*WITH A VINDICATION FROM THE ATTACKS OF MR. B. SMITH AND MR. HOLMES*

EDITED BY HIS BROTHER

### GEORGE H. HODSON, M.A., F.S.A.

VICAR OF ENFIELD, PREBENDARY OF S. PAUL'S
LATE SENIOR FELLOW OF TRINITY COLLEGE, CAMBRIDGE

New and Cheaper Edition

LONDON
KEGAN PAUL, TRENCH, & CO., 1 PATERNOSTER SQUARE
1889

FRANZ HILL, CAMBERLEY.

DEAR MR. HODSON,—

I am much obliged for the perusal of your Preface to the new Edition of your Memoir of your Brother.

I am now, as I have always been, fully convinced of his honour and integrity.

    Believe me,
        Dear Mr. Hodson,
            Yours very truly,
                NAPIER OF MAGDALA.

*Nov. 4th,* 1883.

## To the Memory

OF

## SIR HENRY LAWRENCE, K.C.B.

THE TRUE CHRISTIAN, THE BRAVE SOLDIER,
THE FAITHFUL FRIEND,
THESE EXTRACTS FROM THE LETTERS OF
ONE WHOM HE TRAINED
TO FOLLOW IN HIS FOOTSTEPS, AND WHO NOW
RESTS NEAR HIM AT LUCKNOW,

## Are Dedicated

BY THE EDITOR.

---

They were lovely and pleasant in their lives,
And in their deaths they were not divided.

# INTRODUCTION:

*Containing a Vindication from the Charges made by Mr. Bosworth Smith in his "Life of Lord Lawrence."*

—o—

IN the Life of Lord Lawrence, which has recently appeared, his biographer has gone out of his way to assail the reputation of a man whose brilliant services and romantic exploits have taken a wonderful hold on the popular mind, and raised him to the position of one of his country's heroes—Hodson, of Hodson's Horse. It is difficult to account for the animosity which Mr. Smith has exhibited towards one with whom he could have had no personal relations. Those who knew Lord Lawrence best felt assured that he would have been the last man to sanction his biography being made the vehicle of so cruel an attack on the memory of a brave soldier long dead, and who had done good service to his country.

Many who were themselves prejudiced against Major Hodson, condemned Mr. Smith's ungenerous conduct, in raking up old scandals without any regard to the feelings of his family and friends. Even if the charges themselves had been true, instead of being, as I hope to show, either utterly unfounded, or gross misrepresentations, the line which Mr. Smith has taken would be quite indefensible.

Not contented with what he could find in the papers and correspondence of Lord Lawrence, he appears to have gone round to those whom he knew to have been ill-affected to Hodson in India, and collected all the stories to his discredit which had ever been circulated, with the embellishments which they had received in passing from one to another during the course of twenty-five or thirty years.

It might have been supposed that at any rate he would have felt bound to be scrupulously accurate in retailing what he heard. So far from it, when I have had access to his sources of information, I have been able to convict him of the grossest exaggerations, and of losing sight of the all-important distinction between the evidence of an eye-witness and mere scandalous report. In one case in which Mr. Smith states that a *"high official of scrupulous accuracy"* had *himself* seen an act of atrocious cruelty committed, which in fact only rested on a story told by a discharged servant and was utterly untrue, he has been obliged, when challenged by me, to modify his statement in a later edition, but without any apology for the slander.

The same entire want of honourable feeling has been shown by Mr. Smith with regard to my refutation of one of his cruellest calumnies, viz., that "Hodson was killed in the act of looting in a house at Lucknow." The evidence which I brought forward of its falsehood was so convincing that he could not resist it, but instead of any expression of regret he aggravated his original offence by a number of insinuations, and by repeating other accusations, which, in due course, I shall prove to be equally unfounded.

He defended himself by saying, "that three highly distinguished officers, who, if they were not eye-witnesses, had at least considerable means of learning the truth, told me independently of each other that he was killed in the act of looting." I wish especially to call attention to this statement, as it throws great light upon the whole subject.

If three distinguished officers, with such opportunities, could have themselves believed, as doubtless they did, and reported to Mr. Smith so outrageous a falsehood as to a simple matter of fact, what weight attaches to the other stories of the same character brought forward by him? May they not all be equally false? Even if they cannot be disproved by such conclusive evidence as in this case, is it not at least probable that they owe their origin to the same source—the malignant invention of a party who, both during the siege of Delhi and afterwards, were bent on ruining my brother's reputation by tales "of envy born," to which others lent too easy a credence?

That such tales were told, and such enmity did exist, is no imagination of mine, as Mr. Smith insinuates. It was well known, as regards Delhi, to such men, for instance, as Colonel Baird Smith, then in command of the Engineers, who in a letter before me, speaking of those stories, says that he is "very sceptical regarding them, as there was certainly a strong party employed in throwing as much moral dirt at him as possible." To the same effect Sir James Outram, shortly after his death, wrote—"I was a great admirer of Hodson, and gave no credit to the stories against him."

I am quite aware of the disadvantages under which I labour in taking up my pen in vindication of my brother. I shall naturally be suspected of undue partiality, and being influenced by fraternal affection, in the view I take. To avoid this suspicion I shall as much as possible use documentary evidence, and quote the opinions of others, not my own. Mr. Smith refers to a Life of my brother which I published some years ago, "doubtless," he says, "in entire ignorance of the facts of the case." I beg to assure him that I was perfectly aware of all that was said then, and of all that Mr. Smith has said now, against him that I investigated, and was able to disprove all the charges on the authority of those who were most intimately acquainted with the facts, when they were fresh in remembrance, especially Sir T. Seaton, who shared his tent during the siege. Many of these, unhappily, are now dead, but some remain: among the foremost, Lord Napier of Magdala. No one knew my brother more intimately. He had been on terms of unbroken friendship with him from the time of his first employment in the Punjab in 1846, till his last hours at Lucknow. To him I am indebted for much valuable assistance in this vindication, to which I shall refer hereafter in detail. I will only quote now his general verdict on Mr. Smith's "shameful publication," as he calls it in a letter to me. "The whole of the paragraphs relating to your brother contained in pages 216-220, vol. ii., appear to me most cruelly unjust. . . . My poor friend Hodson has been greatly misjudged and misrepresented by people who have no knowledge and no cause for malevolence."

There is still another disadvantage in this case. To enter into controversy with one who has all Lord Lawrence's papers at his command, is somewhat akin to arguing with the master of thirty legions. However, I take comfort from the very fact of Mr. Smith's manifest animosity, feeling assured, notwithstanding his hints of what there is behind, that if he could have found anything more unfavourable to my brother in Lord Lawrence's papers he would certainly have published it. Nothing is more remarkable than to find that, with the exception of two or three expressions, the exact weight of which depends very much on the context or on the occasion of writing, no charges are made by Lord Lawrence himself. Mr. Smith is obliged to have recourse for his more serious accusations to his "*distinguished officers*," or to the remembrance of long bygone conversations.

## INTRODUCTION.

Before I proceed to deal more in detail with the counts of Mr. Smith's indictment, a few prefatory remarks may be expedient.

The question may be asked, How came such stories as Mr. Smith has collected against Hodson to have been invented and believed? How came he to have made for himself so many and such bitter enemies? The explanation is not difficult. Partly, doubtless, it was owing to jealousy excited by his rapid promotion over the heads of his seniors in standing, and by the unprecedentedly high position to which as a subaltern he had attained. Human nature is human nature in India as elsewhere. Partly too, and perhaps in great measure, he was himself to blame. I do not at all wish to represent my brother as a faultless character.

Coming out to India at a more advanced age, with greater advantage of education, and greater natural abilities than most of his compeers, he was quite conscious of his superiority, and took no pains to conceal it, but, more especially in his earlier days, was overbearing and unconciliatory. His best and dearest friend, Sir H. Lawrence, was quite aware of his failings in this respect, and in one of his published letters, gives an amusing account of the way in which he would lay down the law. Besides this, he had no toleration for meanness or inefficiency or cowardice in others, and would express himself in language which stung deeply at the time, and was never forgiven. Nor was he less outspoken in criticising the conduct of his superiors, and he thus incurred the enmity of those whom it would have been most his interest to propitiate.

Added to all this, the unhappy differences between Sir H. Lawrence and his brother, which drove Sir Henry from the Punjab, had a most injurious effect on his fortunes.

There was much strong party feeling, and my brother was not a man to conceal his sentiments.

And now to return to Mr. Smith. He says of the shooting of the Shahzadahs:—"The deed was worthy of the man, and the man of the deed" (vol. ii. p. 219).

I accept the words, though in a very different sense from Mr. Smith. *The deed was worthy of the man.* Instead of my own judgment, which is worthless, I will give that of a writer in the *Edinburgh Review*, well known as one of the highest legal authorities of the day:—" No more righteous act was ever done. No history in the world records an instance of more heroic courage."* I may add that of the author of "Tom Brown's School Days," a true representative Englishman:—"As for defending the shooting of the Princes, let those do it who feel that a defence is needed, for we believe that no Englishman worth convincing now doubts as to the righteousness and policy of the act. He who did the deed and is gone cared not for hasty or false tongues. Why should we?"†

Yet Kaye, whom Mr. Smith follows, has the audacity to say that he never in England heard the act approved. " I never heard it even defended," though he is forced to confess, what he could not deny, that "some of the best and wisest of our countrymen in India looked on it with approval," and surely they were the best judges. Sir Robert Montgomery, for example, wrote, on receiving the news:— "My dear Hodson,—All honour to you, and your Horse, for catching the King and slaying his sons." Why, then, is Hodson to be branded as a murderer for that which good and wise men in their calmer judgment approved? Is this justice?

* No. 222, April 1859.
† *Fraser's Magazine*, No. 350, February 1859.

## INTRODUCTION.

There probably never was a more remarkable instance of the power, I may say the fascination, exercised by one man of resolute will over a multitude, than that exhibited in the capture of the Princes by Hodson on September 22, 1857. I am tempted, for the benefit of those who may have forgotten or never seen it, to reproduce the narrative of Lieutenant Macdowell, the only other Englishman present:—

"On the 20th the King gave himself up, and was lodged securely in Delhi under a guard. On this day all had evacuated the place, of which we were complete masters. On the 21st a note from Hodson, 'Come sharp, bring one hundred men.' Off I went; time, six o'clock A.M. He told me he had heard that the three Princes (the heads of the rebellion and sons of the King) were in a tomb six miles off, and he intended going to bring them, and offered me the chance of accompanying him. Wasn't it handsome on his part? Of course I went. We started at about eight o'clock, and proceeded slowly towards the tomb. It is called Humayoon's Tomb, and is an immense building. In it were the Princes and about three thousand Mussulman followers, in the suburb close by about three thousand more, all armed; so it was rather a ticklish bit of work. We halted half a mile from the place, and sent in to say the Princes must give themselves up unconditionally, or take the consequences. A long half-hour elapsed, when a messenger came out to say the Princes wished to know if their lives would be promised them if they came out. 'Unconditional surrender' was the answer. Again we waited. It was a most anxious time. We dared not take them by force, or all would have been lost, and we doubted their coming. We heard the shouts of the fanatics (as we found out afterwards) begging the Princes to lead them on against us. And we had only one hundred men, and were six miles from Delhi. At length, I suppose, imagining that sooner or later they must be taken, they resolved to give themselves up unconditionally, fancying, I suppose, as we had spared the King, we would spare them. So the messenger was sent to say they were coming. We sent ten men to meet them, and by Hodson's order I drew the troop up across the road ready to receive them, and shoot them at once if there was any attempt at a rescue. Soon they appeared in a small 'ruth,' or Hindoostanee cart drawn by bullocks, five troopers on each side. Behind them thronged about two thousand or three thousand (I am not exaggerating) Mussulmans. We met them, and at once Hodson and I rode up, leaving the men a little in the rear. They bowed as we came up, and Hodson, bowing, ordered the driver to move on. This was the minute. The crowd behind made a movement. Hodson waved them back; I beckoned to the troop, which came up, and in an instant formed them up between the crowd and the cart. By Hodson's order I advanced at a walk on the people, who fell back sullenly and slowly at our approach. It was touch-and-go. Meanwhile Hodson galloped back, and told the sowars (ten) to hurry the Princes on along the road, while we showed a front and kept back the mob. They retired on Humayoon's Tomb, and step by step we followed them. Inside they went up the steps, and formed up in the immense garden inside. The entrance to this was through an arch, up steps. *Leaving the men outside, Hodson and myself (I stuck to him throughout), with four men, rode up the steps into the arch, when he called out to them to lay down their arms. There was a murmur. He reiterated the command, and (God knows why, I never can understand it) they commenced doing so.* Now you see we didn't want their arms, and under ordinary circumstances would not have risked our lives in so rash a way, but what we wanted was to gain time to get the

Princes away, for we could have done nothing had they attacked us but cut our way back, and very little chance of doing even this successfully. Well, there we stayed for two hours, collecting their arms, and I assure you I thought every moment they would rush upon us. I said nothing, but smoked all the time, to show I was unconcerned; but at last, when it was all done, and all the arms collected, put in a cart, and started, Hodson turned to me and said, 'We'll go now.' Very slowly we mounted, formed up the troop, and cautiously departed, followed by the crowd. We rode along quietly. You will say, Why did we not charge them? I merely say, we were one hundred men, and they were fully six thousand. I am not exaggerating; the official reports will show you it is all true. As we got about a mile off, Hodson turned to me and said, 'Well, Mac, we've got them at last;' and we both gave a sigh of relief. Never in my life, under the heaviest fire, have I been in such imminent danger. Everybody says it is the most dashing and daring thing that has been done for years (not on my part, for I merely obeyed orders, but on Hodson's, who planned and carried it out). Well, I must finish my story. We came up to the princes, now about five miles from where we had taken them, and close to Delhi. The increasing crowd pressed close on the horses of the sowars, and assumed every moment a more hostile appearance. 'What shall we do with them?' said Hodson to me. 'I think we had better shoot them here; we shall never get them in.'

"We had identified them by means of a nephew of the King's, whom we had with us, and who turned king's evidence. Besides, they acknowledged themselves to be the men. Their names were Mirza Mogul, the King's nephew, and head of the whole business; Mirza Kishere Sultamed, who was also one of the principal rebels, and had made himself notorious by murdering women and children; and Abu Bukt, the commander-in-chief nominally, and heir-apparent to the throne. This was the young fiend who had stripped our women in the open street, and, cutting off little children's arms and legs, poured the blood into their mothers' mouths. This is literally the case. There was no time to be lost. We halted the troop, put five troopers across the road behind and in front. Hodson ordered the Princes to strip and get again into the cart. He then shot them with his own hand. So ended the career of the chiefs of the revolt, and of the greatest villains that ever shamed humanity. Before they were shot, Hodson addressed our men, explaining who they were, and why they were to suffer death. The effect was marvellous; the Mussulmans seemed struck with a wholesome idea of retribution, and the Sikhs shouted with delight, while the mass moved off slowly and silently."

Mr. Smith calls it "a stupid, cold-blooded, threefold murder." I am quite ready to admit that it may have been a fair subject of controversy, on which different opinions may have been held, whether Hodson was justified in shooting the Princes. It was an exceptional act, only to be justified by exceptional circumstances, and of these circumstances no one could judge but himself. At any rate, Mr. Smith was bound to state the facts fairly, but with his usual *animus*, he implies that the excuse of necessity was an after-thought. He says, "*When* Hodson found that the deed was condemned, he attempted to justify it on the plea that he feared an attempt at rescue would be made by the crowd."

Now, what are the facts? So far from it being an after-thought, in a letter to his wife written the very next morning, he says, "I came up just in time, as a large mob had collected and were turning on the guard. I intended to have had them hung, but when it came to a question of 'they' or 'us,' I had no time for deliberation." In another letter of the same date, he says, "We should all have been cut in pieces in another moment;" and, again, a few days later, while still the hero of "the crowning mercy," as some called it, "I am much gratified at the congratulations I receive on all sides regarding the capture of the King and the retribution on the Shahzadahs. Their execution could hardly be called one of unresisting enemies, since we were surrounded by an armed host, to whom we should have been most unquestionably sacrificed if I had hesitated for a moment. It was 'they' or 'we.'"

Sir Hugh Gough, V.C., in a letter just received from him, tells me that he heard both from Macdowell and the native officers that it was a "touch-and-go" affair; that Hodson's own men were wavering; and that nothing but his prompt and decisive action could have saved them. More than this, I afterwards heard from Dr. Anderson, the surgeon to the regiment, that the attack had actually begun. "All I can say is, that I dressed the wounds of my own orderly, who came back with his ear half cut off."

It is very easy for men at a distance, and unacquainted with the circumstances, to sit in judgment and pass sentence. Speaking of the affair afterwards, Hodson said, "I recommend those who might cavil at my choice to go and catch the next rebels themselves."

Mr. Smith, writing in his house at Harrow, with his usual self-confidence expresses his opinion that it would have been quite easy to carry the Princes in safety into Delhi. The leader of "Hodson's Horse" on the spot thought it impossible. With the same self-confidence, he takes upon himself to assert that there was no evidence worthy of the name of the Princes' guilt. Here, again, some may be inclined to believe that Hodson, who as head of the Intelligence Department had more accurate information than any other man of what was going on in Delhi, and was said in camp to know every day what the King had for dinner, may have been a better judge of the evidence than Mr. Smith, not to mention that the facts were notorious, and that the Princes owned their identity.

Mr. Smith does not appear to see that in his anxiety to prove Hodson guilty of murder, he overshoots his mark. If the deed were cold-blooded murder, then all the authorities, civil and military, including his own hero, Lord Lawrence, were accessories before or after the fact.

Hodson ought to have been tried by court-martial and dismissed the service at least. Was anything of the kind done? Was there any official expression of disapproval? Nothing of the kind. He was called to account officially for sparing the King's life, but never for shooting the Princes. So far from it, he had congratulations on all sides. I have already quoted Sir R. Montgomery's letter: Sir A. Wilson, to whom blame, if blame there were, would have attached, for he had stipulated that he was not to be bothered with them, in a letter which I have seen, after mentioning that the Princes were shot, so far from expressing censure, goes on, "Hodson, as a partisan officer, has no equal."

Afterwards, when all resistance had ceased, and undoubtedly great severities were practised on the natives without sufficient justification, the tide of feeling began to turn. No distinction was made between such acts done in cold blood and one totally different in character done by a man who had taken his life in his hand.

Again Mr. Smith, following the lead of Kaye and Malleson, endeavours to fasten on Hodson the charge of being bloodthirsty, and "as much a stranger to pity as a tiger with his prey in his talons" (*sic*), on the strength of certain expressions in his letters, such as, "I am not cruel, but I confess I did rejoice at the opportunity of ridding the earth of these wretches."

But surely in judging a man's words the circumstances under which they were spoken or written ought to be taken into account. I do not suppose that there was a man in the army before Delhi who would not have felt the same. Malleson's own words afford the best justification—"The cries of helpless women and children, ruthlessly butchered, had gone home to the heart of every individual soldier, and made their cause his own. There was not an Englishman in those ranks, from first to last, who would have consented to turn his back on Delhi without having assisted in meting out to those bloody rebels the retributive justice awarded them by his own conscience, his country, and his God." *

Why, in the name of justice, is Hodson to be condemned for that which is deemed worthy of praise in others? There was no one who had a fuller knowledge of the atrocities committed by the rebels, and especially by their leaders, the Princes. He had not only public but private wrongs to avenge, for some of his dearest friends had fallen victims. Why, then, is he to be singled out for execration because he expressed his satisfaction at the punishment of such wretches?

So far from being by nature cruel or bloodthirsty, those who study his letters will come to the same conclusion as that arrived at by Dr. Russell of the *Times*, that "he was of a humane and clement disposition, but firm in the infliction of deserved punishment."

Mr. Smith, in his anxiety to throw dirt at Hodson, is not ashamed to repeat the stupid slander, originally of French

* Malleson, vol. ii. p. 85.

origin, that in ordering the Princes to strip he had an eye to their clothes as booty. It may be enough to say in reply, on evidence that cannot be gainsayed, that whatever the value of the garments may have been—and they were of no value at all—they were left behind.

I do not expect to convince Mr. Smith, of whom it may be said, with equal justice as of Colonel Malleson, by his reviewer in the *Times*, " His mind has evidently been poisoned by those who, envious of Hodson's glory, were base enough for that reason to pursue him with their rancour even beyond the tomb, or by those strange philanthropists who prefer every race to their own;" but I do expect that every unbiassed reader will agree with the same reviewer, "that Hodson deserved honour instead of censure for his act."

I proceed now to examine in order the several counts of Mr. Smith's indictment against *the man who had done the deed.*

1. " During his visit in early times with Sir Henry Lawrence to Cashmere, his management of the public purse, which had been intrusted to him, and his money dealings with the native merchants, had been of such a character that Sir H. Lawrence lost all faith in his personal integrity, and told his most intimate friends so" (vol. ii. p. 219).

And in another place, " Hodson's daring and unscrupulous character came out at every step of the journey" (vol. i. p. 358.)

Now, let us hear Sir Henry's own account of the matter in a letter to his brother, Sir George, published in his Life:—

"I have had a very nice tour with Hodson, who makes a good travelling companion, energetic, clever, and well-informed. I don't know why you did not take to him at Peshawur. He has his faults, positiveness and self-will among them, but it is useful for us to have companions who contradict us, and keep us in mind that we are not Solomons."

So far from having lost all faith in him, Sir Henry continued not only to write *to* him in the most affectionate terms, though never hesitating to tell him of his faults, but wrote *of* him to others with strong commendation, and did everything in his power to promote his interests. It was by his influence that the command of the Guides was given to him two years afterwards in 1852. No one who knows anything of Sir Henry's high and honourable character will for one moment believe that this would have been the case had he lost faith in his integrity.

I quote in preference to any private letters one written by him to Lord Hardinge in July 1853, and published in his Life.

"The Guide Corps which you raised at my request has held its ground as the best irregular corps in India. The present commander is a young fellow, Hodson by name, whom you gave me at Lahore in 1847. He is a first-rate soldier, and as your Lordship likes young officers in command, I beg to bring him to your notice for a brevet-majority. Sir Charles Napier thinks highly of him, and I believe held out hopes of the rank. Hodson is a most ambitious and most gallant fellow, and very able in all departments. He was through both the Sikh campaigns, in the latter with the Guides."

In another published letter he says to Sir J. Kaye: "I was very fortunate in my assistants, all of whom were my friends, and almost every one introduced into the Punjab through me.

"George Lawrence, Macgregor, Edwardes, Lumsden, Nicholson, Taylor, Cocks, Hodson, &c., are such men as you will seldom see anywhere; but when collected under one administration were worth double and treble the number taken at haphazard. Each was a good man. The most were excellent officers."

The slight foundation of truth on which Mr. Smith has raised his fabric of calumny is this:—

During the visit to Cashmere, Lieutenant Hodson, carried away, I suppose, by a visitor's enthusiasm, ordered two expensive shawls to be made for him. When some time afterwards they arrived, he was not in a position to pay for them, and as they could not be returned, he sent them to England to be sold, that with the proceeds he might pay the merchants. Unfortunately from some miscarriage there was considerable delay, and meanwhile the merchants applied to Sir H. Lawrence, who was naturally much annoyed, and, I have no doubt, made use of strong language to Lieutenant Hodson, as he often did. Of course, I do not wish to defend Lieutenant Hodson from the charge of thoughtlessness and extravagance, but surely such a piece of indiscretion in a young subaltern ought not to brand a man's character for life with dishonesty, or to be brought forward, as it has been, many years after a glorious career is closed. As to Hodson's *unscrupulous character coming out at every step* of the journey, I have ascertained from Mr. Smith's informant that this is only a piece of fine writing, founded on no fact, but betraying Mr. Smith's *animus*. I can only say with regard to the whole charge, that if Sir Henry Lawrence, in consequence of this visit, lost faith in my brother, his whole conduct belied his belief. His two most intimate friends, and those to whom he would naturally most often speak of him, Lord Napier of Magdala, and Sir R. Montgomery, have both assured me that they never heard any intimation of the sort, nor did his brother-in-law, the Rev. J. Knox Marshall, with whom to the last he most constantly corresponded in England. So far from it, that he wrote in indignation at the accusation: "I well remember the way in which Sir Henry used to write respecting your noble and distinguished brother. Among the many whose character for honour, bravery, and courage those trying times developed, no one stood higher, few so high."

I may also remark, that if it were true that Sir Henry had been estranged from him, it is very remarkable that my brother himself should have had no suspicion of the fact, but continued to write and speak of him as his best and dearest friend, and to mourn his loss as a father.

With regard to another story which was circulated, that Hodson had borrowed money of the Maharajah or his Dewan, I am authorised by Lord Napier to say that he himself inquired of the Dewan, and found that the story was utterly untrue.

2. Again Mr. Smith writes, "In later years his management of the accounts of the regiment had given rise (as I have shown elsewhere) to grave suspicions of a similar kind, to which colour is given by many letters which lie before me" (vol. ii. p. 219).

And in another place—

"Soon other and more painful questions came to the front connected with the account-books of his regiment. . . . The court of inquiry, after protracted examination, arrived at conclusions which were very unfavourable to Hodson's character" (vol. i. p. 430).

The facts so far are correctly stated, but Mr. Smith has dealt with them in a way which entirely destroys his claim to be considered as an impartial historian. He has suppressed other facts, of which he was fully aware, which had a most material bearing on the subject; and, in so doing, he has done his best to justify the complaints, which I made some years ago in my memoir of my brother, of the unfair treatment which he had experienced. Mr. Smith forgets to state that Lieutenant Hodson appealed against the verdict of the court of inquiry, on the ground that it had been given on *ex parte* evidence, and that he had not had the opportunity of producing his accounts; that after some delay the Punjab Government ordered a second inquiry, which was intrusted to one of the most competent and high-minded officers in the service, Major (now General) Reynell Taylor, who, after a patient and minute investigation, drew up a report completely vindicating Lieutenant Hodson on all the charges. A printed copy of this report, addressed to the Military Secretary of the Chief Commissioner, Lahore, lies before me. It is too long and technical to reproduce *in extenso*. It begins, "I have the honour to report that the result of my examination of Lieutenant Hodson's accounts has been quite satisfactory;" and concludes, "If I have entered into more details than was absolutely necessary, I am sure that the fact of Lieutenant Hodson's honesty and honour having been assailed with regard to his regimental accounts, and my examination of the case having convinced me that there was nothing whatever in the accounts to afford grounds for the imputation, and, moreover, that he had unusual difficulties to contend with, will sufficiently account for my doing my best to show that I have demonstrable grounds for the opinions I have formed."

The difficulties here alluded to with which my brother had to contend were of no ordinary kind. His predecessor in the command had gone home, leaving the accounts in confusion. There had been no settlement between them, and within twenty-four hours of his taking the command, my brother had started on a campaign which lasted between six and seven weeks. Further than this, as Lord Napier of Magdala has explained to me, he was engaged in building a fort, and in his anxiety to get his men under cover before the rains—not being able to get the requisite advances from the engineering department—he had borrowed from the regimental chest for the pay of the workmen, which introduced an additional element of confusion. "It is impossible," to use Lord Napier's words, "for those who remain quietly in stations with efficient establishments to make allowance for the difficulties and irregularities entailed by rapid movements on service, and want of proper office means in adjusting accounts for which no organised system had been established."

It was thirteen months after the conclusion of the first court of inquiry before Major Taylor's report was made, and for the whole of that time Lieutenant Hodson had been suspended from his duties, and had lain under the imputation of malversation. Only those who knew him intimately maintained their confidence in his honour and uprightness. It can easily be understood what an opportunity was thus given to his enemies of assailing his reputation. They had succeeded in their immediate object of getting rid of him, and were not backward in following up their success.

But this is not all. Major Taylor's official report, which so completely cleared him from the grievous and unjust imputations which during that time had been cast upon him, and which Sir R. Montgomery declared most triumphant, was in some way or other suppressed.

Whether it was that those in authority did not think it convenient to publish it, or whether the delay was owing to the ordinary workings of red-tape in the wanderings of the document from one office to another, the fact is certain that my brother thus suffered a most grievous wrong.

The report was presented to the Commissioner at Lahore

in February 1856. In April 1857 my brother ascertained from General Anson himself, then Commander-in-Chief, that he had not seen it, though the result of the first court had been communicated to him. And in the same month, Mr. Edmonstone, Secretary to Government, informed Colonel Douglas Seaton, who called on him at Calcutta, that the report had never been submitted to Government, who had no official knowledge of it, and that he had not seen it himself. Colonel Seaton then presented him with a copy, and with good results; for I heard in August 1858 from Mr. Bowring, then private secretary to Lord Canning, "Colonel Birch, the military secretary, informs me that Major Taylor's report was of essential service towards clearing up the cloud which rested on Hodson's transactions. Government adopted it as satisfactory, and the investigation terminated. Lord Dunkellin, through whose hands the paper passed, expressed himself strongly in favour of your brother."

Probably, if my brother's life had been spared, full and public justice would have been done him, and it would have been impossible for such charges to have been raked up again as they have been. But unhappily, after his death, though his brilliant services were fully recognised, no steps were taken to obtain a public acknowledgment of his justification.

In order to show that I have not overstated the injury done to my brother's reputation by the suppression of Major Taylor's report, I will here give an extract from a letter written to me by the Rev. C. Sloggett, formerly chaplain at Dugshai, on the appearance of Mr. Smith's book:—

"Early in April 1857, Hodson called upon me at Dugshai, where I was chaplain, and after telling me of the harshness and injustice with which he had been treated, requested me to read a statement which he had drawn up respecting his case, embodying Major Taylor's report.

"I was so much impressed by the clearness and force of this important document, that I offered to show it to my dear friend, Colonel Chester, then Adjutant-General, with whom I was to stay a few days at Simla. He kindly looked over it at my earnest request, and while doing this, the Judge-Advocate-General, Colonel Keith-Young, came into the room and took part in the conversation. He too, like many men who have made the reputation and greatness of our Indian Government, was possessed of the highest honour and integrity, and at first he spoke to me with scorn respecting the case; the whole matter he said had passed under his own review ere it had been submitted to Government, and the verdict of the court was amply justified by the evidence produced.

"But here Colonel Chester interposed by telling him of this new light thrown upon it, and I left them to go through it together. When they had done so, they were evidently much impressed by it. Colonel Chester promised to show it at once to the Commander-in-Chief, General Anson, and Keith-Young thanked me very earnestly for bringing it under his notice. From that time Keith-Young became one of Hodson's warmest friends, and General Anson was prevailed on by both of them to give him another appointment. Then, of course, the idea only was that he should write on the matter to Lord Canning, which I believe he did, but the letter was lost in transmission through the sudden outbreak of the rebellion.

"It was, I think, just a week after I spoke to them that the mutiny broke out at Meerut, and for months afterwards there was no direct postal communication with Calcutta. General Anson, therefore, gave Hodson a staff appointment on his own responsibility, and he soon justified the selection, for it is doubtful if there was another man in the whole army who could have supplied his place."

I have dwelt the more on this subject as it is essential to a proper understanding of the readiness, on the part of many who did not know him intimately, to believe the ill-natured stories which his enemies circulated.

During the whole time of the siege of Delhi, though he held important commands, there had been no public vindication of his character from the stigma cast on it at Peshawur by the court of inquiry, followed by his removal from his command, and I believe that to this day many are ignorant—as Mr. Smith would wish them to remain—that the verdict of 1856 was so triumphantly set aside.

In order that it may not be supposed that in my view of my brother's character, and of the cruel treatment to which he was subject, I am biassed by affection, I have permission to publish a letter written from Gwalior in 1859 by Lord Napier of Magdala, on the receipt of a copy of "Twelve Years of a Soldier's Life in India," which I sent to him:—

"Every one here was enthusiastic about your poor brother, who is regarded as a hero. Had he had opportunities, his military qualities were of such an order as must have gained him the highest fame and eminence had his career been prolonged.

"There are in your memoir of him opinions regarding the persecution which your brother underwent, and the persons who were concerned in it, which would of course raise the opposition and criticism of all who are concerned with them. But the book will live and be read with admiration—regretful admiration—of the character it describes, long after the detractors shall have been forgotten. . . . I should be very sorry to say that those concerned in the press upon him did not think they were doing their duty. I am very sure some did, and it was one of the sources of my deepest distress that I was *forced* to judge so harshly of the conduct of some whom I had so many reasons to regard; but I feel sure that the more that may be known of the particulars of the case, the more will judgment hereafter decide in favour of your brother, and admiration of the fortitude with which he bore such searching trials and punishments, the heroic courage with which he addressed himself to labour in a comparatively humble position, and to show his value as strongly there as in his former high post.

"Nothing made me feel more for him than this, and I wonder that it did not disarm hostility. God knows! perhaps it did."

3. Another count is this, "In the year 1855 he was deliberately deprived by Lord Dalhousie of all his appointments in the Punjab for his outrageous treatment of a native chief."

True as to the fact, though "outrageous" is due to Mr. Smith; but it must be remembered that, as Hodson always maintained, he was condemned unheard, on the one-sided representations of an official superior, who had made no secret of his wish and determination to get rid of him from Eusofzai, and that the attack was made upon him at a time when he could least defend himself, and when his case was prejudiced by the unfounded charge with regard to his regimental accounts.

At the worst, he was only guilty of an error of judgment. He had what he thought most convincing evidence that a native chief, Kader Khan, was implicated in the assassination of Colonel Mackeson, and in the unsuccessful attempt some months later on Lieutenant Godby, and he had in consequence arrested him and kept him some time in prison. However, when brought to trial before the Chief Commissioner, he was acquitted, which no more proved his innocence than an acquittal of a Fenian by an Irish jury. Still Hodson had to bear the blame of an unjust prosecution, and this was seized on as a reason for his dismissal.

He continued, however, in common with others, to believe in Kader Khan's guilt, as appears from a letter written afterwards:—" Since Kader Khan has been out of jail, there has been a renewal of the former state of uneasiness and excitement, and his people and emissaries are most active in intrigue. Tell Godby to look out for his friend, if he is really at Murree, and to remember that whatever Major Edwardes or any one else may say to the contrary, Kader Khan, and no one else, was the author of the attack on him last December."

I can quite believe that Hodson's restless energy, outspoken criticism, and hatred to red-tape regulations, made him troublesome at times to his official superiors, and I am far from supposing that he was always free from error in his dealings with the wild and savage tribes of the frontier. He could be severe, when severity was the truest mercy, with those who required a mailed hand, and not a silken glove; but that he was cruel I utterly deny.

The kind of men with whom he had to deal may best be seen from Lord Lawrence's own letters. One of the complaints made against him when in command of the Guides was, that he was getting rid of his native officers. Hear Lord Lawrence's own account of one of these, Futteh Khan: "I look upon him as a perfect devil when his blood is up, and that is very often. At such a moment he would murder his nearest and dearest relative or friend."

However unpopular he may have made himself with such characters, he had the power of inspiring enthusiastic attachment and devotion on the part both of officers and men. Sir R. Temple, in the *Calcutta Review*, describes him "as marvellously attaching the Guides to himself by the ties of mutual honour, mutual daring, and mutual devotion."

The reception given to him by his old regiment on their arrival at Delhi sufficiently proved to those who saw it that the charge of unpopularity which had been brought against him was utterly without foundation.

The following words of an officer of Hodson's Horse, written after his death (and I have many others to the same effect), exhibit in a striking manner the feeling entertained towards him:—" Allow me to tell you that we, who have served with him through so many dangers, felt his loss like that of a brother. His was the influence that kept us together, and since he has passed away from us we have all broken up, and another officer and I are the only two in the regiment that have served with him at all, and I am about to leave also. Had he lived it would have been otherwise."

4. I proceed to another count:—" Hodson himself was everywhere to be seen appropriating vast stores of valuables, which were revealed for the first time, in their collective form, to the eyes of those whose painful duty it was to open his boxes after he had met his death at Lucknow" (vol. ii. p. 246).

I will deal with the last part of this charge first, "*the vast stores of valuables*" found in his boxes after his death.

Probably Mr. Smith would picture to himself several vans going about with Hodson laden with spoils. I must disabuse his mind and the minds of his readers.

I have unexpectedly been able to recover the original report of the proceedings of the Committee of Adjustment (which, as usual in the case of a deceased officer, was formed to settle Major Hodson's affairs), signed by the president, now Sir Charles Gough, V.C., K.C.B. To this is attached an inventory of every article in my brother's possession at his death, even to his brushes and sponge.

The effects of the deceased, as Sir C. Gough stated at the

time in a letter to his widow, were opened and examined in the quarters of General, now Lord Napier, who is alive to give evidence. Sir C. Gough is also alive, and can be referred to for the truth of my statement. I have just received a letter from him in India, in which he expresses his indignation at the slanderous attacks made by Mr. Smith, which, he says, "show such animosity and hatred that I cannot but think they will defeat the object of the writer, for they are more likely to rouse a feeling of sympathy."

It appears from the proceedings of the committee that, with the exception of a few memorials, such as his ring, watch, Bible and Prayer-book, and a miniature, &c., which at General Napier's request were handed over to him for the widow, all Major Hodson's effects were sold by auction, and that the whole, exclusive of his horses, consisting of tents, a gig, camp equipage, guns (one rifle valued at £35), swords, telescope, saddles and bridles, &c., realised the sum of R.1774, or less than £170. The only article found in his possession which could possibly have come under the head of "loot" was a native ornament of some flat stones set in silver, worth a few rupees at most, which had probably, as would appear from his letters, been bought from a sowar. This represents "the vast stores of valuables in their *collective form.*"

. 5. After this specimen of the veracity of Mr. Smith or his informers, my readers will probably not attach much weight to his assertion that at Delhi *Hodson was everywhere to be seen appropriating vast stores, &c.*

The following correspondence, however, may throw some light on the origin of such stories. I will only premise that Hodson, as Intelligence officer, was necessarily intrusted with very large discretionary powers, and that in the exercise of them he was peculiarly liable to misrepresentation on the part of those who, as I have already proved, were watching for every opportunity of "throwing dirt at him."

"CAMP, DELHI, *September* 30, 1857.

"MY DEAR GENERAL,—I must confess that I am very much hurt at an order being issued, which conveys a certain amount of censure, before I had an opportunity of explaining matters or replying to the charges which seem to have been brought against me. It would have been more manly had these gentlemen waited till my return, or spoken out before I left Delhi; but it is always safer to accuse a man behind his back. I shall hope to see you when I have got my camp pitched and convince you of the utter falsehood of the stories which have been invented to my prejudice. To the best of my memory and belief, I have neither acted without orders or authority, nor protected any one without permission, and most certainly I have protected no property or houses *from* the prize agents, although I have protected much *for* them at Colonel Seaton's request.—Believe me, my dear General, yours sincerely,   W. S. R. HODSON."

*N.B.*—This Colonel Seaton afterwards fully confirmed.

To which the General replies the same day:—

"MY DEAR HODSON,—I had hoped I had worded the order so that not a particle of censure could be conveyed by it. The charges made against you were by a rascally inhabitant of the city, and I did not therefore believe them. Colonel Seaton never mentioned to me that he had asked you to protect houses; hence the mistake. The enclosed is dated September 14, and must, I think, have been given without authority.—Yours sincerely,   A. WILSON."

Writing two days later, my brother says: " I had a long

talk with the General yesterday, and satisfied him that —— had imposed on him in saying that I had acted without authority. He produced two papers signed by me which, he thought, I had given 'on my own hook;' but, fortunately, I was able to show that he had himself given me the orders to that effect, and that I had written the papers under positive instructions, so that all is clear. But since —— assumed the government, I have experienced difficulties in carrying out my duties, and a system of backbiting and insinuation has commenced."

Amongst the other *canards* circulated was one that he had been bribed by the King of Delhi to spare his life, and others equally monstrous.

I am again indebted to the Rev. C. Sloggett for the following narrative, to the accuracy of which he is prepared to make affidavit. It illustrates the kind of misrepresentations to which he was exposed, and the readiness on the part of many to give credence to them.

Mr. Sloggett says—"Not long after the fall of Delhi, Captain Wriford of Hodson's regiment (1st B. F.) came up to the station of Dugshai, where I was still living. In course of conversation, I asked him how Hodson was getting on; when he said, 'Capitally, I think; but it is wonderful how ready people are to say things against him.' He went on to tell me that in the previous week the General (Sir A. Wilson) had ordered him to go with a company to Hodson's lines and take possession of the regimental treasure chest, and bring it to head-quarters. Hodson himself had been a few days absent on one of his expeditions; but on the morning of the day he left, it had been noticed that twenty troopers of his regiment had brought from the house of a native banker a bag each of 500 rupees, or 10,000 rupees in all, in exchange for an order signed by Hodson releasing him from the liability of having his premises searched for plunder. Inquiries had been made which proved that this sum had not been paid over to the prize agents, and therefore it was assumed that he meant to keep the money. On his way, Wriford met Hodson coming to report himself to the General, and on hearing his errand, Hodson induced him to return with him. On hearing his report, the General burst forth into warmest acclamations of praise. 'If I had many like you,' he said, 'we should soon see the country settled quietly down.' Hodson's reply was, 'Now, sir, I beg you to place me under arrest;' at the same time unbuckling and laying down his sword. The General, astonished, asked what he meant, when he alluded to the order just before given to Wriford. 'Oh,' said the General, 'I had forgotten all about it; yes, I am very sorry, but I was obliged to issue it, because you had signed a release from search to the banker, which no one knew anything about, save that you must have had 10,000 rupees for giving it.' Hodson opened his sabretasch and held out the order for him to do this, signed by the General, and then he showed the second order which had taken him off an hour after on the emergent expedition from which he had that moment returned. The General expressed the deepest contrition; said he believed his mind was going; he could remember nothing from hour to hour, and so on, asked Hodson to forgive him and take up his sword again and continue to give him the benefit of his invaluable services. But (Wriford continued in his story to me), 'would you believe it? This thing is still brought up against him. Some men envy and dislike him so much, they really don't care what they say.'"

As a further illustration of my brother's statement to General Wilson that he had protected much property *for* the prize agents and not *from* them, I will quote one or two passages from amongst many in his private letters, which will show how much prize-money passed through his hands, and how easy it was for maliciously-minded persons to misrepresent his actions :—"Khuda Bux brings me untold money and bullion which he digs up, and is very indignant because I insist on its being handed over to the prize agents." "I have annexed six chests of indigo, worth about 1000 rupees, and I believe have done as much for prize-money as any man, and shall get little or nothing." "We have added a little to the store of 'loot,' 2000 rupees in coin and silver, and seventeen chests of indigo, which ought really to be mine; but of course they go to swell the prize-money."

It may perhaps interest Mr. Smith to have an authentic catalogue of the *vast stores of valuables* which he was supposed to have looted at Delhi.

On October 2 he writes to his wife—"I have to-day packed up a lot of odds and ends to go to Umballa, and will send them to you. Bows and arrows; the king's silver stick (bamboo overlaid with silver); ivory ditto; Cashmere rug; some silver bits, and odds and ends and curiosities; beads and rosaries; two little silver boxes, with bits of Koran in them; lots of silk and gold thread; a pugree, some muslin, and a fur coat. There's a lot of rubbish for you."

I suppose that no one would grudge Hodson the arms, &c., taken with the King, though, according to strict interpretation, they might be considered loot. *He* thought them legitimate spoils of war, and General Wilson and his officers recognised the claim. The General, in a letter to his wife, says:—"Hodson has presented me with the King's sword and dagger and matchlock. I wish I could send them to you." Not only so, but the Queen was graciously pleased to accept two swords of historic value, now at Windsor Castle. The King's shield of steel, damascened with gold, he retained, and it is now in his widow's possession. I have heard of its being gravely asserted, quite recently, by *an eye-witness*, that it was of solid gold.

6. Another story told by Mr. Smith is this:—

"In his brilliant raids after Delhi had fallen, he (Hodson) harried the cattle of the neighbouring tribes with perfect impartiality, sold many of them for his own benefit, and with the proceeds bought a house at Umballa, which became known as the Cow-house, a sufficient indication of the belief which the people who knew him had formed of his integrity" (vol. ii. p. 419).

Here there is a substratum of truth, but just enough to make the calumny the greater and more unjustifiable on Mr. Smith's part, who might have known better. What really occurred was this. When attached to Brigadier Showers's column, which was employed in quieting the country, Hodson had captured and brought into camp a large quantity of cattle, nearly 1700. The General on seeing them was in dismay, and exclaimed, "Hang me! what in the world am I to do with them? I cannot be encumbered with them;" and, as he told Lord Napier afterwards, was never more relieved than when Hodson said, "Sell them to me and I will take my chance." So the bargain was struck for 2 rupees 4 annas a head, and they were sent off under the charge of two or three of Hodson's troopers, and then driven to Delhi, where, contrary to all expectation, they arrived safely, and were sold at a very large profit, out of which he bought, at a ridiculously low price, owing to the state of panic at Umballa, a house which had been worth 20,000 rupees. Mr. Smith will be sorry to hear that the name Cowhouse was given by Hodson himself as a joke, as appears from a letter written by him, at the time, in high glee at the result of his speculation. I have before me the original receipt given to my brother by the prize agent for R.3417, 12, the price of 1519 horned cattle at 2r. 4a. per head: 148 goats were retained. I have also the authority of Sir Donald Stewart, now Commander-in-Chief in India, for saying that there was nothing secret or underhand in the transaction.

There can be no doubt, however, but that the purchase of this house, as well as that of a carriage and horses which he bought at about the same time for his wife, at an equal depreciation, were seized upon as a proof that he had made money by looting. Many other equally unfounded calumnies were put in circulation at the time, to some of which he refers in his letters to his wife:—

"A report has reached me from Simla that you have got some magnificent diamond rings, &c., taken at Delhi. This is rather good, considering that the only rings I sent you were the Princes', and not worth twenty rupees altogether, and the only diamonds were in that little brooch I bought from a sowar more than a month before Delhi was taken. So much for the veracity of our good-natured friends."

It can scarcely be necessary to say more on this subject after so completely refuting all the charges which have taken any specific form; but as I know that there is an impression amongst many who have never taken the trouble to ascertain the facts, that my brother enriched himself by plunder, it may not be amiss to ask the pertinent question, If so, what became of these riches? During the last year of his life he had been in receipt of large pay.  At the time of his death considerable sums were due to him for arrears of pay and "batta," and his executors were thus enabled to pay off debts which he had incurred during the period when he was reduced from the receipt of a good income, as commanding the Guide corps, to the pay of a subaltern; but when this was done, so little remained for his widow, that, as appears from a letter of Lord Lawrence's to her, she was necessitated to apply to the Compassionate Fund for a grant to enable her to go home, which was allowed, much to the surprise of some of those who had given credence to the many stories to his prejudice, which, in Mr. Sloggett's words, "because of his very reputation were too often thoughtlessly repeated and became magnified in the repetition."  Mr. Sloggett says—"The Fund, called the 'Punjab Special Fund,' of which I had been made Honorary Secretary, was under the management of a Committee consisting of the Judicial and Financial Commissioners, the Commissioner of Lahore (at that time Mr., now Sir R. Temple), the Civil Surgeon, and H. C. Perkins, Esq., C.S.—to all of whom every application had to be confidentially submitted, with all particulars, before a grant was made.

"It had happened that Mrs. Hodson, in forwarding to me her application, sent also a statement of accounts drawn up by her husband as a private memorandum, the particulars of which she asked me to explain to her.  I was much affected on looking at it, for it was dated by him on the very morning of the day on which he met his death.  It was a simple statement he had hastily written down of all he owed, and all his available assets.  I forget the exact balance, and on which side it stood of the account; but, in fact, both the debit and credit sides were so nearly equal, that I was able to assure the Committee that, from this most credible source of information, the case was one which required their liberal consideration."

7. Reference has already been made to the concluding paragraph of Mr. Smith's indictment, which more than any other, has aroused a storm of indignation against the writer both at home and in India.

"It only remains to be added that early in the following year he was killed in the act of 'looting' in a house at Delhi."

There has been a general expression of opinion that, even had such a story been true, no man of generous feeling would have raked it up after the lapse of so many years.

But it has been most conclusively proved to be an "unmitigated slander." It is rather remarkable and most fortunate that so many witnesses should have been still alive and ready to come forward and give the details of Major Hodson's death, all agreeing in the important facts, but with just such trifling discrepancies as may always be expected. In the account given at the time by Brigadier Napier, who commanded the Engineers, he told me that "my brother had ridden up to him just as the assault was about to commence and said jokingly, 'I am come to take care of you.' He entered the breach with me as soon as it was practicable, and in a few minutes we were separated in the mêlée, and I saw nothing more of him till I was sent for to him dangerously wounded."

The details of the short period that intervened have been furnished by an old 93rd Highlander, who gives the following graphic account:—

"I was so near to Hodson when he was killed that my hand was almost on his shoulder, and I positively assert that to say he was *looting* is an unmitigated slander. His death happened as follows:—Between 2 and 3 o'clock P.M. on

March 11, 1858, Colonel Napier, now Lord Napier of Magdala, reported the breach of the Begum's palace practicable. My regiment, the 93rd Sutherland Highlanders, was ordered to storm it, and the fighting was without doubt the sternest struggle of the siege of Lucknow. After the palace was carried, many of the enemy took shelter in the dark arched buildings which surrounded the court of the palace, and had to be dislodged by throwing in bags of powder with lighted fuses attached to them. By this time the stormers were broken up, and engaged in a series of such fights all over the palace, and Lieutenant and Adjutant William MacBean, of the 93rd, late Major-General MacBean, got the V.C. for cutting down eleven men escaping out of one of those places. I was at another angle with some sixteen men, several of whom were shot down from a dark room which we tried to enter, for the glare of the afternoon sun was so strong we could not see the position of the enemy when looking into the dark. I made four or five men take post at each side of the door, and sent two back to the breach to bring up a few bags of powder from the engineers, who were preparing and attaching the fuses, to dislodge the enemy from this room. The men sent by me went in search of Colonel Napier, and found Hodson, who was never behind when fighting was to be done, and I believe he had accompanied Napier as his assistant in storming the Begum's palace. Hodson did not wait for the powder bags, but came running up with his drawn sword, and called to me to show him where the rebels were. I pointed to the doorway, and he was about to rush in when I called out, 'Don't, it's certain death; wait for the powder.' He took a step forward; and I put out my hand to seize hold of his shoulder to pull him out of the line of the doorway, when he fell, shot through the chest with two or three bullets. He ejaculated something, either, 'Oh, my wife!' or 'Oh, my mother!' I really could not say which; but being shot through both lungs he was immediately choked with blood. I assisted to lift him into one of the doolies that had by that time commenced to collect the wounded, and sent him to where the surgeons were at work. By this time some bags of powder were brought up, and we dislodged the men who were in the room, and bayoneted them down without mercy —some eighteen or twenty men. That Hodson was killed through his own rashness, I admit, but that he was looting I would deny, even if every authority of the British army were to say so. No looting had then commenced, not even by Jung Bahadoor's Goorkhas."

This account has been confirmed by many in public and private letters, and amongst others by Sir D. Stewart, Bart., Sir Hugh Gough, V.C., Sir J. Hills, K.C.B., V.C. The last says, "I think it my duty, in the interest of truth and honour, to protest against an ungenerous attack on one whose voice can never be heard in his own defence."

It is quite true, as Mr. Smith says, when attempting to justify his charge, that Major Hodson did not belong to the storming party, which was formed by the 93rd, but was there as a volunteer and a friend of Lord Napier's. It is the first time, however, that I have heard it cast in a man's teeth as a reproach that he had volunteered for a dangerous service, though it is much to be regretted that so valuable a life was thus sacrificed.

I have now gone through the various counts of Mr. Smith's indictment, and I feel confident that my readers will agree with me in thinking that there was never a more cruel and unfounded attempt to blacken the reputation of a brave and honourable man. I have, of course, in this vindication only touched on the points in which he has been assailed. But I think that the best vindication will be found in his letters, which I have republished. Those who read them will see that he was not only a born leader in war, but a loving husband, a tender father, a devoted friend, one whose great aim it was to go straight forward and do his duty, regardless alike of danger and of praise or blame. Perhaps, for his own sake, too regardless. I will only add two testimonies to his worth, which will carry weight from the position of the writers. One from Mr. L. Bowring, C.S.I., who was private secretary to Lord Canning during the time of the Mutiny, and therefore had the best opportunities of knowing the truth:—

"No one knew better than I did his admirable qualities, and I am not exaggerating when I say that his death has been universally lamented by every one in India. . . .

"You know that I had a great regard for your brother, and I believe you will appreciate my testimony to his worth as an officer and a gentleman."

The other is from Colonel Baird Smith, R.E.:—

"Some of the best and highest qualifications for command were combined in his character; fearless enterprise, resources always ready for use, and admirably adapted to his object, power to win the absolute trust of his agents, ready resolution in difficulties, a cool head, a strong hand, a quick judgment. These were among the most prominent traits that struck me during the few months we were together at Delhi."

While writing this I have been shown the following extract from the "Life of Sir F. Roberts":—"Into the vexed question of the shooting of the Princes by Lieutenant Hodson we will not enter here further than to remark that, after a careful perusal of Hodson's own account of the affair; of the Memoir of that gallant officer by his brother; of the description of the scene by his subaltern, Lieutenant Macdowell, the only other European eye-witness, who afterwards died the soldier's death; after carefully weighing the considerations that guided Hodson (a man of nerve and not given to panic) in the commission of the act, of the necessity of which he must have been the best judge—we cannot but acquit this gallant soldier of needless bloodshedding. His career at Delhi, achieved as the most brilliant of free lances, was so remarkable, that envy was aroused in breasts where it might least have been expected, and, sad to say, this discreditable feeling was not exorcised even by his death, some months later, in the service of his country, when, surely, any blots in his career—if any there were, and Lord Napier of Magdala denies their existence—might have been buried with him in his grave at Lucknow. This estimate of the character of the late Major Hodson is in agreement with that formed by such distinguished soldiers as Sir Donald Stewart, Sir Frederick Roberts, Sir James Brind, Sir James Hills, and many others of his comrades at Delhi."

For myself I can only say, that the fresh evidence which has now come before me from many different quarters, and letters of his which I have now seen for the first time, have only served to increase the admiration which I expressed twenty-five years ago for my brother's character, and I feel assured that, notwithstanding the efforts of his calumniators, his name will be handed down to posterity as one of whom his country may well feel proud.

I must take this opportunity of expressing my obligations to Lord Napier of Magdala, Sir Robert Montgomery, K.C.B., G.C.S.I.; Sir Charles Gough, V.C., K.C.B.; Sir Hugh Gough, V.C., K.C.B.; Sir James Hills, V.C., K.C.B.; General Anderson; Colonel Alexander, late 93rd; Colonel

Sampson, late Hodson's Horse; Colonel Dyer, R.A.; Captain Verney, R.N.; Lewin Bowring, Esq., C.S.I.; Rev. C. Sloggett, Rev. J. Knox Marshall, Dr. Graves Burton, and other friends, for valuable assistance.

GEORGE H. HODSON.

ENFIELD, *Sept.* 1883.

---

*P.S.*—It has been suggested to me that I ought to take more specific notice of a letter from Sir George Lawrence in the *Daily News*, in which he comes forward to vouch for the accuracy of Mr. Smith's statements. But I think that I have sufficiently shown how little weight should attach to the evidence even of "distinguished officers" when they belong to a party who were prejudiced against Major Hodson, and ready to believe anything to his discredit. It appears from a letter of Sir Henry Lawrence, published in his Life, that Sir George took offence at my brother when he was a subaltern of a few years' standing, and he has now shown that, after thirty-five years, he can neither forgive nor forget.

# PREFACE TO THE FIRST EDITION.

IT can scarcely be needful to make any apology for offering to the public this record of one who has attracted to himself so large a measure of attention and admiration. Many, both in this country and in India, have expressed, and I doubt not many others have felt, a desire to know more of the commander of Hodson's Horse, and captor of the King of Delhi and his sons.

My original intention was to have compiled from my brother's letters merely an account of the part he bore in the late unhappy war. I very soon, however, determined to extend the work, so as to embrace the whole of his life in India.

I felt that the public would naturally inquire by what previous process of training he had acquired, not merely his consummate skill in the great game of war, but his experience of Asiatics and marvellous influence over their minds.

The earlier portions of this book will serve to answer such inquiries; they will show the gradual development of my brother's character and powers, and that those exploits which astonished the world by their skill and daring, were but the natural results of the high idea of the soldier's profession which he proposed to himself, honestly and consistently worked out during ten years of training, in perhaps the finest school that ever existed for soldiers and administrators.

They will explain how it was that, in the midst of a struggle for the very existence of our empire, he was able to call into being and bring into the field around Delhi an "invincible and all but ubiquitous" body of cavalry.

The dragon's teeth which came up armed men, had been sown by him long before in his earlier career in the Punjâb. There, by many a deed of daring and activity, by many a successful stratagem and midnight surprise, by many a desperate contest, he had taught the Sikhs first to dread him as an enemy, and then to idolise him as a leader. Already in 1849 the Governor-General had had "frequent occasions of noticing not only his personal gallantry, but the activity, energy, and intelligence with which he discharged whatever duties were entrusted to him." Even then the name of Hodson, although unknown in England, except to the few who watched his course with the eyes of affection, was a sound of terror to the Sikhs, and a bugbear to their children. In 1852 he earned this high praise from one best qualified to judge: "Lieutenant Hodson, marvellously attaching the Guides to himself by the ties of mutual honour, mutual daring, and mutual devotion, has on every opportunity proved that the discipline of a public school and subsequent university training are no disqualification for hazardous warfare, or for the difficult task of keeping wild tribes in check."

The title given to this book will sufficiently indicate the principle on which, particularly in the first part, I have made selections from my brother's letters. My object has been to show what a soldier's life in India may be, and what in his case it was; how wide and varied is the field which it opens for the exercise of the highest and noblest qualities, intellectual and moral, of our nature; and how magnificently he realised and grasped the conception.

His letters, written in all the freedom of unreserved intercourse, will give a truer notion of his character than the most laboured description; they exhibit the undercurrent of deep feelings that ran through even his most playful moods, the yearning after home that mingled with the dreams of ambition and the thirst for the excitement of war, the almost womanly tenderness that co-existed with the stern determination of the soldier. They show that though his lot was cast in camps, he was not a mere soldier; though a hanger-on on the outskirts of civilisation amidst wild tribes, he had a keen appreciation of the refinement and elegancies of civilised life; that though in India, he remembered that he was an Englishman; that though living amongst the heathen, he did not forget that he was a Christian.

I have not attempted to write a biography, but have allowed my brother to speak for himself, merely supplying such connecting links as seemed absolutely necessary.

Indeed, I could do no otherwise; for unhappily, during the twelve years of his soldier's life—those years in which his character received its mature development—I knew him only by his letters, or by the reports of others: when we parted on board the ship that carried him from England, in 1845, we parted to meet no more in this world. My recollections of him, vivid as they are, are not of the leader of men in council and the battle-field, but of the bright and joyous boy, the life of the home circle, the tender and affectionate son, the loving brother, the valued friend, the popular companion.

Of what he became afterwards my readers will have the same means of judging as myself. He seems to me to have been one of whom not only his family, but his country, may well be proud—a worthy representative of the English name and nation amongst the tribes of India, an impersonation of manly straightforwardness, and unhesitating daring and irresistible power.

I cannot doubt but that the verdict of his countrymen will confirm my judgment.

Many too, I believe, will agree with me in thinking that these pages prove that the poetry and romance of war are not yet extinct, that even the Enfield rifle has not reduced all men to a dead level, but that there is still a place to be found for individual prowess, for the lion-heart, and the eagle eye, and the iron will. One seems transported back from the prosaic nineteenth century to the ages of romance and chivalry, and to catch a glimpse, now of a Paladin of old, now of a knightly hero *sans peur et sans reproche;* now of a northern chieftain, "riding on border foray," now of a captain of free-lances; yet all dissolving into a Christian soldier of our own day.

Most striking of all, it has appeared to me, is the resemblance to the romantic career of that hero of the Spanish ballads, who, by his many deeds of heroic daring, gained for himself the distinguished title of "El de las Hazanas,"— "He of the exploits." Those who are acquainted with the chronicles of the Conquest of Granada, will almost fancy in reading these pages that they are hearing again the story of Fernando Perez del Pulgar; how at one time by a bold dash he rode with a handful of followers across a country swarming with the enemy, and managed to force his way into a beleaguered fortress; how at another he galloped alone up the streets of Granada, then in the possession of the enemy, to the gates of the principal mosque, and nailed a paper to the door with his dagger; how again he turned the tide of battle by the mere charm of his eagle-eye and thrilling voice, inspiring the most timid with a courage equal to his own; how he made the enemy lay down their arms at his word of command; how the Moorish mothers frightened their children with the sound of his name; how he was not only the hairbrained adventurer, delighting in peril and thirsting for the excitement of the fight, but also the courteous gentleman, the accomplished scholar; as profound and sagacious in the council as he was reckless in the field, and frequently selected by the wily Ferdinand to conduct affairs requiring the greatest prudence and judgment.*

It may be, however, that affection has biassed my judgment, and that I shall be thought to have formed an exaggerated estimate of the grandeur and nobleness of the subject of this memoir. Even if this be so, I shall not take much to heart the charge of having loved such a brother too well, and I shall console myself with the thought that I have endeavoured to do something to perpetuate his memory.

If, however, any young soldier be induced, by reading these pages, to take a higher view of his profession, to think of it as one of the noblest fields in which he can serve his God and his country, and enter on it in a spirit of self-sacrifice, with " duty " as his guiding principle, and a determination never to forget that he is a Christian soldier and an Englishman, I shall be abundantly rewarded; my main object will be attained.

COOKHAM DEANE,
   *December* 1858.

---

\* See Washington Irving, &c.

# CONTENTS.

## Part I.

### CHAPTER I.

EARLY LIFE—RUGBY—TRINITY COLLEGE, CAMBRIDGE—GUERNSEY MILITIA . . . . . . . . . . . 1-4

### CHAPTER II.

ARRIVAL IN INDIA—CAMPAIGN ON THE SUTLEJ, BATTLES OF MOODKEE, FEROZESHAH, SOBRAON—OCCUPATION OF LAHORE—1845-6 . . . . . . . . . . . 5-19

### CHAPTER III.

FIRST BENGAL EUROPEAN FUSILIERS — CASHMERE WITH SIKH ARMY — LAWRENCE ASYLUM — APPOINTMENT TO GUIDE CORPS—*June* 1846–*October* 1847 . . . . . . 20-36

### CHAPTER IV.

EMPLOYMENT IN THE PUNJAB AS SECOND IN COMMAND OF THE CORPS OF GUIDES, AND ALSO AS ASSISTANT TO THE RESIDENT AT LAHORE—ROAD-MAKING AND SURVEYING—CAMPAIGN OF 1848-9—CAPTURE OF FORTS—BATTLE OF GUJERAT—ANNEXATION OF PUNJAB—*October* 1847–*March* 1849 . . . 37-69

## CHAPTER V.

ANNEXATION OF PUNJAB — INCREASE OF CORPS OF GUIDES AT PESHAWUR — TRANSFER TO CIVIL DEPARTMENT AS ASSISTANT COMMISSIONER—*April* 1849–*April* 1850 . . . . 70-82

## CHAPTER VI.

TOUR IN CASHMERE AND THIBET WITH SIR HENRY LAWRENCE— TRANSFER TO CIS-SUTLEJ PROVINCES—*June* 1851–*October* 1851 . . . . . . . . . . . . 83-100

## CHAPTER VII.

MARRIAGE—COMMAND OF THE GUIDES—PESHAWUR—EUZOFZAI —FRONTIER WARFARE—MURDÂN—*January* 1852–*November* 1854 . . . . . . . . . . . . 101-121

## CHAPTER VIII.

REVERSES—UNJUST TREATMENT—OFFICIAL ENMITY—LOSS OF COMMAND — SUPPRESSION OF REPORT — RETURN TO REGIMENTAL DUTIES — BETTER PROSPECTS — MAJOR TAYLOR'S REPORT—TESTIMONY OF SIR R. NAPIER—MR. MONTGOMERY —*November* 1854–*May* 1857 . . . . . . 122-141

CONTENTS. lv

## Part II.

*NARRATIVE OF THE DELHI CAMPAIGN, 1857, 1858.*

### CHAPTER I.

PAGE

OUTBREAK OF REBELLION—MARCH DOWN TO DELHI FROM DUGSHAI WITH FIRST EUROPEAN BENGAL FUSILIERS—APPOINTMENT TO INTELLIGENCE DEPARTMENT — RIDE FROM KURNAL TO MEERUT TO OPEN COMMUNICATION—ORDER TO RAISE REGIMENT—DEATH OF GENERAL ANSON—*May 10th–June 8th* . . . . . . . . 143–157

### CHAPTER II.

SIEGE OF DELHI—*June–August* . . . 158–199

### CHAPTER III.

SIEGE OF DELHI, CONTINUED—ROHTUCK EXPEDITION—ASSAULT—DELHI TAKEN—CAPTURE OF KING—CAPTURE AND EXECUTION OF SHAHZADAHS—*August 17th–September 25th* . . 200–236

### CHAPTER IV.

OPERATIONS IN THE NEIGHBOURHOOD OF DELHI — SHOWERS' COLUMN — SEATON'S COLUMN — ACTIONS AT GUNGEREE, PUTTIALEE, MYNPOOREE—RIDE TO COMMANDER-IN-CHIEF'S CAMP — JUNCTION OF FORCES — SHUMSHABAD — *October–January* . . . . . . . . . 237–279

### CHAPTER V.

ALUMBAGH, LUCKNOW—THE BEGUM'S PALACE—BANKS' HOUSE—THE SOLDIER'S DEATH—NOTICES—CONCLUDING REMARKS—*February 24th–March 12th* . . . . . 280–300

# POSTSCRIPT TO INTRODUCTION.

SINCE the Introduction to this volume was written, Mr. Holmes, nothing daunted by the almost universal expression of indignation at Mr. Bosworth Smith's attack on Hodson of Hodson's Horse, has published a Life of him which originally appeared as an article in the *National Review*, August 1884, and was then characterised as "dictated apparently by an artful malevolence, which aims at appearing impartial whilst dealing the cruellest blows possible;" and this may be said with still greater truth of the additions made to the Life in its new form.

Mr. B. Smith may be looked on as holding a brief for Lord Lawrence, but it is difficult to understand what excuse Mr. Holmes can make for himself in attacking the reputation of one to whose brilliant qualities as a soldier he does full justice. It can only be supposed that he has been led away by others, who were too glad to avail themselves of his pen in giving publicity to the vindictive feelings which they had long cherished. It is the more remarkable that he should have lent a ready ear to such stories as he has retailed, since he expresses his conviction "that many of the gravest charges current against Hodson are exaggerated, and may have grown out of random suggestions made by his enemies." This was undoubtedly the case. And yet he does not scruple to make such atrocious charges as these—"that he enriched himself by dishonest means," and "that, heedless of justice, of gratitude, and honour, he was swift to shed innocent blood;" though, while painting him in such dark colours, he is obliged to allow that *brave soldiers* and *high-minded gentlemen* and *noble-minded men* loved him well and mourned for him as for a brother; "that he was capable of loving and winning the love of the good."

If the good and the high-minded loved and esteemed him, as unquestionably they did, and those who knew him most intimately valued him the most, it matters but little what men of a different character thought of him. Undoubtedly, while he inspired the most enthusiastic devotion in his friends, he made many enemies, partly by his high qualities, partly by his faults; for I have no wish to represent him as faultless. I will again quote the words of a general officer, who knew him well, written at the time of his death :—

"He was too noble to pass through the world without detractors. The ambitious envied him because the brilliancy of his actions threw them into the shade; the mean and despicable hated him because they quailed before the eagle-eye that could endure neither dishonesty nor cowardice. Their base slanders were in whispers during his life; now that his gallant spirit is gone, they come forward in unblushing malignity."

And I may add, that during the thirty years which have passed since his death, they have been gathering strength and receiving fresh embellishments as they passed from one to another.

Mr. Holmes, of course, does not allow this, but professes to be actuated by a simple desire for truth; but he has dealt with the subject in a way which completely destroys any claim which he can make to be considered an impartial historian. He, still more than Mr. Smith, accepts every story told against Hodson as gospel, without reference to the character or antecedents of the narrator, whilst any testimony in his favour, even from men of the highest character, is contemptuously set aside as being the biassed judgment of a friend.

Mr. Holmes is unfortunate in those with whom he has been thrown. We gain an insight into the kind of man on whom he relies for some of his most damaging charges, and we cannot be surprised that the commander of the Guides should have been glad to get rid of him.

## POSTSCRIPT TO INTRODUCTION.

No doubt, Hodson, by too openly showing his want of toleration for any backwardness or inefficiency, mortally offended some of his subalterns, who avenged themselves by bringing charges against him which, though believed for a time, were afterwards triumphantly disproved. It is not to be wondered at that such men should even now bear enmity; and yet Mr. Holmes considers it absurd to throw any doubt on their evidence, even as regards conversations which took place more than thirty years ago.

But Mr. Holmes has a worse fault. In his text[1] he makes the gravest accusations as matters of fact, which in his notes he admits cannot be proved.

Again,[2] when speaking of a guarantee which he supposes Hodson to have given for the safety of the King and Queen, he adds, "*Doubtless for a substantial consideration.*" In his Addenda, which most would overlook, he confesses that there is no positive proof of this. He should rather have said there is not a shadow of evidence beyond mere surmise, though to Mr. Holmes' mind it is "*self-evident* that he could not have given the guarantee without a *quid pro quo.*"

Again,[3] he states that the Queen had with her 7000 rupees, which Hodson *appropriated.* This is supposed to rest on the authority of the Queen; but as she could not possibly have said more than that Hodson *took* them, the word *appropriated* shows the animus of the narrator; whereas, in point of fact, the money, whatever it was, was handed over to the prize-agent, Colonel (afterwards Sir Thomas) Seaton. He, from his position as prize-agent after the capture of Delhi, was better able than any one else to form a judgment; and yet no one was more indignant at the charges of looting made against Hodson, or more ready to give them a positive contradiction, as he has repeatedly done to me and to others.

I shall not attempt to refute all the stories to Hodson's discredit which Mr. Holmes and Mr. Smith have so industriously collected. It would be impossible at this distance of time to deal with them all; but I think that the samples given in the former pages of this

[1] Page 178.   [2] Page 208.   [3] Page 299.

Introduction sufficiently show how groundless they are, even when vouched for by three or any number of distinguished officers. I feel sure that even those which seem most damaging can be satisfactorily explained.

The *canards* in circulation at the time of the siege of Delhi were innumerable. A sort of halo of myth had gathered round Hodson, and nothing good or bad was too monstrous to gain credit. If it had been asserted that he used to eat children or had leapt his horse over the wall of Delhi, some would have believed it; and Mr. Holmes, in recording the tale, would have said, "It could not be proved, but doubtless it was true."

But I must deal with Mr. Holmes' accusation that he enriched himself by dishonest means.

I can most positively and emphatically deny that he did enrich himself by any means whatever, for he died quite a poor man. As I have shown above, p. xxxix., the papers of those who administered to his effects prove this beyond contradiction. It is quite true, as Mr. Holmes asserts, that at the outset of the Mutiny he was in pecuniary difficulties, owing to the loss of his command of the Guides, and the consequent reduction of his pay from R.1250 to R.250, and that he had been obliged to borrow from native bankers, and, on the security of his life-policy, from Colonel Welchman, who commanded his regiment, the 1st Bengal Fusiliers, sums amounting altogether to nearly £1800; but during the last months of his life he was again in the receipt of large pay as head of the Intelligence Department and commander of a regiment of horse, and in this way, aided by a successful speculation in prize-cattle, of which I have given an account elsewhere (p. xxxviii.), he was in a position to pay off a considerable portion of his debts during his life, and the arrears of pay and batta due to him at his death enabled his executors to discharge the remainder. But when this was done, so little was left, that his widow was obliged to apply to the Compassionate Fund for assistance, which was granted after due investigation by the Commissioners, of whom Sir Richard Temple was one, much to the surprise of those who had believed the stories that were circulated to his prejudice. I may add, that when his widow died, four years ago, at Hampton Court Palace, where an apartment had been granted her by the Queen in recognition of her husband's services, her whole property was sworn under £400. She had been in receipt of two pensions.

Mr. Holmes, however, in support of his charge, quotes Mr. Smith's story that "vast stores of valuables were found in his boxes after his death at Lucknow."

I thought that I had disposed of this slander to the satisfaction of all reasonable men by bringing forward the report of the Committee of Adjustment (p. xxxi.), which showed conclusively that all his property (except horses), including these "*vast stores of valuables*," was sold for £170.

But Mr. Smith, in a letter to which Holmes refers, returns to the attack with no abatement of animosity. Having found his boxes with *vast stores of valuables* vanish into thin air, he is obliged to resort to the desperate expedient of supposing that the boxes had been pillaged before they were examined by the Committee of Adjustment,—forgetting, what was stated at the time by both Sir H. Daly and Sir C. Gough, that immediately on Hodson's death a guard was placed over his effects till they were removed to the quarters of General Napier, who says there was nothing in his boxes but what an officer might legitimately and honourably have in his possession, and that the story of their having been previously pillaged is impossible.

But Mr. Smith says he has another proof, "possibly most significant of all," and, as usual, on unexceptionable authority, which is this—that Hodson was able to remit to Calcutta, to a place of safety, a very large sum, amounting to some thousands of pounds.

I was able to trace back this story to its origin. The only foundation for this fresh calumny is that when Hodson applied to the paymaster, Captain Tombs, for two months' pay for his regiment, R.60,000, which was sanctioned by General Mansfield, the chief of the staff, he asked to have it in the form of bills on

Calcutta, as these were in great request at that time with the up-country bankers, from whom he drew money for his men. That they were duly paid, all allow.

This may serve as a specimen of the ingenuity of those, who wished to run him down, in twisting everything into a matter of accusation against him.

It is perhaps needless after this to say that it can be proved that no such sum came into the hands of his bankers at Calcutta, or was found by his executors.

And with regard to the charge of looting, so industriously circulated and believed, I may refer again to what I have already said (p. xxxvi.) to show how easy it was for maliciously-minded persons to misrepresent his actions, from the quantity of prize-property which passed through his hands, collected in his different raids, and afterwards handed over by him to the prize-agents. It was patent to all that he had the property; no one troubled himself to ask what became of it.

It is amusing to read Mr. Smith's virtuous indignation at his having sent to his wife two rings, and an amulet taken from the Princes. This seems to him to justify his belief in any amount of plundering. I should like to ask Hodson's accusers whether there is one of them who has not some memento of their campaigns in India or China which may be construed into "loot?" I have never met with one who had not.

Mr. Smith, with his usual positiveness in a matter of which he can know nothing, denies the statement that the rings were only worth a few rupees. Indian Princes, he says, do not wear "ten-shilling rings." I can only say in answer that these Princes *did*, and that Mr. Smith is quite welcome to see the rings, if he likes to judge for himself. It appears further that these very rings were sent to his wife through the prize-agent, Colonel Seaton.

We can see in many of Mr. Holmes' charges how easy it is to twist isolated expressions, taken without the context or the circumstances under which they were uttered, into a sense which they were never intended to bear. It is one thing to say that a man cannot be trusted to keep accounts; quite another to accuse him of dishonesty.

It may be quite possible that Hodson was careless in his accounts. They were certainly not his *forte*. He preferred, as he said himself, the saddle to the desk; and yet, as Sir J. Lawrence himself wrote, "many things are culpable which are not criminal." Whilst blaming him for procrastination, he added his conviction "that nothing could be proved against him unbecoming a gentleman." And as to Sir Henry, though he scolded him at times, it is quite certain that he never in the slightest degree lost confidence in him or doubted his honour.

But we must not, in fairness to him, forget what the difficulties were with which he had to contend in the matter of accounts, of which some notion may be formed from the following letter, written after reading Mr. Holmes' article in August 1884:—

"DEAR MR. HODSON,—I think it right and due to your brother's memory, after the charges brought against him, to tell you what I know of some passages in his history.

"I made acquaintance with your brother when he was a sub-altern with the 1st Bengal Fusiliers at Sabbathoo in 1847. He used then to ride over to the Lawrence Asylum, which had just been commenced, to assist in superintending the construction, at the request of Sir Henry Lawrence, whose benevolent impatience to rescue the soldiers' children from barrack-life and the Plains led him to urge forward the work, and to press every one into the service who could help him. This involved a ride of fourteen miles, with a stiff mountain climb of some 6000 feet, counting both ascents, going and returning, and made no slight addition to a subaltern's duty two or three times a week; but it was cheerfully undertaken to please Sir Henry.

"A European overseer, lent from the Public Works Department to assist your brother, was a very clever man, excellent when sober, but, as was afterwards learnt, liable to fits of intemperance, which ultimately ruined him.

"Labour in India was then paid for in small copper coins, which made the accounts very troublesome from the exchange constantly varying. One day a rupee might be worth $67\frac{1}{2}$ of these coins; a day or two later $69\frac{1}{2}$. I can quite understand, with such a subordinate, that there may have been some confusion in accounts.

"The last thing I should have set your brother to do at that time was a complicated account. His mind was too impetuously active in devouring every kind of information in a country so new to him to let him sit down patiently to a work which was certainly not then taught in English public schools, though he learnt it from bitter experience afterwards. Sir Henry may have thought the buildings expensive, and he may have said so, but I never heard him express a doubt of your brother's honour. Had he really lost confidence in him, he never would have sent him to live with me as my guest to be instructed in work, nor would he have recommended his appointment to the Guides.

"In March 1855, on visiting Peshawur, I found the case of your brother under discussion at Sir J. Lawrence's head-quarters. Feelings were very strong against him, and the loss of his appointment considered so certain, that I feared the decision had been already made. I immediately sought your brother, and found him quite unconscious of his danger, and confident of clearing himself of the accusations brought against him.

"On his showing me his accounts, I saw they were all in Persian, liable to any misconstruction which an ill-disposed interpreter might place on them, and I urged him to translate them into English.

"He said it would take a fortnight, and I therefore rode back to Sir J. Lawrence's camp and asked him to allow that time for translating the accounts. To this he gave consent, which I carried at once to Hodson.

"By working day and night, he accomplished the translation in the time.

"When it is remembered that on his being suspended, notice

was given to every complainant to come forward against him, any one who knows the material contained in the Guides, knows that there were men who might have had enmity to gratify, or hope of positive advantage in bringing accusations before the Court of Inquiry. The investigation afterwards by Reynell Taylor was complete and searching, occupying as it did many months. No man of higher honour or ability could have been chosen for such a duty, high-minded, pure in character, painstaking, and indefatigable.

"That Hodson's full acquittal from the inquiry was not at once accepted and acknowledged, I considered then, and consider still, a grievous wrong. Your brother was left for many months exposed to all the discredit of accusations made against him, and greatly exaggerated by rumours, while his judges' favourable verdict was reserved. To this course I attribute the prejudice against him on the part of many who listened too easily to stories to his discredit.

"Though not agreeing with your brother in all things, I never doubted his honour and integrity, and I maintain my full belief in them now. Those who thought otherwise might have left undisturbed the grave of a gallant soldier who had fought so bravely and successfully for his country.

"Believe me, yours very sincerely,
                    "NAPIER OF MAGDALA."

Another letter of more recent date throws still further light both on his difficulties and the origin of charges made against him. His zeal for the public service often led him to take on himself the responsibility of setting red tape regulations at defiance.

*July 2nd*, 1889.

"DEAR MR. HODSON,—You ask me to write for you the circumstances which I related to you some time ago, connected with the building of the Fort of Kote Murdan. I do not think there is any one else who could give you the information.

## POSTSCRIPT TO INTRODUCTION.

"A fortified cantonment was sanctioned for the Guides' head-quarters at Kote Murdan. A plan for the work was drawn by one of the executive officers. The quarters for the officers and men were thrown into the form of a bastioned enclosure, giving a defensive character sufficient for the protection of the depot and families within it when the corps might be in the field. The plan was approved by the Punjab Government, but I could not spare an engineer officer to build it. Hodson was most anxious to get his men under shelter before the hot weather, and received sanction to construct the work. I was able to make a small advance for preliminary expenses, but could give no more money until the receipt of an estimate.

"Major Hodson was called away on some service, and left the work under charge of an overseer. When he returned he found that matters were not going on well, and there was no estimate, without which I could make no further advance of money. The hot weather was well on, and the setting in of rains threatened to destroy what was done. In this distress Hodson informed me that he advanced money from the Regimental Chest. There was difficulty and delay in getting the money from the Civil Department, and the pay of the Guides became overdue, there being no money in the Regimental Chest.

"Those hostile to your brother immediately assumed a defalcation. These I believe are part of the circumstances leading to the Court of Inquiry on your brother.

"The whole case, as is well known, came under the review of Colonel Reynell Taylor, who fully acquitted your brother of any breach of trust.

"I have read what has been accumulated against your brother by Mr. Bosworth Smith. I remember Colonel Daly finding a pile of papers in your brother's trunk. I do not think I quite realised what they were, but I remarked that if your brother had any evil intentions regarding them, nothing would have been easier than to have destroyed them.

"If Sir Henry Daly's memory is accurate, and your brother at the time he was asked the question denied all knowledge of these papers, I firmly believe that he spoke the truth, and that had he lived he could have explained satisfactorily how they came into his possession. It may be asked why was Reynell Taylor's report to be discounted? No more competent, honourable, or conscientious officer could have been found in the service, and I fully accept his decision.

"Yours very truly,      NAPIER OF MAGDALA."

I proceed now to refute another of Mr. Holmes' cruellest accusations:—"That, heedless of justice, of gratitude, and even of honour, he (Hodson) was swift to shed innocent blood."

Mr. Holmes founds this sweeping charge mainly on a story which he tells of the execution of one Bisharut Ali, an officer of the 1st Irregular Cavalry, who was known to him before, and had become security for a loan. The story, as he tells it, leaves the impression that Bisharut Ali was living quietly on sick-leave at his own village near Delhi. But if we turn to Sir H. Norman's "History of the Siege of Delhi," we get a very different view. He says, "At Rohtuck Hodson managed to surprise and nearly to destroy a party of mutineers, irregular cavalry, sowars of different regiments, including Ressaldar Bisharut Ali, who was taken and shot." This expedition to Rohtuck was one of Hodson's most brilliant exploits, for which he was thanked by the Commander-in-Chief.

Bisharut Ali is not named either by Hodson or by MacDowall, whose account I have before me, but he mentions "that one of the men killed was a brute of the 14th Irregular Cavalry, who committed such butchery at Jhansi."

There certainly is a strong presumption against the innocence of a man found in such company. Mr. Holmes can claim the authority of General Crawford Chamberlain for the main facts of the story, but it must be observed that General Chamberlain was not present; he only professes to have gathered his information afterwards on the spot; and as this information must have come from natives, and presumably friends of the rebels, it may be considered as carrying about as much weight as the accounts of Mr. Balfour's "atrocities," to which we are all accustomed, gathered from eye-witnesses on the spot where evictions have taken place, by sympathising visitors. General C. Chamberlain believed Bisharut Ali to have been innocent, and wished to establish his innocence, misled by his sympathy for a man whom he had known before, and thought well of. Nothing is more remarkable in the history of the Mutiny than the implicit confidence which officers retained in their men up to the very moment when they rose and treacherously murdered them.

It is impossible that General Chamberlain can know what evidence Hodson had of the man's guilt. It may or may not be true that he got information from Shahaboodeen, but doubtless he had other evidence to confirm it. No one at the time doubted Bisharut Ali's guilt, and fresh light has recently been thrown on it in an unexpected manner. One of the native officers who came to England on the occasion of the Queen's Jubilee in 1887, Ressaldar Isree Sing, of the 19th Bengal Lancers, made the following statement to a general officer whom he visited as an old acquaintance:—"That he lived when young in or near Bisharut Ali's village, and remembered him well, and how he used to boast that he could make the Sahib-log believe what he chose; that it was notorious that he was a very dangerous character, disseminating rebel doctrines, and preparing to take a leading part in the event of the rebellion succeeding, while keeping ostensibly on good terms with the authorities, and hoodwinking them. Isree Sing had never heard Major Hodson's conduct in shooting him called in question."

The same officer had been told previously by a native officer of Hodson's Horse, who was present on the occasion, that no one doubted the guilt of the condemned man, and all considered his death a mere act of justice.

If, then, Hodson was satisfied of the man's guilt, is he to be denounced as bloodthirsty because he ordered his immediate execution at a time when he was sent out expressly to clear the country of rebel soldiers, and when (to use Sir N. Chamberlain's own words) the penalty of death or entire release were the only alternatives, as it was impossible to guard or carry about prisoners? Even if on private grounds, in remembrance of past obligations, he might have been inclined to spare him, public considerations required sharp and speedy justice. The very existence of our Empire was trembling in the balance.

No doubt in many cases of wholesale executions the innocent suffered with the guilty, as was inevitable; but there is no reason for believing that it was so in this case, and all Mr. Holmes' righteous indignation may well be spared.

And here I may ask once more why Hodson's acts are always to be judged by so different a standard from those of other men, Edwardes and others, who put down the Mutiny? Mr. Holmes in his History* tells a ghastly story of a civilian who, after "shooting 216 sepoys who were crouching like a flock of wildfowl, shut up sixty-six others in a second Black Hole, so that forty-five were found dead in the morning, and then proceeded to shoot the remaining twenty-one." Here Mr. Holmes has nothing to say of the want of a regular trial or any evidence of guilt. He characterises it as "*a splendid assumption of responsibility*, for which the officer was assailed by the vulgar cries of *ignorant humanitarianism*." What if Hodson had done this?

Mr. Holmes chooses to assume that in one case the sufferers were innocent, and in the other guilty; but this begs the whole question. The officers were as much convinced of the guilt in the one case as in the other.

Was Hodson ever censured at the time for undue severity by those in authority and best able to judge? Did he not receive the highest commendation for his services in quieting the country? The only act for which he was called to account, and for which he had to defend himself, was not one of severity, but sparing the King's life. His execution of the Princes was

* History of the Mutiny, pp. 372-373.

universally applauded at the time, even by so humane a man as Sir Robert Montgomery. Were not the feelings which he expressed of satisfaction at the punishment of the guilty shared at the time by every Englishman in India, including Lord Lawrence? Why are they then brought up against him so persistently to prove his truculent disposition?

Mr. Holmes follows Mr. Smith in quietly assuming that his view of Hodson's character was shared by all those who knew him in India, and Anglo-Indians generally.

Nothing can be more preposterous. I have received letters which would fill a volume, many of them from perfect strangers, expressing their admiration of him from what they had seen and known, and their indignation at the attacks made upon him. One of Mr. Smith's authorities goes so far as to say that he never knew of any friend who believed in him in the Punjab but Colonel Napier. Even had this been true, the fact that such a man, who was thoroughly acquainted with all the details of his career from the beginning to his last moments at Lucknow, should have honoured him with his friendship and esteem, and should have come forward now to express his confidence in his honour and integrity, should be quite sufficient to silence gainsayers. But it is far from being the case. He had many friends. Those most intimate with him in the Punjab were Major James Douglas and Major the Hon. H. Powys, both of the 60th Rifles, and Colonel Douglas Seaton of the 1st Fusiliers, all men of the highest character and models of Christian gentlemen, who would not for a moment have tolerated anything dishonourable. They esteemed him as Napier did, and continued his fast friends and defenders till their deaths.

Lewin Bowring, C.S., who served in the Punjab with him under Sir H. Lawrence, is still alive, and his letter printed at p. xliii. speaks for itself.

I merely mention now those who were his chosen friends in the Punjab, and with whom I was well acquainted. I have spoken elsewhere of the opinion of others better known in later times.

To show what the opinion entertained of him in India is now, I quote from a Lucknow paper an account of a prize-distribution at La Martinière College, in the grounds of which he was buried. When reference had been made by the Principal to Hodson of Hodson's Horse as the *genius loci*, and to the slanderous attacks made on him, General Dillon said, "As one who knew him in the field, and as one who was intimately associated for many years with the greatest soldier of the time, General Sir Robert Napier, now Lord Napier of Magdala, I am in a position not only to give my own opinion, but to state that General Napier was on the most intimate terms with Hodson during almost the whole of the career of that dashing soldier, and that he had the highest opinion of him. I have no hesitation in characterising the attacks that have been made, in the face too of the verdict of such a soldier as Lord Napier of Magdala, as ungenerous, unwarrantable, and atrocious."

To the same effect are the words of a well-known writer, who was himself at Lucknow :—

"The testimony of such a man as Lord Napier of Magdala must count as conclusive refutation of any amount of the idle chatter of irresponsible frivolity, or, worse, the calculated defamation of the jealous malignant."

In conclusion, I may say that I have read carefully Mr. Smith's reply to my Vindication, with the letters of his correspondents, and I see no reason for retracting or modifying anything that I have written; and I am glad to find that Lord Napier agrees with me. Mr. Smith has proved that those who bore enmity against Hodson, and tried to injure him when alive, do so still; that those who were prejudiced against him, and ready to believe stories to his discredit on the strength of general rumour without any proof, are prejudiced still.

It is very natural that those who were more or less connected with the Government should take the official view; that those concerned in the Court of Inquiry should wish to defend the decision at which they arrived, and should be annoyed at its being reversed by Major R. Taylor's report. All alike show their anxiety to depreciate the value of that report, by representing Major Taylor's investigation as unofficial, though it was ordered by the Chief Commissioner (Sir J. Lawrence). They try to make out that he was a "good-natured man," "who was the most guileless and trusting of men," and was influenced by plausible explanations, and allowed himself to be bamboozled; that when Sir R. Montgomery wrote of the report to Hodson as "more satisfactory than any one he ever read, and most triumphant," he could not have known what he was about; that no one acquainted with the proceedings of the Court of Inquiry could possibly have thought it satisfactory, &c., &c., &c.

Happily Sir C. Chamberlain himself furnishes the most complete answer. He quotes the words of Colonel Keith Young, Judge Advocate-General. "The whole matter had passed under his own review ere it had been submitted to the Government, and the verdict of the court was amply justified by the evidence produced." "These," says Sir C. Chamberlain, "are the *sober words of a legal mind.* Will any one consider that he came to his conclusion on *ex parte* evidence?" But observe, these sober words were spoken before he had seen Major Taylor's report; and mark the sequel. The Rev. C. Sloggett tells us, and he is prepared to support his statement by an affidavit, that though Colonel Keith Young had spoken at first of Hodson's case with scorn, yet when he had been shown Major Taylor's report, he was so much impressed by it, that from that time he became one of Hodson's warmest friends. Does not this dispose effectually of the contention that no one acquainted with the proceedings of the Court of Inquiry could possibly have considered Major Taylor's report satisfactory? Does it not confirm my original charge, that Hodson was condemned on *ex parte* evidence, and that the suppression of Major Taylor's report vindicating him did him a grievous injustice?

That it may not be said that Major R. Taylor afterwards altered his opinion, I quote a letter received from him in 1883:—

"You were justified in describing my report as exculpatory, as far as the regimental accounts were concerned, and I have always regarded the doubt and distrust which had arisen regarding that as the most serious charge that had been made against your brother, as it involved a breach of trust. I found him to be quite clear in this matter.

"There had truly been great irregularities in keeping the accounts, but your brother had made strenuous efforts at times to get all into form, and had accomplished a good deal.

"The great difficulty had been caused by the audit of ten months' pay of the whole regiment having been withheld. This had resulted from the fact of the transfer of the regiment from the Civil to the Military Department.

"Through the whole of these ten months the regiment had been living on advances, and that with a regiment like the Guides, having detachments all over the country, was calculated to cause very great confusion in the accounts.

"I remain, yours very truly, REYNELL TAYLOR."

That I may not be supposed to be singular in the view which I have taken of the Punjab authorities, I will quote a passage from the "Life of Lord Lawrence" by William St. Clair:—

"We read of John Lawrence always finding fault with and trying to shunt men against whom he took a dislike. No sentence in Lord Dalhousie's Life appears to have stung him more than being called a 'good hater.' It was true of both Sir Henry and Sir John Lawrence. If they disliked any one, it was hopeless to try and conciliate them. There were Henry's friends and John's friends. Sir Henry's friends were his till death, but John's likings were rather official than personal. The roots of disease ran deep into the soil, and did not wither away till Sir Henry left the Punjab, three years after the Board had been formed. But to two of Sir Henry's friends John was most specially indebted—to the chivalrous Nicholson, who fell mortally wounded at Delhi, and to Hodson, from whom, however, the official mantle of favour had been torn prior to 1857, never to be regained, even by the gallant deeds of the Mutiny and a subsequent death at Lucknow." *

*Note.*—In self-justification I must allude to Mr. Smith's attempt to throw doubt on my good faith. He calls attention to the fact that in the first edition of the Memoir of my brother, 1858, there was a mistake in the version which I gave of Lord Clyde's letter to his widow, written after the funeral. He was represented to have called him, "the most brilliant soldier," instead of what he did write, "one of the most brilliant soldiers." I relied on a copy of the letter hastily made at the time, and sent me by his widow.

Mr. Smith does not mention that in a second edition, published more than twenty years before he wrote, having then the original letter in my possession, I corrected the mistake, and apologised for it to Lord Clyde. I am ready to produce the original of this and all other letters which I have quoted.

* "Life of Lord Lawrence," by William St. Clair, p. 102.

# HODSON OF HODSON'S HORSE;

OR

## Twelve Years of a Soldier's Life in India.

―― o ――

## PART I.

## CHAPTER I.

*EARLY LIFE—RUGBY—CAMBRIDGE—GUERNSEY.*

WILLIAM STEPHEN RAIKES HODSON, third son of Rev. George Hodson, afterwards Archdeacon of Stafford and Canon of Lichfield, was born at Maisemore Court, near Gloucester, on 19th March 1821.

As a boy, his affectionate disposition and bright and joyous character endeared him greatly to his family, and made him a general favourite with all around him, old and young, rich and poor. That which characterised him most was his quickness of observation and his interest in everything going on about him. By living with his eyes and ears open, and never suffering anything to escape his notice, he acquired a stock of practical knowledge which he turned to good account in his after-life. With the exception of a short time spent with a private tutor, the Rev. E. Harland, he was educated at home till he went to Rugby, in his fifteenth year. Home life, however, had not prevented him from growing up an active, high-spirited boy, full of life and energy.

His feats of activity at Rugby still live in the remembrance of his contemporaries and the traditions of the school. The following is an extract from a paper in the "Book of Rugby School," published in 1856:—

Who does not remember the fair-haired, light-complexioned active man, whose running feats, whether in the open fields or on the gravel walks of the Close, created such marvel among his cotemporaries. He has carried his hare and hounds into his country's service, and as commandant of the gallant corps of Guides, has displayed an activity and courage on the wild frontier of the Punjab, the natural development of his early prowess at Crick and Brownsover.

A very similar notice appeared in a periodical during the Indian Mutiny:—

The Rugbœans have had their Crick run. Six miles over heavy country, there and back, to the school gates by the road, is no mean distance to be done in one hour twenty-nine minutes.

There was a day when the gallant leader of "Hodson's Horse" always led in this run. We think we see "larky Pritchard," as he was familiarly designated, in his blue cloth jacket, white trousers, his well-known belt, and his "golden hair," going in front with his nice easy stride (for he never had any very great pace, though he could last for ever), and getting back coolly and comfortably to "Bons" when the rear hounds were toiling a mile behind. There never was such a boy to run over, after second lesson, to Dunchurch to see the North Warwickshire, or to give himself a "pipe-opener" to Lutterworth and back between callings over, till the doctor vowed he would injure his heart.  How true it is that men who have distinguished themselves most in school sports come out the best at last.

It was not, however, only in active sports that he showed ability.  As head of a house, during the later portion of his Rugby life, he gave equal indications of "administrative capacity."

His tutor (Cotton, after Lord Bishop of Calcutta), speaking of his having been transferred to his house, in which there were then no præpostors, "because, from his energetic character and natural ability, he seemed to Dr. Arnold likely to give me efficient help," continues :—"He gave abundant proof that Arnold's choice had been a wise one.  Though he immediately re-established the shattered *prestige* of præpositorial power, he contrived to make himself very popular with various classes of boys.  The younger ones found in him an efficient protector against bullying.  Those of a more literary turn found in him an agreeable and intelligent companion, and were fond of being admitted to sit in his study and talk on matters of intellectual interest.  The democrats had got their master, and submitted with a good grace to power which they could not resist, and which was judiciously and moderately exercised.  The *régime* was wise, firm, and kind, and the house was happy and prosperous.

"From all that I knew of him, both at Rugby and afterwards, I was not surprised at the courage and coolness which the *Times* compared 'to the spirit of a Paladin of old.'  I cannot say how much I regret that I shall not be welcomed in India by the first head of my dear old house at Rugby."

From Rugby my brother went, in October 1840, to Trinity College, Cambridge.  Here, as might have been expected from his previous habits, he took an active interest in boating and other athletic amusements, while at the same time he by no means neglected the more serious and intellectual pursuits of the University. He had a very considerable acquaintance with, and taste for, both classical and general literature, but a constitutional tendency to headache very much stood in the way of any close application to books; and after he had taken his degree in 1844, was one strong reason for his deciding on an active rather than a studious life. The Indian army seemed to offer the best opening, but while waiting for a cadetship, in order to prevent superannuation, he obtained, through the kind introduction of Lord de Saumarez, a commission in the Guernsey Militia from Major-General W. Napier, the Lieutenant-Governor, and there commenced his military life. From the first he felt that the profession of a soldier was one that required to be studied, and took every opportunity of mastering its principles.

On his leaving Guernsey to enter the Honourable East India Company's service, Major-General W. Napier bore this testimony to his character:—"I think he will be an acquisition to any service. His education, his ability, his zeal to make himself acquainted with military matters, gave me the greatest satisfaction during his service with the militia."

# CHAPTER II.

*ARRIVAL IN INDIA—CAMPAIGN ON THE SUTLEJ, 1845-46.*

My brother landed at Calcutta on the 13th of September 1845, and with as little delay as possible proceeded up the country to Agra, where he found a hearty welcome beneath the hospitable roof of the Hon. James Thomason, Lieutenant-Governor of the North-West Provinces, an old family friend and connection, who from that time to his death treated him with as much affection, and took as deep an interest in his career, as if he had been his own son.

He was appointed to do duty with the 2nd Grenadiers, then forming a part of the Governor-General's escort, and accordingly left Agra on November 2. In the following letter he describes his first impressions of camp life in an Indian army.

After mentioning a delay caused by an attack of fever and dysentery on his way to the camp, he proceeds :—

I was able, however, to join the Grenadiers at four o'clock, on the morning of the 7th, and share their dusty march of ten miles to the village near which the Governor-General's camp was pitched. Since that day we have been denizens of a canvas city of a really astonishing extent, seeing that it is the creation of a few hours, and shifts with its enormous population, some ten or fifteen miles a day. I wonder more every day at the ease and magnitude of the arrangements, and the varied and interesting pictures continually before our eyes. Soon after four A.M., a bugle sounds the *reveillé*, and the whole mass is astir at once. The smoke of the evening fires has by this time blown away, and everything stands out clear and defined in the bright moonlight. The Sepoys, too, bring the straw from their tents, and make fires to warm their black faces on all sides, and the groups of swarthy redcoats stooping over the blaze, with a white background of canvas, and the dark clear sky behind all, produce a most picturesque effect as one turns out into the cold. Then the multitudes of camels, horses, and elephants, in all imaginable groups and positions—the groans and cries of the former as they stoop and kneel for their burdens, the neighing of hundreds of horses mingling with the shouts of the innumerable servants and their masters' calls, the bleating of sheep and goats, and louder than all, the shrill screams of the Hindoo women, almost bewilder one's senses as one treads one's way through the canvas streets and squares to the place where the regiment assembles outside the camp.

A second bugle sounds "the assembly." There is a blaze of torches from the Governor's tents; his palanquin carriage drawn by four mules, and escorted by jingling troopers, trots to the front. The artillery thunder forth the morning gun, as a signal that the great man is gone—the guns rattle by—the cavalry push on after them—and then at length our band strikes up. "Forward" is the word, and the red (and black) column moves along, by this time as completely obscured by the dense clouds of dust as though they were in London during a November fog. We are not expected to remain with our men, but mount at once, and ride in a cluster before the band, or ride on a quarter of a mile or so, in twos and threes, complaining of the laziness of the great man's people, and of the dust and cold, as if we were the most ill-used of her Majesty's subjects. As soon as we're off the ground, and the road pretty clear, I dismount, and walk the first eight miles or so, this being the time to recover one's powers of locomotion. The cold is really very great, especially in the hour before sunrise—generally about one and a half or two hours after we start. It soon gets warm enough to make one glad to ride again, and by the time the march is over, and the white city is in sight, the heat is very great, though now diminishing daily. It is a sudden change of temperature, truly—from near freezing at starting, to 90° or 100° at arriving; and it is this, I think, which makes us feel the heat so much in this climate. In the daytime we get on very well; the heat seldom exceeding 86°, and often not more than 84° and 82° in tents. It sounds hot, but a house or tent at 84° is tolerably endurable, especially if there is a breeze. My tent is twelve feet square inside, and contains a low pallet bed, a table, chair, two camel trunks, and brass basin for washing. I will get a sketch of the camp to send you.

*Nov. 18th.*—This nomad life is agreeable in many respects, and very healthy, and one sees a great deal of the country, but it destroys time rather, as the march is not over generally till half-past nine or ten, and then breakfast, a most eagerly-desired composition, and dressing afterwards, do not leave much of the day before the cool evening comes for exercise, or sight-seeing and dining, and by nine most of us are in bed, or near it.

*Dec. 2nd.*—Umbâla.—We had a short march of six miles into Umbâla this morning, and I got leave from our colonel to ride on and see the troops assemble to greet the Governor-General. I never saw so splendid a sight: 12,000 of the finest troops were drawn up in one line, and as I rode slowly along the whole front, I had an excellent opportunity of examining the varied materials of an Indian army. First were the English Horse Artillery; then the dashing dragoons of the 3rd Queen's, most splendidly mounted and appointed; then came the stern, determined-looking British footmen, side by side with their tall and swarthy brethren from the Ganges and Jumna—the Hindoo, the Mussulman, and the white man, all obeying the same word, and acknowledging the same common tie; next to these a large brigade of guns, with a mixture of all colours and creeds; then more regiments of foot, the whole closed up by the regiments of native cavalry; the quiet-looking and English-dressed Hindoo-troopers strangely contrasted with the wild Irregulars in all the fanciful *un*uniformity of their native costume : yet these last are the men *I* fancy for service. Altogether, it was a most interesting sight, either to the historian or soldier, especially as one remembered that these were no men of parade, but assembled here to be poured across the Sutlej at a word.

The "pomp and circumstance" of war were soon to be exchanged for its stern realities, as will be seen in the following letter to his father, dated Christmas Day, 1845 :—

CAMP, SULTANPOOR.

I take the first day of rest we have had to write a few hurried lines to relieve you from any anxiety you may have felt at not hearing from me by the last mails, or from newspaper accounts, which will, I fear, reach you before this letter can. I am most thankful to be able to sit down once more to write to you all but unharmed. Since I wrote, I have been in four general engagements of the most formidable kind ever known in India. For the first time we had to contend with a brave and unconquered people, disciplined, and led on like our own troops by European skill; and the result, though successful to our arms, has been fearful indeed as to carnage. You will see accounts in the papers giving details more accurate than I can possibly furnish, both of our wonderfully rapid and fatiguing marches, and of the obstinate and bloody resistance we met with. On the 10th of this month, on our usual quiet march to Sirhind with the Governor-General's camp, we were surprised by being joined by an additional regiment, and by an order for all non-soldiers to return to Umbâla. From that day we have had the fatigues and exertions of actual warfare in their broadest forms—marching day and night unprecedented distances, scarcity of sleep and food, and all the varieties of cold and heat. I enjoyed all, and entered into it with great zest, till we came to actual blows, or rather, I am (*now*) half ashamed to say, till the blows were over, and I saw the horrible scenes which ensue on war. I have had quite enough of such sights now, and hope it may not be my lot to be exposed to them again. Our loss has been most severe, especially in officers. Our Sepoys could not be got to face the tremendous fire of the Sikh artillery, and, as usual, the more they quailed, the more the English officers exposed themselves in vain efforts to bring them on. The greatest destruction was, however, among the Governor-General's staff—only two (his own son and Colonel Benson) escaped death or severe wounds. They seemed marked for destruction, and certainly met it most gallantly. On the 15th we joined the Commander-in-Chief, with his troops from Umbâla, were put off escort duty, and joined General Gilbert's division. On the 17th we had a march of thirty miles (in the daytime, too), with scanty food; on the 18th, after a fasting march of twenty-five miles, we were summoned, at half-past four in the afternoon, to battle, which lasted till long after dark. Almost the first shot which greeted our regiment killed the man standing by my side, and instantly afterwards I was staggered by a ball from a frightened Sepoy behind me grazing my cheek and blackening my face with the powder—so close was it to my head! We were within twenty, and at times ten, yards of three guns blazing grape into us, and worse than all, the bushes with which the whole ground was covered were filled with marksmen who, unseen by us, could pick us off at pleasure. No efforts could bring the Sepoys forward, or half the loss might have been spared, had they rushed on with the bayonet. We had three officers wounded out of our small party, and lost many of the men. We were bivouacked on the cold ground that night, and remained under arms the whole of the following day. Just as we were going into action, I stumbled upon poor Carey, whom you may remember to have heard of at Price's, at Rugby. On going over the field on the 30th, I found the body actually cut to pieces by the keen swords of the Sikhs, and but for his clothes could not have recognised him. I had him carried into camp for burial, poor fellow, extremely shocked at the sudden termination of our renewed acquaintance. On Sunday, the 21st, we marched before daybreak in force to attack the enemy, who had entrenched themselves behind their formidable artillery. The action began in the afternoon, lasted the whole night, and was renewed with daybreak. They returned again to the charge as often as we gained any advantage, and it was evening before they were finally disposed of by a charge of our dragoons, *and our ammunition was exhausted !*—so near are we in our most triumphant successes to a destruction as complete! The results are, I suppose, in a political point of view, immense indeed. We took from them nearly one hundred large guns, and routed their vast army, prepared, had they succeeded in beating us, to overrun Hindoostan; and it must be owned they had nearly succeeded! It will scarcely be believed, but they had actually purchased and prepared supplies as far into the interior of our country as Delhi, and unknown to our authorities; and the whole of Northern India was, as usual, ready to rise upon us at an hour's notice. On the evening of the 21st, as we rushed towards the guns, in the most dense dust and smoke, and under an unprecedented fire of grape, our Sepoys again gave way and broke. It was a fearful crisis, but the bravery of the English regiments saved us. The Colonel (Hamilton), the greater part of my brother officers, and myself, were left with the colours and about thirty men immediately in front of the batteries! Our escape was most providential, and is, I trust, thankfully acknowledged by us. A ball (from a shell, I fancy) struck my leg below the knee, but happily spared the bone, and only inflicted a flesh wound. I was also knocked down *twice*—once by a shell bursting so close to me as to kill the men behind me, and once by the explosion of a magazine or mine. I am most thankful indeed for my escape from death or maiming. The wound in my leg is nothing, as you may judge when I tell you that I was on foot or horseback the whole of the two following days. Last night we moved on here about five miles from the scene of action, and got some food, and into our beds, after four days and nights on the ground, alternately tried with heat and cold (now most severe at night), and nothing but an occasional mouthful of black native bread. I think, during the four days, all I had to eat would not compose half a home breakfast-loaf, and for a day and night we had not even water; when we did get water, after driving the enemy from their camp, it was found to have been spoiled with gunpowder! It was like eating Leamington water, but our thirst was too great to stick at trifles.

*Dec. 26th.*—We are resting here comfortably again in our tents, and had a turkey for our Christmas dinner last night. The rest is most grateful. We had only nine hours in bed out of five nights, and then the next four were on the ground. So you see I have come in for the realities of a soldier's life pretty early in my career; and since I am spared, it is doubtless a great thing for me in every way. There never has been anything like it in India, and it is not often that an action *anywhere* has lasted thirty-six hours as ours did. It is called a succession of three engagements, but the firing never ceased for a quarter of an hour. Infantry attacking guns was the order of the day, and the loss occasioned by such a desperate resort was fearful. How different your Christmas week will have been from mine! This time last year I was quietly staying at Bisham, and now sleeping on the banks of the Sutlej, with a sea of tents around me for miles and miles! The last few days seem a year, and I can scarcely believe that I have only been four months in India, and only two with my regiment.

At a later period, when it was proposed to erect a monument in Lichfield Cathedral to the 80th Queen's, he wrote with reference to their conduct in one of these actions:—

It is, you know, a Staffordshire regiment, having been raised originally by the Marquis of Anglesey, and has still a great number of Staffordshire men in its ranks. It is a splendid corps, well-behaved in cantonments, and first-rate in action. I lay between them and my present regiment (1st E. B. Fusiliers) on the night of the 21st of December, at Ferozeshah, when Lord Hardinge called out "80th! that gun must be silenced." They jumped up, formed into line, and advanced through the black darkness silently and firmly: gradually we lost the sound of their tread, and anxiously listened for the slightest intimation of their progress—all was still for five minutes, while they gradually gained the front of the battery whose fire had caused us so much loss. Suddenly we heard a dropping fire—a blaze of the Sikh cannon followed, then a thrilling cheer from the 80th, accompanied by a rattling and murderous volley as they sprang upon the battery and spiked the monster gun. In a few more minutes they moved back quietly, and lay down as before in the cold sand; but they had left forty-five of their number and two captains to mark the scene of their exploit by their graves.

---

CAMP, ARMY OF THE SUTLEJ,
*Feb.* 12*th*, 1846.

The fortune of war has again interfered between me and my good intentions of answering all my correspondence by this mail. We have been knocked about for some days so incessantly that there has been no chance of writing anything; and even this scrawl, I fear, will hardly reach you. You will hear publicly of our great victory of the 10th, and of the total and final rout of the Sikh force at Sobraon. But, first, I must tell you that the 2nd Grenadiers were sent back about a week ago to the villages and posts in our rear, to keep open the communication. Not liking the notion of returning to the rear while an enemy was in front, I applied immediately to do duty with another regiment; my petition was granted; and I joined the 16th Grenadiers on the evening of the 9th inst. About three in the morning we advanced towards the Sikh entrenchments along the river's bank. Our guns and ammunition had all come up a day or two before, and during the night were placed in position to shell their camp. At daybreak, seventeen heavy mortars and howitzers, rockets, and heavy guns, commenced a magnificent fire on their position; at half-past eight the infantry advanced—Sir R. Dick's division on the right, and ours (Gilbert's) in front—covered by our fire from the batteries. On we went as usual in the teeth of a dreadful fire of guns and musketry, and after a desperate struggle we got within their *triple* and *quadruple* intrenchments, and then their day of reckoning came indeed. Driven from trench to trench, and surrounded on all sides, they retired, fighting most bravely, to the river, into which they were driven pell-mell, a tremendous fire of musketry pouring on them from our bank, and the Horse Artillery finishing their destruction with grape. The river is literally choked with corpses, and their camp full of dead and dying. An intercepted letter of theirs shows that they have lost 20,000 in killed, wounded, and missing; all their guns remaining in our hands. I had the pleasure myself of spiking two guns which were turned on us. Once more I have escaped, I am thankful to say, unhurt, except that a bullet took a fancy to my little finger and cut the skin off the top of it—a mere pin scratch, though it spoiled a buckskin glove. I am perfectly well: we cross in a day or two, but I fancy have done with fighting.

*To his Sister.*

LAHORE, *Feb. 27th*, 1846.

In honour of your birthday, I suppose, we crossed the Sutlej on the 17th, and are now encamped close to old Runjeet Singh's capital without a shot having been fired on this side the river! The war is over—sixty days have seen the overthrow of the Sikh army, which, when that period commenced, marched from the spot on which the victors are now encamped, with no fewer than 100,000 fighting men, *now*

> "A broken and a routed host,
> Their standards gone, their leaders lost."

So ends the tale of the mightiest army, and the best organised, which India has seen.

I hope you will have got a scrap I wrote after the fight at

Sobraon in hopes it would reach you before the newspapers, as I have no doubt you were all anxious enough on my account, and indeed you well might be, for I can hardly imagine (humanly speaking) how it was possible to go through that storm of bullets and shot unhurt. I have indeed much to be thankful for, and I hope I shall not forget the lesson. A campaign is a wonderful dispeller of false notions and young imaginations, and seems too stern a hint to be soon forgotten.

About this time Mr. Thomason says, in a letter to my father:—

"I hear of William constantly from friends in camp, and am glad to find that he is a great favourite in his regiment. I had some little fear that his great superiority in age and attainments to those of his own standing in the army might make him the object of envy and disparagement. I felt that he had no easy task before him, and that it would be difficult to conduct himself with discretion and becoming humility in such a position. He was quite aware of the difficulty when we talked the matter over at Agra, and I am much pleased to see the success which has attended his prudent exertions."

LAHORE, *March 4th*, 1846.

The army breaks up now very soon, but I shall be posted before that. I am trying to get into the 1st European regiment, now stationed at Umbâla, who have just been styled Fusiliers for their distinguished service. It is the finest regiment in India, with white faces, too, and a very nice set of officers. I have been brigaded with them all along.

It seems an age since the campaign opened. One *day* of fighting such as we have had fastens itself on the memory more than a year of peaceful life. We must really have a natural taste for fighting highly developed, for I catch myself wishing and "asking for more," and grumbling at the speedy settlement of things, and the prospect of cantonments instead of field service. Is it not marvellous, as if one had not had a surfeit of killing? But the truth is, *that* is not the motive, but a sort of undefined ambition. . . . I remember bursting into tears in sheer rage in the midst of the fight at Sobraon at seeing our soldiers lying killed and wounded. Don't let any of my friends forget me yet. I have found a new one, I think, in Major Lawrence (Sir H. Lawrence, K.C.B.), the new President at this Court, thanks to the unwearying kindness of Mr. Thomason.

In a letter of the same date to Hon. J. Thomason, the following sentence occurs:—

I must thank you very much for making me known to Major Lawrence, from whom I have received every sort of attention and kindness. I have been very much struck with his superiority, and freedom from diplomatic solemnity and mystery, which is rather affected by the politicals and officials.

---

CAMP, NUGGUR GHAT, ON THE SUTLEJ,
*March* 27*th*, 1846.

The last returning regiment of the army of the Sutlej crossed that river yesterday morning, and by to-morrow every man will have left its banks, on their way to their stations. It was a most interesting and picturesque sight to see the army filing across the splendid bridge of boats constructed by our engineers at this place. So many of the native corps have been required for the new province and for the Lahore garrison, that we had hardly any but Europeans homeward-bound, which gave an additional and home interest to the passage of the river. Dusty, travel-stained, and tired, but with that cool, firm air of determination which is the most marked characteristic of English soldiers, regiment after regiment passed on, cavalry, artillery, and infantry in succession, their bands playing quick steps and national tunes, as each stepped upon the bridge. To *you* the sight would have been only interesting; but to those of us who had seen the same corps three months ago, their reduced numbers and fearfully thinned ranks told a sadder tale. Regiments cut down to a third, individual companies to a fourth or fifth of their former strength, gave a silent but eloquent reply to the boastful strains of martial music, and to the stirring influence of the pageant. As each regiment moved up on this side the river, our fine old chief addressed a few words of congratulation and praise to each; they pushed on to their tents, and a genuine English cheer, caught up and repeated from corps to corps, and a thundering salute from the artillery, proclaimed the final dispersion, and bid an appropriate farewell to the army of the Sutlej.

Thus ends my first campaign! To-morrow I march with the 26th Native Infantry to Umbála, where I hope to be transferred to the 1st Europeans. I was posted to the 26th a few days ago, but have not joined yet, as I applied at once for an exchange. Marching and living in tents is becoming unpleasantly hot now, and in another fortnight will be very bad. Yesterday we had a regular storm of wind and dust, filling everything with sand, and darkening the air most effectually; one's mouth, eyes, ears, and pockets get filled with dust: you sit down to breakfast, and your plate is ready loaded with sand, your coffee is excellently thickened, and your milk would pass for clotted cream—but for the colour. Then you get a sheet of paper, and vainly imagine you're writing, but the sand conceals the last word you write ere the ink can dry, and your pens split of themselves with the dryness of the air. In truth, it is next to impossible to do anything while the storm lasts, for one's eyes smart and cry with the plenitude of grit; and if you talk, you are set coughing with eating small stones! Yet all this is far better than the damp-exhaling heat of Bengal. Here the ground and air are as dry by night as by day, and no exhalation poisons the freshness of any wind that may be stirring.

UMBÂLA, *April* 13*th*, 1846.

Here I am once more. I am writing in a comfortable house, and actually slept in one last night—the first time I have eaten or slept under a roof since the 3rd of November; and on the 10th I saw a lady again!

I find General Napier has written to his brother about me. Scindh has been given over to the Bombay army, so that Sir Charles can't do anything for me, but still the kindness is all the same. Unfortunately, the note reached me three days after Sir Charles left the army to return to Scindh, or I might have had the pleasure of seeing him and speaking to him.

---

CAMP, MORADABAD, ROHILCUND,
*April* 29*th*, 1846.

It is time indeed to be getting under cover, for we have been in the thick of the "hot winds." This sounds a very mild word, but you should only just try it! Do you remember ever holding your face over a stove when it was full of fire? and the rush of hot air which choked you? Well, something of that sort, of vast volume and momentum, blowing what they call at sea "half a gale of wind," comes quietly up, at first behind a wall of dust, and then with a roar bursts upon you, scorching you, and shrivelling you up as if you were "a rose that was plucked." It feels as if an invisible, colourless flame was playing over your face and limbs, scorching without burning you, and making your skin and hair crackle and stiffen until you are covered with "crackling" like a hot roast pig. This goes on day after day, from about eight or nine o'clock in the morning till sunset; and, accompanied with the full power of the blazing sun of India, produces an amount of heat and dryness almost inconceivable. The only resource is to get behind a tattee (or wet grass mat) hung up at one of the doors of the tent, and to lie on the ground with as little motion as possible, and endeavour to sleep or read it out. *Nunc veterum libris, nunc somno et inertibus horis*—I cannot go on, for the "sweet forgetfulness" of the past is too much to expect! To-day we have a new nuisance in the shape of a plague of wood-lice; our camp is pitched in an old grove of mango-trees, and is literally swarming with huge pale lice, in numbers numberless. You cannot make a step without slaying them, and they have already (noon) covered the whole sides of the tents, chairs, beds, tables, and everything. But one is really getting used to everything, and I hardly expect to be *proud* again. Our rest has been terribly destroyed by this last month's marching, the usual hour for the *réveille* being two A.M., and this morning a quarter to one!! and no power of quizzing can move our worthy major to let us take it easily, though I don't scruple to tell him that he has sold his shadow or his soul to the evil powers, and forfeited the power of sleep, he is such a restless animal! We breakfast at seven, or even a quarter-past six, constantly, and dine at seven P.M.; so one has a fair opportunity of practising abstinence, as I rigidly abstain from eating in the meantime, or drinking. After all, it is very healthy weather, and I imagine there is less harm done to the health in the hot winds than even in the cold weather. I have never been so well in India.

---

NYNEE TAL, *May 14th*, 1846.

I am writing from the last new Hill Station, discovered about three years ago by an adventurous traveller, and now containing forty houses and a bazaar. It is a "tal" or lake, of about a mile in length, lying in a basin of the mountains, about 6200 feet above the sea; the hills rising about 1800 feet on all sides of it, and beautifully wooded from their very summits down to the water's brink. How I got here remains to be told. You will remember that I had applied some time ago to be transferred to the 1st Bengal European Fusiliers. Well, after keeping me in suspense some seven weeks, and sending me the whole way from

Lahore to Bareilly in April and May, I received notice that my application was granted, and a civil request to go back again. I had had enough of marching in the plains, and travelling dâk would have been madness for me, so I determined on going up into the hills, and making my way across the mountain ranges to Subathoo, where my regiment is stationed. A good-natured civilian at Bareilly offered to take me with him to this place, from whence I could make a good start. We started on the morning of the 11th, and drove to Rampoor, stayed there till midnight, and then set off for the hills. By daylight we got to the edge of the "Terai," the far-famed hot-bed of fever and tigers, swamps and timber, along the whole ridge of the Himalayas, stretching along the plains at their feet in a belt of about twenty miles from the Indus to the Burhampootra. Here we found horses awaiting us, and mounting at once, started for a ride of twenty-seven miles before breakfast. The first part of the "Terai" is merely a genuine Irish bog, and the oily, watery ditches and starved-looking cows shout out "Fever" on all sides of you. The last ten miles to the foot of the hills is through a dense mass of ragged trees in all stages of growth and decay, " horrida, inculta, hirsuta,"—moist, unpleasant, and ugly. At length we reached the first low woody ranges of the hills, and following the dry bed of a mountain stream, by noon we doubled the last ridge, and descended upon our lake. None of these hills are to be compared in beauty with Scotland and Wales, though very fine, and inexpressibly refreshing, almost *affecting*, after the dead flat we have lived in so long. As soon as my servants arrive, I start hence by myself, through an unfrequented sea of vast mountains, by way of Landour, or Mussoorie, to Simla and Subathoo. It is about 340 miles, and will take me thirty-two or thirty-four days to accomplish. I mean to take no pony, but trust that my old powers of walking and endurance will revive in the mountain air.

# CHAPTER III.

### *FIRST BENGAL EUROPEAN FUSILIERS—LAWRENCE ASYLUM—APPOINTMENT TO GUIDE CORPS.*

SUBATHOO, *June* 16*th*, 1846.

WHEN I wrote to you last from Sireenuggur, I hoped to have been able to reach this place by way of the hills and Simla; but before I got to Mussoorie, the early setting in of the rains made it so difficult and unpleasant (and likely to be dangerous) to get on, that after spending two days there, I rode down to Deyra Dhoon, and came dâk through Saharunpoor and Umbâla to Kalka, at the foot of these hills, where I found my beast awaiting my arrival, and mounted the seventeen miles of hill at once. Here I am at last with my own regiment, and with the prospect of being quiet for four months. I am eighth Second Lieutenant; a distinguished position (is it not?) at the age of five-and-twenty. The campaign, I am sorry to say, did me no good in the way of promotion, owing to my not having been "posted" permanently before it commenced.

---

SUBATHOO, *July* 3*rd*, 1846.

I hope you will congratulate me on getting into my present splendid corps, the 1st Fusiliers, now, alas! a mere shadow of what it was six months ago. We could only muster 256 men under arms when we were inspected by Sir R. Gilbert on the 1st; but then there was a most picturesque body of convalescents present with their empty sleeves, pale faces, and crutches, but looking proudly conscious of their good conduct, and ready "to do it again." We are under much stricter discipline in this corps, both officers and men, and obliged to be orderly and submissive. No bad thing for us either. I hold there is more real liberty in being under a decent restraint than in absolute freedom from any check. I have been much more reconciled to India since I joined this regiment. It is pleasant to have white faces about one, and hear one's own tongue spoken; and then, besides, there is a home-loving feeling in this corps which I have never met with in India. I believe we would each and all migrate to England, if we had our own way.

---

*To his Father.*

SIMLA, *Sept. 2nd,* 1846.

I came here on the 31st for a week, to stay with Major Lawrence (now a Colonel and C.B.), who dined and slept with me at Subathoo last week, and pressed me to come here. I am nothing loth, as I like him amazingly, and value his friendship very much, and pick up a great deal of information as to India, and Indians black and white. He has kindly offered to take me with him for a tour through Jullunder Doâb, and up to Jummoo, Rajah Gholab Singh's camp and court. He says he can give or get me leave to accompany him. My colonel says he won't give any one leave after the 14th of this month. Which is right remains to be seen, but I think you may calculate that the "Agent to the Governor-General" will prevail, and I shall see Jummoo.

I am now writing in his room with the incessant entrances and exits of natives—rajahs, princes, vakeels, &c. &c., and officers civil and military; and the buzz of business and confusion of tongues, black and white, learned and unlearned, on all subjects, political, religious (at this minute they are disputing what "the Church" means), and military, so that I am tolerably puzzled. I have been taking a tremendously long walk this morning about the hills and valleys, with Mr. and Mrs. Currie, and enjoying the beauties of Simla.

---

SIMLA, *Sept.* 14*th*, 1846.

My original week at Simla has grown into a month, thanks to Colonel Lawrence's pressing, and Colonel Orchard's (*my* colonel's) kindness. I should hardly like staying so long with Colonel Lawrence (especially as I live day and night in the same room with him and his papers, regularly camp fashion), but that he wishes it, and I manage to give him a slight helping hand by making *précis* of his letters, and copying confidential papers. He is amazingly kind, and tells me all that is going on, initiating me into the mysteries of "political" business, and thus giving me more knowledge of things and persons Indian than I should learn in a year of ordinary life; ay, or in three years either. This is a great advantage to my ultimate prospects, of course independently of the power he possesses of giving me a lift in the world when I am of sufficient standing to hold any appointment.

He makes me work at Hindoostanee, and has given me a lesson or two in the use of the theodolite, and other surveying instruments, to the end that I may get employed in the Surveying Department, after two years of which, he says, "I shall be fit for a Political."

I have been very fortunate in many ways, more so than I had any right to expect. If I were only nearer to you all, and had any old friends about me, I should have nothing to regret or wish for. It is *there* that the shoe especially pinches. All minor annoyances are easily got rid of, but one *does* find a wonderful lack of one's old friends and old associations. Society is very different here from ours at home, and different as it is, I have seen very little of it. Nor am I, with my previous habits, age, and education, the person to feel this an indifferent matter; but, on the contrary, all the drawbacks of Indian existence come with redoubled force from the greatness of the contrast. Still I do not let these things annoy me, or weigh down my spirits, but strive, by keeping up English habits, tastes, and feelings, and looking forward to a run home (thus having a motive always in view), to make the best of everything as it occurs, and to act upon the principle, that mere outward circumstances don't make a man's happiness. If I have one feeling stronger than another, it is contempt for a "regular Indian," a man who thinks it fine to adopt a totally different set of habits and morals and fashions, until, in forgetting that he is an Englishman, he usually forgets also that he is a Christian and a gentleman. Such characters are happily rare now, but there are many fragments of it on a small scale, and always must be so, so long as the men who are to support the name and power of England in Asia are sent out here at an age when neither by education or reflection can they have learnt all or even a fraction of what those words imply. It would be a happy thing for India and for themselves if *all* came out here at a more advanced age than now, but *one* alone breaking through the custom in that respect made and provided, must not expect to escape the usual fate, or at least the usual annoyances, of innovators.

I have enjoyed my visit here very much, and though I have not sought them, have made one or two very pleasant acquaintances, or improved them. I have been very little out, and passed my time almost entirely with Colonel Lawrence and his family, *i.e.*, his brother and the two sisters-in-law. Things are not looking well on the frontier. Cashmere and the hill country won't submit to Gholab Singh, to whom we gave them over, and have been thrashing his troops and killing his ministers; and I expect October will see an army assembled to frighten them into submission, or interfere with a strong arm, as the case may be.

We seem bound to see him established on the throne we carved out for him, and it is our only chance of keeping peace and order; though at the best he is such a villain, and so detested, that I imagine it will be but a sorry state of quietness—

"The torrent's smoothness ere it dash below."

In a letter to his wife, during this visit, Sir H. Lawrence says:—

"*Sept. 1st.*—I brought up with me from Subathoo a fine young fellow, by name Hodson, son of the Archdeacon of Stafford. He is now (10 P.M.) sleeping in my little office-room, where I am writing. Thomason recommended him to me, and I have seldom met so promising a young fellow. He left the native branch of the army at the expense of some steps, because he did not like the conduct of the Sepoys. He was for four years with Dr. Arnold, and two in the sixth form under his eye. He speaks most affectionately of him. I will try to get leave for him for a month to accompany me to Lahore and Jummoo in October. . . . I get a good deal of help from Hodson, who works *willingly* and *sensibly*. Perhaps you may meet the family at Lichfield."

LAHORE, *October 14th*, 1846.

As I hoped when I wrote last, I am again writing from the capital of the "Singhs," but, alas for the "lions," their tails are very much down in the world since this time last year, when the "fierce and formidable army" assembled to invade our tempting provinces. Nearly half the garrison has marched across the Ravee, and not more than 5000 or 6000 British troops now hold the far-famed capital of Runjeet Singh.

You must not be alarmed by the accounts you will see in the papers by this mail of the advance of two forces from Lahore and Jullunder towards Jummoo. They are not to take any active part in the operations of Gholab Singh for the recovery of Cashmere from the rebellious Sheikh Imaumoodeen—our troops are to hold the Maharaja's country for him while he advances with his whole disposable force, augmented by a Sikh auxiliary army.

It is probable that the Sheikh will give in without fighting as soon as he hears the preparations made by both powers for his coercion. Indeed, a letter has arrived from Cashmere to say he *has* given in ; but he is a wily fellow, and I mightily distrust him. I only know if *I* was in Cashmere with my army at my back, *I* would not give in as long as a man was left to pull a trigger ! The Agent (Colonel Lawrence) and I start to-morrow evening, going seventy miles the first day, and hope to reach Bhimbur, at the foot of the hills, on the 17th, thence to go up and join the Maharaja, and accompany his army to Cashmere. If he fights we shall see the fun ; if not, we are to accompany him and keep him from excesses and injustice in the valley, and return here, I fancy, in about a month or six weeks. Of course, in event of the two armies coming to blows, it will probably be some time longer ere we return. I am delighted at the thoughts of seeing Cashmere, and am gaining great advantage from being with these " politicals " in the way of learning the languages, and the method of governing the natives. I have been hard at work day and night for some time now, writing for Colonel Lawrence. I left Subathoo on the 1st, and after a ride of some twenty miles through the hills, joined Colonel Lawrence and Mr. Christian, and after a shake-down in a little mud bungalow, and an amusing dinner (served up in two brass basins, standing on a bed), and a breakfast to match, we rode down to Roopur, on the Sutlej. Here we took boat, and floated down the river to Ferozepore, and came across to Lahore during the night in a capital barouche belonging to the Ranee, with relays of horses and an escort of cavalry.

THANNA, AT THE FOOT OF THE PASS
INTO CASHMERE, *Oct.* 26*th*, 1846.

Our tent is pitched on the top of a little spur from the mountain side, and beneath us lie, in quaint picturesque confusion, scattered over the valley and the little staircase-like rice fields, the mingled hosts of Lahore and Jummoo. The spare stalwart Sikh, with his grizzled beard and blue turban of the scantiest dimensions, side by side with the huge-limbed Affghan, with voluminous head-gear and many-coloured garments. The proud Brahmin in the same ranks with the fierce " Children of the Faithful ; " the little active Hill-man ; the diminutive, sturdy, platter-faced Ghoorka, and the slight-made Hindoostanee, collected in the same tents, and all alike clothed in a caricature of the British uniform. I have been very much interested and amused by this march with a native army, so different from our own proceedings and our own military power—albeit the British army will soon be as varied in its composition.

I have seen a great deal of the native Sirdars or chiefs, especially Tej Singh, who commanded the Sikh forces in the war, and of the Maharaja. The former a small, spare little man, marked with the small-pox, and with a thin and scanty beard, but sharp and intelligent, and by his own account *a hero*. The Maharaja is a fine, tall, portly man, with a splendid expressive face, and most gentlemanly, pleasing manner, and fine-toned voice—altogether the most pleasing Asiatic I have seen—to all appearance, the gentlest of the gentle, and the most sincere and truthful character in the world. And in his habits he is certainly exemplary; but he is the cleverest hypocrite in the world; as sharp and acute as possible, devoured by avarice and ambition, and, when roused, horribly cruel. This latter accusation he rebuts, by alleging the necessity of the case and the ferocity of those he has to deal with. To us, however, his fondness for flaying men alive, cutting off their noses and ears and hands, &c., savours *rather* of the inexcusable. He was accused of having flayed 12,000 men, which he indignantly asserted was a monstrous calumny, as he only skinned *three;* afterwards he confessed to *three hundred!* Yet he is not a bit worse, and in many ways infinitely better, than most native princes. Lawrence doubts whether *one* could be found with fewer faults, if placed in similar circumstances. Avitabile, to the disgrace of his European blood, was far more cruel. The stories current in the Punjab of his abominations are horrible. The costumes of these chiefs would delight you. They never make a mistake in colours, and the effect is always good, however bright they may be. This force is (as I told you) moving up to turn the Sheikh

Imaumoodeen, the rebellious vassal of the Lahore Government, out of Cashmere, in virtue of the treaty ceding it to Gholab Singh. Up to yesterday, I expected it would be a fight, but yesterday the Sheikh sent letters to say he was sorry and repentful, and was on his way to tender his submission. So we wait here to receive him. This will not, however, prevent my visit to the valley, as Colonel Lawrence intends to accompany the Maharaja to pacify and take possession.

It is very cold here, though not much above 5000 feet above the sea.

---

*To his Father.*

SHUPYEN, IN CASHMERE,
*Nov. 6th,* 1846.

I write a hurried line to announce my safe arrival in the valley. On the 1st we got hold of the rebellious Sheikh, and sent him down to the plains; and yesterday, Colonel Lawrence, Captain Browne, and myself, rode into the valley, amid the acclamations of an admiring population—of beggars! I am writing at sunrise in a little tent, and in spite of two coats and waistcoats, I am nearly "friz." We crossed the Pir Punjal Pass on the 4th, 12,000 feet above the sea, with snow all around us, and slept on this side in an old serai; I say *slept,* because we went to bed; but sleeping was out of the question, from the cold, and uproar of all our followers and their horses, crowded into a courtyard thirty feet square, horses and men quarrelling and yelling all night long. The view from the top of the Pass was very fine, but the wind far too high to take more than a peep of it without losing one's eyes; but the road from Thanna to the summit was most lovely the whole way, winding up a glen wooded magnificently, and the rocks towering above us on all sides; the trees were all in their varied autumn dress, surmounted by forests of pine; altogether, I never saw so grand a scene. As the Sheikh's submission has cut the Gordian knot of politics here, we shall only stay a few days to see the valley, and instal the Maharaja (who is following us with his force by slow stages), and then rush back to Lahore and Subathoo.

This is said to be the largest town but three in the valley. It is a poverty-stricken scattered hamlet of mud houses with wooden roofs, the upper half being generally rough open lattice-work or railing, with alternate supports of unbaked bricks; low mud enclosures, and open waste spaces between, dedicated to dogs and dunghills. The whole is thickly grown over with fine apple and walnut trees, the staple fruits (with the grape) of the valley, and the food of the people. *They* are a poor wretched set, only good for beasts of burden—and certainly they can carry a vast load—their dress, both men and women, being a loose wide-sleeved smock-frock of dirty sackcloth-looking woollen. The men wear a dirty skull-cap on their shaven "nobs," and the women a crimson machine, like a flowerpot-saucer inverted, from which depends a veil or cloth of the same texture as the frock; legs and feet clothed in their native dirt. The women are atrociously ugly, and screech like the witches in *Macbeth*—so much so, that when the Agent asked me to give them a rupee or two, I felt it my duty to refuse firmly, but respectfully, on the ground that it would be encouraging ugliness! I fancy the climate and the soil are unrivalled, but years of poverty and oppression have reduced to a nation of beggars what ought to be a Paradise. We go hence after breakfast to Islumabad, at the eastern end of the valley; and spend a day or two in looking about us, and floating down the river to Cashmere itself, by which time our "prince" will have arrived. I am the luckiest dog unhung to have actually got into Cashmere. I fancy I am the first officer of our army who has been here, save the few who have come officially. These delightful breezes are most invigorating. I only wish you could all enjoy these travels with me. I expect to be back at Subathoo by the 1st of December.

In a letter to my father about this time, Mr. Thomason says:—

"I am very glad to observe that such an intimacy has sprung up between Colonel Lawrence and your William. He could not be under better direction.

"Colonel Lawrence has evidently taken him entirely into his confidence, which cannot but be of the greatest use to him in his future career. He will have opportunities of observation and instruction now, which very few possess after a long period of service. To be selected, too, as his confidant by a man of Colonel Lawrence's stamp, is no small feather in the cap of any young man. He stands deservedly high also in the esteem of all who know him; and if it please God to spare his life and give him health, his prospects are as good as any man's can be in this country."

Colonel Lawrence having discovered that my brother could *work*, was by no means disposed to let him remain without full occupation, as his next letter will show:—

SUBATHOO, *April 1st*, 1847.

I am wonderfully well and flourishing, and have lots to do. Lawrence has made me undertake the secretaryship of the new Asylum for European Children, building some ten miles hence, at Sunawur, which will give me volumes of correspondence, and leagues, nay latitudes, of riding. Nevertheless, it is well, and it is a good work. The responsibility will be great, as a committee of management, on an average three hundred miles apart, are rather nominal in their supervision of things.

---

SUBATHOO, *April 1st*, 1847.

If my locomotive instinct has been brought into play in India, as you suggest, my constructive organs are likely to have their share of exercise. I have the entire direction and arrangement of the new Hill Asylum on my hands just now. It is seven miles hence, of mountain roads, and what with going and coming, planning, instructing, and supervising, my time is pretty well occupied, to say nothing of my regiment, and private affairs. Building a house in India is a different affair from one's previous experiences. You begin from the forest and the quarry, have to get lime burnt, trees cut down, bricks made, planks sawn up, the ground got ready, and then watch the work foot by foot—showing this "nigger" how to lay his bricks, another the proper proportions of a beam, another the construction of a door, and to the several artisans the mysteries of a screw, a nail, and a hinge. You cannot say to a man, "Make me a wall or a door," but you must with your own hands measure out his work, teach him to saw away here, to plane there, or drive such a nail, or insinuate such another suspicion of glue. And when it comes to be considered that this is altogether new work to me, and has to be excuded by cogitation on the spot, so as to give an answer to every inquirer, you may understand the amount of personal exertion and attention required for the work.

I have the sole direction and control of nearly four hundred and fifty workmen, including paying them, keeping accounts, drawing plans, and everything. I have to get earth dug for bricks, see the moulds made, and watch the progress of them till the kiln is full, get wood for the kiln, and direct the lighting of the same, and finally provide a goat to sacrifice to the demon who is supposed to turn the bricks red! Then I must get bamboos and grass cut for thatching, and string *made* for the purpose; send about the hills for sand for mortar, and limestone to burn, see it mixed and prepared, and then show the niggers how to use it. Then the whole of the woodwork must be set out and made under one's own eye, and a lump of iron brought from the mine to be wrought (also under one's direction) into nails and screws, before a single door can be set up; and when to all this is added the difficulty of getting hands (I mean in the hills), and the bother of watching the idlest and most cunning race on earth, you may suppose my "unpaid magistracy" is no sinecure. I am not exaggerating or indeed telling half the difficulty, for fear you should think the whole a romance. You will naturally ask how I learnt all these trades. I can only say that you can't be more astonished than I am myself, and can only satisfy you by the theory that "necessity is the mother of invention." I am seldom able to sit down from sunrise to sunset, when I get a hasty dinner, and am then only too glad to sleep off the effects of the day. How I have escaped fever during the last month I cannot think, as it has been terribly hot in the sun, even in the hills, and I have lived in the blaze of it pretty constantly. Colonel Lawrence seems determined I shall have nothing to stop me, for his invariable reply to every question is, "Act on your own judgment;" "Do what you think right;" "I give you *carte blanche* to act in my name, and draw on my funds," and so forth.

Are you aware of the nature of the institution? It was started in idea by Colonel Lawrence some two or three years ago, and a sufficient sum of money for a commencement having been raised, he charged me with the erection of the necessary buildings, and the organisation and setting in motion of the great machine which is to regenerate and save from moral and physical degradation, sickness and death, the children of the British soldiers serving in India. The object is to teach them all things useful, while you give them the advantage of a healthy climate, removed from the evil influence of a barrack-room. The children are to remain in the Asylum until their parents return to England, or till old enough to join the ranks, or be otherwise provided for.

Another drag upon my hands is the care of a small European boy who was lately found up in Cabul, and is supposed to be the son of some soldier of the destroyed army. He has been brought up as a Mussulman, and made to believe his father was such, and is a very bigot. Colonel Lawrence sent him to me from Lahore, but forgot to write about him, so I know no more of him than I have seen in the newspapers, and have no idea what to do with him, or where he is to go. He is rather a nuisance, and I shall be glad when he goes, as there is little but his odd fate to interest one in him; and I have considerable doubts as to his genuine origin. He is more like a half-caste than a "European." Our communication is brief, as he speaks but little Hindoostanee, and I less Persian. The Asylum is a much more interesting occupation, as, independently of its object, there is a pleasure in covering a fine mountain with buildings of one's own designing.

A few days later he writes:—

My last few days at the Asylum were enlivened by the arrival of Mrs. George Lawrence, whose tent was pitched close to mine on the hill-top. She is a great acquisition in a forest life, and a very nice person—the wife of the Captain Lawrence who was one of the Cabul prisoners. She is to be superintendress until the arrival of the future man from England. I have fourteen little girls to take care of, by the same token, and listen to the grumblings of their nurses. In short, I don't know myself, and that is the long and short of it. I am going to Simla for a day or two, to see Mr. Thomason.

And again, to his brother:—

The state of things is so provokingly quiet and placid, that there seems but small chance of our being called upon for another rush across country (called a "forced march") like the one of December 1845; and one is obliged to take to anything that offers to avoid the "tædium vitæ" which the want of employment engenders in this "lovely country," in those, at least, who have not learnt to exist in the philosophical medium of brandy and cheroots. Did I tell you, by the by, that I abjured tobacco when I left England, and that I have never been tempted by even a night "al fresco" to resume the delusive habit? Nor have I told you (because I despaired of your believing it) that I have declined from the paths of virtue in respect to beer also, this two years past, seldom or never even tasting that once idolised stimulant!! It has not been caused alone by a love of eccentricity, but by the very sensitive state of my inner man (achieved in India), which obliges me to live by rule. This is all very edifying, no doubt, to *you;* to me it is especially so, for I believe if I get on well in India, it will be owing, physically speaking, to my *digestion.*

---

SUBATHOO, *June* 18*th,* 1847.

I am getting on famously at the Asylum just now, and have succeeded in getting the children under cover before the rains. I have narrowly escaped a bad fever through over-work in the sun, but by taking it in time I got right again. The weather has since taken a turn, and become much cooler, besides which my principal anxiety is over for the season. I have certainly had a benefit of work, both civil and literary, for the Institution, and since Colonel Lawrence put an advertisement in the papers, desiring all anxious persons to apply to me, I have had enough on my hands. It is all very well, but interferes with my reading no little; and I am sure to get more kicks than thanks for my pains from an ungrateful and undiscerning public. However, as long as Colonel Lawrence leaves everything so completely in my hands, and trusts so implicitly to my skill and honesty, it would be a shame not to work "*un*-like a nigger."

It is intended that the children should remain in the Institution until they are eighteen years of age, if their fathers be alive, and until somehow or other provided for, should they be orphans. The majority of the boys will, of course, become soldiers; but my belief is, that having been brought up in the delightful climate of the Himalaya, they will, after ten or fifteen years, settle down in the various stations and slightly elevated valleys in these hills, as traders and cultivators, and form the nucleus of the first British colony in India. My object is to give them English habits from the first, which they have in most cases to learn, from being brought up by native nurses from infancy. Part of the scheme is to make the Institution support itself, and I am very shortly going to start a farm-yard. I have already got a fine large garden in full swing; and here you may see French beans, cabbages, strawberry plants, and fine potatoes (free from disease). I steadfastly refuse the slightest dash of colour in admitting children. People may call this illiberal if they please; the answer is obvious. Half-castes stand the climate of the plains too well to need a hill sanitorium, and by mixing them with English children you corrupt those whom you wish to benefit. The little boy who was lately redeemed from Cabul, and whom Colonel Lawrence consigned to my care, is the plague of my existence. He has the thoroughly lying, deceitful habits, and all the dirt, of the Affghan races, and not a single point of interest to counterbalance them.

In 1854 Sir H. Lawrence wrote in an account of the Asylum:—' As soon as the site was fixed Lieutenant Hodson took much trouble with the buildings. The less said about me the better, but give the credit to my brother, to Edwardes, Hodson, and others, who from the beginning have helped me.'

SUBATHOO, *August* 1847.

I have some hopes, though but faint ones, of being relieved from the necessity of a move to Cawnpore [whither his regiment had been ordered], by obtaining a berth under Colonel Lawrence. I know that he has asked for me, and, I believe, for an appointment which would please me more than any other he could find, as being one of the most confidential nature, and involving constant locomotion, and plenty of work both for head, nerve, and body. But I must not be sanguine, as we have already a large proportion of officers away from the regiment, and I am a young soldier, though, alas! growing grievously old in years.

The appointment alluded to was to the " Corps of Guides," then recently organised by Colonel Lawrence for service in the Punjab. While this question, however, was still pending, there seemed a prospect of Lieutenant Hodson's succeeding to the adjutancy of his regiment, and Colonel Lawrence, as will be seen from the subjoined letter, recommended his accepting it, if offered :—

"SIMLA, *Sept.* 11*th*, 1847.

"MY DEAR HODSON,—I have spoken to the Governor-General about you, who at once replied, 'Let him take the adjutancy.' He wishes you well, but is puzzled by the absentee question. We are all, moreover, agreed on the usefulness to yourself of being employed for a time as adjutant to a regiment. There are always slips, but I know of no man of double or treble your standing who has so good a prospect before him. Favour and partiality do occasionally give a man a lift, but depend upon it that *his* is the best chance in the long run who helps himself. So far you have done this manfully, and you have reason to be proud of being selected at one time for three different appointments by three different men. Don't, however, be too proud. Learn your duties thoroughly. Continue to study two or three hours a day; not to pass in a hurry, but that you may do so two or three years hence with *éclat.* Take advantage of Becher's being at Kussowlee to learn something of surveying. All knowledge is useful; but to soldier or official of any sort in India, I know no branch of knowledge which so well repays the student.

"In Oriental phrase, pray consider that much is said in this hurried scrawl, and believe that I shall watch your career with warm interest.—I am, very sincerely yours,

"H. M. LAWRENCE."

The expected vacancy, however, did not occur, and Colonel Lawrence accordingly renewed his application for my brother's services in the Punjab, and, as will be seen, with success. In the beginning of October he writes :—

I have every reason to expect that before many days I shall be gazetted as attached to the Guide Corps. The immediate result of my appointment will be a speedy departure to Lahore with

Colonel Lawrence, who returns there to arrange matters before going home.

And on the 16th :—

You will, I am sure, rejoice with me at my unprecedented good fortune in being appointed to a responsible and honourable post, almost before, by the rules of the service, I am entitled to take charge of a company of Sepoys. I shall even be better off than I thought; instead of merely " doing duty " with the Guide Corps, I am to be the second in command.

The next chapter will show how well Lieut. Hodson justified Colonel Lawrence's selection of him for so responsible a command, one which the course of events made far more important than could then have been foreseen. It was in this that he laid the foundations of his reputation as an " unequalled partisan leader," and acquired his experience of the Sikhs, and extraordinary influence over them.

# CHAPTER IV.

*EMPLOYMENT IN THE PUNJAB AS SECOND IN COMMAND OF THE CORPS OF GUIDES, AND ALSO AS ASSISTANT TO THE RESIDENT AT LAHORE.*

*From October, 1847, during the Campaign of 1848-9, to the Annexation of the Punjab in March, 1849.*

CAMP, KUSSOOR, *Nov. 15th,* 1847.

I ALMOST forget the many events that have happened since I wrote last: I believe I was "at home" in my snug little cottage in Subathoo, and now I am in a high queer-looking native house among the ruins of this old stronghold of the Pathàns; with orders "to make a good road from Lahore to the Sutlej, distance forty miles," in as brief a space as possible. On the willing-to-be-generally-useful principle this is all very well, and one gets used to turning one's hand to everything, but certainly (but for "circumstances over which I had no control") I always laboured under the impression that I knew nothing at all about the matter. However, Colonel Lawrence walked into my room promiscuously one morning, and said, "O Hodson! we have agreed that you must take in hand the road to Ferozepoor—you can start in a day or two;" and *here I am.* Well, I have galloped across the country hither and thither, and peered into distances with telescopes, and inquired curiously into abstruse (and obtuse) angles, rattled Gunter's chains, and consulted compasses and theodolites, till I have an idea of a road that will astonish the natives not a little. Last night I was up half the night, looking out for fires which I had ordered to be lighted in sundry places along the line of the Sutlej at a fixed hour, that I might find the nearest point. This morning, I had a grand assembly of village "punches," to discuss with them the propriety of furnishing able-bodied men for the work. By a little artful persuasion, I succeeded in raising 700 from a small district, and am going onwards to hold another such " county meeting" to-morrow. The mode and fashion that has always obtained in public works under native governments, has been to give an order to seize *all* the inhabitants, and make them work—*and not pay them then.* These gentry, therefore, have been so bullied by their Sikh masters, that they hardly believe my offers of ready-money payments. My predecessor, an artillery officer, who came here on the same errand, was turned off for resorting to violent measures in his anxiety to get hold of workmen, having hung some of the head men up by the heels to trees *till they were convinced.* He got no good (nor hands either) by his dodge. So I was sent here on the other persuasion, and you will be glad to hear, for the credit of the family, that I am gammoning the dear old punches most deliciously. They'd give me anything, bless their innocent hearts! when I get under the village tree with them, or by the village well, and discourse eloquently on the blessing to society of having destroyed the Sikhs, and on the lightness of their land-tax. I hope to be relieved in a month, and go up to Peshawur to join "the Guides," for this is cruelly hard work, and I have had enough for one year of native workpeople. Besides, I am not strong yet, and have a horrid cold. I would give anything to be able to sit down and read a book quietly, a luxury I have not enjoyed for many a long day. Colonel Lawrence starts for England on the 30th for two years. I hope you will contrive to see him, and make his acquaintance. Sir F. Currie is to be his successor during his absence.

*Dec. 1st.*

I have been at Lahore to receive Colonel Lawrence's parting instructions, and say good-bye to him, poor fellow. He is a genuinely kind-hearted mortal, and has been a brother to me ever since I knew him. I hope to see him back in two years, invigorated and renewed, to carry out the good work which he has so nobly begun.

---

### To his Sister.

CAMP KUSSOOR, *Dec.* 15*th*, 1847.

Your letter met me on my road two days ago, and emerged from the folds of a Sikh horseman's turban, to my great delight. I got off my horse, and walked along, driving him before me till I had read the packet. You must not conclude, because I am writing to you a second time from this place, that I have been here ever since I first commenced operations in these parts. I have been twice to Lahore, and several times to various intermediate and more distant places, since then. In short, you may give up all idea of being able to imagine where I may be at any given time. My work has progressed considerably. In three weeks I have collected and got into working order upwards of a thousand most unwilling labourers, surveyed and marked out some twenty miles of road through a desert and forest, and made a very large piece of it. I am happy to say I am to be relieved in a day or two, and sent to survey another district. I have had one or two visitors the last few days, and therefore not been so lonely as usual; but my time has been even more than ever occupied. My duties are nearly as various as there are hours in the day; at one time digging a trench, at another time investigating breaches of the peace. I am a sort of justice of the peace for general purposes, and have to listen to and inquire into complaints, and send cases which I think worthy of it for trial to Lahore. I caught as neat a case of robbing and murder the other day as ever graced Stafford Assizes; to say nothing of endless modes of theft, more or less open, according to the wealth or power of the stealer. This is the most remarkable scene of ruin I have met with for many a long day; erst, a nest of the abodes of wealthy Pathàn nobles, and now a desert tract, of many miles in extent, covered with ruins, with here and there a dome, or cupola, or minaret, to mark what has once been.

I am happy to say that I have succeeded in obtaining a respite on Sundays. Hitherto, all the works I have had in hand have gone on the same every day, and consequently one's annoyance and responsibility continued equally on Sundays. This is happily put an end to, and I shall have one day's rest a week at least, to say nothing of higher considerations. An order on the subject was issued six months ago, but great difficulties were in the way of its execution.

---

CAMP, DEENANUGGUR, *Jan.* 15*th*, 1848.

Here I am off again like a steam-engine, calling at a series of stations, puffing and panting, hither and thither, never resting, ever starting; now in a cutting, now in a tunnel; first in a field, next on a hill; thus passes day after day, week after week, a great deal of work going through one's hands, and yet one can give very little account of oneself at the end of it. At present I am moving rapidly along the banks of a small canal which traverses the Doâb, between the Ravee and Beas Rivers, for purposes of irrigation; accompanying Major Napier [now Lord Napier of Magdala, K.C.B., G.C.S.I.], to whom the prosecution of all public improvements throughout the Land of the Five Rivers belongs. We (the "Woods and Forests" of the day) have nearly reached the point where the river debouches from the hills, and have put up for the day in a little garden-house of Runjeet Singh's, in the midst of a lovely grove of great extent, through whose dark-green boughs we have a splendid panorama of the snowy range to back our horizon. We have great projects of extending the canal by various branches to feed and fertilise the whole extent of the Doâb, which wants nothing but water to make it a garden, so fertile is the soil. We have come along a strip of beautiful country, richly cultivated, lying along the banks of this life-giving little watercourse, and the weather is perfect, so I am as happy as mere externals can make one. Certainly we whose lot has fallen on this side of India, are much to be envied. Here, all day long, one rides about, clothed as warmly, and even more so, than in England at this season, enjoying the bright clear sunshine, and never troubled with thinking of the sun; whilst at Calcutta they are running into their houses at nine o'clock to avoid the heat of the day! I imagine two years in Calcutta would be more *wearing* than ten up here; by the same token, I have achieved the respectable weight of eleven stone ten pounds, being an increase of seventeen pounds since July. May my shadow never be less!

I live from the arrival of one mail in expectation of the next. I had meant to have written a long series of despatches for this opportunity, and have asked you to do some commissions for me, but I must postpone it now to another time, as Major Napier has lots of work for me. I want a pair of thick blankets; mine were plundered at Ferozeshah, and I have always mourned over them since, when cold nights and long marches come together. In these far countries it is next to impossible to get anything decent.

---

CAMP, RAJA KE BAGH, *Jan. 29th*, 1848.

For some days I was staying in, and intend returning again to, a fine picturesque old castle or fort built by the Emperor Shahjehan. Its lofty walls, with their turrets and battlements, enclose a quadrangle of the size of the great court of Trinity, while from the centre rises a dark mass of buildings three stories high, forming the keep; presenting externally four blank walls pierced with loopholes, but within, arches and pillars and galleries, with an open space in the centre, in which they all face. The summit rises sixty-four feet, which, in addition to the great elevation of the mound on which the castle stands, gives a noble view of mountain, river, and plain, covered with the finest timber, and green with young corn; the whole backed by range on range, peak after peak, of dazzling snow. Another, nearly similar, lies about ten miles to the north, and I am now "pitched" at the foot of a third to the west; all monuments of the taste and grandeur of the Mogul Emperors. That Goth, Runjeet Sing, and his followers have as much to answer for in their way, as Cromwell and his crop-eared scoundrels in England and Ireland. They seem only to have conquered to destroy—every public work, every castle, road, serai or avenue, has been destroyed; the finest mosques turned into powder magazines and stables, the gardens into cantonments, and the fields into deserts. I had a pretty specimen the other day of the way in which things have been managed here. I was desired to examine into, and report on, the accounts of revenue collected hitherto in 180 villages along the "Shah Nahr," or Royal Canal. By a convenient mixture of coaxing and threats, compliment and invective, a return was at last effected, by which it appeared that in ordinary cases about one-half the revenue reached the treasury, in some one-third, and in one district *nothing!* To my great amusement, when I came to this point, the gallant collector (a long-bearded old Sikh) quietly remarked—"Yes, Sahib, this was indeed a great place for us entirely." I said, "Yes, you villain, you gentry grew fat on robbing your master." "Don't call it robbing," he said; "I assure you I wouldn't be dishonest for the world. I never took more than my predecessors did before me." About the most naïve definition of honesty I have had the luck to meet with. I fancy our visit to these nooks and corners of the Punjab has added some £50,000 a year to the revenue. My present *rôle* is to survey a part of the country lying along the left bank of the Ravee and below the hills, and I am daily and all day at work with compasses and chain, pen and pencil, following streams, diving into valleys, burrowing into hills, to complete my work. I need hardly remark, that having never attempted anything of the kind hitherto, it is bothering at first. But one is compelled to be patient under this sort of insult, and I should not be surprised any day to be told to build a ship, compose a code of laws, or hold assizes,—in fact, 'tis the way in India; every one has to teach himself his work, and do it at the same time; if I go on learning new trades as fast during the remainder of my career as I have done at its commencement, I shall have to retire as a Jacksonian professor at least, when "my dog has had its day." Well! I have fairly beaten the cold this time—I turned back one side of the tent, and had a big fire lighted outside, protected from draughts by a canvas screen, and the whole tent is now in a jolly glow; a gipsy light reflected on the trees around, and on the two tall picturesque Affghans who, seated cross-legged on each side of the fire, either replenish it with sticks, fan it into a flame, or watch my pen with the large, black, inquisitive eye of a dog looking out for a crust.

They make much better servants for wandering folks like myself than the Hindoostanee servant-tribe, have fewer or no prejudices (save against clean water), and trudge along the livelong day as merrily as if life was a joke to them, instead of the dull heavy reality it is.

About this time Lieutenant Herbert Edwardes wrote as follows to his family in England:—

"Young Hodson has been appointed to do duty with our Punjab Guide Corps, commanded by Lieutenant Lumsden. The duties of a Commandant or Adjutant of Guides are at once important and delightful. It is his duty in time of peace to fit himself for leading armies during war. This necessitates his being constantly on the move, and making himself and his men acquainted with the country in every quarter. In short, it is a roving commission, and to a man of spirit and ability, one of the finest appointments imaginable.

"I think Hodson will do it justice. He is one of the finest young fellows I know, and a thorough soldier in his heart."

CAMP, *Feb.* 27*th*, 1848.

I really have very little to tell you of my new Guide Corps duties, from the somewhat strange fact that I have never yet actually entered upon them; this will soon come to an end, however, as I have directions to proceed to Peshawur as soon as the survey I have been at work on is completed. The grand object of the corps is to train a body of men in peace to be efficient in war; to be not only acquainted with localities, roads, rivers, hills, ferries, and passes, but have a good idea of the produce and supplies available in any part of the country; to give *accurate* information, not running open-mouthed to say that 10,000 horsemen and a thousand guns are coming (in true native style), but to stop to see whether it may not be really only a common cart and a few wild horsemen who are kicking up all the dust: to call twenty-five by its right name, and not say *fifty* for short, as most natives do. This of course wants a great deal of careful instruction and attention. Beyond this, the officers should give a tolerably correct sketch and report of any country through which they may pass, be *au fait* at routes and means of feeding troops, and above all (and here you come close upon practical duties), keep an eye on the doings "of the neighbours" and the state of the country, so as to be able to give such information as may lead to any outbreak being nipped in the bud. This is the *theory*, what the *practice* may be I'll tell you some day or other when I know. Hitherto I have been making myself generally useful under the chief engineer, and learning to survey. One has to turn one's hand to everything if one wishes to get on.

Meanwhile, I am busily collecting every species of information about the people and the land they live in. Hard work and fatigue, of course, but a splendid opening and opportunity for making oneself known and *necessary*.

DEENANUGGUR, *March* 14*th*, 1848.

The night your letter reached me, Napier (our chief engineer) and I were encamped on a spur of grass land separating two streams of the river "Chukkir," and had been so for some days. That evening it began to rain (if a sluice of water, apparently *struck down from the heavens* by a flood of the fiercest lightning, can be called so), and for thirty-six hours the torrent descended without intermission, as only Asiatic storms can descend. At length a pause ensued, and the sky was visible, and we emerged from our sodden tents only to be threatened with water in a worse form. The hills, valleys, and mountains began to send down to us what they had so plentifully received from above, and the hitherto quiet stream, whose wide stony channel surrounded us, was in a single hour a powerful torrent, tearing over the country as if to prove what it could do. By one of the singular freaks common to all tropical rivers, it dammed up one of its own widest outlets by the quantity of stones which it brought along with it, and came tearing down the one nearest to us. Across this, not a hundred yards from our tents, we had just built a powerful breakwater some sixteen feet wide, but the water quietly walked over, under, and round it; roared, groaned, stormed, and swelled angrily for two hours, and our breakwater was a "thing of history:" meantime, we were gradually getting more and more surrounded with water, it rose and rose until only four inches were wanting to set us well afloat. The pegs of my tent-ropes were undermined, and a notice to quit was as plainly written on the face of the water as ever on a legal process. There was but one way of escape; so, mustering the whole of a neighbouring village, we loaded all our valuables and moveables on their backs, and made a dash at the hamlet. Once having succeeded in turning us out, the valiant Chukkir was content, and we slept in our tents as usual, but not without, as it turned out, considerable risk of finding ourselves landed in some unknown field on waking.

When this flood subsided, it appeared that the scene of our

unfortunate dam had become the deepest part of the channel, and the old course choked with stones and boulders which you and I couldn't lift in a week of Sundays. Is not this an incident?

Since I wrote last, in consequence of representations I sent to headquarters as to the amount of plundering going on, a large party of horse, with one of the principal chiefs, was sent out here, with directions to act on the information I gave them. We have accordingly had a robber-hunt on a large and tolerably successful scale. Numbers have been caught. One shot *pour encourager les autres*, and we have traces of others, so that my quiet practice (originally for my own amusement and information) has been very useful to the State. I found out the greatest part of it by sending clever fellows disguised as "faqueers" (you know what they are, I think—religious beggars) to the different villages to talk to the people and learn their doings. Some of the stories of Sikh violence, cruelty, and treachery which I have picked up are almost beyond belief. The indifference of these people to human life is something appalling. I could hardly get them to give a thought or attempt an inquiry as to the identity of a man whom I found dead, evidently by violence, by the road-side yesterday morning; and they were horrified at the thought of tying up or confining a sacred ox, who had gored his *thirteenth* man the evening before last! They told me plainly that no one had a right to complain of being hurt by so venerable a beast.

In such pursuits, combined with surveying, my time passes away tolerably well. I am alone again, Napier having gone to Lahore; but this is a sweet place, and I am staying in a pleasant summer-house of Runjeet Singh's, in the midst of a fine garden grove of mango and orange trees.

---

CAMP ON RAVEE, *March 29th*, 1848.

Just as I had completed my somewhat lengthy reply to your question, I was interrupted by a camel-rider, who had come in hot haste with a letter from Sir F. Currie at Lahore, with the most agreeable intelligence in the world—*voilà*.

"MY DEAR MR. HODSON,—Pray knock off your present work, and come into Lahore as quickly as you can.

"I want to send you with Mr. Agnew to Mooltan. Mr. Agnew starts immediately w th your acquaintance, Sirdah Sumshere Singh, to assume the government of that province, Moolraj having sent in his resignation of the Nizàmut. Lieutenant Becher is to be Agnew's permanent assistant, but he cannot join just now, and I wish you to go with Agnew. It is an *important mission*, and one that, I think, you will like to be employed in. When relieved by Becher, you will join the Guides at Lahore, and be employed also as assistant to the Resident. The sooner you come the better.—Yours sincerely, F. CURRIE."

The last line of Sir Frederick's letter was not lost on me, and to keep up my character for locomotion, I started at daybreak for Deenanuggur, finishing off my work *en route*, remained there the rest of the day to wind up matters and add my surveying sketch to the large plan I had commenced beforehand, and hurried onwards this morning. You will perceive that I have crossed the Doâb, and am now writing on the banks of the Ravee, some sixty miles above Lahore. I marched twenty-four and a half miles with tent and baggage this morning, and hope to continue at that pace, with the difference of marching by night, the weather having suddenly become very hot indeed.

I am much interested in the thought of going to so new a place as Mooltan—new, that is to say, to Europeans, yet so important from position and commerce. The only drawback is the heat, which is notorious throughout Western India. I am not aware, however, that it is otherwise unhealthy.

As you may suppose, I am much gratified by the appointment, both for its own sake and also as evincing so very favourable and kindly a disposition toward myself on the part of the new potentate.

*To his Sister.*

CAMP, *March* 29*th,* 1848.

Of incidents to amuse you I have not many to narrate, save the usual "moving" ones by "flood and field." On the 18th I was very nearly becoming a damp unpleasant corpse to celebrate my birthday. In attempting a ford, my horse sank up to the girths in a quicksand. I managed to extricate myself, and dry land being near, he got up without damage. Sending a man ahead, I tried again in another place. Here it was fair to the eye but false to the foot. Down he went again, this time in deeper water, and got me under him by struggling. However, I realised the old proverb, and escaped with a good ducking and a mouthful of my native element, *rather* gritty. Next I tried a camel, but the brute went down at the first stride. So giving it up in despair, I put on dry clothes, and *then* waded through the river.

Not content with one attempt on my existence, the horse gave me a violent kick the same evening when I went up to him to ask " How d'ye do." So I completed my year, in spite of myself, as it were.

LAHORE, *April* 2*nd.*

Since the above was written, I have succeeded in reaching the metropolis, as you see, at a greater expenditure of animal heat and fatigue than I have gone through for some time. I was very friendlily and pleasantly greeted by Sir F. and Lady Currie, and tumbled at once again into the tide of civilisation—loaf bread, arm-chairs, hats, and ladies—as philosophically as if I had been for months in the calm and unrestrained enjoyment of such luxuries.

On my arrival, I found that the arrangement proposed in Sir F. Currie's note had already become matter of history, *not* of fact. The new one is still better for me. I am to remain at Lahore, and be an assistant to the Resident, having my Guide duties to discharge also, when Lumsden arrives from Peshawur with the Corps. He is expected in twenty days. Nothing could possibly have been better for me. I shall have the advantage of learning in the best school, headquarters, and have many more opportunities of making myself "generally useful." I am most rejoiced at the plan, and Sir F. Currie's considerate kindness in devising it. We won't say anything of the regularity or consistency of making a man of two and a half year's service, and who has passed no examination, a political officer, nor will we be ungrateful enough to say that he is unfit for the appointment, but that he should do his utmost to show that the rule is more honoured "in the breach than in the observance."

---

RESIDENCY, LAHORE, *April 16th*, 1848.

I shall not have the same variety to chronicle now that I seem to be fixed here, but more interest and a higher style of work. Since I wrote last I have been six hours a day employed in court, hearing petitions and appeals in all manner of cases, civil and criminal, and in matters of revenue, as there are but two officers so employed. You, perhaps, will comprehend that the duty is no sinecure. It is of vast importance, and I sometimes feel a half sensation of modesty coming over me at being set down to administer justice in such matters so early, and without previous training. A little practice, patience, and reflection settle most cases to one's satisfaction, however; and one must be content with substantial justice as distinguished from technical law. In any point of difficulty one has always an older head to refer to, and meantime, one has the satisfaction of knowing that one is independent and untrammelled save by a very simple code. Some things, such as sentencing a man to imprisonment for seven years for killing a cow are rather startling to one's ideas of right and wrong; but then to kill a cow is to break a law, and to disturb the public peace—perhaps cause bloodshed; so the law is vindicated, and one's conscience saved. I have many other duties, such as finishing my map, for which I was surveying at Deenanuggur; occasionally translating an official document; going to Durbars, &c.; and when the Guides arrive (on the 20th) I shall have to assist in drilling and instructing them; to say nothing of seeing that their quarters are prepared, and everything ready for them. I am not, therefore, *idle*, and only wish I had time to read.

On the 26th he writes from Lahore:—

I mentioned to you that Sir F. Currie's plan of sending me to assist Agnew at Mooltan had been altered, and that Anderson had gone with him in my stead. At the time I was disposed to be disappointed; but we never know what is for our good. In this case I should doubtless have incurred the horrible fate of poor Anderson and Agnew. Both these poor fellows have been barbarously murdered by the Mooltan troops.

He then gives a detailed account of their tragical fate, and the treachery of the villain Moolraj, and adds:—

The Sikh Durbar profess their inability to coerce their rebel subject, who is rapidly collecting a large army, and strengthening himself in the proverbially strong fort of Mooltan.

One cannot say how it will end. The necessary delay of five months, till after the rains, will give time for all the disaffected to gather together, and no one can say how far the infection may extend. The Sikhs were right in saying, "We shall have one more fight for it yet."

LAHORE, *May 7th.*

I expect to be busy in catching a party of rascals who have been trying to pervert our Sepoys by bribes and promises. We have a clue to them, and hope to take them in the act. We are surrounded here with treachery. No man can say who is implicated, or how far the treason has spread. The life of no

British officer, away from Lahore, is worth a week's purchase. It is a pleasant sort of government to prop up, when their head men conspire against you and their troops desert you on the slightest temptation.

Lumsden, the commandant of the Guides, and I want something sensible for the protection of our heads from sun and blows, from *coups de soleil* equally with *coups d'épée*. There is a kind of leathern helmet in the Prussian service which is light, serviceable, and neat. Will you try what you can do in the man-millinery line, and send me a brace of good helmets? We don't want ornament; in fact, the plainer the better, as we should always wear a turban over them, but strong, and light as a hat. I have no doubt your taste will be approved. I hope this won't be a bore to you, but one's head wants protecting in these stormy days.

The helmets on their arrival were pronounced "maddening." This was the first of a series of commissions connected with the clothing and arming of the Guide Corps, which was left mainly, if not entirely, in my brother's hands, and was a matter of much interest to him. The colour selected for their uniform was "drab," as most likely to make them invisible in a land of dust. Even a member of the Society of Friends could scarcely have objected to send out drab clothing for 900 men, but to this succeeded directions to select the pattern of, and send out, 300 rifled carbines, which seemed scarcely a clerical business. The result, however, was satisfactory, and in the following year my brother wrote:—

Many thanks for the trouble you have taken about the clothing for the Guides. Sir C. Napier says they are the only properly dressed light troops he has seen in India.

CAMP, DEENANUGGUR, *June 5th*, 1848.

You will hardly have been prepared to hear that I am once more on the move, rushing about the country, despite climate, heat, and rumours (the most alarming).

I wrote last the day after our successful capture of the conspirators, whom I had the satisfaction of seeing hung three days later. I then tried a slight fever as a variety for two days; and on the 14th started to "bag" the Ranee in her abode beyond the Ravee, she having been convicted of complicity in the designs of the conspirators. Lumsden and myself were deputed by the Resident to call on her, and intimate that her presence was urgently required. A detachment was ordered out to support us, in case any resistance should be offered. Fortunately it was not required, as the Ranee complied at once with our "polite" request to come along with us. Instead of being taken to Lahore, as she expected, we carried her off to Kana Kutch, on the Ferozepoor road, where a party of Wheeler's Irregulars had been sent to receive her. It was very hard work—a long night march to the fort, and a fourteen hours' ride across to Kana Kutch, whence I had two hours' gallop into Lahore to report progress, making sixteen hours in the saddle, in May, when the nights are hot. On the next Sunday night I was off again, to try and seize or disperse a party of horse and foot collected by a would-be holy man, Maharaja Singh, said to amount to 400 or 500. I made a tremendous march round by Umritsur, Byrowal-Ghat on the Beas, and up that river's bank to Mokeria, in the Jullundur Doâb, whence I was prepared to cross during the night with a party of cavalry, and attack the rascals unawares. Everything succeeded admirably up to the last, when I found that he had received notice from a rogue of a native magistrate that there would be attempts made to seize him, when he fairly bolted across the Ravee, and is now infesting the Doâb between that river and the Chenab. I have scoured this part of the country (which my late surveys enabled me to traverse with perfect ease), got possession of every boat on the Ravee from

Lahore to the Hills, placed horsemen at every ferry, and been bullying the people who supplied the Saint with provisions and arms. I have a regiment of Irregular Horse (Skinner's) with me, and full powers to summon more, if necessary, from the Jullundur Doâb. Meantime, a party from Lahore are sweeping round to intercept the fellow, who is getting strong by degrees; and I am going to dash across at midnight with a handful of cavalry, and see if I cannot beat up the country between this and Wuzeerabad. I am very well, hard at work, and enjoying the thing very much. I imagine this will be the sort of life we shall lead about once a week till the Punjab is annexed. Every native official has fraternised with the rebels he was ordered to catch.

LAHORE, *July 5th,* 1848.

I wrote last from Deenanuggur, on the eve of crossing the Ravee to look after the Gooroo, Maharaja Singh. I remained in the Rechnab Doâb some days, hunting up evidence and punishing transgressors.

I was very fairly successful in obtaining information of the extent of the conspiracy, which has been keeping the whole country in a ferment these two months past. All that has occurred is clearly traceable to the Ranee (now happily deported) and her friends, and has been carried out with a fearful amount of the blackest treachery and baseness. There have been stirring events since I wrote last. Twice within a fortnight has Herbert Edwardes fought and defeated the Mooltan rebels in pitched battles, and has succeeded, despite of treacherous foes and doubtful friends, in driving them into the fort of Mooltan. His success has been only less splendid than the energy and courage which he has shown throughout, especially that high moral courage which defies responsibility, risks, self-interest, and all else, for the good of the State, and which, if well directed, seems to command fortune and ensure success. I have been longing to be with him, though after my wonderfully narrow escape of being murdered with poor Agnew at Mooltan, I may well be content to leave my movements in other hands. I was summoned into Lahore suddenly (as usual!) to take command of the Guides and charge of Lumsden's duties for him, as he had been sent down the river towards Bhawulpoor. I came in the whole distance (one hundred miles), with bag and baggage, in sixty hours, which, considering that one can't travel at all by day, and not more than four miles an hour by night, required a great amount of exertion and perseverance. It is strange that the natives always knock up sooner than we do on a march like this. The cavalry were nine days on the road, and grumbled then! I know few things more fatiguing than when exhausted by the heat of the day, to have to mount at nightfall, and ride slowly throughout the night, and for the two most disagreeable hours of a tropical day, viz., those after sunrise. One night, on which I was making a longer march than usual, had a fearful effect on a European regiment moving upon Ferozepoor; the same hot night-wind which had completely prostrated me for the time, fell upon the men as they halted at a well to drink; they were fairly beaten, and lay down for a few minutes to *pant*. When they arose to continue their march, a captain and nine or ten men were left dead on the ground! It was the simoom of Africa in miniature. I have happily escaped fever or sickness of any kind, and have nothing to complain of but excessive weakness. Quinine will, I trust, soon set me up again.

---

LAHORE, *Sept. 3rd*, 1848.

We have had stirring times lately, though I personally have had little share in them. Mooltan is at last invested, and we expect daily to hear of its fall. Meanwhile, a new outbreak has occurred in Huzàra, a wild hilly region on the left bank of the Indus, above Attok, where one of the powerful Sirdars has raised the standard of revolt.

I suppose I may say to you at so great a distance, what I must not breathe here, that it is now morally certain that we have only escaped, by what men call chance and accidents, the effects of a general and well-organised conspiracy against British supremacy in Upper India. Our "ally" Gholab Singh, the creature of the treaty of 1848, the hill tribes, the whole Punjab, the chiefs of Rajpootana, and the states round Umbâla and Kurnàl, and even the King of Cabul, I believe, have been for months and months securely plotting, without our having more than the merest hints of local disturbances, against the supremacy of the British Government. They were to unite for one vast effort, and drive us back upon the Jumna. This was to be again the boundary of British India. The rising in Mooltan was to be the signal. All was prepared, when a quarrel between Moolraj and the treacherous khan, Singh Mán, who was sent to commence the war, spoilt their whole scheme. The proud Rajpoot, Gholab Singh, refused to follow in the wake of a Mooltan merchant, and the merchant would not yield to the soldier. We have seen the mere ebullitions of the storm, the bubbles which float at the surface. I believe that now we are safe from a general rising, and that the fall of Mooltan will put a stop to mischief. If, however, our rulers resort again to half measures, if a mutinous army is retained in existence, the evil day will return again. Absolute supremacy has been, I think, long demonstrated to be our only safety among wild and treacherous races. *Moderation*, in the modern sense, is the greatest of all weakness.

*Sept.* 18*th*, 1848.

You will have seen that our troops have been hard at it in Mooltan, and now I have to tell you that it has all been in vain; Rajah Shere Singh, and the whole of our worthy Sikh allies, have joined the rebel Moolraj, and General Whish has been compelled to raise the siege and retire.

I have just despatched every available Guide to try and get quietly into the far-famed fort of Govindghur, and hope in a few hours to hear of their success. They have forty friends inside, and only a few score wavering enemies. I have not a moment which I can call my own, and have put off this (which is merely an assurance that I am alive and very well) to the last moment, so as to give you the latest tidings. I am all agog at the prospect of stirring times, and the only single drawback is the fear that you all will be very anxious. I shall not, however, run my head unnecessarily into a scrape, and see no cause for your frightening yourselves.

One comfort is, that the farce of native government has been played out. It was an experiment honestly tried, and as honestly a failure.

A few days later he says:—

My Guides have covered themselves with glory (and dust) by the way in which they got into, and got possession of, the famed fort of Govindghur. A hundred of my men, under a native officer —a fine lad of about twenty, whom I have petted a good deal— went up quietly to the gates, on pretence of escorting four State prisoners (whom I had put in irons for the occasion), were allowed to get in, and then threw up their caps, and took possession of the gateway, despite the scowls, and threats, and all but open resistance of the Sikh garrison. A day afterwards a regiment marched from Lahore, and went into garrison there, and so Runjeet Singh's treasure-fort is fairly in our hands.

*Nov. 1st,* 1848.

I left Lahore—but stay, I must get there first. Well, I wrote from Ramnuggur, on the Chenab, last; whence, after a fruitless *séjour* of six days, in the vain hope of meeting Mrs. George Lawrence, I returned suddenly to Lahore by an order which reached me the evening of the 5th. I started at sunset, and pushing my way on various borrowed steeds across that dreary region during the night, accompanied by a single camel-rider, I reached Lahore, a distance of seventy miles, by nine the following morning.

## RUNGUR NUGGUL.

On the 8th I was off again at daybreak on a longer journey still, having to cross the country to Brigadier Wheeler's camp in the Jullundur Doâb, to convey orders to him, relative to the reduction of two rebellious forts in the Doâb, between the Ravee and Beas. A "grind" of some twenty-six hours on *camel-back*, with the necessary stoppages, took me to the camp, whence (because I had not had enough) I recrossed the Beas the same night, after examining and reporting on the state of the ferries by which the troops were to follow me. This time I was escorted by a troop of Irregular Horse, and being thereby, according to *my* estimation of Sikh prowess, rendered tolerably independent, I marched the next morning for the fort of Rungur Nuggul, some fourteen miles from the right bank of the Beas.

On approaching it, and the village which covered one side of it, I was welcomed by a discharge of matchlocks, &c., as a sort of bravado, which served to point out exactly the range of my friends' pieces. I lost no time in getting the horsemen into a secure position (which means, one equally good for fighting or running away), and advanced under shelter of the trees and sugar-canes to within easy distance of the fort. Hence I despatched a message to the rebels, to say that if they did not come to reason within an hour, they should have no choice but that between cold steel or the gallows. The hour elapsed without result, so mentally consigning the garrison to annihilation, I set to work to reconnoitre the ground round the fort. This accomplished—with no further interruption than a shower of unpleasant bullets when I ventured too near—I sat down, and drew a little pencil plan of the ground and fort, despatched a trooper with it to the Brigadier, and then retired to a little village about a mile off for the night. Another day and night passed in this precarious fashion, without (as is my usual fate), servants, clothes, or traps, until at length my own men (Guides) arrived from Lahore with my baggage and horses. I could now muster a hundred rifles and eighty horsemen, so we set to work to *invest the place*, being the only way to render the escape of the rebels difficult or impossible. The fort, though very small, was immensely strong, and well garrisoned with desperadoes, and we had sharp work of it during the two nights and day which elapsed before the Brigadier appeared with his troops. By keeping my men scattered about in parties, under cover, the superiority of their weapons enabled them to gall the defenders of the fort whenever they showed their heads, day or night, and whenever they made a sally they got driven back with the loss of one or two of their companions. At last the Brigadier appeared, pounded the place with his guns during the day, and let the garrison escape at night. Then came the bore of destroying the empty fort, a work which consumed a week of incessant labour, and forty-one mines loaded with an aggregate of 8000 pounds of powder. Having destroyed house, fort, stables, and everything, and removed the grain and property, we at length moved on to a second fort, called "Morara," about a mile from the left bank of the Ravee, near this place. I cannot now go into details of the second failure of the Brigadier in attempting to punish the rebels, for they bolted before he fired a shot, nor of my attempts to prevent their escape. I have had loads of work, what with soldiering, providing supplies for the force, and all the multifarious duties which come on the shoulders of a "political" out here. I am quite well, and the weather is lovely, so work is easy comparatively, and an active life like this is, as you know, my particular weakness. I hope to cross the Ravee in a few days with the troops collecting to punish the rebel (or patriot) Sikh army. We want Sir C. Napier sadly. What with the incapacity shown at Mooltan, and the dilatory proceedings at headquarters, our reputation is suffering cruelly, and every one knows that that is a stain only to be dyed out in blood. Every week's delay adds thousands to our present foes and future victims.

*Extract from Despatch of* BRIGADIER WHEELER *to the* ADJUTANT-GENERAL.

"CAMP, RUNGUR NUGGUL, *Oct.* 15*th*, 1848.

"Lieut. W. S. Hodson, with his detachment of Corps of Guides, has done most excellent service, and by his daring boldness, and that of his men, gained the admiration of all."

---

*To his Sister.*

DEENANUGGUR, *Dec.* 4*th*, 1848.

You must not suppose that because I have written twice from this place that therefore I have been here all the time. On the contrary, I have been incessantly on the move; so much so as to have pretty nearly established a claim to the medal for discovering perpetual motion. I have been moving in an orbit whose gyrations have been confined to a space bounded by the Chenab and the Beas, and a line drawn E. and W. through Umritsur and Lahore. Nearly the whole of this vast "*track*" of country has been under my sole charge. I have had also to feed an army daily of 3000 odd fighting men, 2000 odd horses, and 14,000 to 15,000 camp followers. Also to take care of and work my Guides; to point out the haunts and obtain information of the strength of "the enemy," and give him over to the tender mercies of fire and sword; *item*, to fight him personally; *item*, to destroy six forts, and sell by auction the property therein found; *item*, to be civil to all comers; *item*, to report all the said doings daily to Government; *item*, to march ten to twenty miles a day at a slow pace; *item*, to eat, drink, dress, and sleep, to rest oneself from all these labours. In the above compendious epitome of the work of that much-abused and ill-used class called "politicals" in India, you will, I trust, observe no vacant places or "hiati" in which you would expect to see inscribed, "*item*, to write to one's friends." No; one is a white slave, and no mistake; day and night, early or late, week day or Sunday, one is the slave of the public, or rather of the Government, to a degree which cannot be credited until it is experienced. The departure of Brigadier Wheeler across the Beas, and therefore out of my beat, has made a slight break in the work, but there is still more than I can get through in the day. I am grinding my teeth all the time at being kept away from the scene of what must be the grand struggle between the cow-killers and cow-worshippers on the banks of the Chenab.

On the 8th of last month I marched hence to overtake Brigadier Wheeler and his troops, and accompany them across the Ravee. On reaching the river, I represented to the Brigadier (who of course does not know friend from foe until he is told) the urgent necessity of attacking a party of insurgents who were within fourteen miles of us, but could not persuade him to do so. The old gentleman was intent on pushing on the main army, flattering himself he was going to command a division of it. When within twenty-five or thirty miles of the headquarter camp at Ramnuggur, I rode over to Lahore, and talked to Sir F. Currie, who was just despatching an express to me about these very people we had left unattacked two days before. He sent me off there and then to see the Commander-in-Chief, who was very polite; asked my opinion (and acted on it too!); told me all his plans for carrying on the war; and on my telling him the facts of the case, sent an order to the Brigadier to retrace his steps, and attack the party he had passed by at once, with something very like a rap over the knuckles. After a delay of some days, caused by a sudden counter-summons to move to reinforce Colin Campbell (afterwards Lord Clyde), who was vainly expecting that the Singhs would fight, we at length turned back for Kulállwála, the name of the fort occupied by my friends. We got within twenty-five miles of it on the 20th, and I urged the Brigadier to move on like lightning, and crush them. He would not, and began to make short marches, so I was compelled to out-manœuvre him by a bold stroke. On the morning of the 21st I left his camp, and pushed on some ten miles to a place on the straight road for Kulállwála. Here was a fort belonging to a doubtful Sirdar, and I determined to get possession of it if possible. I had with me only 100 men, and the enemy was only eight miles off with 4000—rabble, to be sure, and fellows who have no heart for fighting; but the odds were great, and it was necessary to put a bold face on matters. I therefore "boned" the Chief's two confidential servants, who were in his dwelling-house outside the fort, and taking one on each side of me, walked up to the gateway, and demanded admission; they hesitated, and made excuses. I significantly hinted that my two companions should be responsible if a shot was fired; the stout Sikh heart failed, and I was admitted. My proceeding was justified, and rendered most opportune, by the discovery that the garrison were preparing munitions of war, mounting guns, and looking saucy. I turned them out by the same means as I had gained admittance, viz., by hinting that if any resistance was made the headmen by my side were doomed. Putting in sixteen of my Guides to hold it until further orders, I took up my quarters outside for the night, and prepared to attack another small mud fort near at hand in the morning.

However, my friends ran away in the night in a fright, and thus I had opened the road to Kulállwála without firing a shot. In the morning I marched with my little party towards the enemy, sending back a messenger to the Brigadier to say that I was close to the place, and that if he did not come on sharp they would run away or overwhelm me. He was dreadfully angry, but came on like a good boy! When within a mile or so of the fort, I halted my party to allow his column to get up nearer, and as soon as I could see it, moved on quietly. The *ruse* told to perfection; thinking they had only 100 men and myself to deal with, the Sikhs advanced in strength, thirty to one, to meet me, with colours flying and drums beating. Just then a breeze sprung up, the dust blew aside, and the long line of horsemen coming on rapidly behind my party burst upon their senses. They turned instantly, and made for the fort, so leaving my men to advance quietly after them, I galloped up to the Brigadier, pointed out the flying Sikhs, explained their position, and begged him to charge them. He melted from his wrath, and told two regiments of Irregulars to follow my guidance. On we went at the gallop, cut in amongst the fugitives, and punished them fearfully. The unfortunate wretches had cause to rue the day they turned rebels, for we left them thickly on the ground as we swept along. I had never charged with cavalry before, or come so directly into hand to hand conflict with the Sikh, save of course in the trenches at Sobraon. About 300 to 400 escaped into the fort, while the remainder threw down their arms and dispersed over the country. The garrison ran away during the night, unfortunately, and we had only to take peaceful possession in the morning. We had killed some 250 to 300 of them, which will be a lesson to them, I hope. My men got into the village contiguous to the fort early, while we pitched into those of the enemy who remained behind, to a great extent. Since then we have been pursuing other parties, but only came into collision with them to a very trifling extent once. They had learnt how to run away beautifully. The Brigadier has grown quite active, and *very fond of me* since that day at Kulállwála, though he had the wit to see how very "brown I had done him" by making him march two marches in one.

---

*Extract from an Order issued by* BRIGADIER-GENERAL WHEELER.

CAMP, KULÁLLWÁLA, *Nov.* 23*rd*, 1848.

"The detachment of the Corps of Guides moved in the morning direct on the village, whilst the other troops were moving on the fort. It was occupied in force by the enemy, who were dislodged in a most spirited manner, and the place afterwards retained as commanding the works of the fort, the men keeping up a sharp fire on all who showed themselves. The thanks of the Brigadier-General are due to Lieut. Hodson, not only for his services in the field, but for the information with which he furnished him, and he offers them to him and to his men."

---

*Jan.* 1849.

I have just completed the first series of my duties in this Doâb, by driving the last party of the insurgents across the Chenab.

As soon as I had settled matters a little at Deenanuggur, and made some arrangements to prevent further troubles if possible, I crossed the Ravee again, and got upon the track of the rebel party who had given us so much trouble. On the 15th, I heard that a large party had collected at a village called Gumrolah (near Dufferwal), but they had so many spies in my camp, that it was difficult to avoid their ken; at the same time their tendency to run away made a surprise the only feasible mode of reaching them. We therefore turned *in* as usual at night, but soon after midnight I aroused my men, and got them under arms and off before any one was aware of our move. I had with me 100 of my Guides and fifteen sowars.

We marched quietly but swiftly all night, and came upon the insurgents just at daybreak. I had ridden forward about half-a-mile, with a couple of sowars, to reconnoitre, and got unobserved within 250 yards of the insurgents, numbering at least 150 horse and foot.

They looked at me, and hesitated whether to come at me or not, apparently, while I beckoned to the remaining sowars to come up. I was in great hopes that they would have waited for ten minutes, by which time my men would have been up, with their rifles, and we should have given a good account of them. However, before five minutes had elapsed, they moved off sulkily like a herd of frightened deer, half alarmed, half in doubt. I saw at once that there was but one chance left, and determined to go at them as I was—though 15 to 150 is an imprudent attempt.

The instant we were in motion they fled, and had gone half-a-mile before we could overtake them; the mounted men got off, but a party of Akhalees (Fanatics) on foot stopped and fought us, in some instances very fiercely. One fine bold "Nihung" beat off four sowars one after another, and kept them all at bay. I then went at him myself, fearing that he would kill one of them. He instantly rushed to meet me like a tiger, closed with me, yelling, "Wah Gooroo ji," and accompanying each shout with a terrific blow of his tulwar. I guarded the three or four first, but he pressed so closely to my horse's rein that I could not get a fair cut in return. At length I pressed in my turn upon him so sharply that he missed his blow, and I caught his tulwar backhanded with my bridle hand, wrenched it from him, and cut him down with the right, having received no further injury than a severe cut across the fingers; I never beheld such desperation and fury in my life. It was not *human* scarcely. By this time the rest of the party had gone a long way, and as we had already pursued further than was prudent, where the spectators even were armed, and awaiting the result, I was obliged to halt, not without a growl at General Wheeler for having left me without any men. We had killed one more than our own number, however, and five more were so severely wounded that they were removed on "charpoys."

I insert here a portion of Sir F. Currie's despatch to the Governor-General with reference to this affair, with the Governor-General's reply.

They will show the high opinion entertained at the time of my brother's services by his superiors.

"LAHORE PRESIDENCY, *Jan. 6th*, 1849.

"The affair at Buddee Pind was a most gallant one—far more so than Lieutenant Hodson's modest statement in his letter would lead me to suppose. I have accounts from parties who were eye-witnesses to the personal gallantry and energy of Lieutenant Hodson, by whose hand, in single conflict, the Akhalee, mentioned in paragraph 5, fell, after he had beaten off four horsemen of the 15th Native Cavalry, and to whose bold activity and indefatigable exertions, and the admirable arrangements made by him, with the small means at his disposal, the successful issue of this expedition is to be attributed."

To this his Lordship replied as follows, through his secretary :—

*From the* SECRETARY TO GOVERNMENT *to* SIR F. CURRIE, BART.
"*Jan.* 14*th*, 1849.

"I am directed to request that you will convey to Lieutenant Hodson the strong expression of the Governor-General's satisfaction with his conduct, and with the mode in which he discharges whatever duty is entrusted to him. The Governor-General has had frequent occasions of noticing the activity, energy, and intelligence of his proceedings, and he has added to the exercise of the same qualities on this occasion an exhibition of personal gallantry which the Governor-General has much pleasure in recording and applauding, although Lieutenant Hodson has modestly refrained from bringing it to notice himself. The Governor-General offers to Lieutenant Hodson his best thanks for these services.

(Signed) "H. M. ELLIOTT,
"*Secretary to the Government of India with the Governor-General.*"

---

CAMP UNDER THE HILLS ON THE RAVEE,
*Jan.* 18*th*, 1849.

. . . A few days afterwards, Lumsden having joined me with our mounted men, we surprised and cut to pieces another party of rebels, for which we have again been thanked by Government. Since then I have been with Brigadier-General Wheeler's force again, employed in hunting after one Ram Singh and his followers, and have been day and night at work—examining the hills and rivers, trying fords, leading columns, and doing all the multifarious duties thrust on that unhappy combination of hard work, a "Guide" and "Political" in one. Ram Singh's position was stormed on the 16th, and I had been chosen to lead one of the principal columns of attack; but we had to march by a circuitous route across the hills, darkness came on, accompanied by dreadful rain, the rivers rose and were impassable, and after twenty-four hours of the most trying work I ever experienced, in which cold, hunger, and wet were our enemies, we succeeded in reaching our ground just in time to be too late; however, I had done all that human nature could effect under the circumstances, and one cannot always be successful. Two poor fellows, one a nephew of Sir R. Peel's, were killed; otherwise the loss was trifling on our side.

We have just received intelligence of another great fight between the army under Lord Gough and the Sikhs (Chillianwalla, January 13th, 1849), in which the latter, though beaten, seem to have had every advantage given away to them. Our loss has been severe, and the mismanagement very disgraceful, yet it will be called a victory and lauded accordingly. Oh for one month of Sir Charles Napier!

---

*Extract from an Order issued by* BRIGADIER-GENERAL WHEELER, C.B., *dated*

"CAMP BELOW DULLAH, *Jan.* 17*th*, 1849.

" This order cannot be closed without the expression of the Brigadier-General's high opinion of the services of Lieutenants Lumsden and Hodson, who have spared no labour to obtain for him an accurate knowledge of the mountain of Dullah and its approaches; and Lieutenant Hodson has entitled himself to the sincere thanks of the Brigadier-General for his endeavours to lead a column to turn the enemy's position, which failed only from causes which rendered success impracticable."

---

DEENANUGGUR, *Feb. 4th,* 1849.

I had one of my narrowest escapes two days ago; I went into Lahore for a few days to see Sir H. Lawrence (who is again the Resident), and laid relays of horses along the road to this place, so as to ride in at once. I left Lahore on the morning of the 31st, and stopping at Umritsur to breakfast, reached my camp at nightfall, having ridden one hundred miles in ten hours and a half. A party of Sikhs had collected at a village by the roadside to attack me and "polish" me off, but not calculating upon the rapidity of my movements, did not expect me until the morning. I am sorry to say that they surrounded my horses, which were coming on quietly in the morning, asked for me, and finding I had escaped, stole my best horse (a valuable Arab, who had carried me in three fights), and bolted, not, however, without resistance, for two horsemen (Guides) of mine who were with the horse tried to save it. One got four wounds and the other escaped unhurt. Had I ridden like any other Christian instead of like a spectre horseman, and been the usual time on the road, I should have been a "body." We gave chase from hence as soon as we heard, and rode for eleven hours and a half in pursuit! which was pretty well after a hundred miles' ride the day before.

> "But my horse it is another's,
> And it never can be mine!"

---

CAMP, WUZZEERABAD, *Feb.* 19*th*, 1849.

I have at length reached the "army of the Punjab," almost by accident, as it were, though I was most anxious to be present at the final grand struggle between the Khalsa and the British armies. I am at present with my men, attached to a brigade encamped on this (the left) bank of the Chenab, to prevent the enemy crossing until Lord Gough is ready to attack them on the right bank, where he is now encamped with his whole force minus our brigade. The Sikhs quietly walked away from him the other day, and instead of having their backs to the Jhelum, passed round his flank, and made steadily for this place, intending, boldly enough, to march upon Lahore. I came across the Doâb with a handful of men, and reached this place just as they took up a position on the opposite bank of the river. At the same moment a brigade arrived by a forced night march from Ramnuggur, and for the present the Sikhs have been *sold*. Yet I should not be surprised at their evading us again, and going off to a higher ford. The game is getting very exciting, and I am quite enjoying the stir and bustle of two large armies in the field. The grand finale must, one would think, come off in a day or two. It is possible, however, that, as I say, the Sikhs may out-manœuvre us and prolong the campaign. The Affghans have joined the Sikhs, contrary to the expectations of every one (but myself), and there is now no saying where the struggle will end.

The Affghans are contemptible *in the plains*, generally speaking; but numbers become formidable, even if armed with broomsticks.

This was written two days before the decisive engagement of Goojerat, at which he was present, attached to the personal staff of the Commander-in-Chief. His letter giving an account of the action was unfortunately lost, but I subjoin a despatch from the Commander-in-Chief to the Governor-General :—

"CAMP, KULLALA, *March* 15*th*, 1849.

"On the re-perusal of my despatch relative to the operations of February 21st at Goojerat, I regret to find that I omitted to mention the names of Lieutenants Lumsden and Hodson of the corps of Guides, and Lieutenant Lake of the Engineers, attached to the Political Department. These officers were most active in conveying orders throughout the action, and I now beg to bring their names to the favourable notice of your Lordship."

# CHAPTER V.

*ANNEXATION OF PUNJAB—INCREASE OF CORPS OF GUIDES AT PESHAWUR—TRANSFER TO CIVIL DEPARTMENT AS ASSISTANT COMMISSIONER.*

*April* 17*th,* 1849.

You will have heard of the great events of the last month; how, on the 26th March, the Punjab became "for ever" a British Province, governed by a Triumvirate; and how the Koh-i-noor was appropriated as a present to the Queen—and all the rest of it: you may imagine the turmoil and unrest of this eventful time; but I defy you to imagine the confusion of the process which converts a wild native kingdom into a police-ridden and civilian-governed country.

I had anticipated and wished for this measure. I did not, however, expect that it would be carried out so suddenly and so sweepingly as it has been. . . .

I have been *annexed* as well as the Punjab! my "occupation's gone," and although efforts have been and are making for my restoration to "the department," yet at present I am shelved. I shall know more next month. Meanwhile, I am off with the new Commissioner to instruct him in the details of his province, which I had governed and *won* from the rebels during the last six months, but in which I am not now accounted worthy to be a humble assistant. There's fame! Well, something will turn up, I suppose. I hope to remain here, however, under the Commissioner, for a time, that I may get acquainted with this wonderful civil system. It is as well to know how the mill works.

I got quite fond of Lord Gough. I was his guest at Lahore for a month, and his noble character and fire made one condone his mistakes.

We are now on the "*qui vive*" for his successor. I long for Sir C. Napier, but the Court of Directors seem determined to hold out.

The Guides are at Peshawur, where I shall probably join them.

Lieutenant Hodson's descent in position upon the annexation of the Punjab was perhaps unavoidable, though it was very natural that he should feel it. So soon as the country was placed under the government of the East India Company, the regulations of the service with regard to seniority of course took effect, and it was not to be expected that a subaltern of less than five years' standing should be continued in so important a charge, however well qualified he might have proved himself for it in the most trying times. His position altogether had been a peculiar and exceptional one.

We shall see, however, that his disappointment did not prevent his throwing himself with his usual energy into whatever duties were assigned to him.

---

*To his Brother.*

PESHAWUR, *May* 14*th*, 1849.

My stay here is very uncertain. I merely came to settle affairs with Lumsden relative to the increase of the Guides. Meantime, I have been much interested with my first visit to this Affghan province and to the Indus. You will see at once that though it gives us a very strong military frontier, only passable to armies in half a dozen points, and therefore infinitely less difficult to hold than a long line of river, which is ever "a silent highway for nations," yet, at the same time, we have once more established a footing in Affghanistan from which there is no receding, as we did when we went as allies to the puppet Shah Soojah. Our next stride must be to Herât, I fancy; *when* the day will come no man can say, but "the uncontrollable principle," which, according to Sir R. Peel, took us there before, will not be the less active in its operation now that we have no longer the court and camp of Runjeet Singh between us and these wild tribes. It is to be hoped that "the uncontrollable principle" will not appear so *very* like an *un*controllable want of it as it did in days gone by! However, go we must, and shall *some* day—so hurrah for Cabul!

I wish you would hit upon some plan for keeping me more *au fait* with the events of your home world. My time has been occupied so constantly since I came to India, that though I may have made some progress in the knowledge of *men*, I have made but little in that of *books*. We are sadly off for military works in English, and few sciences require more study than the art of war. You might get me a list of good works from the "United Service Institution" at Charing Cross. I want the best edition of Cæsar procurable; also Xenophon and Arrian. I fancy the last has been very well edited.

---

PESHAWUR, *June 8th*, 1849.

This is the first time I have written to you from Affghanistan. Who shall say whence my letters may be directed within a few months. Are we to advance on Cabul and Candahar, and plant the Union Jack once more on the towers of Ghuznee? or are we to lie peacefully slumbering on the banks of the Indus? Are our conquests at an end? or will it be said of Lord Dalhousie—

> "Ultra et Garamantas et Indos
> Proferet imperium?"

My own belief is, that I shall live to see both the places I have mentioned, and Herât, occupied by British troops; at least I hope so.

I think I told you how it had pleased the Governor-General to reward "my distinguished services," toils, troubles, and dangers, by kicking me out of the coach altogether. Did I not? Well, after that close to my civil duties, after having "initiated" the new Commissioner into his duties, I was sent up hither to augment recruits and train the Guides. And now daily, morning and evening, I may be seen standing on one leg to convince their Affghan mind of the plausibility and elegance of the goose step. I am quite a sergeant-major just now, and you will well believe that your wandering brother is sufficiently cosmopolised to drop with a certain *aplomb* into any line of life which may turn up in the course of his career. I was always fond of "soldiering," and there is a species of absurdity in dropping from the minister of a province into a drill-sergeant, which is enlivening. By the next mail I may have to report my transformation into some new animal. So "*vive la gloire.*"

------

PESHAWUR, *July* 19*th*, 1849.

I hope that you got my letter about sending me books. There is a remarkable dearth of them here just now. You know it was a flying column which came on here after Goojerat, composed of regiments hurried up to the field from Bombay, Scinde, and Hindoostan. They came in light marching order. Books are not a part of that style of equipment. Suddenly a Government order consigned them to Peshawur, for seven months at least— 10,000 men, with an unusually large number of Europeans and officers, *and no books!* Pleasant during the confinement caused by the hot season. I was better off, because, being a nomad by profession, I carry a few books as a part even of the lightest equipment, but I have read them all till I am tired, except Shakspeare. *My* time is pretty fully occupied, but there are dozens of regimental officers who have not an hour's work in two days, and I do pity them from my heart. Then, of course, there are no ladies here, and consequently no society, or *réunions* (as they are called when people *live* together), and people are pitched headlong on to their own resources, and find them very *hard falling indeed!* I have nothing personal to tell you, except that when the last mail went out I was in bed with a sharp attack of fever, which left me without strength, flesh, or appetite—a regular blazing eastern fever, the sort of thing which burns so fast, that if it don't stop quickly, it burns you well down into the socket, and leaves you there without strength to splutter or flicker, and you go out without the satisfaction of a last flare-up at expiring. I am thankful to say I am well again now, and picking up strength fast.

They are increasing our corps of Guides to 1000 men, so that I shall have enough on my hands, especially as our Commandant leaves almost everything to me. Sir H. Lawrence writes from Simla that I am to be appointed an Assistant Commissioner under the new Board of Administration. I was the only one of the late Assistants to the Resident who was not included at first in the new *régime*.

---

LAHORE, *Sept.* 3rd, 1849.

On my arrival here I found your note of 18th June. You may imagine how wild I was with pleasure at seeing your handwriting again, as I had been deeply anxious since the arrival of my father's and George's letters of the 4th June. These brought me the first tidings of our darling's death. Happily I saw no newspaper by that mail, and the black edges first startled me from the belief that you were all well and happy. The blow was a bitter one indeed, and its utter suddenness was appalling. Indeed the prevailing impression on my mind for days was simple unbelief of the reality of that sweet child's actual death. I have been so long *alone*—home has been for so long a time more a pleasant dream than a reality—I have been for so many a weary day, as it were, dead to you all, and the sense of separation has grown so completely into one's being, that I find it difficult to separate that which it is possible to see again from that which is impossible. Thus it seems to me incredible that any greater barrier can sever me from this darling child than that ever-present one which divides me from all of you. Can you understand this? I know it to be a delusion, and yet I cannot shake it off. Yet 'tis a good delusion in one way. It deadens the sense of grief which the full realisation of her death would overwhelm me with.

I have been unfortunate again, and had a second sharp attack of fever since my arrival. I am about again, but not able to work. Sir H. Lawrence is very unwell: I fear that his constitution is utterly broken down, and that he will either have to go away from India for two years or more, or that another hot season will kill him. He is ten years older in every respect than he was during our Cashmere trip in 1846. This is a hard, wearing, dry climate, which, though preferable to Hindoostan, is destructive to the weak and sickly. It is quite sad to feel how, little by little, one's strength and muscle and energy fade, and how one can perceive age creeping in upon one so early.

---

LAHORE, *Sept.* 24*th*, 1849.

You know that I have left the Guides (alas!) and have been transformed into a complete civilian, doomed to pass the rest of my career in the administrative and executive duties of the Government of this last acquisition of the English in India. To tell the truth, I had much rather have remained with the Guides; a more independent, and very far pleasanter life, and I think one that will in the end be more distinguished. However, I was guided by Mr. Thomason's and Sir H. Lawrence's advice, and must take the consequences. It would be difficult to define or explain the exact nature of my new calling, but in brief, you will comprehend that in their respective districts the Deputy Assistant Commissioners perform the whole of the judicial, fiscal, and magisterial duties which devolve upon the Government of a country in Europe, with the addition of collecting from the cultivators and landholders the rent of all lands under cultivation and pasture, and the duties which in Europe devolve on an owner of landed property. Police, gaols, quarter sessions, committals to prison, jury, judge, excise, stamps, taxes, roads, bridges, ferries, woods and forests, and finally rent! Think what these imply, and you will form some idea of the employment of an official in the Punjab under the "Board of Administration." I have not yet dipped very deep into this turbid stream of ever-recurring work, since the great amount of arrears consequent on the break-up of one Government, and the establishment of another, including the paying-up and discharge of vast civil and military establishments, have rendered it necessary to employ any available head and pair of hands for some months at headquarters. The army has fallen to my share, and I have to examine into the claims of innumerable fine old hangers-on of the Lahore State to grants or pensions, to record their rights, and report on them for the decision of Government. Then there are upwards of 2000 old women, wives and mothers of soldiers killed in war, whom I have to see and pay the pittance decreed by their masters. Lord Dalhousie and his secretaries and officials are stern and hard taskmasters, and are not unworthily represented by the new Board, the only merciful member of which (Sir H. Lawrence) is left in a minority, and is, moreover, too ill to do much.

---

CAMP, PATANKOTE, *Jan. 21st*, 1850.

I at length got away from Lahore on the 7th. I had been ordered merely to seek change of air, but Sir H. Lawrence was starting on a long tour of inspection, and offered me the option of accompanying him, and doing a little work by the way, which I very much preferred; so here we are, after visiting the sacred city of Umritsur, and the scenes of my last year's adventures in Butala, Deenanuggur, and Shahpoor, all between the Ravee and Beas: and are now on our way to the mountain stations of Kangra, &c. We then go to the westward again, and I hope to see

> "Our coursers graze at ease,
> Beyond the blue Borysthenes,"

as I have dubbed the Indus, ere we again return to civil life, which does not suit my temperament or taste half as well as this more nomad life. I am able to ride again, though not quite with the same firmness in the saddle as of yore. I have no doubt, however, that ere we do see the "Borysthenes," I shall be as "game" for a gallop of one hundred miles on end, as I was last year at this season.

---

UMRITSUR, *March 4th,* 1850.

I am at last in a fair way of being stationary for a time at Umritsur, the sacred city of the Sikhs, and a creation entirely of their genius. Lahore, as of course you know, was the old Mussulman capital, and was not built by the Sikhs, though used by them as the seat of government and headquarters of the army. Umritsur is larger than Lahore by a third or more of people, and half as much again of space. It is five miles in circumference, very strongly fortified, and covered by the fortress of Govindghur on the west, and by a large fortified garden on the north. I am Assistant Commissioner under the Deputy-Commissioner in charge of the district, Mr. Saunders, a civilian, a very nice sort of fellow, with an exceeding pretty and nice wife. Mr. Montgomery is our Commissioner. I like all I have seen of him very much indeed. He is a very able man, and at the head of his service in many respects. Lahore is only about thirty-five miles hence—quite within visiting distance in India.

You must not talk of getting "acclimatised." There is no way of becoming so but by avoiding the climate as much as possible. I have had a bad time of it since I left Peshawur, three and a half months almost entirely on my back, which reduced me terribly. Then just as I was getting well, the other day I had a fit of jaundice, which has only just left me: altogether, in health and in prospects I have come "down in my luck" to a considerable extent; not that, *per se*, I ought, as a subaltern of not quite five years' service, to grumble at my present position, if I was now starting in the line for the first time; but I can't forget that I came into the Punjab two years and a half ago, and have had no little of the "burden and heat of the day" to bear, when to do so required utter disregard of comfort and personal safety and of rest. It is now two years since I was made an Assistant to the Resident, and within a few months of that time I took absolute charge of a tract of country (in a state of war, too) comprising three modern districts, in one of which I am now playing third fiddle. Surely annexation was a "heavy blow and a great discouragement" to me at least. In the military line, too, I have been equally unlucky, from the fact of my services having been with detachments instead of with the main army. I held my ground (and cleared it of the enemy, too) for weeks, with only 120 men at my back, and when every officer, from General Wheeler downwards, entreated me to withdraw and give it up; I fed 5000 men and horses for six months by personal and unremitting exertion; collected the revenues of the disturbed districts, and paid £15,000 over and above into the treasury, from the proceeds of property taken from the rebels. Besides this, I worked for General Wheeler so satisfactorily, that he has declared publicly that he could have done nothing without me. So much were the Sikhs enraged at my proceedings, that party after party were sent to "*polish*" me off, and at one time I couldn't stir about the country without having bullets sent at my head from every bush and wall. However, I need not go on with the catalogue, I have been egotistical enough as it is. The "reward" for these services was losing my civil appointment, and being reduced to half pay or little more for three months, and the distinction of being the only subaltern mentioned in despatches for whom nothing has been done either *in presenti* or *in prospectu*.

Speaking of the system of the Indian army:—

## SYSTEM OF PROMOTION.

*March 18th,* 1850.

At the age at which officers become colonels and majors, not one in fifty is able to stand the wear and tear of Indian service. They become still more worn in mind than in body. All elasticity is gone; all energy and enterprise worn out; they become, after a fortnight's campaign, a burden to themselves, an annoyance to those under them, and a terror to every one but the enemy! The officer who commanded the cavalry brigade which so disgraced the service at Chillianwalla, was not able to mount a horse without the assistance of two men. A brigadier of infantry, under whom I served during the three most critical days of the late war, could not see his regiment when I led his horse by the bridle until its nose touched the bayonets; and even then he said faintly, "Pray, which way are the men facing, Mr. Hodson?" This is no exaggeration, I assure you. Can you wonder that our troops have to recover by desperate fighting, and with heavy loss, the advantages thrown away by the want of heads and eyes to lead them?

A seniority service, like that of the Company, is all very well for poor men; better still for fools, for they must rise equally with wise men; but for maintaining the discipline and efficiency of the army in time of peace, and hurling it on the enemy in war, there never was a system which carried so many evils on its front and face.

I speak strongly, you will say, for I feel acutely; though I am so young a soldier, yet the whole of my brief career has been spent in camps, and a year such as the last, spent in almost constant strife, and a great part of it on detached and independent command, teaches one lessons which thirty years of peaceful life, of parades and cantonments, would never impart.

There are men of iron, like Napier and Radetzky, aged men, whom nothing affects; but they are just in sufficient numbers to prove the rule by establishing exceptions. Depend upon it, that for the rough work of war, especially in India, your leaders must be young to be effective.

If you *could* but see my beautiful rough-and-ready boys, with their dirt-coloured clothes and swarthy faces, lying in wait for a Sikh, I think it would amuse you not a little. I must try and send you a picture of them. Alas! I am no longer a "Guide," but only a big-wig, administering justice, deciding disputes, imprisoning thieves, and assisting to hang highwaymen, like any other poor old, fat, respectable, humdrum justice of the peace in Old England.

———

UMRITSUR, *April 5th,* 1850.

I quite agree with all you say about Arnold. His loss was a national misfortune. Had he lived, he would have produced an impression on men's minds whose effects would have been felt for ages. As it is, the influence which he did produce has been most lasting and striking in its effects. It is felt even in India; I cannot say more than *that*.

You should come and live in India for five years if you wished to feel (supposing you ever doubted it) the benefit of our "established" forms of Christianity. Even the outward signs and tokens of its profession—cathedrals, churches, colleges, tombs, hospitals, almshouses—have, I am now more than ever convinced, an influence on men's minds and principles and actions which none but those who have been removed from their influence for years can feel or appreciate thoroughly. The more I think of this, the more strongly I feel the effect of mere external sights and sounds on the inner and better man. Our Gothic buildings, our religious-looking churches, have, I am sure, a more restraining and pacifying influence than is generally believed by those who are habituated to them, and have never felt the want of them. A few cathedrals and venerable-looking edifices would do wonders in our colonies. Here we have nothing physical to remind us of any creed but Islamism and Hindooism. The comparative purity of the Moslem's creed is shown admirably in the superiority in taste and form of their places of prayer. Christianity alone is thrust out of sight! A barrack-room, a ball-room, a dining-room, perhaps a court of justice, serve the purpose for which the "wisdom and piety of our ancestors" constructed such noble and stately temples; feeling, justly, that the human mind in its weakness required to be called to the exercise of devotion by the senses as well as by reason and will; that separation from the ordinary scenes of everyday life, its cares, its toils, its amusements, is necessary to train the feelings and thoughts to that state in which religious impressions are conveyed. I have not seen a church for three years and more, nor heard the service of the Church read, save at intervals, in a room in which, perhaps, the night before, I had been crushed by a great dinner-party, or worn out by the bustle and turmoil of suitors. The building in which one toils becomes intimately associated with the toil itself. That in which one prays should at least have some attribute to remind one of prayer. Human nature shrinks for long from the thought of being buried in any but consecrated ground; the certainty of lying dead some day or other on a field of battle, or by a roadside, has, I have remarked, the most strange effect on the soldier's mind. Depend upon it, the same feeling holds good with regard to consecrated places of worship. You may think this fanciful, but I am sure you would feel it more strongly than I do, were you to live for a time in a country where everything *but religion* has its living and existent memorials and evidences.

But to return to reality: I have just spent three days in Sir Charles Napier's camp, it being my duty to accompany him through such parts of the civil district as he may have occasion to visit. He was most kind and cordial; vastly amusing and interesting, and gave me even a higher opinion of him than before. To be sure, his language and mode of expressing himself savour more of the last than of this century—of the camp than of the court; but, barring these eccentricities, he is a wonderful man; his heart is as thoroughly in his work, and he takes as high a tone in all that concerns it, as Arnold did in his; that is to say, the highest the subject is capable of. I only trust he will remain with us as long as his health lasts, and endeavour to rouse the army from the state of slack discipline into which it has fallen. On my parting with him he said, "Now, remember, Hodson, if there is any way in which I can be of use to you, pray don't scruple to write to me." I didn't show him his brother's (Sir W. Napier) letter—that he might judge for himself first, and know me *per se*, or rather *per me;* I will, however, if ever I see him again.

# CHAPTER VI.

*TOUR IN CASHMERE AND THIBET WITH SIR HENRY LAWRENCE — PROMOTION AND TRANSFER TO CIS-SUTLEJ PROVINCES.*

CAMP, EN ROUTE TO CASHMERE,<br>
*June* 10*th*, 1850.

YOUR letter from Paris reached me just as I was preparing to start from Umritsur to join Sir Henry Lawrence and accompany him to Cashmere. I fought against the necessity of leave as long as possible, but I was getting worse and worse daily, and so much weakened from the effects of heat and hard work acting on a frame already reduced by sickness, that I was compelled to be off ere worse came. We yesterday arrived at the summit of the first high ridge southward of the snowy range, and have now only some sixty miles to traverse before entering the valley. To me, travelling is life, and in a country where one has no home, no local attractions, and no special sympathies, it is the greatest comfort in the world. I get terribly *ennuyé* if I am in one place for three months at a time; yet I think I should be just as tame as ever in England, quite domestic again.

---

CASHMERE, *July* 8*th*, 1850.

You would enjoy this lovely valley extremely. I did not know it was so beautiful, having only seen it before in its winter dress. Nothing can exceed the luxuriant beauty of the vegetation, the plane trees and walnuts especially, except the squalor, dirt, and poverty of the wretched Cashmerians. The King is avaricious, and is old. The disease grows on him, and he won't look beyond his money bags. There is a capitation tax on every individual practising any labour, trade, profession, or employment, collected *daily*. Fancy the Londoners having to go and pay a fourpenny and a sixpenny bit each, per diem, for the pleasure of living in the town. Then the tax on all shawls, goods, and fabrics is about seventy-five per cent., including custom duty; and this the one solitary staple of the valley. The chief crops are rice, and of this, what with one-half taken at a slap as "revenue," or rent, and sundry other pulls for dues, taxes, and offerings, so little remains to the farmer, that in practice he pays *all*, or within a few bushels of all, his produce to the King, and secures in return *his food*, and that not of the best. Thus the farmer class or "Zemindars" are reduced pretty well to the state of day-labourers; yet the people are all well clothed, and fuel is to be had for the asking. What a garden it might be made. Not an acre to which the finest water might not be conveyed without expense worth naming, and a climate where all produce comes to perfection, from wheat and barley to grapes and silk. We go northwards on the 20th, first to Ladâkh and Thibet, thence to Iskardo, and then across the Indus to Gilghit, a *terra incognita* to which, I believe, only one European now living has penetrated. Sir Henry Lawrence is not well, and certainly not up to this trip, but he has made up his mind to go. I do not gain strength as fast as I could wish, but I fancy when once thoroughly unstrung, it takes a long time to recover the wonted tone.

We shall have another frontier war in the cold weather evidently, and I fancy a more prolonged and complete affair than the last. The cause of the only loss sustained in the last scrimmage was the panic of the Sepoys. They are as children in the hands of these Affghans and hill tribes. Our new Punjab levies fought "like bricks," but the Hindoostanee is not a hardy enough animal, physically or morally, to contend with the sturdier races west of the Sutlej, or the active and fighting " Patháns." The very *name* sticks in John Sepoy's throat. I must try and see the next contest, but I do not quite see my way to it at present.

---

### *To his Sister.*

CAMP, NEAR LADÂKH, *August 4th*, 1850.

Who would have thought of my writing to you from Thibet. I am sitting in a little tent about eight feet long, which just takes a narrow cot, a table, and chair of camp dimensions, and my *sac-de-nuit*, gun, &c., and a tin box containing books, papers, and the materials for this present epistle. Under the same tree (a veritable chestnut) is Sir Henry Lawrence's tent, a ditto of mine, in which he is comfortably sleeping, as I ought to be; outside are my pets—that is, a string of mules who accompany me in all my travels, and have also in the mountains the honour of carrying me as well as my baggage. The kitchen is under a neighbouring tree; and round a fire are squatting our gallant guards, a party of Maharaja Gholab Singh's household brigade. Some of his people accompany us, and what with followers, a Moonshee or two for business, and their followers, I daresay we are a party of two or three hundred souls of all colours and creeds—Christians, Mussulmans, Hindoos, Buddhists, Sikhs, and varieties of each. The creeds of the party are as varied as their colours; and that's saying a good deal, when you contrast my white face and yellow hair with Sir Henry's nut-brown, the pale white parchmenty-colour of the Cashmeree, the honest brunette tinge of the tall Sikh, the clear olive-brown of the Rajpoot, down through all shades of dinginess to the deep black of the low-caste Hindoo. I am one of the whitest men in India, I fancy, as instead of burning in the sun, I get blenched like endive or celery. How you would stare at my long beard, moustache, and whiskers. However, to return from such personalities to facts. The Indus is brawling along 500 feet below us, as if in a hurry to get " out of that ; " and above, one's neck aches with trying to see to the top of the vast craggy mountains which confine the stream in its rocky channel. So wild, so heaven-forsaken a scene I never beheld ; living nature there is none. In a week's journey, I have seen three marmots, two wagtails, and three jackdaws ; and we have averaged twenty miles a day.

We met a lady the other day, in the most romantic way possible, in the midst of the very wildest of glens, and almost as wild weather. She is a young and very pretty creature, gifted with the most indomitable energy and endurance (except as regards her husband, whom she *can't* endure, and therefore travels alone). But conceive, that for the last three months she has been making her way on pony-back across a country which few *men* would like to traverse, over the most formidable passes, the deepest and rapidest rivers, and wildest deserts in Asia. For twenty days she was in the extreme wilds of Thibet, without ever seeing a human habitation ; making such long day's journeys as often to be without food or bedding, traversing passes from 16,000 to 18,000 feet above the sea, where you can hardly breathe without pain ; enduring pain, sickness, and every mortal ill, yet persevering still! Poor creature, she is dying, I fear. It is evident that she is in a deep consumption, created by a terrible fall she had down a precipice, at the commencement of her journey. Well, one day we met her between this place and Cashmere. She was sixteen or twenty miles from her tents, and the rain and darkness were coming on apace ; the thermometer down below fifty degrees. So we persuaded her to stop at our encampment. I gave her my tent and cot ; acted lady's maid ; supplied her with warm stockings and shoes, water, towels, brushes, &c., and made her comfortable, and then we sat down to dinner ; and a pleasanter evening I never spent. She was as gay as a lark, and poured out stores of information and anecdotes, and recounted her adventures in the "spiritedest" manner. After an early breakfast the next morning, I put her on her pony, and she went on her way, and we saw her no more. I hope she will live to reach the end of her journey, and not die in some wild mountain-side unattended and alone.

Another letter of same date :—

CAMP, KULSEE IN LADÂKH, *August 4th*, 1850.

... Until you cross the mountain chain which separates Cashmere from Tibet (or Thibet), all is green and beautiful. It is impossible to imagine a finer combination of vast peaks and masses of mountain, with green sloping lawns, luxuriant foliage, and fine clustering woods, than is displayed on the sides of the great chain which we usually call the Himalaya, but which is better described as the ridge which separates the waters of the Jhelum, Chenab, Ravee, and Beas from those of the Indus. When once, however, you have crossed this vast barrier, the scene changes as if by magic, and you have nothing but huge convulsive-looking masses of rock, tremendous mountains, glaciers, snow, and valleys which are more vast watercourses than anything else. On the more open and less elevated spots along these various feeders of the Indus, one comes to little patches of cultivation, rising from the banks of the rivers in tiers of carefully-prepared terraces, and irrigated by channels carried along the sides of the hill from a point higher up the stream. Here, in scattered villages ten and twenty miles apart, live the ugliest race on earth, I should imagine, whom we call Thibetians, but who style themselves "Bhots" or "Bhods," and unite the characteristic features, or rather want of them, of both Goorkhas and Chinese. I went yesterday to see a monastery of their Llamas, the most curious sight, as well as *site*, I ever beheld. Perched on the summit of a mass of sandstone-grit, conglomerate pudding-stone, worn by the melting snows (for there is no rain in Tibet) into miraculous cones, steeples, and pinnacles rising abruptly from the valley to the height of 600 feet, are a collection of queer little huts, connected together by bridges, passages, and staircases. In these dwell the worthies who have betaken themselves to the life of religious mendicants and priests. They seem to correspond exactly with the travelling friars of olden times. Half stay at home to perform chants and services in their convent chapel, and half go a-begging about the country. They are not a distinct race like the Brahmins of India, but each Bhot peasant devotes one of two or three sons to the church, and he is thenceforward devoted to a life of celibacy, of shaven crown, of crimson apparel, of mendicancy, of idleness, and of comfort. They all acknowledge spiritual allegiance to the Great Llama at Lhassa (some two months' journey from Ladâkh), by whom the abbot of each convent is appointed on a vacancy occurring, and to whom all their proceedings are reported. Nunneries also exist on precisely the same footing. I saw a few of the nuns, and their hideous appearance fully justified their adoption of celibacy and seclusion. From their connection with almost every family, as I have said, they are universally looked up to and supported as a class by the people. Even Hindoos reverence them; and their power is not only feared, but I fancy tolerably freely exercised. Their chapel (a flat-roofed square building supported on pillars) is furnished with parallel rows of low benches to receive the squatting fathers. Their services consist of chants and recitative, accompanied by the *dis*cord of musical (?) instruments and drums, while perpetual lamps burn on the altars before their idols, and a sickly perfume fills the air. Round the room are rude shelves containing numberless volumes of religious books; not bound, but in separate leaves secured between two painted boards. I will try and send you one, if I can corrupt the mind of some worthy Llama with profane silver. They are genuine *block books*, strange to say, apparently carved on wood, and then stamped on a Chinese paper. The figures of their images, and their costume and head-dress (*i.e.*, of the images), are Chinese entirely, not at all resembling the Bhot dress, or scarcely so, and though fashioned by Thibetian hands, you might fancy yourself gazing on the figures in the Chinese Exhibition at Hyde Park Corner. Their language is a sealed book to me, of course, and though they all read and write well, yet they were unable to explain the meaning of the words they were repeating. The exterior appearance and sites of their conventual buildings reminded me very strongly of the drawings I saw in a copy of Curzon's "Monasteries of the Levant," which fell in my way for five minutes one day. I need hardly say that, in a country composed of mountains ranging from 14,000 feet upwards, the scenery is magnificent in the extreme, though very barren and savage. Apricots and wheat are ripening in the valley whence I now write (on the right bank of the Indus, some fifty miles below the town of Ladâkh), and snow is glistening on the summits above me; the roads have been very easy indeed, and enabled us to make long day's marches, from sixteen to twenty-five miles. This is more than you could do in two days in the ranges south of the Himalaya, with due regard for your own bones, and the cattle or porters which carry your traps and tents. I am very seedy, and twenty miles is more than I can ride with comfort (that I should live to say it). I have not as yet derived much, if any, benefit from change of climate.

From Ladâkh we go to Iskardo, some twelve marches lower down the Indus, where it has been joined by the water of Yarkund; and thence to Gilghit, a valley running up from that of the Indus, still lower down, and bordering on Budakhstan. We (Sir Henry Lawrence and I) then return to Cashmere; I expect it will be two more months' journey. We have already been out a fortnight, and it is very fatiguing. I am not sure that I was wise in undertaking it, but he (Lawrence) is a greater invalid than I am, and two or three men fought shy of the task of accompanying him.

---

CAMP, ISKARDO (IN LITTLE THIBET),
*August 25th*, 1850.

Only think of my sitting down peaceably to write to you from this outside world. Had I lived a hundred years ago, I should have been deemed a great traveller, and considered to have explored unknown countries, and unknown they are, only the principal danger is past, seeing that they have been subdued by a power (Gholab Singh) with whom we have "relations." Yet if I were to cross the mountains which stare me in the face a few miles off, I should be carried off and sold for a slave. It were vain to try to compress the scenes of a two months' journey into a sheet of note-paper. We have travelled very rapidly: few men go the pace Sir Henry Lawrence does. So we have covered a great extent of country in the past month; and seeing that the valleys are the only inhabited parts of the country, the rest being huge masses of mountains, one really sees in these rapid flights all that is to be seen of the abodes of man. We have collected a good deal of information too, which, if I had time to arrange it, might be of value. We were eleven long days' journey from Cashmere to Ladâkh, besides halts on the way at Ladâkh itself, or, as the people call it, "Leh." We remained a week, and saw all the "foreigners" who came there to sell furs and silk. It is called the "Great Emporium" of trade between Yarkund and Kashgar, and Llassa and Hindoostan. Fine words look well on paper, but to my unsophisticated mind the "leading merchants" seemed *pedlars*, and the "emporium" to be a brace of hucksters' shops. However, 'tis curious, that's a fact, to see (and talk to) a set of men who have got their goods from the yellow-haired Russians at the Nishni-Novogorod fair, and brought them across Asia to sell at Ladâkh. It is forty days' journey of almost a continuous desert for these caravans from Yarkund to Leh: and there is no small danger to life and limb by the way. The current coin is lumps of Chinese syce silver of two pounds weight each. I bought a Persian horse for the journey, and paid for it in solid silver four pounds weight, 166 rupees, or about £16. I shall sell it for double the money when the journey is over. Leh is a small town, of not more than 400 houses, on a projecting promontory of rock stretching out into the valley formed by one of the small feeders of the Indus. For the people, they are Bodhs, and wear tails, and have flat features like the Chinese, and black garments. The women, unlike other Asiatics whom I have seen, go about the streets openly, as in civilised countries; but they are an ugly race, and withal dirty to an absolutely unparalleled extent. They wear no head-dress, but plait their masses of black hair into sundry tails half-way down their backs. Covering the division of the hair from the forehead back and down the shoulders, is a narrow leathern strap, universally adorned with rough turquoises and bits of gold or silver. The old Ranee whom we called upon had on this strap (in her case a broader one, about three fingers wide) 156 large turquoises, worth some hundreds of pounds. Over their ears they wear flaps of fur which project forward with precisely the effect of blinkers on a horse.

The climate is delightful; it never rains; the sky is blue to a fault, and snow only falls sparingly in winter, though the climate is cold, being 10,000 feet (they say) above the sea. In boiling water the thermometer was only 188°. I never felt a more exhilarating air. That one week quite set me up, and I have been better ever since. The Llamas or monks, with their red cardinals' hats and crimson robes, look very imposing and monastic, quite a travestie of the regular clergy, and they blow just such trumpets as Fame does on monuments in country churches. Jolly friars they are, and fat to a man. From Leh we crossed the mountain-ridge which separates the two streams of the Indus, and descended the northern (or right) stream to this place, the capital of Bultistan or Little Thibet. It is a genuine humbug. In the middle of a fine valley some 6000 feet above the sea, surrounded by sudden rising perpendicular mountains 6000 feet higher, stands an isolated rock washed by the Indus, some two miles by three-quarters: a little Gibraltar. The valley may be ten miles by three, partially cultivated, and inhabited by some two hundred scattered houses. There's Iskardo. There *was* a fort on the rock, but that is gone, and all, as usual in the East, bespeaks havoc: only Nature is grand here. The people are Mussulmans, and not Bodhs, and are more human-looking, but not so well clad. It is warmer by far, much more so than it ought to be. The thermometer was at 92° in our tents to-day, a thing for which

I cannot possibly account, since there is snow now on all sides of us. We go hence across the Steppe of Deo Sole towards Cashmere for four days' journey, and then strike westward to cross the Indus into Gilghit, whence we return to Cashmere by the end of September. We have been making very fast marches, varying from sixteen to thirty-two miles a day—hard work in a country with such roads, and where you must take things with you. I enjoy it very much, however, and after a year's sickness, the feeling of returning health is refreshing. I shall return to work again by the 1st of December; but I propose paying a flying visit to Mr. Thomason in October, if possible; but the distances are so vast, and the means of locomotion so absent, that these things are difficult to achieve. I suppose I have seen more of the hill country now than ninety-nine men out of a hundred in India. Indeed, not above four Europeans have been here before. But travelling suits my restless spirit. Sir Henry and I get on famously together.

On October 7th, 1850, he writes from Simla to his father:—

I have had a long and fatiguing march from Cashmere across the mountains and the valleys of the "five rivers," nearly 400 miles, which I accomplished in fifteen days. I left Sir Henry Lawrence in Cashmere. I have since heard from him, urging me to use all the influence I can muster up here to procure a brevet majority in *posse* (*i.e.*, on attaining my regimental captaincy), and a *local* majority, in *esse* for "my services in the late war;" and adding, that if I did not find civil employment to suit me, he would, when I had given it a fair trial, try and get me the command of one of the regiments in the Punjab. I am going to consult Mr. Thomason on the subject, and will let you know the result. I hate the least suspicion of toadyism, and dislike asking favours, or I should have been better off ere now; but on Sir Henry Lawrence's suggestion, I will certainly use any opportunity which may offer. I thought, however, you would be gratified with the opinion which must have dictated so perfectly spontaneous an offer. I confess that I very much prefer the military line myself, although I like civil work much, and it is the road to competence. Nevertheless, military rank and distinctions have more charm for me than rupees; and I would rather *cut* my way to a name and poverty with the sword, than *write* it to wealth with the pen.

There is something to me peculiarly interesting in the *forming* and *training* soldiers, and in acquiring that extraordinary influence over their minds, both by personal volition and the aid of discipline, which leads them on through danger, even to death, at your bidding. I felt the enthusiasm of this power successfully exerted with the Guides during the late war; and having felt it, am naturally inclined to take advantage of it on future occasions.

---

*To his Sister.*

SIMLA, *Oct.* 21*st*, 1850.

It is rather too late to tell you "all about Cashmere," as you desire; but I *can* say that I saw some beauties this time who were really so to no common extent; and that I was much more pleased with the valley than on my first visit, which was a winter one. If you see what wonderfully out-of-the-way places we got into, I think you will marvel that I managed to write at all. We traversed upwards of 1500 miles of wild mountainous countries, innocent of roads, and often for days together of inhabitants, and carrying our houses on our backs. The change to the utter comfort and civilisation of this house was something "stunning;" and I have not yet become quite reconciled to dressing three times a day, black hat, and patent-leather boots. I need hardly say, however, that I have very much enjoyed my visit and my "big talks" with Mr. Thomason. He is very grey, and looks older than when I saw him in 1847, but otherwise he is just the same, working magnificently, and doing wonders for his province. Already the North-West Provinces are a century in advance of the Bengal Proper ones. As a Governor he has not his equal; and in honesty, high-mindedness, and indefatigable devotion to the public good, he is *facile princeps* of the whole Indian service. Nor is there a household in India to match his; indeed, it is about the only "big-wig" house to which people go with pleasure rather than as a duty. I saw Sir Charles Napier, too, and dined with him last week. He is very kind and pleasant, and I am very sorry on public grounds that he is going away.

---

KUSSOWLEE, *Nov. 4th*, 1850.

I had a most pleasant home-like visit to Mr. Thomason, and was most affectionately entertained. He will have told you of the power of civility I met with at Simla from the "big-wigs," and that even Lord Dalhousie waxed complimentary, and said that "Lumsden and Hodson were about the best men he had" (that I write it that shouldn't!), and that he promised to do his best to get me a brevet majority as soon as I became, in the course of time, a regimental captain. And Sir Charles Napier (the best-abused man of his day) was anxious to get for me the Staff appointment of Brigade-Major to the Punjab Irregular Force— *i.e.*, of the six newly raised cavalry and infantry regiments for frontier service. He did not succeed, for the berth had been previously filled up unknown to him; but he *tried to do so*, and that's a compliment from such a man. I hope I need not say that this good deed of his was as spontaneous as a mushroom's birth.

---

*To his Father.*

KUSSOWLEE, *Nov. 6th*.

I am to be here next year, I find, by tidings just received, which will be a splendid thing for my constitution. My connection with Umritsur is dissolved by my having been appointed to act as personal assistant to the Commissioner of the Cis-Sutlej States, which is, I believe, a piece of promotion. The great advantages are, first, the capital opportunity it affords of experience in every kind of civil work, and of being under a very able man—Mr. Edmonstone; and secondly, that the Commissioner's headquarters are "peripatetic" in the cold weather, and in the hills during the remainder of the year. But I confess that I hanker after the "Guides" as much as ever, and would catch at a good opportunity of returning to them with honour. I fear I have been remiss in explanations on this subject. The matter lies in this wise—I left the Corps and took to civil employment, at the advice of Sir Henry Lawrence, Mr. Thomason, and others, though against my own feelings on the subject. The man or men who succeeded me are senior to me in army rank. When one of them resigned six months ago, I was strongly disposed and urged to try and succeed to the vacancy. There was a hitch, however, from the cause I have mentioned, and Lumsden was anxious that his lieutenants should not be disgusted by supercession. I might have had the appointment, but withdrew to avoid annoying Lumsden. *Now*, both Sir Henry Lawrence and Mr. Thomason are very sorry that I ever left the Corps, and that they advised the step. Things have taken a different turn since then, and it is confessedly the best thing a young soldier can aspire to. I know that my present line is one which leads to more pecuniary advantages; but the other is the finer field, and is far more independent. I shall work away, however, cheerfully in the civil line until I see a good opening in the other; and *then*, I fear you will hardly persuade me that sitting at a desk with the thermometer at 98° is better than soldiering—*i.e.*, than *commanding* soldiers made and taught by yourself! I will give you the earliest warning of the change.

---

UMRITSUR, *Nov.* 24*th*, 1850.

I returned here on the 16th, and have been up to the neck in work ever since, having the whole work, civil, criminal, police,

&c. &c., on my shoulders, Sanders, the Deputy Commissioner, my superior, being engaged dancing attendance on the Governor-General, who is here on his annual tour of inspection; and Macleod, my co-assistant, dead. Directly the Governor-General has gone onwards I shall be relieved here, and join my new appointment with Mr. Edmonstone.

LAHORE, *Jan. 2nd*, 1851.

I broke up from Umritsur early in December, and came into Lahore to join my new chief. He did not arrive till the 18th, so I had a comparative holiday. I have got into harness, however, again now, and am up to the elbows in work and papers. The work is much more pleasant than that I had at Umritsur, and more free from mere routine.

LAHORE, *Feb. 21st*.

This is an interesting anniversary to many of us, and an overwhelming one to this country—that of the day on which "the bright star of the Punjab" set for ever. It has been curiously marked by the announcement that the net balance of receipts over expenditure for the past year for the newly acquired provinces has reached upwards of a million sterling. Lord Dalhousie's star is in the ascendant. His financial measures are apparently all good, when tried by the only standard admissible in the nineteenth century—their success.

KUSSOWLEE, *March 22nd*, 1851.

I broke down again most completely as soon as the hot weather began, but my flight to this beautiful climate has wonderfully refreshed me. Talk of Indian luxuries! there are but two—cold water and cool air! I get on very comfortably with my new "Chief." He is a first-rate man, and has a most uncommon appetite for work, of which there is plenty for both of us. We cover a good stretch of country—comprising five British districts and nine sovereign states; and as the whole has been in grievous disorder for many years, and a peculiarly difficult population to deal with, you may imagine that the work is not slight. My principal duty is hearing appeals from orders and decisions by the district officers in these five districts. It is of course not *per se*, but as the Commissioner's personal assistant, that I do this. I prepare a short abstract, with my opinion on each case, and he issues his orders accordingly. I was at work a whole day lately over one case, which, after all, involved only a claim to about a quarter of an acre of land! You will give me credit for ingenuity in discovering that the result of some half-dozen quires of written evidence was to prove that *neither* of the contending parties had any right at all! If that's not "justice to Ireland," I don't know what is! I have been staying with Captain Douglas, 60th Rifles, and I hope I shall see a great deal of him. There is not a better man or more genuine soldier going. This may appear faint praise, but rightly understood, and conscientiously and boldly worked out, I doubt whether any other profession calls forth the higher qualities of our nature more strongly than does that of a soldier in times of war and tumults. Certain it is that it requires the highest order of man to be a good general, and in the lower ranks (in this country especially), even with all the frightful drawbacks and evils, I doubt whether the Saxon race is ever so pre-eminent, or its good points so strongly developed, as in the "European" soldier serving in India, or on service anywhere.

---

KUSSOWLEE, *April 7th*, 1851.

I have the nicest house here on a level spot on the very summit of the mountain ridge, from which a most splendid view is obtainable for six months in the year. In the immediate foreground rises a round-backed ridge, on which stands the former work of my hands, the "Lawrence Asylum;" while to the westward, and down, down far off in the interminable south, the wide glistening plains of the Punjab, streaked with the faint ribbon-like lines of the Sutlej and its tributaries, and the wider sea-like expanse of Hindoostan, stretch away in unbroken evenness beyond the limits of vision, and almost beyond those of faith and imagination. On the other side you look over a mass of mountains up to the topmost peaks of Himalaya. So narrow is the ridge, that it seems as though you could toss a pebble from one window into the Sutlej, and from the other into the valley below Simla. I like the place very much. I have seven or eight hour's work every day, and the rest is spent (as this one) in the society of the 60th Rifles, the very nicest and most gentlemanly regiment I ever met with.

---

KUSSOWLEE, *May 4th*, 1851.

Your budget of letters reached me on the 2nd. It is very pleasant to receive these warm greetings, and it refreshes me when bothered, or overworked, or feverish, or disgusted. I look forward to a visit to England and *home* with a pleasure which nothing but six years of exile can give.

The Governor-General has at last advanced me to the higher grade of "assistants" to Commissioners. The immediate advantage is an increase of pay—the real benefit, that it brings me nearer the main step of a Deputy-Commissioner in charge of a district. It is satisfactory, not the less so that it was extorted from him by the unanimity of my official superiors in pressing the point upon him, Mr. Edmonstone having commenced attacking him in my favour before I had been under him four months. I am not in love with the kind of employment—I long with no common earnestness for the more military duties of my old friends the "Guides:" but I am not therefore insensible to the advantages of doing well in this line of work. Ambition alone would dictate this, for my success in this civil business (which is considered the highest and most arduous branch of the public service) almost ensures my getting on in any other hereafter.

## To Rev. E. Harland.

KUSSOWLEE, *June* 11*th*, 1851.

I fancy the change is as great in myself as in either. The old visions of boyhood have given place to the vehement aspirations of a military career and the interests of a larger ambition. I thirst now not for the calm pleasures of a country life, the charms of society, or a career of ease and comfort, but for the maddening excitement of war, the keen contest of wits involved in dealing with wilder men, and the exercise of power over the many by force of the will of the individual. Nor am I, I hope, insensible to the vast field for good and for usefulness which these vast provinces offer to our energies, and to the high importance of the trust committed to our charge.

---

## To his Father.

KUSSOWLEE, *Oct.* 20*th*, 1851.

I am much stronger now, and improving rapidly. By the end of next summer I hope to be as strong as I ever hope to be again. That I shall ever again be able to row from Cambridge to Ely in two hours and ten minutes, to run a mile in five minutes, or to walk from Skye (or Kyle Hatren Ferry) to Inverness in thirty hours, is not to be expected, or perhaps desired. But I have every hope that in the event of another war I may be able to endure fatigue and exposure as freely as in 1848. One is oftener called upon to ride than to walk long distances in India. In 1848 I could ride one hundred miles in ten hours, fully accoutred, and I don't care how soon (saving your presence!) the necessity arises again! I have no doubt that matrimony will do me a power of good, and that I shall be not only better, but happier, and more care-less than hitherto.

I have been deeply grieved and affected by the death, two days ago, of Colonel Bradshaw, of the 60th Rifles. He will be a sad loss, not only to his regiment, but to the army and the country. He was the *beau ideal* of an English soldier and gentleman, and would have earned himself a name as a general had he been spared. A finer and nobler spirit there was not in the army. I feel it as a deep personal loss, for he won my esteem and regard in no common degree.

# CHAPTER VII.

### MARRIAGE—COMMAND OF THE GUIDES—FRONTIER WARFARE—MURDAN.

On the 5th of January, 1852, Lieutenant Hodson was married, at the Cathedral, Calcutta, to Susan, daughter of Captain C. Henry, R.N., and widow of John Mitford, Esq. of Exbury, Hants. By the first week in March he had resumed his duties at Kussowlee as Assistant Commissioner. On the breaking out of the war with Burmah he expected to rejoin his regiment (the First Bengal European Fusiliers), which had been ordered for service there, but in August he writes from Kussowlee:—

My regiment is on its way down the Ganges to Calcutta, to take part in the war, but the Burmese have proved so very unformidable an enemy this time, that only half the intended force is to be sent on from Calcutta; the rest being held in reserve. Under these circumstances, and in the expectation that the war will very speedily be brought to a close, the Governor-General has determined not to allow officers on civil employment to join their regiments in the usual manner. I am thus spared what would have been a very fatiguing and expensive trip, with very little hope of seeing any fighting.

It was not long, however, before an opportunity of seeing active service presented itself, and in a way, of all others, most to his taste. His heart had all along been with his old corps, "the Guides," as his letters show. He had taken an active share in raising and training them originally, and as second in command during the Punjab campaign of 1848-49, had contributed in no small degree to gain for the corps that reputation which it has recently so nobly sustained before Delhi.

The command was now vacant, and was offered to him; but I must let him speak for himself:—

KUSSOWLEE, *Sept.* 23rd, 1852.

Lumsden, my old commandant in the Guides, goes to England next month, and the Governor-General has given me the command which I have coveted so long. It is immense good fortune in every way, both as regards income and distinction. It is accounted the most honourable and arduous command on the frontier, and fills the public eye, as the papers say, more than any other.

This at the end of seven years' service is a great thing, especially on such a frontier as Peshawur, at the mouth of the Kyber Pass. You will agree with me in rejoicing at the opportunities for distinction thus offered to me.

Mr. Thomason writes thus: "I congratulate you very sincerely on the fine prospect that is open to you, and trust that you will have many opportunities of showing what the Guides can do under your leadership. I have never ceased to reproach myself for advising you to leave the corps, but now that you have the command, you will be all the better for the dose of civilianism that has been intermediately administered to you."

KUSSOWLEE, *Oct.* 7th, 1852.

Here I am still, but hoping to take wing for Peshawur in a few days. It is only 500 miles; and as there are no railways, and only nominal roads, and fine vast rivers to cross, you may suppose that the journey is not one of a few hours' lounge.

I am most gratified by the appointment to the command of the Guides, and more so by the way in which it was given me, and the manner of my selection from amidst a crowd of aspirants. It is no small thing for a subaltern to be raised to the command of a battalion of infantry and a squadron and a half of cavalry, with four English officers under him! I am supposed to be the luckiest man of my time. I have already had an offer from the Military Secretary to the Board of Administration to exchange appointments with him, although I should gain, and he would lose £200 a year by the "swop;" but I would not listen to him; I prefer the saddle to the desk, the frontier to a respectable, wheel-going, dinner-giving, dressy life at the capital; and —— ambition to money!

But though his "instincts were so entirely military" (to use his own words), this did not prevent his discharging his civil duties in a manner that called forth the highest eulogium from his superiors, as the subjoined letter from Mr. Edmonstone, now Secretary to Government at Calcutta, will testify:—

"KUSSOWLEE, *Oct.* 12*th*, 1852.

"MY DEAR HODSON,—I am a bad hand at talking, and could not say what I wished, but I would not have you go away without thanking you heartily for the support and assistance which you have always given me in all matters, whether big or little, since you joined me, now twenty months and more ago. I have in my civil and criminal reports for the past year recorded my sense of your services, and your official merits, but our connection has been peculiar, and your position has been one which few would have filled either so efficiently or so agreeably to all parties. You have afforded me the greatest aid in the most irksome part of my duty, and have always with the utmost readiness undertaken anything, no matter what, that I asked you to dispose of, and I owe you more on this account than a mere official acknowledgment can repay adequately. I hope that though your present appointment will give you more congenial duties and better pay, you will never have occasion to look back to the time you have passed here with regret; and I hope too that all your anticipations of pleasure and pride in commanding the corps which you had a chief hand in forming, may be realised. —Believe me to be, with much regard, yours very sincerely,

"G. F. EDMONSTONE."

---

CAMP IN HUZARA, BLACK MOUNTAINS, *Dec.* 16*th*, 1852.

I took command of the Guides on the 1st November, and twenty-four hours afterwards marched "on service" to this country, which is on the eastern or left bank of the Indus, above the parallel of Attok. We are now in an elevated valley, surrounded by snowy mountains, and mighty cold it is, too, at night. We have come about 125 miles from Peshawur, and having marched up the hill, are patiently expecting the order to march down again. We have everything necessary for a pretty little mountain campaign but an enemy. This is usually a *sine quâ non* in warfare, but not so now. Then we have to take a fort, only it has ceased to exist months ago; and to reinstate an Indian ally in territories from which he was expelled by some neighbours, only he won't be reinstated at any price.

My regiment consists of five English officers, including a surgeon, Dr. Lyell, a very clever man. Then I have 300 horse, including native officers, and 550 foot, or 850 men in all, divided into three troops and six companies,* the latter armed as riflemen. My power is somewhat despotic, as I have authority to enlist or dismiss from the service, flog or imprison, degrade or promote any one, from the native officers downwards, always remembering that an abuse of power might lose me the whole. This sort of chiefdom is necessary with a wild sort of gentry of

* No two troops or companies were of the same race, in order to prevent the possibility of combination. One company was composed of Sikhs, another of Affreedees, others of Pathans, Goorkhas, Punjabee Mohammedans, &c., with native officers, in each case, of a different race from the men.

various races and speeches, gathered from the snows of the Hindoo Koosh and the Himalaya, to the plains of Scinde and Hindoostan, all of whom are more quick at blows than at words, and more careless of human life than you could possibly understand in England by any description. I am likely to have civil charge as well as military command of the Euzofzai district, comprising that portion of the great Peshawur valley which lies between the Cabul river and the Indus. So you see I am not likely to eat bread of idleness, at least. I will tell you more of my peculiar duties when I have more experience of their scope and bent. . . . I am, I should say, the most fortunate man in the service, considering my standing. The other candidates were all field officers of some standing.

Our good friend and guest, Captain Powys, of the 60th, who has spent the first six months of our married life under our roof, is on the way to England. He will see you very soon, and give you a better account of us than you could hope for from any one else.

In a letter to his wife, then staying with Sir H. Lawrence at Lahore, he says:—

I have been much cheered by the arrival in camp of my dear friend Colonel Napier. He is the most lovable man I know in this country, and a Bayard in generosity and courage. I am sure you will like him. I am anxious about your journey, but I am sure that Sir Henry will do all he can to start you comfortably.

Notwithstanding all appearance to the contrary at its opening, the campaign lasted seven weeks, and supplied plenty of fighting. It was afterwards characterised by my brother as the hardest piece of service he had yet seen. One engagement lasted from sunrise to sunset. He had thus an opportunity of displaying his usual gallantry and coolness, and showing how well he could handle his "Guides" in mountain warfare. They suffered much from cold, as the ground was covered with snow for a part of the time, and from want of supplies.

Colonel (now Lord) Napier, speaking afterwards of this expedition, said:—

"Your brother's unfailing fun and spirits, which seemed only raised by what we had to go through, kept us all alive and merry, so that we looked back upon it afterwards as a party of pleasure, and thought we had never enjoyed anything more."

In reply to congratulations on his appointment to the Guides, my brother wrote from—

PESHAWUR, *March* 13*th*, 1853.

I have certainly been very fortunate indeed, and only hope that I may be enabled to acquit myself of the trust well and honourably, both in the field and in the more political portion of my duties. It was a good thing that I had the opportunity of leading the regiment into action so soon after getting the command, and that the brunt of the whole should have fallen upon us, as it placed the older men and myself once more on our old footing of confidence in one another, and introduced me to the younger hands as their leader when they needed one. Susie says she told you all about it; I need therefore only add that it was the hardest piece of service, while it lasted, I have yet seen with the Guides, both as regards the actual fighting, the difficulties of the ground (a rugged mountain, 7000 feet high, and densely wooded), and the exposure. You will see little or no mention of it publicly, it being the policy of Government to make everything appear as quiet as possible on this frontier, and to blazon the war on the eastern side of the empire (some 2000 miles away) as much as they can. I am, as you justly imagined, to be employed both civilly and in a military capacity—at least, it is under discussion. I was asked to take charge of the wild district of "Euzofzai" (forming a large portion of the Peshawur province), where the Guides will ordinarily be stationed. I refused to do so unless I had the exclusive civil charge in all departments, magisterial, financial, and judicial, instead of in the former only, as proposed, and I fancy they will give in to my reasons. I shall then be military chief, and civil governor, too, as far as that part of the valley is concerned, and shall have enough on my hands, as you may suppose. In the meantime, I shall have the superintendence of the building of a fort to contain us all—not such a fortress as Coblentz, or those on the Belgian frontier, but a mud structure, which answers all the purposes we require at a very, very small cost.

---

PESHAWUR, *April 30th*, 1853.

I am sorry to say my wife is ordered to the hills, and we shall again be separated for five or six months. My own destination for the hot season is uncertain, but I expect to be either here, or on the banks of the Indus.

---

CAMP, NEAR PESHAWUR, *June 4th*, 1853.

. . . I hope to get away from work and heat in August or September for a month, if all things remain quiet. But for this sad separation, there would be much charm for me in this gipsy life. To avoid the great heats of the next three months in tents, we are building huts for ourselves of thatch, and mine is assuming the dignity of mud walls. We are encamped on a lovely spot, on the banks of the swift and bright river, at the foot of the hills, on the watch for incursions or forays, and to guard the richly-cultivated plain of the Peshawur valley from depredations from the hills. We are ready, of course, to boot and saddle at all hours; our rifles and carbines are loaded, and our swords keen and bright: and woe to the luckless chief who, trusting to his horses, descends upon the plain too near our pickets! Meanwhile, I am civil as well as military chief, and the natural taste of the Euzofzai Pathans for broken heads, murder, and violence, as well as their litigiousness about their lands, keeps me very hard at work from day to day. Perhaps the life may be more suited to a careless bachelor than to a husband with such a wife as mine; but even still it has its charms for an active mind and body. A daybreak parade or inspection, a gallop across the plain to some outpost, a plunge in the river, and then an early breakfast, occupy your time until 9 A.M. Then come a couple of corpses, whose owners (late) had their heads broken over-night, and consequent investigations and examinations; next a batch of villagers to say their crops are destroyed by a storm, and no rents forthcoming. Then a scream of woe from a plundered farm on the frontier, and next a grain-dealer, to say his camels have been carried off to the hills. "Is not this a dainty dish to set before—your brother?" Then each of my nine hundred men considers me bound to listen to any amount of stories he may please to invent or remember of his own private griefs and troubles; and last, not least, there are four young gentlemen who have each his fancy; and who often give more trouble in transacting business than assistance in doing it. However, I have no right to complain, for I am about, yes, quite, the most fortunate man in the service; and have I not the right to call myself the happiest also, with such a wife and such a home?

At this time he received the following letter from Sir H. Lawrence, dated July 13th, 1853:—

"MY DEAR HODSON,—I hope Mrs. Hodson and yourself are alive. Perry informed me of the fact and of your whereabouts, &c. &c.

"By last mail I wrote to Lord Hardinge, and asked him to get you brevet rank. You had better write to Sir C. Napier (but don't use my name, or it might do you harm), and say that if he moves in your favour, you think Lord Hardinge will agree. If you could get local rank till you are a captain it would be a great matter. Say nothing to any one on the matter. . . .

Has the star fort been built yet? We hope Mrs. Hodson likes border life. Give her our kind regards.—Yours, &c.

"H. LAWRENCE."

---

CAMP, NEAR PESHAWUR, *August* 1853.

It is very trying that I cannot be with Susie at Murree; but with a people such as these it is not safe to be absent, lest the volcano should break out afresh. Since I began this sheet a dust-storm has covered everything on my table completely with sand. My pen is clogged and my inkstand choked, and my eyes full of dust! What am I to do? Oh, the pleasures of the tented field in August in the valley of Peshawur! It has been very hot indeed, lately. We have barely in our huts had the thermometer under 100°, and a very steamy, stewy heat it is, into the bargain.

---

MURREE, *Sept.* 14*th*, 1853.

I am enjoying a little holiday from arms and kutchery up in the cool here with Susie. Murree is not more than 140 miles from Peshawur. You say that you do not know "what I mean by hills in my part of India." This is owing to the badness of the maps. The fact is, that the whole of the upper part of the country watered by the five rivers is mountainous. The Himalaya extends from the eastern frontiers of India to Affghanistan, where it joins the "Hindoo Koosh," or Caucasus. If you draw a line from Peshawur, through Rawul Pindee, to Simla or Subathoo, or any place marked on the maps thereabouts, you may assume that all to the north of that line is mountain country. Another chain runs from Peshawur, down the right bank of the Indus to the sea. At Attok the mountains close in upon the river, or, more correctly speaking, the river emerges from the mountains, and the higher ranges end there. The Peshawur valley is a wide open plain, lying on the banks of the Cabul river, about sixty miles long by forty broad, encircled by moun tains, some of them covered with snow for eight or nine months of the year. Euzofzai is the north-eastern portion of this valley, embraced between the Cabul river and the Indus. Half of Euzofzai (the "abode of the children of Joseph") is mountain, but we only hold the level or plain part of it. Nevertheless, a large part of my little province is very hilly. In the north-east corner of Euzofzai, hanging over the Indus, is a vast lump of a hill, called "Mahabun" (or the "great forest"), thickly peopled on its slopes, and giving shelter to some 12,000 armed men, the bitterest bigots which even Islam can produce. The hill is about 7800 feet above the level of the sea. This has been identified by the wise men with the Aornos of Arrian, and Alexander is supposed to have crossed the Indus at its foot. Whether he did so or not, I am not "at liberty to mention," but it is certain that Nadir Shah, in one of his incursions into India, marched his host to the top of it, and encamped there. This gives colour to the story that the Macedonian did the same; as in all ages there are dominating points which are seized on by men of genius when engaged in the great game of war. The great principles of war seem to change as little as the natural features of the country. Well, you will see how a mountain-range running "slantingdicularly" across the Upper Punjab contains many nice mountain tops suited to Anglo-Saxon adventurers. If you can find Rawul Pindee on the maps, you may put your finger on Murree, about twenty-five miles, as the crow flies, to the northeast. You should get a map of the Punjab, Cashmere, and Iskardo, published by Arrowsmith in 1847. George sent me two of them. They are the best published maps I have seen. As to the Euzofzai fever, that is, I am happy to say, now over. It was terrible while it lasted. Between the 1st March and the 15th June 1853, 8352 persons died out of a population of 53,500. It was very similar to typhus, but had some symptoms of yellow fever. It was confined to natives.

Poor Colonel Mackeson, the Commissioner at Peshawur (the chief civil and political officer for the frontier), was stabbed, a few days ago, by a fanatic, while sitting in his verandah reading. The fellow was from Swât, and said he had heard that we were going to invade his country, and that he would try to stop it, and go to heaven as a martyr for the faith. Poor Mackeson is still alive, but in a very precarious state, I fear. I hope this may induce Government to take strong measures with the hill tribes.

He had soon to mourn the loss of a still more valued friend:—

*Oct. 15th, 1853.*

You will have been much shocked at hearing of poor dear Mr. Thomason's death.

It is an irreparable loss to his family and friends, but it will be even more felt in his public capacity. He had not been ill, but died from sheer debility and exhaustion produced by overwork and application in the trying season just over. Had he gone to the hills, all would have been right. I cannot but think that he sacrified himself as an example to others. You may imagine how much I have felt the loss of my earliest and best friend in India, to whom I was accustomed to detail all my proceedings, and whom I was wont to consult in every difficulty and doubt.

On the 2nd November he wrote from Rawul Pindee to announce the birth of a daughter. He had been obliged previously to return to his duties; but, by riding hard all night, had been able to be with his wife at the time, and, after greeting the little stranger, had immediately to hasten back to his Guides on the frontier.

The Government, with a view to secure the Kohat Pass, were now preparing an expedition against the refractory tribe of the Borees, one of the bravest and wildest of the Affghan race, in order to prove that their hills and valleys were accessible to our troops.

Accordingly, a force consisting of 400 men of Her Majesty's 22nd, 450 Goorkhas, 450 Guides, and the mountain train, marched at 4 A.M. on the morning of the 29th November, under the command of Brigadier Boileau, to attack the villages in the Boree valley.

I must supply the loss of my brother's own account by a letter from an officer with the expedition :—

"Our party, after crossing the hills between Kundao and the main Affreedee range at two points, reunited in the valley at 10.30 A.M., and with the villages of the Borees before us at the foot of some precipitous crags. These it at once became apparent must be carried before the villages could be attacked and destroyed. The service devolved on two detachments of the Goorkhas and Guides, commanded by Lieutenants Hodson and Turner, and the style in which these gallant fellows did their work, and drove the enemy from crag to rock and rock to crag, and finally kept them at bay from 11 A.M. to 3 P.M., was the admiration of the whole force. We could plainly see the onslaught, especially a fierce struggle that lasted a whole hour, for the possession of a breastwork, which appeared inaccessible from below, but was ultimately carried by the Guides, in the face of the determined opposition of the Affreedees, who fought for every inch of ground.

"Depend upon it, this crowning of the Boree heights was one of the finest pieces of light infantry performance on record. It was, moreover, one which Avitabile, with 10,000 Sikhs, was unable to accomplish. During these operations on the hill, the villages were burnt, and it was only the want of powder which prevented the succession of towers which flanked them being blown into the air. The object of the expedition having been thus fully achieved, the skirmishers were recalled at about three, and then the difficulties of the detachment commenced; for, as is well known, the Affghans are familiar with the art of following, though they will rarely meet an enemy. The withdrawal of the Guides and Ghoorkhas from the heights was most exciting, and none but the best officers and the best men could have achieved this duty with such complete success. Lieutenant Hodson's tactics were of the most brilliant description, and the whole force having been once more re-united in the plain, they marched out of the valley by the Turoonee pass, which, though farthest from the British camp, was the shortest to the outer plains. The force did not return to camp till between ten and eleven at night, having been out nearly eighteen hours, many of the men without food, and almost all without water, the small supply which had been carried out having soon been exhausted, and none being procurable at Boree.

"Not an officer of the detachment was touched, and only eight men killed and twenty-four wounded. When the force first entered the valley, there were not more than 200 Borees in arms to resist; but before they returned, the number had increased to some 3000, tens and twenties pouring in all the morning from all the villages and hamlets within many miles, intelligence of the attack being conveyed to them by the firing."

Sir J. Lawrence, who witnessed the operations from an opposite hill, says:—

"The Afreedees fought desperately. The way in which the Guides and Goorkhas carried the heights was the admiration of all. These are the right sort of fellows."

My brother's services on this occasion were thus acknowledged by the Brigadier commanding (Colonel Boileau, Her Majesty's 22nd Regiment), in a despatch dated Nov. 29th, 1853.

"To the admirable conduct of Lieutenant Hodson in reconnoitring, in the skilful disposition of his men, and the daring gallantry with which he led his fine corps in every advance, most of our success is due; for the safety of the whole force while in the valley of the Tillah depended on his holding his position, and I had justly every confidence in his vigilance and valour.

(Signed) "J. B. BOILEAU,
*Brigadier Commanding the Force at Boree.*"

"To Lieutenant W. S. R. Hodson, I beg you will express my particular thanks for the great service he rendered the force under your command, by his ever gallant conduct, which has fully sustained the reputation he has so justly acquired for courage, coolness, and determination.

(Signed) "W. M. GOMM,<br>
*Commander-in-Chief.*"

Before Christmas, to his great delight, he was joined in camp by his wife and child. The following letters bring out still more prominently the tender loving side of his character, both as a father and a son :—

*To his Father.*

CAMP, MURDAN, EUZOFZAI, *Jan.* 2*nd*, 1854.

I have been sadly long in answering your last most welcome letter, but I have been so terribly driven from pillar to post, that I have always been unable to sit down at the proper time. My long holiday with dear Susie, and journeyings to and fro to see her at Murree, and our short campaign against the Affreedees in November, threw me into a sea of arrears which was terrible to contemplate, and still worse to escape from. I am now working all day and half the night, and cannot as yet make much impression on them.

I wish you could see your little grand-daughter being nursed by a rough-looking Affghan soldier or bearded Sikh, and beginning life so early as a dweller in tents. She was christened by Mr. Clarke, one of the Church Missionaries who happened to be in Peshawur.

You evidently do not appreciate the state of things in these provinces. There are but two churches in the Punjab; and there will be an electric telegraph to Peshawur before a church is commenced there, though the station has been one for four years. . . . My second in command, Lieutenant Godby, was stabbed in the back by a fanatic the other day while on parade, and has had a wonderful escape for his life.

You would so delight in your little grand-daughter. She is a lovely good little darling; as happy as possible, and wonderfully quick and intelligent for her months. I would give worlds to be able to run home and see you, and show you my child, but I fear much that, unless I find a "nugget," it is vain to hope for so much pleasure just now. Meantime, I have every blessing a man can hope for, and not the least is that of your fond and much-prized affection.

*To his Wife, shortly afterwards.*

Godby is out of danger. I have been all day busy inquiring into the perpetrators and abettors of the deed, and have decided on seizing one of the principal chiefs of Euzofzai and sending him into Peshawur. The murderer was a servant of this Kader Khan, and certainly did not come of his own idea. I shall have plenty of circumstantial evidence at least against him.

A few months later, again apologising for long silence, he says, writing home:—

*May 1st.*

In addition to the very onerous command of 876 wild men and 300 wild horses, and the charge of the civil administration of a district almost as lawless as Tipperary, I have had to build, and superintend the building of, a fort to give cover to the said men and horses, including also within its walls three houses for English officers, a police station, and a native collector's office.

Our poor little darling had a very severe attack of fever the other day, but is now well again, and getting strong. I never see her without wishing that she was in her grandfather's arms. You would so delight in her little baby tricks and ways. She is the very delight of our lives, and we look forward with intense interest to her beginning to talk and crawl about. Both she and her dear mother will have to leave for the hills very soon, I am sorry to say. We try to put off the evil day, but I dare not expose either of my treasures to the heat of Euzofzai or Peshawur for the next three months. . . . The young lady already begins to show a singularity of taste—refusing to go to the arms of any native woman, and decidedly preferring the male population, some of whom are distinguished by her special favour. Her own orderly, save the mark, never tires of looking at her "beautiful white fingers," nor she of twisting them into his black beard—an insult to an Oriental, which he bears with an equanimity equal to his fondness for her. The cunning fellows have begun to make use of her too, and when they want anything, ask the favour in the name of Lilli Bâbâ (they cannot manage "Olivia" at all). They know the spell is potent.

The following letters from his wife's pen give a lively picture of "domestic" life in the wilderness:—

"*April* 15*th*, 1854.

"You ask for some detail of our life out here, and the history of one day will be a picture of every one, with little variation.

"At the first bugle, soon after daylight, W. gets up and goes to parade, and from thence to superintend the proceedings at the fort.

"By nine o'clock we are both ready for breakfast, after which W. disappears into his business tent, where he receives regimental reports, examines recruits, whether men or horses, superintends stores and equipments, hears complaints, and settles disputes, &c. &c. The regimental business first despatched, then comes 'kutcherry,' or civil court matters, receiving petitions, adjusting claims, with a still longer &c. You may have some small idea of the amount of this work, when I tell you that during the month of March he disposed of twenty-one serious criminal cases, such as murder, and 'wounding with intent,' and nearly 300 charges of felony, larceny, &c. At two o'clock he comes in for a look at his bairn, and a glass of wine. Soon after five a cup of tea, and then we order the horses, and in the saddle till nearly eight, when I go with him again to the fort, the garden, and the roads, diverging occasionally to fix the site of a new village, a well, or a watercourse.

"You can understand something of the delight of galloping over the almost boundless plain in the cool fresh air (for the mornings and evenings are still lovely), with the ground now enamelled with sweet-scented flowers, and the magnificent mountains nearest us assuming every possible hue which light and shadow can bestow. On our return to camp, W. hears more reports till dinner, which is sometimes shared by the other officers, or chance guests.

"When we are alone, as soon as dinner is over, the letters which have arrived in the evening are examined, classified, and descanted on, sometimes answered; and I receive my instructions for next day's work in copying papers, answering letters, &c. And now do you not think that prayers and bed are the fitting and well-earned ending to the labours of the day?

"When you remember, too, that in building the fort, roads, and bridges, W. has to make his bricks and burn them, to search for his timber and fell it, you will not deny that his hands are full enough; but in addition, he has to search for workmen, and when brought here, to procure them food and means of cooking it. Some are Mussulmans and éat meat, which must be killed and cooked by their own people. Some are Hindoos, who only feed on grain and vegetables, but every single man must have his own chula or fireplace, with an enclosure for him and his utensils, and if by chance any foot but his own overstep his little mud wall, he will neither eat nor work till another sun has arisen. Then some smoke, while others hold it in abhorrence; some only drink water, others must have spirits; so that it is no easy matter to arrange the conflicting wants of some 1100 labourers. I shall be very thankful when this Murdân Kôte is finished, for it will relieve my poor husband of half his labour and anxiety.

"By way of variety, we have native sports on great holidays—

such as throwing the spear at a mark, or 'Nazabaze,' which is, fixing a stake of twelve or eighteen inches into the ground, which must be taken up on the spear's point while passing it at full gallop, or putting an orange on the top of a bamboo a yard high, and cutting it through with a sword at full speed. W. is very clever at this, rarely failing, but the spears are too long for any but a lithe native to wield without risking a broken arm. The scene is most picturesque—the flying horsemen in their flowing many-coloured garments, and the grouping of the lookers-on, make me more than ever regret not having a ready pencil-power to put them on paper.

"The weather has been particularly unfavourable to the progress of the fort, so that we are still in our temporary hut and tents. Of course we feel the heat much more so domiciled. W. is grievously overworked; still his health is wonderfully good, and his spirits as wild as if he were a boy again. He is never so well pleased as when he has the baby in his arms."

*To his Sister.*

ATTOK, *June 9th,* 1854.

. . . We are so far on the way to Murree, and here, I grieve to say, we part for the next three months. I hope to rejoin them for a month in September, and accompany them back to our new home, for by that time I trust that my fortified cantonment will be ready, and our house too. This said fort has been a burden and a stumbling-block to me for months, and added grievously to my work, as I am sole architect. It is built regularly, but of earth-works and mud, and as it covers an area of twelve acres, you may believe that it has been no slight task to superintend its construction. It is a sad necessity, and the curse of Indian life, this repeatedly recurring separation, but anything is better than to see the dear ones suffer. I am fortunately very well, and as yet untouched by the unusual virulence with which the hot weather has commenced this year.

*To his Father.*

MUREE, *July* 17*th*, 1854.

I was summoned from Euzofzai to these hills, on the 26th June, by the tidings of the dangerous illness of our sweet baby. I found her in a sinking state, and though she was spared to us for another fortnight of deep anxiety and great wretchedness, there was, from the time I arrived, scarcely a hope of her recovery. Slowly and by imperceptible degrees her little life wasted away, until, early on the morning of the 10th, she breathed her soul away, so gently that those watching her intently were conscious of no change. The deep agony of this bereavement I have no words to describe. We had watched her growth, and prided ourselves on her development with such absorbing interest and joy; and she had so won our hearts by her extreme sweetness and most unusual intelligence, that she had become the very centre and light of our home life, and in losing her we seem to have lost everything. Her poor mother is sadly bowed down by this great grief, and has suffered terribly both in health and spirits.

I have got permission to remain with her a few days, but I must return to my duty before the end of the month.

We had the best and kindest of medical advice, and everything, I believe, which skill could do was tried, but in vain. She was lent to us to be our joy and comfort for a time, and was taken from us again, and the blank she has left behind is great indeed.

I dare not take Susie down with me, much as she wishes it, at this season, and in her state of health. I must therefore leave her here till October. It is very sad work to part again under these circumstances, but in this wretched country there is no help for us. Your kind and affectionate expressions about our little darling, and your keen appreciation of the "unfailing source of comfort and refreshment she was to my wearied spirit," came to me just as I had ceased to hope for the precious babe's life.

... It has been a very, very bitter blow to us. She had wound her little being round our hearts to an extent which we neither of us knew until we woke from the brief dream of beauty, and found ourselves childless.

---

CAMP, MURDAN, *Sept.* 17*th*, 1854.

I am alone now, having none of my officers here save the doctor. But the border is quiet, and except a great deal of crime and villainy, I have not any great difficulties to contend with. My new fort to hold the regiment and protect the frontier is nearly finished, and my new house therein will be habitable before my wife comes down from Murree. So after two years and a quarter of camp and hutting, I shall enjoy the luxury of a room and the dignity of a house.

---

FORT, MURDAN, *Oct.* 31*st*, 1854.

I can give better accounts of our own state than for many a long day. Dear Susie is much better than for a year past, and gaining strength daily, and I am as well as possible. We are now in our new house in this fort, which has caused me so much labour and anxiety; and I assure you a most comfortable dwelling we find it. Our houses (I mean the European officers') project from the general front of the works at the angles of the bastions, and are quite private, and away from the noisy soldiers; and we have, for India, a very pretty view of the hills and plains around us. Above all, the place seems a very healthy one. To your eye, fresh from England, it would appear desolate from its solitude, and oppressive from the vastness of the scale of scene. A wide plain, without a break or a tree, thirty miles long, by fifteen to twenty miles wide, forms our immediate foreground on one side, and an endless mass of mountains on the other.

We have just heard by telegraph of the engagement at Alma, but only a brief electric shock of a message, without details. We are in an age of wonders. Ten months ago there was not a telegraph in Hindoostan, yet the news which reached Bombay on the 27th of this month was printed at Lahore, 1200 miles from the coast, that same afternoon.

---

MURDAN, *Nov. 16th*, 1854.

As yet, we have only felt the surging of the storm which convulses Eastern Europe. The only palpable sign of the effects of Russian intrigue which we have had has been the commencement of negotiation with the Dost Mahomed Khan, of Cabul, who, under the pressure from without, has been fain to seek for alliance and aid from us. Nothing is yet known of his demands, or the intentions of Government, but one thing is certain, that the commencement of negotiations with us is the beginning of evil days for Affghanistan.

In India, we must either keep altogether aloof or absorb. All our history shows that sooner or later connection with us is political death. The sunshine is not more fatal to a dew-drop than our friendship or alliance to an Asiatic Kingdom.

# CHAPTER VIII.

### REVERSES—UNJUST TREATMENT—LOSS OF COMMAND—RETURN TO REGIMENTAL DUTIES.

UP to this time my brother's career in India, except so far as health was concerned, had been one of almost uninterrupted prosperity. He had attained a position unprecedented for a man of his standing in the service, and enjoyed a reputation for daring, enterprise, and ability, only equalled by the estimation in which he was held by all who knew him, for high principle and sterling worth. He was, as he described himself, the most fortunate and the happiest man in India. But now the tide of fortune turned.

A storm had for some time been gathering, the indications of which he had either overlooked or despised, till it burst with its full force upon him, and seemed for the moment to carry all before it, blasting his fair fame and sweeping away his fortunes. Many circumstances had conspired to bring about this result, some of which will only be fully appreciated by those who are acquainted with the internal politics of the Punjab at that period. His appointment to the command of the Guides, over the heads of many of his seniors, had from the first excited much jealousy and ill-will among the numerous aspirants to so distinguished a post. In India, more than in any other country, a man cannot be prosperous or fortunate without making many enemies; and every ascent above the level of your contemporaries secures so many additional "good haters;" nor is there any country where enmity is more unscrupulous in the means to which it has recourse. This mattered comparatively little to my brother, so long as Sir Henry Lawrence, to whose firm and discriminating friendship he owed his appointment, remained in power. He, however, had been removed from the administration of the Punjab, and those who had effected his removal, and now reigned supreme, were not likely to look with very favourable eyes upon one who, like my brother, was known as his *protégé* and confidant, and had not perhaps been as guarded, as in prudence he ought to have been, in the expressions of his opinion on various transactions. More recently still, Colonel Mackeson, the Resident at Peshawur, his immediate superior, for whom he entertained the highest regard and affection, which was, I believe, reciprocated, had fallen a victim to the dagger of the assassin. This had, if possible, a still more injurious influence on my brother's position, as the new Resident was, both on public and private grounds, opposed to him, and made no secret of his wish to get rid of him from the charge of the frontier.

With the prospect of such support, my brother's enemies, more especially one officer of his regiment whom he had mortally offended, were not likely to be idle. Several references to this officer's conduct had been made in his letters at the time :—

It is quite a relief getting rid of ———. He seems to have exhibited greater rascality lately than ever. I shall be glad when he is cleared out of the valley.

Again—

I have had a note from Major Macpherson, in which he seems to take a less favourable view if possible of ———'s letter than I did. He says it is most disgraceful to the writer, and he dare not characterise it. The matter seems far worse than I thought, for he knew the truth and was told it when he wrote the letter.

He had been warned more than once of their undermining operations; but strong in conscious integrity, and unwilling to suspect others of conduct which he would have scorned himself, he "held straight on" upon his usual course, till he found himself overwhelmed by a mass of charges affecting his conduct, both in his military and civil capacity.

Every trifling irregularity or error of judgment was so magnified that a mighty fabric was raised on a single grain of truth; and the result was, that towards the close of the year he was summoned before a court of inquiry at Peshawur.

How little he feared inquiry will be seen from the following letter written at the time:—

Pray impress upon John Lawrence's mind that I am not in the smallest degree disposed to shrink from the strictest inquiry into any act of mine in the command of the Guides. I am much to blame for letting things go the length they did without bringing up ——, but that was good-natured folly, and neither dishonest nor unsoldier-like. It is true that I am annoyed at the trouble and bother of courts of inquiry, but nothing more; and if John Lawrence would come to overhaul everything connected with my command I should be infinitely satisfied, and you may tell him so.

That which seemed principally to give colour to the charges against him was, that there was undeniably confusion and irregularity in the regimental accounts; but this confusion, far from having originated with him, had been very materially rectified. He had succeeded to the command in October 1852, and within twenty-four hours started on a campaign which lasted between seven and eight weeks, without any audit of accounts between himself and his predecessor, who had, immediately on making over the command, left for England; so that he found a mass of unexplained confusion (as Sir John Lawrence himself admitted), which he had been endeavouring, during his period of command, gradually to reduce to some order. This he had to a certain extent accomplished, though under great difficulties from the want of proper office and staff, and from the constant calls incident to border warfare. Further, he had continually to complain of the delays in getting money for the payment of his workmen, which led to complications, when summoned to undergo an investigation and meet the gravest accusations.

I will, however, in preference to any statements of my own, which might not unnaturally be suspected of partiality, insert here, though it was written at a later period, a letter giving an account of the whole affair, from one whose opinion must carry the greatest weight with all who know him, either personally or by reputation, Sir R. Napier (now Lord Napier of Magdala). It has somewhat of an official character, as it was addressed to the colonel of the 1st Bengal European Fusiliers, when my brother subsequently rejoined that regiment.

And I may here observe, with regard to anything which I may now or hereafter say reflecting on the conduct and motives of those concerned in this attempt to ruin my brother's prospects, that I should not have ventured to make these remarks simply on his authority, unless I had had them confirmed, and more than confirmed, by men of the highest character, both civil and military, who were cognisant of all the transactions, and did not scruple to express their indignation at what they characterised as a most cruel and unjust persecution.

*From* COLONEL NAPIER, *Chief Engineer, Punjab, to* COLONEL WELCHMAN, *1st Bengal Fusiliers.*

"UMBALA, *March* 1856.

"MY DEAR COL. WELCHMAN,—I have great pleasure in meeting your request, to state in writing my opinion regarding my friend Lieutenant Hodson's case. Having been on intimate terms of friendship with him since 1846, I was quite unprepared for the reports to his disadvantage which were circulated, and had no hesitation in pronouncing my utter disbelief in, and repudiation of them, as being at variance with everything I had ever known of his character. On arriving at Peshawur in March 1855, I found that Lieutenant Hodson had been undergoing a course of inquiry before a special military court, and on reading a copy of the proceedings, I perceived at once that the whole case lay in the correctness of his regimental accounts; that his being summoned before a court, after suspension from civil and military duty, and after an open invitation (under regimental authority) to all complainants in his regiment, was a most unusual ordeal, such as no man could be subjected to without the 'greatest disadvantage; and notwithstanding this, the proceedings' did not contain a single substantial case against him, provided he could establish the validity of his regimental accounts; and that he could do this I felt more than confident. The result of Major Taylor's laborious and patient investigation of Lieutenant Hodson's regimental accounts has fully justified, but has not at all added to, the confidence that I have throughout maintained in the honour and uprightness of his conduct. It has, however, shown (what I believed, but had not the same means of judging of) how much labour Lieutenant Hodson bestowed in putting the affairs of his regiment in order. Having seen a great deal of the manner in which the Guide Corps has been employed, I can well understand how difficult it has been to maintain anything like regularity of office; and how impossible it may be for those who remain quietly in stations with efficient establishments to understand or make allowance for the difficulties and irregularities entailed by rapid movements on service, and want of proper office means in adjusting accounts for which no organised system had been established. The manner in which Lieutenant Hodson has elucidated his accounts since he had access to the necessary sources of information, appears to be highly creditable. I have twice had the good fortune to have been associated with him on military service, when his high qualities commanded admiration. I heartily rejoice, therefore, both as a friend and as a member of the service, 'at his vindication from most grievous and unjust imputations.' And while I congratulate the regiment on his return to it, I regret that one of the best swords should be withdrawn from the frontier service.—I remain, yours very sincerely,

"R. NAPIER."

On the receipt of Major Reynell Taylor's report, to which reference is here made, Mr. Montgomery (then one of the Commissioners for the Punjab, now Sir Robert, K.C.B., G.C.S.I.), one of the men who, under God, saved India, wrote as follows:—

"To me the whole report seemed more satisfactory than any one I had ever read; and considering Major Taylor's high character, patience, and discernment, and the lengthened period he took to investigate every detail, most triumphant. This I have expressed to all with whom I have conversed on the subject."

All this, however, is an anticipation of the due order of events. I must go back again to the court of inquiry, in order to show more clearly the injustice to which Lieutenant Hodson was exposed. The proceedings of the court terminated on the 15th January 1855. Till they were submitted to the Governor-General, no decision could be given, nor any report published, though every publicity had been given to the accusations made. Up to the last week in July, the papers had not been forwarded from Lahore to be laid before him, though Sir John Lawrence states that it was not his fault. Meanwhile, not merely had my brother been suspended from civil and military duty during the inquiry, but without waiting for the result, he had (in consequence of charges brought against him by Major Edwardes, of harshness in his treatment of Kadir Khan), been superseded in his command of the Guides, on the ground that his continuing in Euzofzai, where his corps was stationed, was inconsistent with the public interest. But worse remains behind.

Seven months after the conclusion of the inquiry, in consequence of repeated applications from my brother for a minute investigation of his accounts, Major Taylor, as has been mentioned, was appointed to examine them, and on the 13th February 1856, made his report to the Chief Commissioner at Lahore. The document itself is too long and technical for publication, but the written opinions I have already quoted of Sir R. Napier and Mr. Montgomery are sufficient to show that it completely established Lieutenant Hodson's innocence, and cleared him from the grievous and unjust imputations cast upon him. Yet in March 1857, he discovered that this report had never been communicated to the Commander-in-Chief, or Secretary to Government. It had been quietly laid aside in some office, and no more notice taken. Lord Dalhousie left India, having heard all that could be said against him, and nothing in his vindication, and it was the same with the Directors at home. He was thus left for more than two years labouring under unjust imputations, and looked on with suspicion by all who were not acquainted with the facts, or who had not confidence in his integrity. I might give many other details illustrative of the manner in which, even in the nineteenth century, official enmity can succeed in crushing one who is so unfortunate as to be its victim, but I will not weary my readers with them.

I give a few extracts from my brother's letters at different times in the course of these proceedings, to show the spirit in which he bore this trial, bitter though it was, peculiarly grievous to one of his sensitive feelings on all points of honour.

In August, 1855, he wrote to me:—

They have not been able, with all their efforts, to fix anything whatever upon me; all their allegations (and they were wide enough in their range) have fallen to the ground; and the more serious ones have been utterly disproved by the mere production of documents and books. The most vicious assertion was, that I had been so careless of the public money passing through my hands, that I had not only kept no proper accounts, but that paper had never been inked on the subject, and consequently it would be impossible to ascertain whether or not any deficiency existed in my regimental treasure chest; and this after I had laid my books on the table of the Court, and begged that they might be examined, and after I had subsequently officially applied for their examination by proper accountants. Well, after seven months' delay, I was offered the opportunity of producing them; and thus I have now at last a chance of bringing out the real state of the case. Up to the present time, the most critical and hostile examination, lasting a month, has only served to prove my earliest assertion, and my only one, that I could give an ample account of every farthing of money intrusted to me whenever it might please the powers that be to inquire into it. The sum total of money represented by my account amounts to about £120,000 passing through my hands in small fractional sums of receipt and expenditure.

Not only do they find that I have regular connected accounts of everything, but that these are supported by vouchers and receipts. It has been a severe trial, and the prolonged anxiety and distress of the past nine months have been nearly insupportable.

I almost despair of making you, or any one not on the spot, understand the ins and outs of the whole affair; and I can only trust to the result, and to the eventual production of all the papers, to put things in their proper light. In the meantime I must endeavour to face the wrong, the grievous, foul wrong, with a constant and unshaken heart, and to endure humiliation and disgrace with as much equanimity as I may, and with the same soldier-like fortitude with which I ought to face danger, suffering, and death in the path of duty.

Again, during the course of the second investigation :—

I never felt the whole humiliation of the business so much as since I have been here. It is pretty nearly, I think, as sharp a moral torture as could be inflicted, and I am obliged to exert the whole power of self-restraint, and to work mightily to endure and hope on, to prevent throwing up the whole thing in disgust.

---

NAOSHERAH, *Nov. 4th*, 1855.

Your two sad letters came close upon one another, but I could not write then. The blow\* was overwhelming; coming, too, at a time of unprecedented suffering and trial, it was hard to bear up against. What a year this has been! What ages of trial and of sorrow seem to have been crowded into a few short months. Our darling babe was taken from us on the day my public misfortunes began, and death has robbed us of our father before their end. The brain-pressure was almost too much for me, coming as the tidings did at a time of peculiar distress. . . . The whole, indeed, is so peculiarly sad that one's heart seems chilled and dulled by the very horror of the calamity. . . . I

\* The news of his father's death.

look with deep anxiety for your next letters, but the mail seems exclusively occupied with Sebastopol, and to have left letters behind.

Again, to his sister, some months later :—

I trust fondly that better days are coming ; but really the weary watching and waiting for a gleam of daylight through the clouds, and never to see it, is more harassing and harder to bear up against than I could have supposed possible. I have been tried to the utmost, I do think. A greater weight of public and private calamity and sorrow surely never fell at once on any individual. But it has to be borne, and I try to face it manfully and patiently, and to believe that it is for some good and wise end.

By the way, I was much gratified and surprised at seeing, in an article in the "Calcutta Review" written and signed by Sir Henry Lawrence, a most flattering testimony* to my character. Coming at such a time it is doubly valuable.

In another letter he says :—

It is pleasant indeed to find that not a man who knows me has any belief that there has been anything wrong. They think I have been politically wrong in not consulting my own interests by propitiating the powers that be, and they know that I am the victim of official enmity in high places ; but I am proud to say, that not one of them all (and indeed I believe I might include my worst foes and accusers in the category) believes that I have committed any more than errors of judgment,† and that, owing to the pressure of work which came upon me all at once, and which was more than one man could manage at once, without leaving something to be done at a more convenient season.

\* Lieutenant Hodson, who has succeeded to the command of the Guides, is an accomplished soldier, cool in council, daring in action, with great natural ability improved by education. There are few abler men in any service.
† I may truly add that I have often expressed an opinion that nothing injurious to your character as a gentleman would be proved.—Letter from Sir John Lawrence.

I can honestly say, that for months before I was summoned into Peshawur for the inquiry, I had never known what a half hour's respite from toil and anxiety was; in fact, ever since I first traced the lines of the fort at Murdan, in December 1853, I was literally weighed down by incessant calls on my time and attention, and went to bed at night thoroughly exhausted and worn out, to rise before daylight to a renewed round of toil and worry.

I remember telling John Lawrence, that if they got rid of me, he would require three men to do the work which I had been doing for Government; and it has already proved literally true. They have had to appoint three different officers to the work I had done single-handed, and that, too, after the worst was over!

---

UMBÂLA, *March 25th,* 1856.

Of myself I have little to tell you: things have been much in *statu quo.* Major Taylor's report, of which I am going to send you a copy, is most satisfactory. He was obliged to steer clear of giving offence to others, and has spoken with great quietness and moderation, though most decisively and triumphantly for me. There is much which you will probably not understand in the way of technicalities, but the general purport will be clear to you.

I expect to join my regiment in about three weeks. They are marching up from Bengal to Dugshai, a hill station sixty miles from hence, and ten from Kussowlee and Subathoo respectively, so I shall be close to old haunts. I am very glad we shall be in a good climate, for though I have not given in or failed, I am thankful to say, still the last eighteen months have told a good deal upon me, and I am not up to heat or work. If the colonel (Welchman) can, he is going to give me the adjutancy of the regiment, which will be a gain in every way, not only as showing to the world that, in spite of all which has happened, there is nothing against my character, but as increasing my income, and giving me the opportunity of learning a good deal of work which will be useful to me, and of doing, I hope, a good deal of good amongst the men. It will be the first step up the ladder again, after tumbling to the bottom.

Soon afterwards, Lieutenant Hodson rejoined the 1st Fusiliers at Dugshai. It may be necessary, for the sake of unprofessional readers, to explain that during the whole time that he had been Assistant-Commissioner in the Punjab, or in command of the Guides, he had continued to belong to this regiment, as political or staff appointments in India do not dissolve an officer's connection with his own regiment.

On April 8th, 1856, he writes from Dugshai:—

. . . . I have but little to tell you to cheer you on my account. My health, which had stood the trial wonderfully, was beginning to fail, but I shall soon be strong again in this healthy mountain air, 7000 feet above the sea.

This is a great thing, but it is very hard to begin again as a regimental subaltern after nearly eleven years' hard work. However, I am very fond of the profession, and there is much to be done, and much learnt, and under any other circumstances, I should not regret being with English soldiers again for a time. Every one believes that I shall soon be righted, but the "soon" is a long time coming. I was much gratified the other day by an unexpected visit from Mr. Charles Raikes, one of the Punjab Commissioners, who was passing through Umbâla, on his way to take a high appointment at Agra. I had no personal knowledge of him, but he came out of his way to call upon me, and express his sympathy and his appreciation of (what he was pleased to call) my high character.

He said much that was encouraging and pleasing, which I need not repeat. It served pleasantly, however, to show that the tide was turning, and that in good men's minds my character stood as high as ever.

In addition to his other troubles, my brother was suffering all this time from a dislocated ankle. He says in June:—

I have nothing to tell you of myself, save that I have to-day, for the first time for eight weeks, put my foot to the ground; I cannot, however, yet walk a yard without crutches.

---

DUGSHAI, *Sept.* 24*th*, 1856.

I strive to look the worst boldly in the face as I would an enemy in the field, and to do my appointed work resolutely and to the best of my ability, satisfied that there is a reason for all, and that even irksome duties well done bring their own reward, and that if not, still they are duties.

But it is sometimes hard to put up with the change! I am getting a little stronger on my ankle, but am still unable, at the end of five months, to do more than walk about the house. Fancy my not being able to walk 200 yards for half-a-year.

---

DUGSHAI, *Nov.* 6*th*, 1856.

I yearn to be at home again and see you all, but I am obliged to check all such repinings and longings, and keep down all canker cares and bitternesses, and set my teeth hard, and will earnestly to struggle on and do my allotted work as well and cheerfully as may be, satisfied that in the end a brighter time will come.

I know nothing in my brother's whole career more truly admirable, or showing more real heroism, than his conduct at this period while battling with adverse fates.

Deeply as he felt the change in his position, he accommodated himself to it in a manner that won the admiration and esteem of all. Instead of despising his regimental duties, irksome and uninteresting, comparatively speaking, as they were, he discharged them with a zeal and energy, as well as cheerfulness, which called forth the following strong expressions of commendation from the colonel of his regiment. They are taken from a letter addressed to the Adjutant-General of the army :—

"UMBÂLA, *Jan.* 18*th*, 1857.

. . . "I consider it a duty, and at the same time feel a great pleasure, in requesting you to submit, for the consideration of his Excellency the Commander-in-Chief, this my public record and acknowledgment of the very essential service Lieutenant Hodson has done the regiment at my especial request. On the arrival of the regiment at Dugshai I asked Lieutenant Hodson to act as quartermaster. I pointed out to him that, mainly owing to a rapid succession of quartermasters when the regiment was on field-service, the office had fallen into very great disorder ; . . . and that he would have to restore order out of complicated disorder, and to organise a more efficient working system for future guidance and observance. To my great relief and satisfaction, Lieutenant Hodson most cheerfully undertook the onerous duties ; he was suffering at the same time severe bodily pain, consequent on a serious accident, yet this did not in any way damp his energy, or prevent his most successfully carrying out the object in view. . . . It is impossible to do otherwise than believe that this officer's numerous qualifications are virtually lost to the State by his being employed as a regimental subaltern, as he is fitted for, and capable of doing great justice to, any staff situation ; and I am convinced, that should his Excellency receive with approval this solicitation to confer on him some appointment suited to the high ability, energy, and zeal which I fear I have but imperfectly brought to notice, it would be as highly advantageous to the service as gratifying to myself. An officer whose superior mental acquirements are fully acknowledged by all who know him ; who has ably performed the duties of a civil magistrate in a disturbed district ; whose knowledge of engineering has been practically brought into play in the construction of a fort on the North-western frontier ; whose gallant conduct in command of a regiment in many a smart engagement has been so highly commended, and by such competent authorities, is one whom I have confidence in recommending for advancement; and in earnestly, yet most respectfully, pressing the recommendation, I plead this officer's high qualifications as my best apology. . . .—I have, &c.

 (Signed)     "J. WELCHMAN,
   *Lieut.-Col. Commanding 1st Bengal Fusiliers."*

Quite as strong was the testimony borne by Brigadier-General Johnstone:—

 *To the* ADJUTANT-GENERAL *of the Army.*

   "SIRHIND DIVISION, HEAD-QUARTERS, UMBÂLA,
    *Jan.* 30*th,* 1857.

"SIR,—My mere countersignature to Colonel Welchman's letter in favour of Lieutenant Hodson seems so much less than the occasion demands, that I trust his Excellency will allow of my submitting it in a more special and marked manner. I beg to accompany Colonel Welchman's letter with a testimony of my own to the high character of the officer in question.

"Rejoining his regiment as a lieutenant, from the exercise of an important command calling daily for the display of his energy, activity, and self-reliance, and frequently for the manifestation of the highest qualities of the partisan leader, or of the regular soldier, Lieutenant Hodson, with patience, perseverance, and zeal, undertook and carried out the laborious minor duties of the regimental staff as well as those of a company; and with a diligence, method, and accuracy such as the best trained regimental officers have never surpassed, succeeded in a manner fully justifying the high commendation bestowed on him by his commanding officer. As a soldier in the field, Lieutenant Hodson has gained the applause of officers of the highest reputation, eye-witnesses of his ability and courage. On the testimony of others, I refer to these, and that testimony so honourable to his name I beg herewith to submit to his Excellency.

"On my own observation, I am enabled to speak to Lieutenant Hodson's character and qualities in quarters, and I do so in terms of well-earned commendation, and at the same time in the earnest hope that his merits and qualifications will obtain for him such favour and preferment at the hands of his Excellency as he may deem fit to bestow on this deserving officer.—I have, &c.

(Signed) "M. C. JOHNSTONE,
*Brigadier-General, &c.*"

I must add a few more extracts from Lieutenant Hodson's letters to myself and others, to complete this part of his history:—

DUGSHAI, *April 7th*, 1857.

Your letter written this day three months reached me at Umbâla, at our mildest of "Chobhams" in the middle of February, and deserved an earlier reply, but I have been taken quite out of the private correspondence line lately, by incessant calls on my time. Regimental work in camp in India, with European regiments, no less than in quarters, is contrived to cut up one's time into infinitesimal quantities, and keep one waiting for every other half-hour through the day. I had more time for writing when I commanded a frontier regiment, and governed a province! These winter camps are very profitable, however, and not by any means unpleasant; and as Umbâla was very full, we had an unusual amount of society for India, and some very pleasant meetings. I was too lame to dance, but not to dine, and take part in charades or tableaux, and so forth, and so contrived to keep alive after the day's work was over. I got some κῦδος and vast kindness for performing the more strictly professional *rôle* of brigade-major to one of the infantry brigades, and had excellent opportunities of learning the essential, but so seldom taught or learned art, of manœuvring bodies of troops. My service has been so much on the frontier and with detached corps, that I had previously had but small opportunities for the study. I had an interview with General Anson the other day, and I hope a satisfactory one. He is a very pleasant mannered and gentlemanly man, open and frank in speech, and quick to a proverb in apprehension, taking in the pith of a matter at a glance. As I always thought, it turned out that Major Taylor's report had never reached the Commander-in-Chief, and they had only the old one-sided story to go upon. I explained the whole to him, and as he had already very kindly read the papers relating to the matter, he quite comprehended it, and begged me to give him a copy of Taylor's report, when he would, if satisfied, try and see justice done me. I trust, therefore, that at last something will be done to clear me from all stigma in the matter. As soon as that is done he will give me some appointment or other, unless Government do it themselves. Sir Henry Lawrence writes to me most kindly, and is only waiting a favourable opportunity to help me.

We are in a state of some anxiety, owing to the spread of a very serious spirit of disaffection among the Sepoy army. One regiment (the 19th of the line) has already been disbanded, and, if all have their dues, more yet will be so before long. It is our great danger in India, and Lord Hardinge's prophecy, that our biggest fight in India would be with our own army, seems not unlikely to be realised, and that before long. Native papers, education, and progress are against keeping 200,000 native mercenaries in hand.

A letter from Rev. J. Sloggett, which will be found elsewhere (Preface, p. xxvi), will confirm my brother's statement with regard to the suppression of Major Taylor's report and the injury occasioned thereby.

*To a Friend in Calcutta.*

DUGSHAI, *May 5th,* 1857.

Unless I hear of something to my advantage meanwhile, I propose starting for Calcutta about the middle of this merry month of May, with the object of endeavouring to effect, by personal appeal and explanations, the self-vindication which no mere paper warfare seems likely to extort from Government. I had waited patiently for nearly two years, " striving to be quiet and do my own business," in the hope that justice, however tardy, would certainly overtake me, when an incident occurred which showed that I must adopt a more active mode of procedure if I wished for success. On applying for employment with the force in Persia, I met with a refusal, on the ground of what had occurred when in command of the Guides.* This, you will allow, was calculated to drive a man to extremities who had been under the impression all along that his conduct, whensoever and howsoever called in question, had been amply vindicated.

It appeared that while everything to my disadvantage had been carefully communicated by the Punjab authorities to army headquarters, they had suppressed "in toto" the results of the subsequent inquiry which had, in the opinion of all good men, amply cleared my good name from the dirt lavished on it. Even the secretaries to Government had never heard of this vindication, and were going on believing all manner of things to my discredit; Lord Canning also being utterly ignorant of the fact that subsequently to Lord Dalhousie's departure, the results of the second investigation had been communicated to the Punjab Government.

There were clearly three courses open to me, "*à la* Sir Robert Peel."

1st. Suicide.

2nd. To resign the service in disgust and join the enemy.

3rd. To make the Governor-General eat his words and apologise.

I chose the last.

The first was too melodramatic and foreign; the second would have been a triumph to my foes in the Punjab; besides, the enemy might have been beaten!

I have determined, therefore, on a trip to Calcutta.

You will, I have no doubt, agree with me that I am perfectly right in taking the field against the enemy, and not allowing the Government to rest until I have carried my point.

* Referring to the charge made against him in the case of Kader Khan.

In another letter of the same date :—

I have had another interview with General Anson at Simla, and nothing could have been more satisfactory. He was most polite, even cordial, and while he approved of my suggestion of going down to Calcutta to have personal explanations with the people there, and evidently thought it a plucky idea to undertake a journey of 2500 miles in such weather (May and June), yet he said that I had better wait till I heard again from him, for he would write himself to Lord Canning, and try to get justice done me.

I do trust the light is breaking through the darkness, and that before long I may have good news to send you, in which I am sure you will rejoice.

It did break from a most unexpected quarter.

This was the last letter received in England from my brother for some months. Six days after it was written, the outbreak at Meerut occurred, and almost immediately India was in a blaze.

"Fortunate was it" (my brother afterwards said) "that I was delayed by General Anson till he received an answer from Lord Canning, or I should undoubtedly have been murdered at some station on the road. The answer never came. It must have been between Calcutta and Allygurh when disturbances broke out, and was, with all the dâks for many days, destroyed or plundered."

Most fortunate, too, was it (if we may use such an expression), that in the hour of India's extremity, Lieutenant Hodson was within reach of the Commander-in-Chief, and available for service. It was no longer a time to stand on official etiquette. In that crisis, which tried the bravest to the utmost, when a strong will and cool head and brave heart were needed, he at once rose again to his proper place in counsel and in action.

But I must not anticipate what belongs to the next chapter. One fact, however, I cannot refrain from stating here, as an appropriate conclusion of this narrative, that within six weeks of the date of the last letter, Lieutenant Hodson was actually commanding in the field, before the walls of Delhi, by General Barnard's special request, the very corps of Guides from which he had been so unjustly ousted two years before.

"Was there ever," he says in reference to it, "a stranger turn on the wheel of fortune? I have much cause to be grateful, and I hope I shall not forget the bitter lessons of adversity."

# Part II.

## NARRATIVE OF THE DELHI CAMPAIGN, 1857.

### CHAPTER I.

#### MARCH DOWN TO DELHI.

ON the 10th of May occurred the outbreak at Meerut, closely followed by the massacre at Delhi.

On the 13th, orders were received at Dugshai, from the Commander-in-Chief, for the 1st Bengal European Fusiliers to march without delay to Umbâla, where all the regiments from the hill stations were to concentrate. They set out that afternoon, and reached Umbâla, a distance of sixty miles, on the morning of the second day. From this point Lieutenant Hodson's narrative commences. It is compiled from the letters or bulletins which he sent day by day to his wife, written as best they might, in any moments which he could snatch from the overwhelming press of work, sometimes on the field, sometimes on horseback. It is almost unnecessary to observe, that they were not intended for the public eye, and would never have been published had my lamented brother been alive, as he had the greatest horror of any of his letters appearing in print. Now, unhappily, the case is different, and I feel, in common with many of his friends, that in justice both to himself and to the gallant band who formed the "army before Delhi," this record of heroic fortitude and endurance ought not to be withheld. It does not profess to be a history of the siege, or military operations connected with it; though it is a most valuable contribution to any history, as Lieutenant Hodson, from his position as head of the Intelligence Department, knew better, probably, than any other man what was going on both amongst the enemy and in our own force; and his incidental notices will tell, better perhaps than the most laboured description, what our men did and what they suffered. Full justice will probably never be done them, nor their trying position appreciated as it ought to be; besiegers in name, though more truly besieged; exposed to incessant attacks night and day; continually thinned in numbers by the sword, the bullet, the sunstroke, and cholera, and for many weeks receiving no reinforcements; feeling sometimes as if they were forgotten by their countrymen, and yet holding their ground against a nation in arms, without murmuring or complaining, and with unshaken determination. All accounts agree in speaking of the cheerful and "plucky" spirit that prevailed, both amongst officers and men, notwithstanding fatigue, privation, and sickness, as something quite remarkable even amongst British soldiers. And if there was one more than another who contributed to inspire and keep up this spirit, if there was one more than another who merited that which a Roman would have considered the highest praise, that he never despaired of his country, it was Lieutenant Hodson. I have seen a letter from a distinguished officer, in which he says:—

"Affairs at times looked very queer, from the frightful expenditure of life. Hodson's face was then like sunshine breaking through the dark clouds of despondency and gloom that would settle down occasionally on all but a few brave hearts, England's worthiest sons, who were determined to conquer."

If any should be disposed to think that my brother, in these letters, speaks too exclusively of his own doings, they must remember, in the first place, to whom they were addressed; and secondly, that in describing events—*quorum pars magna fuit*—it would be almost impossible not to speak of himself.

He himself, even in writing to his wife, thinks it necessary to apologise for being "egotistical." I believe, on the other hand, that the highest interest of the following narrative will be found to consist in its being a *personal* narrative, a history of the man, an unreserved outspeaking of his mind and feelings; nor am I afraid of others thinking apology called for. Nor, however much they may disagree from his criticisms on men and measures, will they deny that he was well qualified, both by his opportunities of observation at the time, and his past experience of Asiatic character, to form a judgment and express an opinion without exposing himself to the charge of presumption.

UMBÂLA, *May* 15*th*, 1857.

We got here after two nights of very harassing marching. We started badly, the men having been drinking before they came to parade, and they were hurried too much in going down hill, consequently there was much straggling; but thanks to tattoos (ponies) and carts and elephants sent out to meet us, we got in to-day in tolerable completeness. Affairs are very serious, and unless very prompt and vigorous measures are taken, the whole army, and perhaps a large portion of India, will be lost to us. Delhi is in the hands of the mutineers—no European that we can hear of being left alive there—men, women, and children, all who were caught, have been butchered! Brigadier Graves,

Abbott, and some others have escaped. Willoughby, the Ordnance Commissary in charge of the magazine and arsenal, is said to have fired it himself to prevent the mutineers having possession of the contents to arm themselves with—of course, sacrificing his own life to such a duty. A lac and a half of muskets would otherwise have been in the hands of the insurgents. The Commander-in-Chief came in this morning. Here alarm is the prevalent feeling, and conciliation, of men with arms in their hands and in a state of absolute rebellion, the order of the day. This system, if pursued, is far more dangerous than anything the Sepoys can do to us. Fortunately the Maharaja of Puttiala is stanch, and so are other Sikh chiefs hereabouts. We shall go on to Delhi in a few days. That city is in the hands of the insurgents, and the king proclaimed Emperor of Hindoostan! I do trust that the authorities will act with vigour, else there is no knowing where the affair will end. Oh for Sir Charles Napier now!

*16th.*—Little is known for certain of what is going on, as there is no communication with, or from below Meerut. At present, the native troops have all gone off bodily; none remain in cantonments. We march, I believe, on Monday—9th Lancers, 75th Queen's, 1st Fusiliers, and nine guns, taking the 5th, 60th Native Infantry and 4th Cavalry with us—nice companions! However, they can do us no harm, and they might do great mischief if left here. There has been an outbreak at Ferozepoor, but the magazine and bridge are safe in the hands of her Majesty's 60th, and the authorities at Jullundur sent off a party of Europeans and Horse Artillery at once, who secured the fort at Philour; otherwise we should have had no ammunition but what the soldiers carried in their pouches. The times are critical, but I have no fear of aught save the alarm and indecision of our rulers. All here is sheer confusion, and there is a tendency to treat these rebellious Sepoys with a tenderness as misplaced as it would be pernicious. There is actually a talk of concentrating troops, and waiting to be joined by others before marching on Delhi; and they utterly refuse to detach even a party on Kurnâl to protect the officers and treasury there. This is all very sad, and sometimes makes one disposed to question whether we are not suffering from the "dementia" which Providence sends as the forerunner of ruin. However, our course is not yet run, and whatever clouds may gather over us, there are good results in store. The Punjab is quiet. The native troops at Mean-Meer were quietly disarmed, and do their guards with bayonets only. This excellent arrangement is Sir John Lawrence's doing, who, to do him justice, has sense and courage. Nothing is known of Lucknow, or indeed of any place below Meerut. Allygurh is supposed to have gone. Some details of the massacre at Delhi, which I have just heard from one of the escapees, are awful beyond belief. Charlie Thomason is said to have escaped; Mr. Jennings, the chaplain, and his daughter were among the victims. Mr. Beresford, his wife, and five daughters all massacred. Poor Colonel Ripley lived long enough to say he was killed by his own men.

*17th.*—We are all terribly anxious about the hill stations, reports having reached us that the Goorkhas have mutinied and attacked Simla. A hundred men, with ammunition, have gone off this morning to Kussowlie. Dugshai is easily defended. Simla is most to be feared. . . . All this has put out of my head for the time the good news for us. Yesterday I was sent for by the Commander-in-Chief, and appointed Assistant Quartermaster-General on his personal staff, to be under the immediate orders of his Excellency, and with command to raise 100 horse and 50 foot, for service in the Intelligence Department, and as personal escort. All this was done, moreover, in a most complimentary way, and it is quite in my line. I am prepared to set to work vigorously; but I confess my anxiety on account of the reports we hear respecting Simla makes me cruelly anxious. . . . General Anson, it seems, wrote about me to Talbot, but could get no answer before the outbreak occurred, which makes this act of his, on his own responsibility, the more complimentary. It is very uncertain now when we move on. All is quiet in the Punjab, I am thankful to say, and the rebels have had a lesson read them at Ferozepoor which will do good. The 45th Native Infantry were nearly cut to pieces by the 10th Light Cavalry, who pursued them for twelve miles, and cut them to pieces. This last is a great fact. One regiment at least has stood by us (they afterwards mutinied), and the moral effect will be great: nothing known yet from below. Poor Macdonald, of the 20th Native Infantry, his wife, and their three babes murdered, with adjuncts not to be mentioned. John Lawrence is acting with great vigour, and they have organised a movable force at Jhelum, composed of her Majesty's 24th and 27th, the Guides, Kumàon Battalion, and other Irregulars, to move in any required direction. Montgomery writes in great spirits and confidence from Lahore. I am just sent for by the Chief.

KURNÂL, *May 18th.*—According to orders I left Umbâla at 8.30 P.M., and reached here at 4.30 A.M., having prepared everything at Peeplee *en route.* I had only "Bux" (his bearer), with me, and did not apprehend any danger until within a few miles of Kurnâl, but nothing whatever happened; the road was deserted, and not a soul to be seen. I am sheltered in a house occupied by the refugees from Delhi and the civil officers of Kurnâl, about fifteen in all, with Mrs. Wagentrieber, her husband, and sundry sergeants, &c. The European troops will be here to-night. What would I not give for a couple of hundred of my old Guides! I flatter myself I could do something then. As it is, I must bide my time until I can get a few good men together on whom I can depend. I have been so busy all day, writing letters on my knee, sending off electric messages, *cum multis aliis.* I can but rejoice that I am employed again; certain, too, as I am, that the star of Old England will shine the brighter in the end, and we shall hold a prouder position than ever. But the crisis is an awful one!

*May 19th.*—This morning the Commander-in-Chief ordered me to raise and command an entire new regiment of Irregular Horse. I do not know who or what has been at work for me, but he seems willing enough to give me work to do, and I am willing enough to do it. The 1st Bengal Fusiliers arrived this morning

(I sent a telegraphic message to say so); and the Rajah of Jheend, with his men, last night. I have offered to clear the road and open the communication to Meerut and Delhi with the Rajah's Horse. If the Chief will consent, I think I am sure of success. It is believed that nothing has occurred at Agra. The Punjab all quiet up to last night; as long as that is the case we shall do. With God and our Saxon arms to aid us, I have firm faith in the result.

*20th.*—Deep anxiety about the safety of the hill stations continues unabated; no letters—no certainty—only rumours. Were it not for this I should enter with full zest into the work before me, and the fresh field which I owe to General Anson's kindness. He has at last consented to my trying to open communication with Meerut, so I start this afternoon to try to make my way across with a party of the Jheend Horse; and I have, under Providence, little doubt of success, though I would rather have a party of my dear old Guides. There has been an outbreak at Agra, but all the Europeans are shut up in the fort; Allygurh and Moradabad have mutinied, but by God's help we shall get safely through.

*20th,* 2 P.M.—Just one line to say I am starting, and shall not be able to write to-morrow or next day. Still no tidings from the hills! This is a terrible additional pull upon one's nerves at a time like this, and is a phase of war I never calculated on.

*May 24th.*—I returned from my expedition to Meerut late last night. It was eminently successful, and I am off immediately to Umbâla to report progress to the Chief. Much relieved by a letter from you.

*25th.*—A hurried line only to say I am safe and well, but dead beat. I went yesterday to Umbâla by mail-cart to report to the Commander-in-Chief. Got there at 6 P.M., and started back again at 11 P.M. As I have only had one night in bed out of five, I am tolerably weary. The Commander-in-Chief arrived this morning. I will give you more particulars when I have slept.

From a letter written from camp before Delhi, in August, to Colonel D. Seaton:—

... As soon as the Commander-in-Chief reached Umbâla he sent for me, and put me in charge of the Intelligence Department, as an Assistant Quartermaster-General under his personal orders. I left Umbâla by mail-cart that night for Kurnâl, ascertained the state of things, made arrangements for the protection and shelter of the advanced party, and offered to open the road to Meerut, from Kurnâl. He replied by telegraph. Seventy-two hours afterwards, I was back in Kurnâl, and telegraphed to him that I had forced my way to Meerut, and obtained all the papers he wanted from the general there. These I gave him four hours later in Umbâla. The pace pleased him, I fancy, for he ordered me to raise a Corps of Irregular Horse, and appointed me commandant.

*Letter from an Officer.*

"When the mutiny broke out, our communications were completely cut off. One night, on outlying picket at Meerut, this subject being discussed, I said, 'Hodson is at Umbâla, I know; and I'll bet he will force his way through, and open communications with the Commander-in-Chief and ourselves.' At about three that night I heard my advanced sentries firing. I rode off to see what was the matter, and they told me that a part of the enemy's cavalry had approached their post. When day broke, in galloped Hodson. He had left Kurnâl (seventy-six miles off) at nine the night before, with one led horse and an escort of Sikh cavalry, and, as I had anticipated, here he was with despatches for Wilson! How I quizzed him for approaching an armed post at night without knowing the parole. Hodson rode straight to Wilson, had his interview, a bath, breakfast, and two hours' sleep, and then rode back the seventy-six miles, and had to fight his way for about thirty miles of the distance."

Another officer, writing to his wife at this time, says:—

"Hodson's gallant deeds more resemble a chapter from the life of Bayard or Amadis de Gaul, than the doings of a subaltern of the nineteenth century. The only feeling mixed with my admiration for him is envy."

---

*May 25th, Evening.*—I wrote this morning a few hurried lines to keep you from anxiety. I was too tired to do more, the continued nightwork had wearied me out, and when I got back here at half-past six this morning I was fairly dead beat. Poor Charlie Thomason is with me. I am happy to have been in some measure instrumental in getting him in in safety, by offering a heavy sum to the villagers. He had been wandering about in the jungles, with several other refugees, for days, without food or shelter. I am deeply grieved for him, poor fellow! The state of panic at Meerut was shocking; all the ladies shut up in an enclosed barrack, and their husbands sleeping in the men's barracks for safety, and never going beyond the sentries.

My commission is to raise a body of Irregular Horse on the usual rates of pay and the regular complement of native officers, but the number of troops to be unlimited—*i.e.*, I am to raise as many men as I please; 2000 if I can get them. The worst of it is, the being in a part of the country I do not know, and the necessity of finding men who can be trusted. Mr. Montgomery is aiding me wonderfully. He called upon some of my old friends among the Sirdars to raise men for me. Shumshere Singh is raising one troop; Tej Singh ditto; Emaumoodeen ditto; Mr. Montgomery himself one or two ditto. All these will be ready in about three weeks. Kauh Singh Rosah, my old friend who commanded the Sikh cavalry at Chilianuale, will be here in a day or two. I have asked to remain Assistant Quartermaster-General, attached to the Commander-in-Chief. This allows me free access to him at any time, and to other people in authority, which gives me power for good. The

Intelligence Department is in my line, and I have for this Sir Henry's old friend, the one-eyed Moulvie, Rujub Alee, so I shall get the best news in the country. Montgomery has come out very, very strong indeed, and behaved admirably. The native regiments at Peshawur have been disarmed. As yet the Punjab is quiet, and the Irregulars true. The Guides are coming down here by forced marches.

CAMP, PANEEPUT, 27*th.*—You will have heard of the sad death of General Anson. He was taken with cholera yesterday, and died without pain from collapse this morning. He made over command to General Barnard with his last breath, who only arrived from Umbâla just in time. His death is politically a vast misfortune just at this crisis, and personally I am deeply grieved, and the natives will be highly elated. I am now hard at work, raising my men, or taking means to do so, and have already had applications for officers; but I shall not settle on officers till the men begin to collect, and this time I will take care to have none but gentlemen, if I can help it. I am going downwards to-night with the Jheend Horse and Chesney to look after the bridge at Bhâgput on this side of Delhi, about thirty miles hence, by which the Meerut troops will move to join us. Colonel T. Seaton is commanding the 60th Native Infantry, and will be here to-night with them. I don't envy him his new command, but he is a good man, and a brave soldier, and if any man can get them over the mess, he will do it. Sir H. Barnard is a fine gentlemanly old man, but hardly up to his work. However, we must all put our shoulders to the wheel, and help him over the crisis. I trust he will act with vigour, for we have delayed far too long already.

29*th.*—There is nothing new. I travelled eighty miles between 2 P.M. yesterday and ten this morning, besides heaps of business. I am tired, I confess, for the heat is awful. The treasuries are empty, and no drafts are to be cashed, so how we are to get money I cannot imagine. I ought to have R.1000 a month as Commandant, and we ought to save half toward paying our debts. We hear that a request has gone to Lord Canning to send for Pat

Grant as Commander-in-Chief, pending instructions. I grieve for poor General Anson, and I ought to do so, for he was a good friend to me.

SUMALKA, 30*th*.—My earnest representations and remonstrances seem at last to have produced some effect, for at 7 P.M. yesterday we got an order to move on. The headquarters follow us to-night from Kurnâl. The " we " means three squadrons of 9th Lancers, Money's troop of Horse Artillery, and 1st Fusiliers. Brigadier Hallifax is in command, but so ill from heat and anxiety, that I begin to be anxious about him, and whether he will be able to remain with the force is doubtful. Colonel T. Seaton is gone on to Rohtuck with the 60th Native Infantry, who, I have no doubt, will desert to a man as soon as they get there. It is very plucky of him and the other officers to go; and very hard of the authorities to send them. The old Guides under Daly are to be here on the 8th or 10th to join us. The heat here is a caution, and writing in this melting climate anything but easy, especially as chairs and tables are not common. Chesney and I live together. This regiment (1st Fusiliers) is a credit to any army, and the fellows are in as high spirits and heart, and as plucky and free from croaking as possible, and really do good to the whole force.

KUSSOWLEE, *May* 31*st*.—Here we are one more stage on our road to Delhi; we are, however, to halt a couple of days or so at the next stage (Raee), to await the arrival of General Barnard. Poor Brigadier Hallifax was so ill that he would clearly have died had he remained here, so we had a medical committee, put him into my shigram (a travelling waggon), and sent him off to Kurnâl for Umbâla and the hills. I sent a telegraphic message for Mrs. Hallifax to meet him at Umbâla. This is but the beginning of this work, I fear; and before this business ends, we who are, thank God, still young and strong shall alone be left in camp; all the elderly gentlemen will sink under the fatigue and exposure. I think of asking for Mr. Macdowell as my second in command; he is a gentleman, and only wants opportunity to become a gallant soldier. The whole onus of work here is on my shoulders; every one comes to me for advice and assistance, which is purely absurd. I shall do all the work and others get the credit, as usual; but in these days we cannot afford to spare ourselves. The Empire is at stake, and all we love and reverence is in the balance. I tried to persuade them to send General Johnstone to Meerut to supersede Hewitt. I wish he had been there and was here; we have few as good.

I insert here an extract from the "Lahore Chronicle" of this date:—

"Hodson himself is working away with all his well-known courage and energy, and it must be allowed that whatever General Anson's faults were, he showed both tact and discrimination in securing at once to the State, in a prominent position, the services of this well-deserving and much-injured officer—would that we had more like him, and some others I could name. Men who can be in the saddle fifteen hours out of the twenty-four at this time of the year, form a glorious contrast to those whom, I hear, are still skulking in safety at Simla and elsewhere in the hills."

RAEE, *June 1st.*—I have just been roused up from the first sleep I have had, for I don't know how long (lying under a peepul tree, with a fine breeze like liquid fire blowing over me), by the news that the dâk is going, so I can only say that all is well, and that we are here, about twenty miles from Delhi, and I hope ere night to capture some of the rascals who stripped and ill-treated two ladies near this the other day on their flight to the hills.

Colonel Hope Grant has arrived to command the force until General Barnard comes, which will be on the 4th, and the Meerut people also. The Delhi mutineers marched out ten miles, and attacked Brigadier Wilson on the night of the 30th, at Ghazee-nuggur, on his way to this place. He drove them back, and captured all their guns. Some 8000 or 10,000 of them came out, and he had only about a thousand men. Long odds this; but of course all his men were Europeans. I fear the 14th Irregulars have joined the mutineers. If they would only make haste and get to Delhi, we might do something.

RAEE, 2nd.—You will have been as much shocked as I was by the tidings of poor Brigadier Hallifax's death at Kurnâl, only a few hours after I put him into the carriage, with the comfortable assurance that his wife would meet him at Umbâla. He died from congestion of the brain. I have been much affected by this, for I had a warm regard for him, and his very helplessness the last few days seemed to strengthen the tie. I feel deeply for his poor wife and children. Colonel Mowat of the artillery is dead too, of cholera. The weather is undoubtedly very trying for old and infirm men; but we are all well here, and there is no sickness to speak of among the troops. All will be here to-morrow. Headquarters, 75th Queen's, and remainder of 9th Lancers; the heavy guns and 2nd Fusiliers are only a short way behind. Colonel Hope Grant commands. The Meerut folks have had another fight (on the 31st) with the Delhi mutineers, and again beaten them; but this constant exposure is very trying to Europeans I wish we were moving nearer Delhi more rapidly, as all now depends on our quickly disposing of this mighty rose. I wish from my heart we had Sir Henry Lawrence here; he is the man for the crisis. We are all in high spirits; only eager to get at the villains who have committed atrocities which make the blood run cold but to think of. I trust the retribution will be short, sharp, and decisive.

Another batch of half-starved, half-naked Europeans, men, women, and children (a deputy collector and his family), were brought into camp to-day, after wandering twenty-three days in the jungle.

RAEE, 3rd.—Things are so quiet in the Punjab that I begin to hope that, if we do but make haste in disposing of Delhi, the campaign may not be so long, after all. Everything depends on that; we dare not, however, calculate on such good fortune either to our arms or ourselves. The headquarters' people joined this morning; they seem to stand it better than I expected. Congreve complains a good deal, but Colonel Chester and Arthur Becher are well. I have not yet seen Sir H. Barnard. I was kept up and out half the night, and then out again at daybreak, so I am too tired and busy to pay visits. There has been no further fight that we know of. Charlie Thomason rejoined us this morning; he has picked up a little since his starvation time ended, and does not look so like a wild beast as he did. Still good news from Agra; there are, however, reports which tend to show disturbances in the Allygurh and Bolundshur districts.

ALEEPORE, *June 5th.*—You must not be anxious on my account: I am in as good a position as possible for a subaltern to be, unless indeed I had my regiment ready for service. I am second only to Becher in the Quartermaster-General Department, and the Intelligence Department is entirely my own. If we could but get all the seventy-four native infantry regiments in one lump we could manage them, but they will never stand after we get our guns to work. I rode right up to the Delhi parade-ground this morning to reconnoitre, and the few Sowars whom I met galloped away like mad at the sight of one white face. Had I had a hundred Guides with me I would have gone up to the very walls.

ALEEPORE, *June 6th.*—All the force is assembled to-day save the Meerut portion, and they will be up to-night; the heat is severe, but not unhealthy. The siege guns came in this morning, and the 2nd European Bengal Fusiliers and we are all ready to move on. About 2000 of the rebels have come out of Delhi, and put themselves in position to bar our road. Even your pride would be satisfied at the cry when I ride to the front or start on any little excursion. I think I am more than appreciated by the headquarters' people. I had barely finished the word when I was sent for by the General, and had a pretty strong proof of the estimation I am held in. He had been urged to one particular point of attack; and when I went into the tent, he immediately turned to the assembled council, and said, "I have always trusted to Hodson's intelligence, and have the greatest confidence in his judgment. I will be guided by what he can tell me now." So the croakers, who had been groaning, were discomfited. This is of course for your own eye and ear alone, but it is pleasant, as the General has only known me since he has now joined the force.

ALEEPORE, *June 7th.*—I have little to do with the "Jheend Rajah's troops," further than that I am empowered to demand as many as I want, and whenever I want them. I have twenty-five men on constant duty with me, and to-day have asked for double that number for extra duty; beyond this, I have not, and do not wish to have, further to do with them. All Rohilcund is in mutiny. In fact, the district of Agra is the only one in the North-West Provinces now under our control. What a terrible lesson on the evils of delay! It will be long yet, I fear, ere this business is over. Oh for Sir Henry Lawrence! Yet personally I have no reason to complain.

CAMP, DELHI, *June 8th*, 1857.—Here we are safe and sound, after having driven the enemy out of their position in the cantonments up to and into the walls of Delhi! I write a line in pencil on the top of a drum to say that I am mercifully untouched, and none the worse for a very hard morning's work. Our loss has been considerable, the rebels having been driven from their guns at the point of the bayonet. Poor Colonel Chester killed at the first fire. Alfred Light (who won the admiration of all) wounded, but not severely. No one else of the staff party killed or wounded; but our general returns will, I fear, tell a sad tale. Greville slightly hurt. The enemy's guns captured, and their dispersion and route very complete. God has been very good to me. May His gracious protection still be shown.

# CHAPTER II.

### *SIEGE OF DELHI.*

CAMP BEFORE DELHI, *June 9th.*

I WROTE you a few hurried lines on the field of battle yesterday, to say that we had beaten the enemy, and driven them back five miles into Delhi. How grateful rest was after such a morning! The Guides came in to-day, and it would have done your heart good to see the welcome they gave me—cheering and shouting and crowding round me like frantic creatures. They seized my bridle, dress, hands, and feet, and literally threw themselves down before the horse with the tears streaming down their faces. Many officers who were present hardly knew what to make of it, and thought the creatures were mobbing me; and so they were—but for joy, not for mischief.* All the staff were witnesses of this, and Colonel Becher says their reception of me was quite enough to contradict all the reports of my unpopularity † with the regiment. There is terrible confusion all along the road, and we can only get the dâks carried at all by bribery stage by stage.

*June 10th.*—When I hastily closed my letter yesterday, I hoped to be able to write a long one for to-day's dâk, and to have had some hours' quiet to myself; but before the post had well started, our troops were again under arms, the mutineers having thought proper to attack our position; consequently I was on horseback

---

\* One of the officers who witnessed this scene told me that the acclamation of the men on meeting him was, "Burra Lerai-wallah," or Great in battle.—*Ed.*

† This had been one of the unfounded charges against him two years before.

the whole day, and thankful to get at night a mouthful of food and a little rest. I had command of all the troops on our right, the gallant Guides among the rest. They followed me with a cheer for their old commander, and behaved with their usual pluck; but I grieve deeply to say that poor Quintin Battye was mortally wounded. He behaved most nobly, Daly tells me, leading his men like a hero. Poor Kauh Singh Rosah, who had come down from the Punjab to join me only the same morning, was badly shot through the shoulder. Indeed, I did *not* expose myself unnecessarily, for having to direct the movements of three or four regiments, I could not be in the front as much as I wished. God has mercifully preserved me, and I humbly pray will continue His gracious care. The warmth of the reception again given me by the Guides was quite affecting, and has produced a great sensation in camp, and had a good effect on our native troops, insomuch that they are more willing to obey their European officers when they see their own countrymen's enthusiasm. Numbers of the men want to come and join my new regiment—in fact, the largest proportion of the cavalry; but of course I cannot take them now, nor until this business is over. I am wonderfully well, and only a little anxious about the hill stations, though I have full confidence in Lord William Hay's management. There is not much sickness in camp, though many wounded, and there will be many more, I fear, before we get into Delhi. We have been fortunate in the weather hitherto.

The enemy are at least four or five times our strength, and their numbers tell when we come near them, despite their want of discipline. They are splendid artillerymen, however, and actually beat ours in accuracy of fire.

Light works on magnificently, despite a severe and painful wound in the head. I was very nearly coming to grief once this morning, for the sabre I thought such a good one went the first blow, and the blade flew out of the handle the second, the handle itself breaking in two. I had to borrow a sword from a horse artilleryman for the remainder of the day.

The Jheend men with me fought like excellent soldiers. The good General came up when it was over, and shook hands with each of them. Their Rajah has given the native officer a pair of gold bangles, and doubled his pay. This is the way to encourage soldiers, European as well as native: reward them, if but with thanks, on the spot.

Colonel Thomas Seaton is at Rohtuck, in command of the 60th Native Infantry. How much longer they will refrain from mutiny one cannot say; certainly not long; though if any man can keep them steady, Seaton will. I hear some 300 or 400 men are ready for me; a few have already arrived with Kauh Singh. Meantime my position is Assistant Quartermaster-General on the Commander-in-Chief's personal staff. I am responsible for the Intelligence Department, and in the field, or when anything is going on, for directing the movements of the troops in action, under the immediate orders of the General; I have no other master, and he listens to my suggestions most readily. Charlie Thomason is here, working away as an engineer. Macdowell is well and merry, and much gratified at my having asked for him.

*June* 14*th.*—We were roused up three times during the night, and I have been deep in business with the General all the morning. I was also interrupted by the mournful task of carrying poor Battyè to his grave. Poor fellow! he had quite won my heart by his courage and amiable qualities, and it is very, very sad, his early death. It was a noble one, however, and worthy of a soldier. We have just been excited in camp by the hasty arrival of Colonel Seaton and the officers of the late 60th Native Infantry, which mutinied yesterday, and, spite of all Seaton could do, they fired on their officers, who, however, all escaped, and came into camp safe, after a ride of fifty miles. Seaton is with me, looking terribly worn and harassed, but he says quite well in health, though disgusted enough. I am much vexed at the "Lahore Chronicle" "butter," and wish people would leave me alone in the newspapers. The best "butter" I get is the deference and respect I meet with from all whose respect I care for, and the affectionate enthusiasm of the Guides, which increases instead of lessening.

*June* 12*th.*—We were turned out early this morning by an attack on our outposts and position generally by the rebel army. A sharp fight ensued, which lasted some four hours. The enemy came on very boldly, and had got close to us, under cover of the trees and gardens, before they were seen; however, the troops turned out sharp, and drove them back quickly from our immediate vicinity; they were then followed up, and got most heartily thrashed. They have never yet been so punished as to-day. I estimate their loss in killed alone at 400, while our loss was comparatively trifling. The Guides behaved admirably, so did the Fusiliers, as usual. Jacob's wing was the admiration of all; one officer (Captain Knox, 75th) was killed and one or two wounded. I do not know how many European soldiers; but on the whole the affair was a very creditable one. I am safe and sound still, and again have to thank the Almighty for my preservation.

Yesterday I was ordered by the General to assist Greathed and one or two more engineers in forming a project of attack, and how we would do to take Delhi. We drew up our scheme and gave it to the General, who highly approved, and will, I trust, carry it out; but how times must be changed, when four subalterns are called upon to suggest a means of carrying out so vitally important an enterprise as this, one on which the safety of the Empire depends! Wilberforce Greathed is next senior engineer to Laughton. Chesney is Major of the Engineer Brigade, and Maunsell commands the Sappers, so they had official claims to be consulted.

I was added, because the General complimentarily told me he had the utmost value for my opinion, and though I am known to counsel vigorous measures, it is equally well known I do not urge others to do what I would not be the first to do myself. It is a much more serious business than was at first anticipated. Delhi is a very strong place, and the vast resources which the possession of our arsenal has given the mutineers has made the matter a difficult one to deal with, except by the boldest measures; the city should be carried by a *coup-de-main*, and that at once, or we may be many weeks before Delhi, instead of within it. All is safe at Agra, and the 3rd Europeans are quietly under cover. I have just been listening to a letter from Lord W. Hay, in which he speaks in the highest terms of the conduct of some of the ladies at Simla, and says that the sense and courage exhibited by one or two of them has given a severe lesson to those who ought to know better than to require it from the weaker sex.

*June* 13*th*.—We were to have taken Delhi by assault last night, but a "mistake of orders" (?) as to the right time of bringing the troops to the rendezvous prevented its execution. I am much annoyed and disappointed at our plan not having been carried out, because I am confident it would have been successful. The rebels were cowed, and perfectly ignorant of any intention of so bold a stroke on our part as an assault; the surprise would have done everything. I am very vexed, though the General is most kind and considerate in trying to soothe my disappointment—too kind, indeed, or he would not so readily have pardoned those whose fault it is that we are still outside Delhi.

*June* 14*th*.—There was another smart engagement last night, the 60th Native Infantry having thought fit to signalise their arrival at Delhi by an attack upon our position; they suffered for it, as usual, but also, as usual, we lost several good men whom, God knows, we can ill spare. Mr. Kennedy was wounded, and a Subadar and some men of the Guides killed. I was not very much under fire, though I had to run the gauntlet now and then of a rain of shot and shells with which the rebels belaboured us. Our Artillery officers themselves say that they are outmatched by these rascals in accuracy and rapidity of fire; and as they have unlimited supply of guns and ammunition from our own greatest arsenal, they are quite beyond us in many respects. I am just returned from a long ride to look after a party of plunderers from the city, who had gone round our flank; I disposed of a few.

*June 16th.*—Everybody here is infinitely disgusted at learning the truth about the report of a riot at Simla, and the opinion is universal that ——— ought to be removed. Neville Chamberlain is Adjutant-General of the army, and Pat Grant Commander-in-Chief. I do not think either of them will approve of any "soldier" showing his prowess in frightening helpless women and children, or of one whose only courage is exhibited on a peaceful parade, or when an unfortunate subaltern is to be bullied.

The weather is intense to-day, and I am uncomfortable from having caught a heavy cold, but it will soon go off, I dare say.

*June 18th.*—I was not able to write yesterday, for the cold, I mentioned as having caught in common with many others in camp, turned into a sharp attack of bronchitis, or inflammation on the chest, and I was really very ill for some hours. To-day I am thankful to say I am much better, though very weak: the inflammation has disappeared, and I hope to be on my horse again to-morrow in spite of all the doctor says. Every one is very kind, the General particularly so; he insists on having me in his own tent, as being so much larger than my own, and he takes the most fatherly care of me.

*June 19th.*—I am up and dressed, and crawling about a little to-day, but much weaker than I fancied, and dizzy with quinine, and vexed at being useless at such a time. The General nurses me as if I were his son. I woke in the night, and found the kind old man by my bedside, covering me carefully up from the draught. The delay and absolute want of progress here is very disheartening. There have been repeated attacks upon us; all of course with the same result (but, for that matter, we are as nearly besieged as the rebels themselves are), and we lose valuable lives in every encounter, the sum total of which would swell the catalogue to the dimensions of that of a general engagement. I fear there is no room to doubt that Dr. Hay is dead; he was actually hung, with other civilians, in the market-place at Bareilly, after going through a mock form of trial. All the Europeans at Shahjehanpoor have, we hear, been murdered while they were in church, at the same moment as nearly as possible that the Bareilly tragedy was going on.

*June 20th.*—I am much better to-day, but still very weak, yet work I must. There was a sharp fight again last evening. The enemy came down and attacked our rear, and a sharp conflict ensued between some 2000 Sepoys with six guns and 300 Europeans with one gun. The result was as usual, but two events occurred which were important for me. Colonel Becher (Quartermaster-General) was shot through the right arm, and Captain Daly badly hit through the shoulder.

The consequence is, that I have in effect to see to the whole work of the Quartermaster-General of the army; and in addition, the General has begged me as a personal favour to take command of the Guides until Daly has recovered. I at first refused, but the General was most urgent, putting it on the ground that the service was at stake, and none was so fit, &c., &c. I do feel that we are bound to do our best just now to put things on a proper footing, and after consulting Seaton and Norman, I accepted the command. If I can but keep it till Delhi is taken I shall be satisfied, for I think I shall be able to do something towards so favourable a result. Shebbeare was appointed second in command at my request. He is an excellent soldier. General Barnard * has written most strongly in my favour, and has voluntarily pledged himself to get me

---

\* *From* MAJOR-GENERAL SIR H. BARNARD, *Commanding Field Force, to the* ADJUTANT-GENERAL *of the Army.*

"CAMP, DELHI, *June* 16*th*, 1857.

"SIR,—While enclosing for the information of the Commander-in-Chief the reports of the late attack made by the enemy on the force under my command, I would wish to bring to his notice the assistance I have received in every way from the services of Lieut. W. S. Hodson, 1st Bengal European Fusiliers.

"Since the arrival of his regiment at Umbâla, up to the present date, his untiring energy and perpetual anxiety to assist me in any way in which his services might be found useful, have distinguished him throughout, and are now my reasons for bringing this officer thus specially to the notice of the Commander-in-Chief.     (Signed)     H. M. BARNARD,
*Major-General.*"

my majority as soon as ever I am a captain. I confess I feel a little proud at being earnestly requested to take again the command of which the machinations of my enemies had deprived me. Our loss altogether last night was not more than 50 killed and wounded; we took two guns—enemy's loss about 500.

*June* 21*st.*—I have been on horseback to-day for the first time since this attack of illness, so I may be considered finally recovered, only I still feel considerable weakness. It is very annoying not to be quite up to the mark in these stirring times, especially when so much work has fallen to my lot. I am fortunate, however, in not being, like many of our poor fellows, laid up with wounds and serious ailments. God has been very good to me, and in nothing more so than in preserving what is most precious to me from the horrible danger and suffering of so many of our poor countrywomen and children. How thankful I am now that Reginald exchanged into an European corps. I never see any of these unhappy refugees, as we call the poor officers whose regiments have mutinied, wandering about the camp, without uttering a mental thanksgiving that he is safe from that at least. I feel more strongly every hour that I should not have been justified in refusing the command of the Guides under present circumstances. We are, in point of fact, reduced to merely holding our own ground till we get more men. The drain on our resources has been enormous, while those of the enemy have proved so much greater, both in men, ammunition, and strength of position, than we expected, and they have fought us so much more perseveringly than was deemed possible, that it has become imperatively necessary to be stronger before striking the final blow. General Johnstone is to be here by the 23d, we hope with considerable reinforcements, and more will follow. I trust that a few days then will end this business, as far as Delhi is concerned, and so enable a part at least of the force to move on towards Allygurh, and reopen the roads and dâks, and restore order for the time; but when the end will be who can say?

The rising in Rohilcund will, I fear, assume formidable proportions and give us much trouble, as I think we shall scarcely be able to do anything there before the cold weather. There is, in fact, every prospect of a long and tedious campaign. May God's wisdom direct and His mercy defend us.

*June 22nd.*—The hottest day we have had yet; but while I know that you are safe, I can bear anything with equanimity. The rumours down here, of all that has been doing and feared at Simla, have been enough to unnerve any one who does not know the truth. Personally, I cannot but feel gratified at the marked pleasure all hands, high and low, have shown at my renewed command of the Guides. All congratulate me as if they were personally interested; and as to the men themselves, their vociferous, and I really believe honest, delight is quite overpowering. The wounded generally are doing well, poor fellows, considering the heat, dirt, and want of any bed but the dry ground. Their pluck is wonderful, and it is not in the field alone that you see what an English soldier is made of. One poor fellow who was smoking his pipe and laughing with the comrade by his side, was asked what was the matter with him, and he answered in a lively voice, "Oh, not much, sir, only a little knock on the back; I shall be up and at the rascals again in a day or two." He had been shot in the spine, and all his lower limbs were paralysed. He died next day. Colonel Welchman * is about again; too soon, I fear, but there is no keeping the brave old man quiet. Poor Peter Brown * is very badly wounded, but he is cheerful, and bears up bravely. Jacob * has "come out" wonderfully. He is cool, active, and bold, keeps his wits about him under fire, and does altogether well. We are fortunate in having him with the force. Good field-officers are very scarce indeed; I do not wonder at people at a distance bewailing the delay in the taking of Delhi. No one not on the spot can appreciate the difficulties in the way, or the painful truth that those difficulties increase upon us. The very large reinforcements which the enemy are receiving (the whole Bareilly and

* 1st European Bengal Fusiliers.

Rohilcund force, some 5000 men, are on their way to join) more than counterbalance the aid which can reach us, so that when the last party arrives, the odds will still be immensely against us. It would not so much signify if we could but get them into the open field, but for every gun we can bring to bear upon them they can bring four heavier ones against us. We drive them before us like chaff in the field, but they can and do attack us in two or three quarters at once, and our unfortunate soldiers are worked off their legs. I do not say this to make matters look gloomy, for I am as confident as ever of the result; but we may be a long while yet, and a weary while too, before that result is arrived at. Baird Smith will be here as Chief Engineer in a day or two, and if we can manage to get some batteries made suddenly, we may carry the city shortly; but there are great obstacles. I regret more than ever that the assault was not made on the night of the 11th, when they were unprepared for us, and so much fewer in numbers. Now they increase daily, and the city is so overflowing, that the rascals are encamped outside the gates under cover of their formidable batteries, and in the glacis; so much for giving our arsenal into native keeping. All is well at Agra; beyond that, we know nothing.

*June 23rd.*—The rebels came out again this morning in considerable force, with the avowed intention of attacking us on all sides. They have been frustrated, however, save on one point, and firing is still going on. Sarel, of the 9th Lancers, came in this morning, in an incredibly short space of time, from his shooting expedition in the interior, ten days' journey beyond Simla. He reports all quiet there, thank God. I am sadly weak, I find, and have been obliged to change my work from the saddle to the pen more than once to-day. This want of physical strength depresses me. It is a burden to me to stand or walk, and the excessive heat makes it difficult for me to recover from that sharp attack of illness. The doctors urge me to go away for a little to get strength—as if I could leave just now, or as if I would if I could.

*June* 24*th*.—I have been in the saddle nearly all day, though obliged occasionally to rest a bit when I could find shelter. One of my halts was by the side of Alfred Light, who has behaved magnificently under trial and difficulty. It does me good to see him working away at his guns, begrimed with dust and heat, ever cheery and cool, though dead beat from fatigue and exposure. He is one of a thousand, and a host in himself.

The enemy turned us out very early, and the firing continued without intermission till dark, and such a day; liquid fire was no name for the fervent heat. Colonel Welchman got an ugly wound in the arm, and Dennis was knocked down by the sun, and numbers of the men; but nothing less than a knock-down blow from sun, sword, or bullet stops a British soldier. How well they fought to-day; and, to do them justice, so did my old Guides and my new Sikhs, while the little Goorkhas vied with any in endurance and courage; but the mismanagement of matters is perfectly sickening. Nothing the rebels can do will equal the evils arising from incapacity and indecision.

Fortunately Neville Chamberlain has arrived, and he ought to be worth a thousand men to us. I am neither down-hearted nor desponding when I say that with our present chiefs I see no chance of taking Delhi. It might have been done many days ago, but they have not the nerve nor the heart for a bold stroke requiring the smallest assumption of responsibility. Horses are very scarce here, and I have the greatest difficulty in getting my own men mounted. Mr. Montgomery is helping me wonderfully with men, and I receive offers for service daily, but in these mutinous times it is necessary to be cautious. A telegram from Agra says, "Heavy firing at Cawnpore; result not known."

*June* 25*th*.—There is little doing to-day, save a vain fire of long shots, and I fear nothing effective will be done till the 8th and 61st arrive. I hope much from Chamberlain. The General, though one of the kindest and best of men, has neither health nor nerve enough for so responsible, and really very difficult, a position as that he is now in. Our loss in officers and men bears a sadly large proportion to our successes. In the 1st Fusiliers it is too melancholy: Colonel Welchman with a very bad hit in the arm, in addition to his sickness when he came to Delhi from Dugshai; Greville down with fever; Wriford with dysentery; Dennis with sun-stroke; Brown with wounds. Jacob and the "boys" have all the work to themselves, and well indeed do the boys behave, with a courage and coolness that would not disgrace veterans. Little Tommy Butler, Owen, Warner all behave like heroes, albeit with sadly diminishing numbers to lead. I am vexed at the mistakes or falsehoods of the newspaper reports. So far from having been wounded in the fight of the 19th, I was not even present, but ill in bed. When Colonel Becher came into camp wounded, I got up and struggled into the saddle, and tried to get far enough to send up fresh troops, but I had not got ten yards before I fell from my horse, and was all but carried back to my tent again.

I am more and more convinced that I was right not to persist in my refusal to take again the command of the Guides. It was so pressed on me, and surely the best eradication of the reproach of removal was the being asked to re-assume it in times of difficulty and danger like these.

That this is the general view of the case is shown by the warm and hearty congratulations I meet with on all sides. There is but one rule of action for a soldier in the field, as for a man at all times—to do that which is best for the public good; to make that your sole aim, resting assured that the result will in the end be best for individual interest also. Never mind if you do not see your husband's name in despatches; be content if he can perform his duty truly and honestly, and be thankful to the Almighty if he is spared for future labours or future repose.

The story prevalent in the hills, that 7000 of the enemy are pitched in the open plain, is a mere magnification of the simple fact, that a surplus portion of the rebels have encamped under cover of their guns, and close up under the wall of the city, and remain there all night, but this is on the side opposite us. We are not very well off *quant à la cuisine*. I never had so much trouble in getting anything fit to eat, except when I dine with the General. Colonel Seaton* lives in my tent, and is a great companion; his joyous disposition is a perpetual rebuke to the croakers. Don't believe what is said about our batteries doing no harm. The same was said of Muttra, yet when we entered, scarcely a square yard was unploughed by our shot. One of the native officers of the Guides (you know how ingenious they are at disguise) got into the city as a spy, and remained there four days. He reports great dissension and quarrelling among themselves. Robbery and fighting, and everything that is bad, between the newly arrived rebels and the city people. This account my own native news letters confirm. The 9th Native Infantry had already decamped, and thousands would follow if they dared. This last I doubt; the spirit of bravado, if not of bravery, is as yet too strong. The rascals in the last engagement came out in their red coats and medals!

*June* 26*th*.—I have been so hard at work the whole day, that I can only find time to say the enemy has made no sortie to-day, but Pandy amuses himself with firing long shots incessantly; all well, however.

27*th*.—We were turned out before I had hardly turned in, by another attack of the rebels. This time a faint one, which has been already repulsed with trifling loss on our side. For a short time, however, the cannonade was very heavy, and I have seldom been under a hotter fire than for about three-quarters of an hour at our most advanced battery, covered every moment with showers, or rather clouds of dust, stones, and splinters; but we kept close, and no one was hurt. There has been an outcry throughout camp at ——'s having fled from Bhágput, the bridge which caused me so much hard riding and hard work to get, some time ago. A report came that a portion of the mutineers were moving in that direction, and he fairly bolted, leaving boats, bridge and all! Yet he had with him all the Rajah of Jheend's men, horse, foot, and

* Sir Thomas Seaton, K.C.B.

guns, and never even saw the twinkle of a musket. In fact, it is not at all sure that an enemy was ever near him. By this conduct he has not only cut us off from all communication with Meerut, but actually left the boats to be used or destroyed by the enemy. Our reinforcements are in sight, at least the camp of the 8th, and I do trust no further delay will take place in our getting possession of Delhi. The only formidable part of the enemy is their artillery, which is amazingly well served, and in prodigious abundance, as my experience this morning abundantly proved. All quiet at Agra, we believe, but no particulars known.

*June 28th.*—I have just got orders to proceed to Bhágput, some twenty-five miles off on the Jumna, and see what the real state of affairs is, and try to save the boats; so I have only time to say I am much better and stronger, which is a great comfort, for I could not have ridden the distance a few days ago. The rains have begun, and the air is colder and more refreshing, though not exactly what one could wish. Certainly the hot season in India is not the pleasantest time in the year for campaigning, and this the rascally mutineers were fully aware of before they begun. Colonel Greathed and the 8th came in this morning, and the 61st will be here to-morrow.

*June 29th.*—I was thirteen hours and a half in the saddle without intermission yesterday, and got back to camp after midnight, very tired, but none the worse; fortunately, I had a cloudy day and a tolerably cool breeze for my work. I recovered the boats and found all quiet, in spite of ——'s disgraceful flight. He had not even the sense or courage to draw the boats over to our side of the river, consequently three were burnt and the whole place plundered.

The fight of the 23rd was a much more severe one than was reported. It was not over till dark, and our loss was the heaviest we have yet had to deplore since we got here on the 8th.

Everything quiet to-day, no firing on either side. I do hope this part of the business will soon be over, and that they will only wait for the 61st and Coke's regiment, both of which will be here to-morrow or next day. All was safe at Cawnpore and Lucknow up to our last news.

*July 2nd.*—I have been quite unable to write since the 29th, on the night of which I was ordered off again to Bhágput, to try to bring the boats down to camp, either to make a bridge here or a "stop" for the enemy. The order was given with the complimentary addenda from the General, "because I can trust your judgment quite as much as your energy." I expected to be back in good time on the 30th, but the winds and waves were against me, and I could not get my fleet of boats down the river.

Shebbeare was with me, and we worked like a couple of "navvies," passing the two days and one night on the banks of the river, without shelter, and almost without food, for we had nothing but a couple of "chupatties" each, and a small tin of soup and a little tea, which I fortunately took with me. Poor Shebbeare would soon lose the graceful rotund of his figure if he were long on such short commons, but I do not think any amount of starvation could reduce my horizontal dimensions.

All's well that ends well, however, and I succeeded in getting every boat safe into camp last night. I missed the skirmish of the 30th by being at Bhágput. The 61st have arrived, rich in twenty officers. We are getting more supplies now, and I have set myself up with plates and dishes for the small charge of one rupee. Colonel Seaton's traps and servants will be here to-day, and then we shall be comfortable, for hitherto a very limited allowance for one has been but small accommodation for two. For my new regiment three complete troops are on their way from Lahore and will be here on the 8th, and another troop from Jugraon should be here in a week. Two more troops are preparing at Lahore.

Montgomery takes the most kind interest in my new Corps, and I am rejoiced and comforted to find that he cordially approves of my having accepted the Guides. I have as much confidence in his judgment as in his kindness.

*July 3rd.*—Sir E. Campbell arrived here to-day by mail-cart, and will be a valuable addition to the 60th, or he will belie his descent from the Bourbons and Fitzgeralds. He is a man you can always trust, which is saying something in these hard times.

Whatever I may have sacrificed of pride and personal feeling to a sense of duty, I shall be fully rewarded by entering Delhi at the head of the Guides. Here at least there is but one opinion on the subject. My poor gallant Guides! they have suffered severely for their fidelity to our cause, above a fourth of the whole having been killed or wounded, including some of our best men. Koor Singh, the little Goorkha Subadar who won the Order of Merit in that stiff affair at Boree in '53, is gone, and others whom we could ill afford to lose, now that so much depends on the fidelity of the native officers—the Guides more than all. Surely, then, I am right, knowing and feeling that my influence with them is so great, to sink every personal consideration before the one great end of public safety, which implies that of ourselves and those dear to us. If we fail here at Delhi, not a soul in the Punjab or Upper Provinces would be safe for a day. I cannot think of self when so much is at stake.

*July 5th.*—It was impossible for me to write by yesterday's dâk, for the rebels got into our rear during the night of the 3d, and attacked Alipoor, the first stage from hence on the Kurnâl road. I was out reconnoitring, and saw them moving out some five miles on our right. I reported their position at 7 P.M. on the 3d, but not until 3 A.M. of the 4th were any measures taken, by which time of course they had attained their end, and were in full march back to Delhi. At daybreak yesterday I pointed out their exact whereabouts to Coke (who commanded the party sent to attack them), and I did not get back to camp till 8 P.M.; a hard day's work, especially as I had no breakfast, nor indeed food of any kind, and hunger makes the heat tell.

We beat 5000 of the rebels in the morning, and were twice attacked by upwards of 3000 in the course of the day. I took the Guides in pursuit (as soon as our guns had driven the enemy from their position), and drove them into a village.

Our loss was about thirty or forty Europeans, and three of my native officers temporarily disabled. Both men and horses were terribly knocked up towards the end of the day, and could hardly crawl back to camp; and no wonder. I was mercifully preserved, though I am sorry to say my gallant "Feroza" was badly wounded twice with sabre-cuts, and part of his bridle cut through, and a piece of my glove shaved off; so it was rather close work. My men, who were the most engaged of all, escaped with the loss of one killed and six wounded, and six horses put *hors de combat.* I am dissatisfied with the day's work, inasmuch as more might have been done, and what was done is only satisfactory as a proof of the ease with which Anglo-Saxons can thrash Asiatics at any odds. Yesterday they were at least from ten to fifteen to one against us. To-day General Barnard has been attacked with cholera, I grieve to say; and Colonel Welchman is very ill indeed. The doctors dread erysipelas, which at his age would be serious; beyond this, the wounded are generally doing well.

*July 6th.*—Poor General Barnard died last night, and was buried this morning. He sank rapidly, for anxiety, worry, over-exertion, and heat had prepared his system, and it was impossible for him to bear up against the virulence of cholera. Personally, I am much grieved, for no kinder or more considerate or more gentlemanly man ever lived. I am so sorry for his son, a fine brave fellow, whose attention to his father won the love of us all. It was quite beautiful to see them together.

The present state of things is terrible, enough to fret one to death—no head, no brains, no decision. Neville Chamberlain, though of decided excellence as a man of action, is, I begin to fear, but a poor man of business. Prompt decision in council is what we want; there is no lack of vigorous action. There are plenty to obey; but we want some one to command. We have seen nothing of the enemy outside the walls since the 4th. I am worked off my legs all the same, and the day is not half long enough for what I have to do. To make matters worse, too, poor Macdowell is down with fever; a sad loss just now to "Hodson's Horse," as they call my growing corps. I am sadly off for clothes, as we of course are only too glad to help the poor refugees who come into camp with none.

*July* 8*th.*—We left camp at 2 A.M. with a considerable force, and marched to a bridge some ten miles off, which we blew up to prevent the enemy annoying us, and then marched back again. I tried hard to induce Chamberlain, who commanded, to march back by another road, which I had reconnoitred, and which would have brought us close along the rear and flank of the enemy, but he would not do so, though admitting that I was right. We have had eleven hours in the saddle and in the sun, merely for this trifling gain. My face is like "General Gascoigne's," and my hands perfectly skinless. I must get some dogskin gloves, for it is as much as I can do to hold a sword, much less a pen. There has been no fighting since the 4th, and my news-writers from the city speak of much disheartenment, and symptoms of a break-up; but I doubt this latter being more than a report, while the enemy are so well provided both with *matériel* and *personnel.*

*July* 10*th.*—We are nearly flooded out of camp by the rain, and everything is wet and wretched but ourselves. I have no respite from work, however, and have only time to say that the ladies in the hills could not employ themselves better or in a greater work of charity than in making flannel-shirts for the soldiers, for our stores are either in the enemy's hands or not come-at-able. The soldiers bear up like men, but the constant state of wet is no small addition to what they have to endure from heat, hard work, and hard fighting. I know by experience what a comfort a dry flannel shirt is.

Mr. Saunders arrived in camp to-day, looking as fat and well as possible, though he and his pretty wife had a narrow escape and hard day's riding from Moradabad.

*July* 11*th.*—Pen-work again all day, as the enemy seem to prefer keeping under cover from the rain.

Colonel Greathed's story is so far true, that I did earnestly urge the construction of a bridge with the boats I brought down from Bhágput, but without success. There are difficulties,

I admit, and great ones, but I humbly think they might be overcome now, as they certainly could three weeks ago, when our plan of assault was suggested, and adopted by General Barnard. Light has just come in off duty, so begrimed with smoke and powder as scarcely to be distinguished even by his own men. He is admitted to be one of the best of our officers, and certainly one of the hardest working. Tombs always distinguishes himself.

*July* 12*th*.—300 of my new regiment have just arrived. 100 more left Lahore on the 7th, and 100 will be here very soon from the Sutlej. Mr. Montgomery has done me most essential service, as I could never by myself have got so many men together; and everything he does is so complete. He sends figured statements giving all details regarding men and horses, which will save me much time and labour hereafter. He has been really most kind, and has, moreover, during this troublous time, evinced an energy, decision, and vigour for which I believe the world hardly gave him credit. For officers, I hope to have permanently, Macdowell, Shebbeare (now acting as my second in command of the Guides, and a most excellent officer), and Hugh Gough of the 3d Cavalry. Saunders came to me to recommend a good officer to command the Jheend troops. I named that merry grig, George Hall, who is, I believe, available, and a really good soldier. I have got a very nice lad "*pro tem*," in the Guides, young Craigie, who promises very well indeed. I have seven officers attached to the Guides, but two are wounded, and Chalmers is very ill. Young Ellis of the 1st Fusiliers is down with cholera, poor boy; and Colonel Welchman dangerously ill and in great agony. I grieve deeply for the brave old man, for I fear we shall lose him.

*July* 13*th*.—We have had news from Agra to-day up to the 7th. The Neemuch rebels and others approached Agra from the south. The 3d Europeans and D'Oyley's battery went out to meet them with the Kotah Contingent. The Contingent turned against us as soon as they came in sight of the enemy. A fight ensued, in which the mutineers got well beaten, despite the treachery and great disparity of numbers; two of their guns were taken. On our side we lost one gun, the tumbrils having been blown up and the horses killed. All our men's ammunition was expended, and they had to retire in good order into the fort. D'Oyley was killed and two officers wounded. Thirty casualties in all. The mutineers then rushed into cantonments, which they burnt and pillaged; then broke open the great jail and released the prisoners. They did not venture near the fort, but marched off towards Muttra, and will, I suppose, come here. The delay here is sickening; if it continues much longer, we shall be too weak-handed to attempt to take the place until fresh regiments arrive.

I inspected my three new troops this morning; very fine-looking fellows, most of them. I am getting quite a little army under me, what with the Guides and my own men. Would to Heaven they would give us something more to do than this desultory warfare, which destroys our best men, and brings us no whit nearer Delhi, and removes the end of the campaign to an indefinite period.

*July 14th.*—Only time * to say I am again mercifully preserved, safe and unhurt, after one of the sharpest encounters we have yet had. Shebbeare got wounded early in the fight, so I led the Guide Infantry myself in the skirmish of the villages and suburbs. I charged the guns with some eight horsemen, a party of the Guide Infantry and 1st Fusiliers. We got within thirty yards, but the enemy's grape was too much for our small party. Three of my officers, Shebbeare, Hawes, and De Brett, slightly wounded, and several men; but though well to the front, my party suffered proportionably least.

Of the Fusiliers who were with us, some sixty men were wounded; Daniell's arm broken by a shot, Jacob's horse shot dead under him, Chamberlain shot through the arm, little Roberts wounded, and several more. Everybody wonders I was not hit; none more than myself. God has been very merciful to

---

\* *Extract from Letter of* COLONEL (NOW SIR T.) SEATON, *from Camp, at this time:—*

"Hodson's courage and conduct are the admiration of all, and how he gets through the immense amount of work and fatigue he does is marvellous.

He has the soundest heart and clearest head of any man in camp."

me. To-day even I say you have no need to be ashamed of your husband.

*July* 15*th.*—I could only write a few words last night on my return from the fight, worn out as I was with a severe day's work. It is pretty much the same now, and while I write I am obliged to have two men to keep the candle alight with their hands, for the breeze gets up at night, and we have all the "Kanats" of the tents down to enable us to breathe; and having no shades to the candlesticks, it is rather difficult to write even that I am safe.

*July* 16*th.*—I have just bade good-bye to Colonel Welchman. The poor old man is better, but sadly pulled down and aged. The doctors now think his arm may be saved, that it may remain on, but it will never be of the slightest use to him again, the elbow-joint is so much injured. He and Captain Brown start to-morrow night with a convoy of sick and wounded men and officers for Umbâla and the hills. Of these, the 1st Fusiliers form a sad proportion. With one or two exceptions, nothing could be better or more gallant than the conduct of this regiment. Jacob, Greville, Wriford, all admirable in the field, and the younger officers beyond all praise; Butler, F. Brown, Owen, and Warner, markedly so. In all the worst of the awful heat, dust, fatigue, work, and privation—and all have been beyond description—our plucky fellows have not only kept up their own spirits, but been an example and pattern to the camp. If any one was down in his luck, he had only to go to the Fusiliers' mess and be jolly.

The story in the papers about the boot was essentially correct for once, though how they should have got hold of it I do not know, for I never mentioned it even to you, since it certainly could not be called a wound, though a very narrow escape from one. A rascally Pandy made a thrust at my horse, which I parried, when he seized his "tulwar" in both hands, bringing it down like a sledge-hammer; it caught on the iron of my anti-gropelos legging, which it broke into the skin, cut through the stirrup-leather and took a slice off my boot and stocking; and yet, wonderful to say, the sword did not penetrate the skin. Both my horse and myself were staggered by the force of the blow, but I recovered myself quickly, and I don't think that Pandy will ever raise his "tulwar" again. I should not have entered into all these details about self but for those tiresome papers having made so much of it. The fight on that day (the 14th) was the old story. An attack in force on the right of our position; the enemy were allowed to blaze away, expending powder, and doing us no harm, until 4 P.M., when a column was sent down to turn them out of the gardens and villages they had occupied, and drive them back to the city. I had just returned from a long day's work with the cavalry, miles away in the rear, and had come back as far as Light's advanced battery. I was chatting with him for a few minutes *en passant*, when I saw the column pass down. I joined it, and sent for a few horsemen to accompany me, and when we got under fire, I found the Guide Infantry, under Shebbeare, had been sent to join in the attack. I accompanied them, and while the Fusiliers and Coke's men were driving the mass of the enemy helter-skelter through the gardens to our right, I went, with the Guides, Ghoorkhas, and part of the Fusiliers, along the Grand Trunk Road leading right into the gates of Delhi. We were exposed to a heavy fire of grape from the walls, and musketry from behind trees and rocks; but pushing on, we drove them right up to the very walls, and then were ordered to retire. This was done too quickly by the artillery, and some confusion ensued, the troops hurrying back too fast. The consequence was, the enemy rallied, bringing up infantry, then a large body of cavalry, and behind them again two guns to bear on us. There were very few of our men, but I managed to get eight horsemen to the front. Shebbeare, though wounded, aided me in rallying some Guide Infantry, and Greville and Jacob (whose horse had just been shot) coming up, brought a few scattered Fusiliers forward. I called on the men to fire, assuring them that the body of cavalry coming down would never stand. I got a few men to open fire: my gallant Guides stood their ground like men; Shebbeare, Jacob, Greville, and little Butler came to the front, and the mass of the enemy's cavalry, just as I said, stopped, reeled, turned, and fled in confusion; the guns behind them were for the moment deserted, and I tried hard to get up a charge to capture them; we were within thirty paces; twenty-five resolute men would have been enough; but the soldiers were blown, and could not push on in the face of such odds, unsupported as we were, for the whole of the rest of the troops had retired. My eight horsemen stood their ground, and the little knot of officers used every exertion to aid us, when suddenly two rascals rushed forward with lighted portfires in their hands, fired the guns, loaded with grape, in our faces, and when the smoke cleared away, we found to our infinite disgust and chagrin, that they had limbered up the guns and were off at a gallop. We had then to effect our retreat to rejoin the column, under a heavy fire of grape and musketry, and many men and officers were hit in doing it. I managed to get the Guides to retire quietly, fighting as they went, and fairly checking the enemy, on which I galloped back and brought up two guns, when we soon stopped all opposition, and drove the last Pandy into Delhi. My Guides stood firm, and, as well as my new men, behaved admirably; not so all who were engaged, and it was in consequence of that poor Chamberlain got wounded; for seeing a hesitation among the troops he led, who did not like the look of a wall lined with Pandies, and stopped short instead of going up to it, he leaped his horse clean over the wall into the midst of them, and dared the men to follow, which they did, but he got a ball in the shoulder. There is not a braver heart or cooler head in camp; his fault is too great hardihood and exposure in the field, and a sometimes too injudicious indifference to his own life or that of his men. We are in a nice fix here; General Reed is so ill he is ordered away at once; Chamberlain is on his back for six weeks at least; Norman, however, is safe and doing admirably; were he to be hit, the "headquarters" would break down altogether. There will be no assault on Delhi yet; our rulers will now less than ever decide on a bold course; and truth to tell, the numbers of the enemy have so rapidly increased, and ours have been so little replenished in proportion, and our losses, for a small army, have been so severe, that it becomes a question, whether now we have numbers sufficient to risk an assault. Would to Heaven it had been tried when I first pressed it.

*July* 17*th.*—But little private writing for me to-day, as I have only just come back from Brigadier Hope Grant's tent, whither I went on business, and I have been fully occupied with news-writers *cum multis aliis.* I begin to think of giving up this Quartermaster-General's work now that times are so changed. I began with poor General Anson, " under his Excellency's personal orders ; " I continued this work under General Barnard at his request, and now for these last days under General Reed; but he too is incapacitated by sickness, age, and anxiety, and goes off to the hills to-night. Colonel Curzon left for Simla yesterday. Colonel Congreve also goes, so the headquarters of the army are finally breaking up. The Adjutant-General (Chamberlain) is badly wounded, the Quartermaster-General (Colonel Becher) ditto, though he does work a little in-doors, if one may use such an expression of a tent, but he ought not to do even that much, so badly hurt as he is. Colonel Young, Norman, and myself are therefore the only representatives of the headquarter staff, except the doctors and commissaries. The headquarters of the army are now at Calcutta, General Pat Grant's arrival having been announced, and this army has dropped into merely a field force, commanded by Brigadier Wilson as senior, with the rank of Brigadier-General. I can hardly reconcile myself to throw up the Intelligence Department now that I have had the trouble of getting it into working order ; but for my own sake I must do so, for it is a terrible drag on me, and ties me down too much. I am wonderfully well, thank God ! and able to get through as much work as any man ; but commanding two regiments, and being eyes and ears of the army too, is really too much ! Shebbeare and Macdowell are appointed to my regiment in general orders—the former as second in command, but to continue for the present with the Guides ; the latter as adjutant, but to act as second in command also, for the present. I hope to have another officer or two in a few days, as more now devolves on poor Mac than his fragile frame can well stand. I wish his bodily strength was equal to his will and courage. It is hot, oh! how hot, and we can have nothing but a hand punkah occasionally; if our servants were to make off, we should indeed be in a pretty predicament, but hitherto they have been faithful and unmurmuring.

*July 19th.*—I was quite unable to write yesterday, as I went out long before daylight; so with the exception of a few minutes at 8 A.M. I was in the saddle until dark! We had a smart engagement in the afternoon. I was sent for to take the Guide cavalry down into the suburbs to support some guns, and assist in driving the enemy back into the city. My own men, whose duty was the difficult one of enduring a very hot fire without acting, behaved admirably, and I had the satisfaction of losing only one killed, and two wounded, besides a few horses, who generally come off second best where bullets are flying about. My poor "Feroza" was hit by one, but not dangerously, and I was again most mercifully preserved unharmed. I was out again early this morning reconnoitring, and have only just returned in time to write even so much, too much of myself as usual for my own feeling, but you will have it so.

*July 20th.*—I had a very fatiguing, because sunshiny, ride yesterday, and a troublesome species of reconnaissance, to prevent the enemy getting into our rear. Their name is indeed "legion" compared with us. I should say, from all I can ascertain by the newsletters, that there cannot be less than 36,000 * fighting men in Delhi, while we are barely a fifth of that number, including cavalry and all! Our position, however, is much strengthened, and we now beat them with half the trouble we had at first, their appetite for fighting being considerably lessened by having been so repeatedly driven back; but alas! we only drive them back, while we do not advance an inch. The odds have, moreover,

* It was ultimately ascertained that there were 70,000 or 75,000 !

fearfully increased against us by their continued accessions, and I confess I now see less and less hope of success in an assault; when I first urged it, the enemy had not more than 7000 Sepoys in the city, while we had two thousand infantry alone. Now, as I said before, the case is very different; for even were we to undertake an assault with a reasonable prospect of success, if they should in despair determine to defend the city inch by inch or street by street, we should not have men enough to secure our hold upon it. In that case the city people (all of whom are armed) would join in the fray, and considering what the consequences of failure would be, and farther, that to do this much we should be obliged to use up every man available, leaving no one, or next to none, to protect our camp, sick and wounded, from any attempt of the enemy, or of our questionable friends the country-people, it becomes a matter of serious and painful consideration. A want of success, moreover, would now be productive of infinite mischief. From hence to Allahabad, the fort of Agra and the Residency of Lucknow are the only spots where the British flag still flies. We are more to be considered now as an isolated band, fighting for our very name and existence in the midst of an enemy's country, than as an avenging army about to punish a rebel force. Sir H. Lawrence is holding out at Lucknow, but Cawnpore has fallen into the hands of the rebels. Sir Hugh Wheeler, after three weeks' contest, with, we hear, only 150 Europeans, in an evil hour capitulated, on condition of being provided with boats and a free passage to Allahabad; as soon as they were on board the boats, the whole were massacred! What became of the women and children we know not: it is hoped they might have been sent away earlier and escaped; otherwise it is horrible to think of what may have been their fate. Troops are collecting fast at Allahabad, and I hope moving on towards Cawnpore; some think we shall be forced to await their arrival at or near Delhi, before we can do anything effective. I trust earnestly that the city will not hold out so long. The people within it are immensely disheartened, and dissensions are rife among them. A split between the Hindoos and fanatic Mohammedans is almost inevitable, and above all, money is getting scarce. Meantime, this "waiting race" is very wearying to heart and body.

.... I have determined on giving up the Assistant Quartermaster-Generalship. It gives me more work than I really can manage in such weather, in addition to the command of two regiments. Macdowell promises admirably, and I trust there is every hope of our having a nice body of officers with "Hodson's Horse." Nothing further from Agra, beyond the assurance that all was well there.

*July 21st.*—Just returned from a long *reconnaissance*, and the post going out, so I have time but for little. Do not believe what the idle gossips say, of my "doing the work of two or three men." I strive to do my duty, but I cannot consider I do more. I do not run wanton risks, but I cannot stand by and see what ought to be done without risking something to do it. Had I not attempted what I did on the 14th, even with the insufficient means at my command, we should have been exposed to a disastrous loss of life, and to the discredit of a reverse. That we cannot afford. It is not only the possession of India which is at stake, not only our name and fame as Englishmen, but the safety, life, and honour of those nearest and dearest to us; were we to fail here, the horrible scenes of Meerut, Delhi, Rohilcund, Jhansee, and others, would be repeated in the Punjab and hill stations. Who, then, as husband, brother, father, son, would hesitate to face any danger, any risk, which tended to secure victory? I saw that our men were retiring (by order) in great confusion, that five minutes more and the whole party would be destroyed, and the fate of the column sealed, for the enemy's cavalry and guns were opening on us at speed. It was a natural impulse to rush forward, and nobly was I aided by Jacob and Greville, and my handful of gallant Guides; the tide was turned by the suddenness of the act; the enemy was driven back, and our men had time to breathe. This was not much to do, but it was a great deal to gain.

*July 22nd.*—Again but a few lines, for I have been regularly hunted all day. I told you that Sir H. Wheeler had capitulated, and been treacherously destroyed with his party; we have since heard that a force from Allahabad had reached Cawnpore under Colonel Neill of the Madras Fusiliers, that Sir H. Lawrence has been succoured, and that, in point of fact, our power up to Agra had been re-established. God grant this be true. Agra is safe, and all well; the troops which attacked it are afraid to come on here, and have halted at Muttra. The force in Delhi is much disheartened, and fights with gradually decaying energy. Already we have beaten them back in twenty-three fights, besides a few such affairs on my own private account, and though with considerable loss to us, yet with comparative ease, when you consider their overwhelming numbers. We had an engagement on the evening of the 20th, in which Colonel Seaton commanded our column, the 1st Fusiliers, 61st Foot, and Guides as usual. I had command of the Guide infantry, and led the advance as well as covered the retreat; and though we pushed close up to Delhi, we never had a shot fired from the walls until we had set out on our return to camp some way. Then they came howling after us like jackals, but the Guides were mindful of their old leader's voice, and steadily kept them in check during the whole distance, so completely that not a European soldier was under fire, and I only lost four men slightly wounded, while the enemy returned in utter discomfiture. Poor Light has been very ill, and Thompson has a bullet through his leg. Bishop is also wounded; he retains the same calm composure of manner under the hottest fire and hardest work, as he habitually exhibited on the Mall. These are excellent officers, but Tombs and Light are really splendid. I hope Chamberlain's arm will be saved; he is a noble fellow, but of course has his weaknesses.

*July 24th.*—I was unable to write yesterday. Pandy chose an unusually inconvenient hour for his attack, and kept us out until the afternoon, and then I was busied in attending to our poor friend Colonel Seaton, who, I grieve to say, was badly wounded, a musket-ball having entered his left breast and come out at his back, providentially passing outside the ribs instead of through his body; his lungs are, however, slightly injured, either by a broken rib or the concussion, and until it is ascertained to what extent this has gone, he is considered in danger. I do not myself think there is danger, as no unfavourable symptom has yet appeared, except a slight spitting of blood; but he is so patient and quiet that all is in his favour. I am deeply sorry for him, dear fellow! and fervently pray that he may be spared to us. There was little actual fighting; the rascals ran the instant they came into contact with our men; the only firing being behind banks and garden-walls. Colonel Drought, late 60th Native Infantry, was wounded; Captain Money of the Artillery got a bad knock on the knee-joint, and Law of the 10th Native Infantry killed; two killed and five wounded in the 1st Fusiliers, who as usual bore the brunt. After many discussions pro and con, it has been arranged that I retain the Intelligence Department and give up the Guides. My own men require great attention, as they are now in considerable numbers; so the General has begged me to relinquish the Guides instead of the Assistant Quartermaster-Generalship; the command of two regiments being an anomaly. I am very ready to do this, though I regret the separation from the men, and should have liked to have led my old corps into Delhi; but it is best as it is. You at least will rejoice that it greatly diminishes the risk to life and limb, which, I confess, lately has been excessive in my case. The General was very complimentary on my doings while commanding the Guides, and "trusted to receive equally invaluable services from my new regiment." I have little doubt of this, if I am spared. I find General Barnard reported no less than four times on my doings in the highest terms; and the last public letter he ever wrote was a special despatch to Government in my favour. It was, in fact, the only letter of the kind he ever wrote, for death intervened just as he was setting to work to bring those who had done well to the notice of Government.

They tell me I shall get pay for the Assistant Quartermaster-

General's Department, as well as my command allowance. For the Guides, of course I shall get nothing; but, I must say, I work, not like a "nigger," considering their work usually amounts to nil, but like a slave, in the Intelligence Department. There is no Paymaster here. We get money as we want it, from the field chest, as advances. I have been deeply shocked to hear that poor Christian, his young wife, and babes were among the murdered in Oudh. Also Colonel Goldney. . . . All is well at Agra; there are about 6000 individuals in the fort, with provisions for six months: they are probably relieved by now, for we hear that six English regiments were at Cawnpore on the 11th instant. This cheers up the men, and makes them think that Government has some thought for the gallant fellows here and elsewhere.

*July 25th.*—Well, yes, I did offer to go down the Doâb towards Agra and Cawnpore, to open the communication, and ascertain exactly where the reinforcements were, and assist them with cavalry in coming up towards Delhi. It would have been of real use, and not so dangerous as this eternal potting work here. I proposed to take 600 of my Horse, 250 infantry of the Guides, and four guns; could I not have made my way with these? I humbly opine I could. I do not mean to say it was not a bold stroke, but in Indian warfare I have always found "toujours l'audace" not a bad motto. I can never forget how much we have at stake, that we have a continent in arms against us; and I do think that every man should do not only his duty but his utmost in a crisis like the present.

*July 26th.*—A parcel with flannel shirts, &c., arrived last night. Those for the men I sent off to the hospital at once, to the doctors' great delight. Macdowell declares that the cap, his "jumpers," and the "baccy" must be in the box, and demands them imperiously. He is doing admirably, and promises to be a first-rate officer of light horse. He rides well, which is one good thing, and is brave as a lion's whelp, which is another. I only fear whether he has physical strength for such work in such weather. The whole country is a steaming bog. I keep my health wonderfully, thank God! in spite of heat, hard work, and exposure; and the men bear up like Britons. We all feel that Government ought to allow every officer and man before Delhi to count every month spent here as a year of service in India. There is much that is disappointing and disgusting to a man who feels that more might have been done, but I comfort myself with the thought, that history will do justice to the constancy and fortitude of the handful of Englishmen who have for so many weeks—months, I may say—of desperate weather, amid the greatest toil and hardship, resisted and finally defeated the worst and most strenuous exertions of an entire army and a whole nation in arms,—an army trained by ourselves, and supplied with all but exhaustless munitions of war, laid up by ourselves for the maintenance of our Empire. I venture to aver that no other nation in the world would have remained here, or have avoided defeat had they attempted to do so. The delay as yet has been both morally and politically bad in many ways, and the results are already beginning to be manifest, but in the end it will increase our prestige and the moral effects of our power. A nation which could conquer a country like the Punjab so recently with an Hindoostanee army, and then turn the energies of the conquered Sikhs to subdue the very army by which they were tamed; which could fight out a position like Peshawur for years in the very teeth of the Affghan tribes; and then, when suddenly deprived of the regiments which effected this, could unhesitatingly employ those very tribes to disarm and quell those regiments when in mutiny,—a nation which could do this is destined indeed to rule the world : and the races of Asia must succumb. This is a proud feeling, and nerves one's arm in many a time of difficulty and danger, as much almost as the conviction that we must conquer, or worse than death awaits us. The intelligence of Sir H. Wheeler's destruction came to us from too true a source to be doubted—it was in dear Sir Henry Lawrence's own handwriting; and has been confirmed, alas, too surely. All we do not know is whether the women and children were massacred with the men, or whether they escaped, or were reserved for a worse fate.

One of my news-letters reports that eighteen women are in prison under the care (?) of Nana Sahib (Bajee Rao Peishwar's adopted son), who attacked Cawnpore. You must remember at the artillery review a very "swell"-looking native gentleman, accompanied by another educated native, who spoke French and other European languages, and was talking a good deal to Alfred Light. Well, this was the identical Nana Sahib who has done all this, and who must even at that very time have been meditating the treachery, if not the murders.

There is not a word of truth in the report of "the King of Delhi coming out for a final struggle." Rumour has been saying so for weeks with no foundation; the truth is, the King is a mere puppet, a "ruse." He is old and well-nigh impotent, and is only used as authority for all the acts of rebellion and barbarity enacted by his sons. The rascals talk (in the city) of coming round on our rear, and attacking us in the field. I only wish they would, for in the open plain we should hunt them down like jackals. They escape us now by flying back into the city, or under cover of the heavy batteries from its walls. When (if ever) they do come out, the General has proposed to put the whole of the Irregular Cavalry under my command, and I trust to give a tolerable account of the enemy, and show that "Hodson's Horse" are capable of something even already.

Colonel Seaton is doing admirably, I am thankful to say. He is patient and gentle in suffering as a woman, and this helps his recovery wonderfully.

*July* 27*th*.—Since the 23d, hardly a shot has been fired here. The news-letters from the city mention meetings in the market-place and talkings at the corners of the streets, with big words of what they intend to do; but they (the people) are actually cowed and dispirited, while their rulers issue orders which are never obeyed.

I fear our movements wait upon theirs. We have no one in

power with a head to devise or a heart to dare any enterprise which might result in the capture of Delhi; and alas! one cannot but admit that it would require both a wise head and a very great heart to run the risk with so reduced a force as we have here now. 2200 Europeans and 1500 Native Infantry are all that we now can muster. We have reliable news from below, that on or about the 14th, General Havelock, with the first portion of the European force, met and attacked the villain Nana, near Futteypore (between Allahabad and Cawnpore), and beat him thoroughly, capturing his camp, twelve guns, and seven lac of rupees. The China troops had arrived: Lord Elgin having consented to the employment of the whole.

Sir P. Grant is coming up with these troops, "on dit," so that in six weeks from the date of the Meerut massacre, 11,000 European troops will have landed in India: what a providential arrival, and what a lesson to Asiatics that they can never contend with England.

This news has put the whole camp, even the croakers, of whom there are not a few, in high spirits. I only hope it is not too good to be true.

As a set-off against this, news has arrived that Tudor Tucker, his wife, and Sam Fisher are among the victims of this horrible insurrection, also poor James Thomason: and of his brother-in-law's, Dr. Hay's execution, there can be no longer a doubt. When shall we see the last; when know the full extent of these horrible atrocities? The accounts make one's blood run fire. Our dear Douglas Seaton has arrived in England, much restored by the voyage, but not, I fear, sufficiently recovered to return, as soon as he would hear of the outbreak. A sad blow for him, poor fellow, for had he been here to command the regiment, he would probably have been a full Colonel and C.B. at the end. I am seriously uneasy at receiving no letters from England, though mail after mail must have arrived, and some people get their letters! therefore, why not I mine? We get none even from Agra, and of course not below it, except by "Kossid," and they but little scraps, written half in Greek characters, to mislead or deceive, if the unfortunate bearer is stopped. They conceal them very ingeniously between the leather of their shoes, or tied up in their hair. I enclose one that came in even a more singular letter-bag than either, rolled up in a piece of wax and packed into a hollow tooth.

Norman tells me that —— was furious at my having the Guides, but was compelled to acquiesce in it, "as it was undoubtedly the best thing for the public service." How he must have winced when he was forced to confess that.

*July* 28*th*.—I have no news. The Pandies have not attacked us since the 23rd, and are much dispirited. In reply to your and Mrs. ——'s wish to come to Delhi as nurses, I must say honestly that there is no necessity for such a sacrifice. Our position here is very different from that in the Crimea and at Scutari. There the men died from want of care and of the ordinary necessaries of life. Here there is no absolute want of anything, except a genial climate and well-built hospitals, neither of which you could supply. The men are attended to immediately they are sick or wounded; and within an hour, sometimes half that time, of his being wounded, a soldier is in his bed, with everything actually necessary, and the greatest medical attention. Unless any unforeseen emergency should arise, I would strongly dissuade any lady from coming to camp.

The flannel garments are invaluable, and this is all that can be done for us by female hands at present. I send you to-day by post a little souvenir from Delhi. A Sepoy picked it up in a field and I bought it from him.

*July* 29*th*.—I have been so occupied with business all day that I have only time to say we have had no more fighting, and the whole atmosphere is still, but hot, oh, so hot. General Wilson is unwell, and will probably break down, like the rest. These sexagenarians are unfit for work in July. I expect Napier will be with the advancing troops. I sincerely hope so. He is the man to do something, if they will but let him.

*July* 31*st.*—I intended writing more fully to make up for my late shortcomings, but the Pandies permit it not. They made an attempt on our position this morning; nothing more, however, than a distant cannonade. A large party have moved round in our rear, and this has kept me in the saddle all day. I have just returned, after some hours of the heaviest rain I was ever out in, drenched to the skin, of course, and somewhat tired, so judge what a comfort a dry flannel shirt must be. There was no actual fighting, so with the exception of keeping us out so long, and a great expenditure of powder and shot, no harm was done.

*August* 1*st.*—The continued heavy rain promises to give me more time for pen work to-day, if no more takes place on this side of Pandy-monium. I had a long letter from Colonel Curzon last night, saying what I wished about my appointment to the Guides, and a good deal of pleasant assurance of General Anson's good-will towards me. We have fresh accounts from below that every European woman and child have been ruthlessly murdered at Cawnpore. The details are too revolting to put on paper and make one's blood boil. Mothers with infants in their arms murdered with fiendish cruelty, and worse than all, two young girls just arrived from England are said to have been only saved to meet a worse fate in some Mussulman's zenana. There will be a day of reckoning for these things, and a fierce one, or I have been a soldier in vain. You say there is a great difference between doing one's duty and running unnecessary risks, and you say truly; the only question is, what is one's duty. Now, I might, as I have more than once, see things going wrong at a time and place when I might be merely a spectator, and not " on duty," or ordered to be there, and I might feel that by exposing myself to danger for a time I might rectify matters, and I might therefore think it right to incur that danger; and yet if I were to get hit, it would be said "he had no business there;" nor should I, as far as the rules of the service go, though in my own mind I should have been satisfied that I was right. These are times when every man should do his best, his utmost, and not say, "No; though I see I can do good there, yet, as I have not been ordered and am not on duty, I will not do it." This is not my idea of a soldier's duty, and hitherto the results have proved me right. Poor Eaton Travers, of Coke's regiment, was killed this morning. He had just come from England *via* Bombay, with a young wife, whom he left at Lahore. Poor young thing, a sad beginning and end for her. We send off convoys of the sick and wounded to Umbâla, where we hear they are well tended and are doing well. Even here everything possible is done for them; Dr. Brougham is an excellent man and first-rate surgeon, quite the man of the camp in his line; clever, indefatigable, and humane. So also is Dr. Clark who joined us yesterday. Reynell Taylor is at Kangra, and doing good work there.

*2nd.*—The rebels attacked us about 5 P.M. yesterday, and kept us at it till seven or eight this morning. Our people kept steadily at their posts and behind entrenchments, and drove them back with steady volleys every time they came near. The result was, that they were punished severely, while our loss was a very trifling one, not more than half-a-dozen Europeans killed and wounded; it is next to impossible ever to ascertain accurately what the enemy's loss is.

Colonel Seaton is doing well; in three weeks' time I hope he will be about again. Before this surely our rulers will consent to take Delhi. Sickness is on the increase, and we have been nearly losing another General. General Wilson was very ill for a few days, but is now better. He is older, however, by ten years than he was. The responsibility and anxiety of what is certainly a very difficult position, have been too much for him, and he has got into the way of being nervous and alarmed, and over-anxious even about trifles, which shakes one's dependence on his judgment. These men are personally as brave as lions, but they have not big hearts or heads enough for circumstances of serious responsibility. This word is the bugbear which hampers all our proceedings. Would we could have had Sir Henry Lawrence as our leader; we should have been in Delhi weeks ago. I hope Colonel Napier is coming up with the force. He has head, and heart, and nerve, and the moral courage to act as if he had; we hear that the crisis is passing; all below Cawnpore is safe, and all above Kurnâl to Peshawur; while Lord W. Hay keeps the more important hill stations steady. When all is over, our power will be stronger than ever, principally because we shall have got rid of our great sore, a native army.

*3rd.*—4 P.M. and I have only just got out of the saddle, and found on my arrival in camp the heaviest news that has yet reached us. Report says that Sir Henry Lawrence is dead! The news wants confirmation.

*4th.*—God grant, for his country's sake and for mine, that it be not true. To the country his death would be worse than the loss of a province; to me it would be the loss of my truest and most valued friend. I hope, yet fear to hope, that it may be a false report; yet what soldier would wish a more noble, a more brilliant end to such a career? Havelock has captured all the enemy's guns, and inflicted severe punishment. The destruction of Sir Hugh Wheeler and his party is fully confirmed, and Havelock was too late to save the unfortunate women and children, who were massacred in their prison, before his arrival, by their guards. Such fiends as these our arms have never met with in any part of the world. May our vengeance be as speedy as it will unquestionably be sure!

We (Hodson's Horse) are getting on very comfortably, and are going to start a mess on our own account, so as to be ready to march without difficulty when required.

*5th.*—The letter I annex* from Colonel Tytler gives good

---

* "CAWNPORE, *July* 26*th.*

"General Havelock has crossed the river to relieve Lucknow, which will be effected four days hence.

"We shall probably march to Delhi to-morrow, with 4000 or 5000 Europeans, and a heavy artillery, in number, *not* weight.

"The China force is in Calcutta, 5000 men. More troops expected immediately. We shall soon be with you.—Yours truly,

"B. A. TYTLER,
*Lieut.-Col. Quartermaster-General,
Movable Column.*"

news, and the man who brought the letter says there were fourteen steamers and flats at Cawnpore when he left. The troops had taken Bithoor, the Nana's place, and at first it was uninjured, but the bodies of some English women were found inside the Nana's house, on which the European soldiers, excited to irresistible fury, destroyed every human being in the place, and then demolished the building, not leaving one stone upon another. The Nana himself, with his family, took refuge in a boat on the river, and the native accounts add that he sunk it, and all were drowned. This I strongly doubt; such Spartan heroism could scarcely exist in the mind of one who could violate and massacre helpless women and children.

*6th.*—Small chance of much writing to-day, for just as I have got into camp, after some hours' attendance on the pleasure of the Pandies, who came out in force and threatened an attack, I find that I have to start on a long reconnoitring expedition, from which I cannot return till late at night. This is unfortunate, as I have much pen work on hand, my necessary official writing being very onerous. I was obliged to write as long a letter as I could to Lord W. Hay, if but to thank him, in my own and others' name, for the comforts he so thoughtfully sent us.

*7th.*—I returned at three o'clock this morning from a forty miles' ride over the worst and wettest country I was ever in, and I am thoroughly exhausted, though everybody is wanting something, and I must attend to business first, and then to rest.

*8th.*—I could write nothing but official papers all the sedentary part of yesterday. I did not get in till 9 P.M. I do trust that when the 52nd arrive, we may be allowed to do something better than this pot-shot work. Nicholson has come on a-head, and is a host in himself, if he does not go and get knocked over as Chamberlains did. The camp is all alive at the notion of something decisive taking place soon, but I cannot rally from the fear of dear Sir Henry's fate. How many of my friends are gone. My heart is divided between grief for those precious victims, and deep gratitude to God for my own safety and that of those dearest to me. May He in His mercy preserve me for further exertion and an ultimate reunion, and if not, His will be done. I have a letter from an unfortunate woman, a Mrs. Leeson, who was saved from the slaughter at Delhi, on May 11th, by an Affghan lad, after she had been wounded, and her child slaughtered in her arms. She is still concealed in the Affghan's house  I heard that there was a woman there, and managed to effect a communication with her, through one of the Guides, and to send her money, &c., and so I think the poor creature may be preserved till we enter Delhi, if we fail in getting her free before. I fear she is the only European, or rather the only Christian (for she herself is hardly European), left alive from the massacre. Her husband was the son of Major Leeson, and a clerk in a Government office in Delhi. I have sent one of our few prisoners up to Forsyth at Umbâla, whom we ironically call the "Maid of Delhi," though her age and character are questionable, and her ugliness undoubted. She actually came out on horseback, and fought against us like a fiend. The General at first released her, but knowing how mischievous she would be among those superstitious Mohammedans, I persuaded him to let her be recaptured, and made over for safe custody.

Our General since his illness has got a still greater dread of responsibility, and ceased to be nearly as vigorous even as heretofore. Would indeed that we had had Sir H. Lawrence here: that he may have been, and still be spared to us, is my prayer! The consequences of longer delay will be more and more disastrous to the health of the troops. Captain Daly has not formally reassumed command of the Guides, though he virtually does all the sedentary work. By an arrangement which I cannot but think unwise, and which deprives the corps of two-thirds of its value, they have separated the regiment into two, putting the cavalry into the Cavalry Brigade under Hope Grant, and the infantry at the other end of the camp under Shebbeare.

The Guides should not be separated, and should be kept as much apart as maybe from other corps. No regiment in the world have done or will do better than they, with a little prudence, and under an officer whom they like and can trust. My own regiment is also in the Cavalry Brigade, and is very hardworked. It is bad for a young and unformed corps, but there is such a scarcity of cavalry here, that I cannot even remonstrate, and I get no small amount of κῦδος for having so large a number of men fit to be put on duty within two months of receiving the order to raise a regiment. I shall have two more troops in with the 52nd, and Nicholson has given me fifty Affghans, just joined him from Peshawur, which, added to thirty coming with Alee Reza Khan from Lahore, will complete an Affghan troop as a counterpoise to my Punjabees.*

We expect the movable column on the 12th or 13th, weather permitting, and some other troops a day or two after. Sir P. Grant is supposed to be at Cawnpore, but we have no tidings later than Colonel Tytler's letter. There is no actual fighting going on here, nothing except the usual cannonade. The rebels being out, guns on all sides, and fire away day and night, but bring no troops forward, and as we act strictly on the defensive, we merely reply to their guns with ours. The whole affair is reduced to a combat of artillery, our leader's favourite arm, excellent when combined with the other two, but if he expects to get into Delhi with that alone, I guess he will find himself mistaken. The news of disaffection in the city is daily confirmed. On the 7th a powder manufactory exploded, and they suspended the minister, Hakeem Ahsanoolah, and searched his house; there they found a letter which had been sent him, concocted by Moulvie Rujub Alee, which confirmed their suspicions, so they plundered and burnt his house, while he himself was only saved by taking refuge in the palace with the king, his master, who it seems is kept close prisoner there, his sons giving all orders, and ruling with a rod of iron. They say, however, that the king has got leave to send his wives and women out of the Ajmere gate to the

---

* The uniform of "Hodson's Horse" was a dust-coloured tunic, with a scarlet sash worn over the shoulder, and scarlet turban, which gained them the name of "The Flamingos."

Kootub. I trust it may be so, for we do not war with women, and should be sadly puzzled to know what to do with them as prisoners.

*August* 11*th*.—The bridge over the Jumna resists all efforts for its destruction. Our engineers have tried their worst, and failed. I have tried all that money could do, to the extent of 6000 rupees, but equally in vain. So there it remains for the benefit of the enemy, whose principal reinforcements come from that side of the city. Two messengers of my own, arrived from Lucknow, leave little hope of dear Sir Henry's life having been spared. I grieve as for a brother. . . . Talking of jealousies, one day, under a heavy fire, Captain —— came up to me, and begged me to forget and forgive what had passed, and only to remember that we were soldiers fighting together in a common cause. The time and place, as well as his manner, appealed to my better feelings, so I held out my hand at once. Nowadays, we must stand by and help each other, and forget all injuries, and rise superior to them, or, God help us! we should be in terrible plight.

*August* 12*th*.—This morning a force under Colonel Showers moved down before daybreak towards the city, or rather the gardens outside the city gates, and gave the enemy, who had been ensconced behind the garden walls for a couple of days, and given our pickets annoyance, a good thrashing, taking four of their guns, and inflicting a heavy loss. All were back in camp by seven P.M., so it was a very comfortable little affair. Our fellows did admirably. Captain Greville captured one gun with a handful of men, getting slightly wounded in the act. Showers himself, Coke, and young Owen, were also wounded, and poor young Sheriff of the 2nd mortally so; the loss among the men was small in proportion to the success. The return to camp was a scene worth witnessing, the soldiers bringing home in triumph the guns they had captured, a soldier with musket and bayonet fixed riding each horse, and brave young Owen astride one gun, and dozens clinging to and pushing it, or rather them, along with might and main, and cheering like mad things. I was in the thick of it by accident, for I was looking on as well as I could through the gloom, when

Coke asked me to find Brigadier Showers and say he was wounded, and that the guns were taken. I found Showers himself wounded, and then had to find a field officer to take command, after which, I assisted generally in drawing off the men—the withdrawal or retirement being the most difficult matter always, and requiring as much steadiness as an attack.

*August* 13*th.*—I wish I could get some pay, but money is terribly scarce and living dear, my favourite beverage, tea, particularly so. I have therefore sent to Umbâla for some.

Poor Light has been brought very low by dysentery, and can hardly crawl about, but about he persists in going, brave fellow as he is. Greville is, I am thankful to say, not badly wounded, and as plucky as ever. All well at Agra: no news from below.

*August* 14*th.*—On returning from a rather disheartening reconnaissance to-day, I found letters which soothed and comforted my weary spirit, just as a sudden gleam of sunlight brightens a gloomy landscape, and brings all surrounding objects into light and distinctness.

A letter from good Douglas Seaton was among them. He little thought that so soon after his departure we should all be moving downwards, and that I should receive his letter in his brother's tent in "Camp before Delhi:" his own dearly loved regiment (1st European Bengal Fusiliers) "next door" to us. How wonderfully uncertain everything is in India. I am interrupted by orders to start to-night for Rohtuck, and must go and make arrangements.

## CHAPTER III.

*SIEGE OF DELHI, CONTINUED—ROHTUCK EXPEDITION— ASSAULT—DELHI TAKEN—CAPTURE OF KING—CAPTURE AND EXECUTION OF SHAHZADAHS.*

BOHUK, NEAR ROHTUCK, *August* 17*th*.

I HAVE been unable to write since we left Delhi, as we have been incessantly marching, and had no means of communicating with any one. Even now I am doubtful whether this will reach camp. We left Delhi during the night of the 14th–15th, and marched to Khurkundah, a large village, in which I had heard that a great number of the rascally Irregulars had taken refuge. We surprised and attacked the village. A number of the enemy got into a house, and fought like devils; but we mastered them and slew the whole. Yesterday we marched on here, intending to reconnoitre and harass "à la Cosaque" a large party of horsemen and foot, with two guns, who have been moving along from Delhi, plundering the wretched villagers *en route*, and threatening to attack Hansie. They, however, thought discretion the better part of valour, and hearing of our approach, started off at a tangent before we got near enough to stop them.

We have been drenched with rain, so I am halting to dry and feed both men and horses, and then we go on to Rohtuck. I have nearly 300 men and five officers — Ward, Wise, the two Goughs, and Macdowell—all first-rate soldiers. I have eighty Guides, and the rest my own men, who do wonderfully, considering how sadly untrained and undisciplined they are. We are roughing it in more ways than one, and the sun is terribly hot; but we are all well and in high spirits, for though it is a bold game to play, I am too careful to run unnecessary risks, or get into a fix. I have done a good deal already, and shall, I hope, recover Rohtuck to-day, when I do trust the authorities will consent to keep it, and not let us have the work to do twice over, as at Bhâgput.

---

*To* COLONEL BECHER, *Quartermaster-General.*

MY DEAR COLONEL,—We are getting on very well. I hope to take Rohtuck to-day, and I trust arrangements will be made for keeping it. The country will then be quiet from Hansie to Delhi. The Jheend Rajah should be told to take care of the district. I believe Greathed did make this arrangement, but Barnes put some spoke in the way, so that the Rajah is uncertain how to act. Please tell Greathed from me that there is nothing now to prevent the restoration of order here. I wish I had a stronger party, for though I feel quite comfortable myself, yet I should like more troops, for the sake of the men, who are not quite so easy in their minds. The road by Alipore, Boanah, and Khurkundah is the best. The canal is easily fordable at Boanah, and just below that place (at the escape) it is quite dry, the banks having given way. We polished off the Khurkundah gentry in style, though they showed fight to a great extent. It has had a wonderfully calming effect on the neighbourhood. I hope the Jheend troops, or some troops, may be sent here. The Jheend men would more than suffice.—Yours very sincerely, W. S. R. HODSON.

---

CAMP, DUSSEEAH, NEAR ROHTUCK, 19*th August.*

This is the first rest since Bohur; we have had very hard work, great heat, and long exposure; but, thank God, are all well and safe, and have done some business. I marched from Bohur on the evening of the 17th. On reaching Rohtuck, we found the Mussulman portion of the people, and a crowd of Irregulars drawn up on the walls, while a considerable party were on a mound outside. I had ridden forward with Captain Ward and a few orderlies to see how the land lay, when the rascals fired, and ran towards us. I sent word for my cavalry to come up, and rode slowly back myself, in order to tempt them out, which had partly the desired effect, and as soon as my leading troop came up, we dashed at them and drove them helter-skelter into the town, killing all we overtook. We then encamped in what was the Kutcherry compound, and had a grateful rest and a quiet night. The representatives of the better-disposed part of the population came out to me, and amply provided us with supplies for both man and beast. The rest were to have made their "amende" in the morning; but a disaffected Rangur went off early, and brought up 300 Irregular horsemen of the mutineers—1st, 13th, 14th, and other rebels—and having collected about 1000 armed rascals on foot, came out to attack my little party of barely 300 sabres and six officers. The Sowars dashed at a gallop up the road, and came boldly enough up to our camp. I had a few minutes before fortunately received notice of their intentions, and as I had kept the horses ready saddled, we were out and at them in a few seconds. To drive them scattering back to the town was the work of only as many more, and I then, seeing their numbers, and the quantity of matchlocks brought against us from gardens and enclosures, determined to draw them out into the open country; and the "ruse" was eminently successful. I had quietly sent off our little baggage unperceived half-an-hour before, so that I was, as I intended, perfectly free and unfettered by *impedimenta* of any sort. I then quietly and gradually drew off troop after troop into the open plain about a mile to the rear, covering the movement with skirmishers. My men, new as well as old, behaved coolly and admirably throughout, though the fire was very annoying, and a retreat is always discouraging, even when you have an object in view. My officers, fortunately first-rate ones, behaved like veterans, and everything went on to my complete satisfaction. Exactly what I had anticipated happened. The enemy thought we were bolting, and came on in crowds, firing and yelling, and the Sowars brandishing their swords as if we were already in their hands, when suddenly I gave the order, "Threes about, and at them." The men obeyed with a cheer; the effect was electrical; never was such a scatter. I launched five parties at them, each under an officer, and in they went, cutting and firing into the very thick of them. The ground was very wet, and a ditch favoured them, but we cut down upwards of fifty in as many seconds. The remainder flew back to the town, as if, not the Guides and Hodson's Horse, but death and the devil were at their heels. Their very numbers encumbered them, and the rout was most complete. Unfortunately I had no ammunition left, and therefore could not without imprudence remain so close to a town filled with matchlock men, so we marched quietly round to the north of the town, and encamped near the first friendly village we came to, which we reached in the early afternoon. Our success was so far complete, and I am most thankful to say with very trifling loss, only two men rather severely wounded, eight in all touched, and a few horses hit. Macdowell did admirably, as indeed did all. My new men, utterly untrained as they are, many unable to ride or even load their carbines properly, yet behaved beyond my most sanguine expectations for a first field, and this success, without loss, will encourage them greatly.

This morning I was joined by a party of Jheend horse, whom my good friend the Rajah sent as soon as he heard I was coming Rohtuck-wards, so I have now 400 horsemen, more or less, fresh ammunition having come in this morning, and am quite independent. I hear also that the General has at my recommendation sent out some troops in this direction; if so, order will be permanently restored in this district. In three days we have frightened away and demoralised a force of artillery, cavalry and infantry some 2000 strong, beat those who stood or returned to fight us, twice, in spite of numbers, and got fed and furnished forth by the rascally town itself.* Moreover, we have thoroughly cowed the whole neighbourhood, and given them a taste of what more they will get unless they keep quiet in future. One of the men killed was a brute of the 14th Irregular Cavalry, who committed such butchery at Jhansi. No letters have reached me since I left camp, and I am not sure that this will reach there safely. It is a terribly egotistical detail, and I am thoroughly ashamed of saying so much of myself, but you insisted on having a full, true, and particular account, so do not think me vainglorious.

LURSOWLIE, *August 22nd.*—I rode over to this place from our little camp at Sonput, eight miles off, to see Saunders and Colonel Durnsford. I find that two of my new troops have been detained on the road, but will reach Delhi in a day or two, and others from Lahore will soon arrive. I think the business at Rohtuck has been very creditable to us, but I can write no more than the assurance of our safety and well-being.

CAMP, SONPUT, *August 23rd.*—I could only write a few hurried lines yesterday. Late in the evening I got a note from General Wilson, desiring me to look out for and destroy the 10th Light Cavalry mutineers from Ferozepoor. He authorised my proceeding to Jheend, but without going through the Rohtuck district. Now, as to do this would involve an immense detour, and insure my being too late, and consequently having a long and fatiguing march for my pains, I wrote back to explain this, and requested more definite instructions. He must either say distinctly "do

---

\* *Extract from Letter of* MAJOR-GENERAL WILSON.

"The Major-General commanding the force having received from Lieutenant Hodson a report of his proceedings and operations from the 14th, when he left camp, till his return on the 24th, has much pleasure in expressing to that officer his thanks for the able manner in which he carried out the instructions given him. The Major-General's thanks are also due to the European and native officers and men composing the detachment, for their steady and gallant behaviour throughout the operations, particularly on the 17th and 18th inst., at Rohtuck, when they charged and dispersed large parties of horse and foot."

this or that," and I will do it; or he must give me *carte blanche* to do what he wants in the most practicable way, of which I, knowing the country, can best judge. I am not going to fag my men and horses to death, and then be told I have exceeded my instructions. He gives me immense credit for what I have done, but "almost wishes I had not ventured so far." The old gentleman means well, but does not understand either the country or the position I was in, nor does he appreciate a tenth part of the effects which our bold stroke at Rohtuck, forty-five miles from camp, has produced. "*N'importe*," they will find it out sooner or later. I hear both Chamberlain and Nicholson took my view of the case, and supported me warmly.

I am much gratified by General Johnstone's exertions in my favour, though I have not the slightest idea that they will eventuate in anything; but the motive is the same. Let me do what I will, I have made up my mind to gain nothing but the approval of my own conscience. I foresee that I shall remain a subaltern, and the easy-going majors of brigade, aides-de-camp, and staff officers will all get brevets, C.B.s, &c., for simply living in camp, and doing their simple duties mildly and without exertion. The Victoria Cross, I confess, is the highest object of my ambition, and had I been one of fortune's favourites I should have had it ere now even, but I have learnt experience in a rough school, and am prepared for the worst; but whether a lieutenant or lieutenant-general, I trust I shall continue to do my duty, to the best of my judgment and ability, as long as strength and sense are vouchsafed to me.

CAMP, DELHI, *August* 24*th*.—I returned here this morning at 2 P.M., very tired and unwell, and not able to write much, for I have been obliged to have recourse to the doctor.

I am to have a surgeon attached to my regiment at once, as I represented how cruel it was to send us out on an expedition without a doctor or a grain of medicine. We had eight wounded men, and two officers had fever on the road, and nothing but the most primitive means of relieving them. I asked for Dr. Charles, but there are so many senior to him waiting for a turn, that I must be content for the present with what I can get. I hope, however, to have Charles ultimately, for he is skilful, clever, a gentleman, and a Christian.

Nicholson has just gone out to look after a party of the enemy with twelve guns, who had moved out yesterday towards Nujjufghur, threatening to get into our rear. I wanted to have gone with him, but I was laughingly told to stay at home and nurse myself, and let some one else have a chance of doing good service. This was too bad, especially as Nicholson wished me to go.

*26th.*—It is 4 P.M., and I am only just free from people and papers, but good news must make up for brevity. General Nicholson has beaten the enemy gloriously at Nujjufghur, whither he pushed on last evening. He has taken thirteen guns, and all the camp equipage and property. Our loss was small for the gain, but two of the killed were officers—young Lumsden of Coke's Corps, a most promising fellow, and Dr. Ireland. The victory is a great one, and will shake the Pandies' nerves, I calculate. All their shot and ammunition were also captured. The 1st Fusiliers were as usual "to the fore," and did well equally as usual. I am much disappointed at not having been there, but Mactier would not hear of it, as the weather was bad, and I should have run the risk of another attack of dysentery, from which I have been suffering. I cannot sufficiently condemn the idle tongues and foolish brains that concocted such absurd stories about me in the Rohtuck business. We were never in any extremity whatever, nor did I ever feel the slightest anxiety, or cease to feel that I was master of the situation. Danger there must always be in war, but none of our own creating, as the fools and fearful said, ever existed.

*August 27th.*—I have been up to my eyes in work all day again, and not had the pen out of my hand all day, except when on horseback with the men. Two troops arrived yesterday, and I have 250 spare horses to mount them, so that we are getting on by degrees. Such an experiment as raising a regiment actually in camp on active (and very active) service, was never tried before.

*28th.*—I am somewhat surprised at not hearing from Agra, but I cannot be sure that my letter reached there, as several of the "Kossids" have been "scragged" on the road. Sir P. Grant will not have a long course to run, as Sir Colin Campbell has been sent out to command, and is in India, I fancy, by this time. Havelock, we hear, has retreated, leaving Lucknow still unrelieved. I cannot understand this, but we have not sufficient information to enable us to judge. After all, Nicholson is the general after my heart.

*29th.*—I have just returned from a ride of twelve hours, leaving camp at three A.M., on a reconnoitring expedition, and have only time before the dâk closes to say that I am safe and well. I found no enemy, and everything quiet in the direction of Nujjufghur, where I was to-day, over and beyond Nicholson's field of battle of the 25th.

*30th.*—I have been writing and listening all this morning till I am tired, a man having come in from Delhi, with much assurance and great promises; but he was sent back rather humbler than he came, for he fancied he should make terms, and could not get a single promise of even bare life for any one, from the king downwards. If I get into the palace, the house of Timur will not be worth five minutes' purchase, I ween; but what my share in this work will be, no one can say, as there will be little work for horsemen, and I do not now command any infantry to give me an excuse. I hope Sir C. Campbell will be here to lead us into the city, which seems probable at our present rate of no-progress. He is a very good man for the post of Commander-in-Chief, as he has had great experience in India and elsewhere, and that, recent experience. Mansfield comes out with him as chief of the staff, with the rank of Major-General.

*31st.*—I have little public news for you: all is expected here. The siege train will be in by the 3rd or 4th, I fancy, and then I trust there will be no more waiting.

The letters from Agra show that a much greater and more formidable amount of insurrection exists than we were prepared to believe. Large bodies of insurgents have collected in different places all over the country, all well supplied with arms and guns. These are under the orders of different Nawabs, Rajahs, and big men, who think that now is their time for rule. None of these will be formidable as soon as the army is disposed of, but for a long time to come we shall have marching and fighting, punishing and dispersing, and it is to be expected that bodies of the fugitives from Delhi will join the standards of these insurgent leaders, and give us trouble here and there. The fall of Delhi will not be the end, but rather the beginning of a new campaign in the field; but the very day the active portion of the work is over, I shall ask to go to some good station, and organise and discipline my regiment, and get it properly equipped, and fit for service. At present it is merely an aggregation of untutored horsemen, ill-equipped, half clothed, badly provided with everything, quite unfit for service in the usual sense of the term, and only forced into the field because I have willed that it shall be so; but it would take six months' constant work to fit it properly for service. Generally when a regiment is raised, it is left quietly at one station until the commanding officer reports it "fit for service," and it has been inspected and reported on by a general officer, when it is brought "on duty" by order of the Commander-in-Chief. My idea of being able to raise a regiment when in the field, and on actual, and very active service, was ridiculed and pooh-poohed, but I stuck to it that it could be done, and General Anson was only too willing I should try, hitherto with success, and with the considerable gain, to an army deficient in cavalry, of having a good body of horsemen brought at once on duty in the field. How long it may be before I am able to get to a quiet station for the purpose required it is impossible to foresee. I shall try to get sent to Umbâla, or as near the Punjab as possible, because my men are all drawn from thence, and it will be easier to recruit, than at a greater distance from Sikhland. I have got six full troops, and another is on its way down.

*September 1st.*—This is muster-day, and a very busy one to me, but I have written a minute letter to go by Kossid to Agra once more. The poor wretch who took my last was murdered on the road, so of course the letter never reached Agra. The dâk by Meerut is again suspended, so we can only send by Kossid. I have to-day got a new subaltern, a Mr. Baker, late of the 60th Native Infantry, and a doctor, so we are seven in all. I could not succeed in getting Dr. Charles just yet, but hope to do so eventually. Little Nusrut Jung has been allowed to come to me from the Guides, and I have made him a jemadar at once. More than half the Guides want to come to my new corps, but this is of course out of the question. I am sending for Heratees, and Candaharees, the farther from Hindoostan the better. Mr. Ricketts, too, is collecting men from his district. I have at present 200 spare horses, but as I am to raise 1200 or 1400 men, I fear mounting them will be a difficulty; it is very difficult to work in a camp on service where so little can be got or bought. Here come more news-letters from the city, and myriads of notes, besides post time and parade, all at once! I shall be glad when Delhi falls, and I cease to be *Times*, *Morning Chronicle*, and *Post* all in one!\*

2*nd.*— . . . "Hodson's Horse" made a very respectable show indeed last evening, when paraded altogether for the first time, and I was much complimented on my success; there are some in the last batch from Lahore whom I shall ultimately get rid of, wild low-caste fellows, and they did not behave very well the other day at the Ravee with Nicholson; but, taken altogether, I am very well satisfied, and trust they will eventually turn out well, and do credit to the hard work I have with them. Colonel Seaton is better—*i.e.*, his wound is healed—but he suffers much pain from the tender state of the scarce united muscles when he moves. The weather is very trying just now, and very unhealthy. Poor Macdowell is unwell, and I fear he will have to go away sick: he is far from strong, which is his only fault, poor boy. I like him increasingly, he is a thorough gentleman. For myself, I am wonderfully well, that is, as well as most in camp, though some-

\* Referring to his charge of the Intelligence Department.

what pulled down by heat, fatigue, and dysentery, and I am literally one of the "lean kine." All is quite quiet here; only a few occasional shots from the batteries. The Pandies are quarrelling among themselves, and are without money; they cannot hold together much longer, and I fear will break up if we do not speedily take the place. The train is to be here to-morrow or next day, and fifty-six guns are to open on the walls at once. We hear that Captain Peel of Crimean celebrity is on his way up to Allahabad, with a naval brigade and some sixty-eight pounders from his ship the *Shannon*.

*September 3rd.*—Nothing is going on here of public importance, and everything is stagnant, save the hand of the destroying angel of sickness; we have at this moment 2500 in hospital, of whom 1100 are Europeans, out of a total of 5000 men (Europeans), and yet our General waits and waits for this and that arrival, forgetful that each succeeding day diminishes his force by more than the strength of the expected driblets. He talks now of awaiting the arrival of three weak regiments of Ghoolab Singh's force under Richard Lawrence, who are marching from Umbâla. Before they arrive, if the General really does wait for them, we shall have an equivalent to their numbers sickened and dying from the delay in this plague spot. "Delhi in September" is proverbial, and this year we seem likely to realise its full horrors. The train will be here to-morrow or next day, and I hope our General will not lose a day after that.

*September 4th.*—There is nothing to tell of public news, and even if there were I have no time to tell it, for I am very busy and hard-worked, and only too thankful to get a few minutes to say I am safe and well.

*September 5th.*—Poor Macdowell has had a bad attack of fever, which has brought him very low. He will have to go to the hills, I very much fear. The amount of sickness is terrible; we have 2500 men in hospital, and numbers of officers beside. Another of the 61st, Mr. Tyler, died of cholera to-day. I would give a great deal to get away, if but for a week, but I must go where I can do most towards avenging the past, and securing our common safety for the future. No arrangements are making for any movements after the capture of Delhi; we sadly want a head over us.

*September 6th.*—To-night I believe the engineers are really to begin work constructing batteries, so that in two or three days Delhi ought to be taken. If General Wilson delays now, he will have nothing left to take; all the Sepoys will be off to their homes, or into Rohilcund, or into Gwalior. News from Cawnpore to 25th August has been received. Up to that date Lucknow was safe, but with only fifteen days' provisions left; and apparently no vigorous measures being taken to relieve the place. Of public news I have none beyond this, and I am still, like every one else, in the dark as to what we do after Delhi is taken, or where and when we go. If the campaign lasts very long I shall be forced to go home next year, for even my health will not stand against many more months of wear and tear like the last. Yet who can say what even a day may bring forth, or can venture to make plans for a future year, after the experiences of the last? God's merciful providence has hitherto preserved me most wonderfully from myriads of no common dangers, and I humbly pray that I may be spared to see my home, and those who make home so dear, once more. Home, altered and bereaved as it is since I left it, still holds the precious sisters and brothers of the past, and the bright new generation with whom I long to make acquaintance. To-day I have letters from home, the first I have had since the war began. I have also a nice letter from Napier which I was quite rejoiced to get. You see his ever-ready kindness was at work for me as soon as he landed.

*September 7th.*—News has just been received up to the 27th from Cawnpore; the garrison in Lucknow had been attacked by the enemy in vast numbers, headed by a lot of "Ghazees." They were repulsed with such severe loss that the enemy would not venture to try that game again, were the siege to be protracted for two years; they say 150 Ghazees and between 400 and 500 Sepoys were killed. Colonel Otter was appointed commandant of Allahabad, at which I rejoice, for he will "come out strong" whenever he has a chance. One of our batteries was armed (*i.e.*, guns put into it) last night, and the bigger one will be made to-night; so that by the 9th I trust Delhi will be ours.

*September 8th.*—To-day, two new batteries, constructed during the night for the heavy guns, opened on the walls and bastions of the city, and the cannonade on both sides has been very heavy; to-morrow other batteries will be ready, and on the following day fifty guns, I trust, will be at work on the doomed city. Very little loss was experienced during the night, only two men being hit; and the casualties to-day have been surprisingly few. I cannot believe there will be any serious resistance when once the enemy's guns are silenced. There is at present nothing to lead one to suppose that the enemy have any intention of fighting it out in the city, after we have entered the breach. All, I fancy, who can, will be off as soon as we are within the walls. The General has not decided yet on the operations which are to succeed Delhi; he says he shall send a strong column in pursuit, which I hope will be under Nicholson, but he has not settled who is to go, or who to stay. I trust I may be among the pursuers. I am constantly interrupted by business, and the necessity of watching the enemy, lest any attempt should be made to turn our flank while we are busied with the batteries in front. For myself, I am not necessarily much exposed to fire, except every now and then; I never run into danger unless obliged to do so for some rightful purpose, and where duty and honour call.

*September 9th.*— . . . To descend to life's hard struggle; our guns are blazing away, but only in partial numbers as yet, the work having been necessarily distributed over two nights instead of one. The garrison at Lucknow is all well, and likely to continue so, for they have plenty of wheat, though no European supplies. However, British soldiers have worked and fought on bread and water ere now, and will do it again: and I have no doubt the gallant 32nd will keep up their spirit and their fame. Reinforcements were reaching Cawnpore, and Sir J. Outram was on his way up with 1500 more soldiers and some artillery. Cholera, their worst enemy, had disappeared, and their communication with Calcutta was quite open. Sir Colin had reached Calcutta, and taken command of the army. I do hope he will come up country at once, and Colonel Napier with him. Poor Alfred Light, after five weeks' severe illness, leaves to-night for the hills, to save his life. Hay has been written to, to take him in; if he cannot, I am sure you will do so. Poor fellow! I have a real regard for him, and it is a terrible disappointment that he cannot be at the actual taking of Delhi, having been so long before the walls. Sickness is terribly on the increase, and Wilson talks of getting into Delhi on the 21st. If the sickness does increase he won't have a sound man left by the 21st.

I was up till 2 A.M. in the trenches, examining the work, and helping what little I could,\* and almost ever since I have been on horseback, and a terrible hot day it has been in all ways. Some of the enemy's horse came out and began to poach on our preserves, and I had to go after them; they are such essential cowards that it is impossible to bring them to a regular fight; they will not come from within reach of their shelter, running off at once to cover, where it would be madness to go after them. The new batteries did not begin to-day, after all; they were not quite ready, and the engineers would not let them open fire. . . . I am very much pleased with ———'s letter, and rejoice that he is out on an expedition: the change of air will do him good after that frightful cholera. His story † of the soldier might be matched by many a rough compliment I get from the men of the

\* An artillery officer told me of my brother, that even when he might have taken rest he would not; but instead, would go and help work at the batteries, and exposed himself constantly in order to relieve some fainting gunner or wounded man.—ED.

† The story referred to was told by an officer: visiting the sick in hospital in the fort at Agra, he asked a man severely wounded whether he could do anything for him. "Oh yes, sir," was the answer, "if you would be so good as read us anything in the papers about that Captain Hodson; he's always doing something to make us proud of our country, and of belonging to the same service as that noble fellow; it makes one forget the pain."

1st Fusiliers; the most genuine perhaps, certainly the most grateful to my feelings, of any I receive; a soldier is generally the best and shrewdest judge of an officer's qualifications.

*September* 11*th*.—There is no public news, except that the batteries are working away at the walls; but our engineers have failed terribly in their estimate of the time required for the works, and all the batteries are even yet not finished. It is now, however, only a question of days, one or two more or less, and Delhi must be ours. I shall be very thankful to get away from here. I look upon this as the very worst climate I have ever been in, and another month would make us all ill. Another of my officers, Captain Ward, is very ill, and two more are ailing. Macdowell, I am thankful to say, is a little better. The natives too are very sick, and a large number are in hospital; in short, we want to be in Delhi.

*September* 12*th*.—I was interrupted in the midst of my pen-work this morning by an alarm (which proved to be a false one) of an attack of cavalry on our rear; it turned us all out, and kept me in the saddle till now, 5 P.M., so I can only say I am safe and unhurt. I trust in three days Delhi will be ours. I fancy my share in the assault will be one of duty rather than of danger. The cavalry have but small work on these occasions. I cannot yet tell what will occur after the capture. I fancy a column under Nicholson will be pushed on to Agra or Cawnpore, and I hope my regiment will be of the party.

*September* 13*th*.—I find I am to accompany Nicholson's column at his own request, but where we are to go is unknown; whether in pursuit of the rebels who are fast evacuating Delhi, or towards Agra, we know not; Nicholson strongly urges the former. I am very glad for my own sake that I am to go on, for this place is dreadfully unhealthy, and I feel that I shall certainly be ill if I remain here much longer. In fact, I had made up my mind not to remain if possible, and when Nicholson urged my going on with him I was only too ready to second the motion, for I am able to work and to fight, and I must do so as long as I can.

*September* 15*th.*—I was totally unable to leave the field yesterday until dark, and long after post time, but I ascertained that a telegraphic message was sent to Simla. I sent one up as soon as possible, for transmission to you through Lord W. Hay, but Colonel Becher had forestalled me. . . . The breaches made by our artillery were successfully stormed early in the morning, with but little loss then; our loss subsequently, however, I grieve to say, was most distressing, and that, in attempting unsuccessfully the capture of the Puhareepore and Kishengunge suburbs. The whole extent of our loss is not yet known, but that already ascertained is grievous to a degree. First, poor Nicholson most dangerously wounded, at a time, too, when his services were beyond expression valuable. The 1st European Bengal Fusiliers was the most tried, and suffered out of all proportion, save in the especial case of the Engineers, of whom ten, out of the seventeen engaged, have been killed or wounded. Chesney and Hovenden among the latter, though not badly. Of the Fusiliers, poor Jacob was mortally wounded, since dead, I grieve to say: Greville, badly; Owen, severely; Wemyss and Lambert, slightly; Butler, knocked down and stunned; F. Brown and Warner, both grazed. Of officers attached to the regiment, Captain Mac Barnett was killed; Stafford, wounded; Speke, mortally so; what a frightful list! Besides this, Captain Boisragon was wounded badly, with the Kumaon battalion; so that of the officers of the 1st Fusiliers engaged yesterday, only Wriford, Wallace, and myself escaped untouched. My escape was miraculous. For more than two hours we had to sit on our horses under the heaviest fire troops are often exposed to, and that too, without the chance of doing anything but preventing the enemy coming on. Brigadier Hope Grant commanded, and while I doubt his judgment in taking cavalry into such a position, I admit that it was impossible for any man to take troops under a hotter fire, keep them there more steadily, or exhibit a more cool and determined bravery than he did. My young regiment behaved admirably, as did all hands. The loss of the party was of course very severe. Of Tombs' troop alone, twenty-five men (out of fifty) and seventeen horses were hit. The brigadier and four officers composing his staff all had their horses killed, and two of the five were wounded. The brigadier himself was hit by a spent shot; Tombs escaped, I am delighted to say, from a similar spent ball. Our success on the whole was hardly what it should have been, considering the sacrifice, but the great end of getting into Delhi was attained. About one-third of the city is in our power, and the remainder will shortly follow, but that third has cost us between 600 and 700 killed and wounded.* I am most humbly and heartily grateful to a merciful Providence that I was spared. May the God of battles continue His gracious protection to the end, and enable me once more to be re-united to all most precious to me on earth.

---

*Letter from* LIEUTENANT MACDOWELL, *Second in command Hodson's Horse.*

"DELHI.

"On the night of the 13th September, final preparations were made for the assault on the city. Brigadiers and commanding officers (our little army boasts of no generals of divisions) were summoned to the general's tent, and then received their instructions. At 1 o'clock A.M. on the 14th the men all turned out silently, no bugles or trumpets sounding, and moved down in silence to the trenches. The batteries all this time kept up an unceasing fire on the city, which responded to it as usual. On arriving at the trenches the troops lay down, awaiting the signal, which was to be given at daybreak, and which was to be the blowing in of the Cashmere Gate, towards which a party of engineers and sappers moved off at about 3 A.M. The assault was to be made in three columns; the first was to blow open the Cashmere Gate, the second to escalade the Water Bastion, and the third to escalade the Moree Bastion, both of which had been pronounced practicable. As I was with the cavalry all the time, I saw nothing of

* 66 officers, 1104 men, was the official return.

the storming, but it is sufficient to say it succeeded on every point, and by 8 A.M. we were inside the walls, and held all their outworks.

"Now began the difficulty, as from the small force we had, it was very hard work to drive a large body of men out of such a city as Delhi. It took four days to accomplish, but at length, on the morning of the 20th, the flag of old England floated gracefully out over the palace of the Great Mogul. And now for what we (the cavalry) did. At 3 A.M. on the 14th, we moved down in column of squadrons to the rear of our batteries, and waited there till about 5 A.M., when the enemy advanced from the Lahore Gate with two troops of artillery, no end of cavalry, and a lot of infantry, apparently to our front. I think they intended to try and take our old position now that we had got theirs. In an instant horse artillery and cavalry were ordered to the front, and we went there at the gallop, bang through our own batteries, the gunners cheering us as we leapt over the sand-bags, &c., and halted under the Moree Bastion, under as heavy a fire of round shot, grape, and canister, as I have ever been under in my life. Our artillery dashed to the front, unlimbered, and opened upon the enemy, and at it they both went 'hammer and tongs.' Now you must understand we had no infantry with us. All the infantry were fighting in the city. They sent out large bodies of infantry and cavalry against us, and then began the fire of musketry. It was tremendous. There we were (9th Lancers, 1st, 2nd, 4th Sikhs, Guide Cavalry, and Hodson's Horse) protecting the artillery, who were threatened by their infantry and cavalry. And fancy what a pleasant position we were in, under this infernal fire, and never returning a shot. Our artillery blazed away, of course, but we had to sit in our saddles and be knocked over. However, I am happy to say we saved the guns. The front we kept was so steady as to keep them back until some of the Guide infantry came down and went at them. I have been in a good many fights now, but always under such a heavy fire as this with my own regiment, and there is always excitement, cheering on your men, who are replying to the enemy's fire; but here we were in front of a lot of gardens perfectly impracticable for cavalry, under a fire of musketry which I have seldom seen equalled, the enemy quite concealed, and here we had to sit for three hours. Had we retired, they would at once have taken our guns. Had the guns retired with us, we should have lost the position. No infantry could be spared to assist us, so we had to sit there. Men and horses were knocked over every minute. We suffered terribly. With my usual good luck I was never touched. Well, all things must have an end. Some infantry came down and cleared the gardens in our front, and as their cavalry never showed, and we had no opportunity of charging, we fell back, and (the fire being over in that quarter) halted and dismounted.* All this time hard fighting was going on in the city. The next day, and up to the morning of the 19th, we did nothing (I am now speaking exclusively of the cavalry brigade) but form in line on the top of the ridge, ready to pursue the enemy should they turn out of the city in force." †

---

*September 16th.*—I have just returned from a very long and terribly hot ride of some hours to ascertain the movements, position, and line of retreat of the enemy, and I can do no more than report my safety. I grieve much for poor Major Jacob; we buried

---

\* One of the officers present on this occasion, speaking of it in a letter to his wife, says, "I found time, however, for admiration of Hodson, who sat like a man carved in stone, and as calm and apparently as unconcerned as the sentries at the Horse Guards, and only by his eyes and his ready hand, whenever occasion offered, could you have told that he was in deadly peril, and the balls flying amongst us as thick as hail."

---

† *Extract from the Despatch of* BRIGADIER HOPE GRANT,
*Commanding Cavalry Division.*

"HEADQUARTERS, DELHI, *Sept.* 17*th*, 1857.

"The behaviour of the Native Cavalry was also admirable. Nothing could be steadier, nothing more soldier-like, than their bearing. Lieutenant Hodson commanded a corps raised by himself, and he is a first-rate officer, brave, determined, and clear-headed."

him and three sergeants of the regiment last night; he was a noble soldier, and delighted us all by his bearing. His death has made me a captain, the long-wished-for goal: but I would rather have served on as a subaltern than gained promotion thus. Greville and Owen are doing well, but I much fear there is no hope for poor Nicholson; his is a cruel wound, and his loss would be a material calamity. You may count our real officers on your fingers now—men, I mean, really worthy the name. General Wilson is fairly broken down by fatigue and anxiety, he cannot stand on his legs to-day; fortunately, Chamberlain is well enough to go down and keep him straight; and Colonel Seaton also—two good men, if he will be led by them. All is going on well; the magazine was carried by storm this morning, with nominal loss, and our guns are knocking the fort and palace about. All the suburbs have been evacuated or taken. I have just ridden through them, and all the enemy's heavy guns have been brought into camp. In forty-eight hours the whole city, I think, with its seven miles of *enceinte*, will be ours: our loss has been very heavy, 46 officers killed and wounded, 200 men killed, and 700 or 800 wounded.

*September* 17*th.*—All is going on well, though slowly; the Sepoys still occupy a portion of the city, and are being gradually driven backwards, while the palace and fort are continually played upon by shell and shot; not above 3000 or 4000 of the rebel troops remain in the city. Headquarters are there, and I am going down immediately to take up my quarters with the staff. I expect to-morrow will see the last of it, but there is no calculating with anything like certainty on the proceedings of these unreasoning wretches. I am thankful to say Nicholson is a little better to-day, and there appears some hope of his recovery, though a very slight one. Mr. Colvin is dead: another celebrity taken away in this time of trial. The home mail of the 10th of August has arrived, but brought no letters for me as yet, but very few have arrived in all. The Government at home seem at last awaking to a sense of the importance of this crisis in Indian affairs.

*September* 18*th.*—There is nothing worth speaking of doing here. We are still shelling the fort and palace, but as slowly, alas, as possible. I shudder at the terrible sights which met my soldiers' eyes. It quite unmans me. I cannot think of it even, or it will quite unfit me to incur rightful risks. Poor Nicholson is lying in a terribly dangerous state. I would give a year's pay to know he would recover, so deeply do we feel his loss at a time like this.

*September* 19*th.*—We are making slow progress in the city. The fact is, the troops are utterly demoralised by hard work and hard drink, I grieve to say. For the first time in my life I have had to see English soldiers refuse repeatedly to follow their officers. Greville, Jacob, Nicholson, and Speke were all sacrificed to this. We were out with all the cavalry this morning on a reconnaissance, or rather demonstration, for some miles, and got a wetting for our pains ; however, rain at this season is too grateful to be complained of.

*September* 20*th.*—I have been much shocked (even familiar as I have become with death) by poor Hervey Greathed's sudden death yesterday from cholera ; the strongest and healthiest man in camp snatched away after a few hours' illness. Sir T. Metcalfe also is very ill with the same cruel disease : what a harvest of death there has been during the past four months, as if war was not sufficiently full of horrors. The rebels have fled from the city in thousands, and it is all but empty; only the palace is still occupied, and that we hope to get hold of immediately, and so this horribly protracted siege will be at an end at last, thank God. None but those who fought through the first six weeks of the campaign know on what a thread our lives and the safety of the Empire hung, or can appreciate the sufferings and exertions of those days of watchfulness and combat, of fearful heat and exhaustion, of trial and danger. I look back on them with a feeling of almost doubt whether they were real or only a foul dream. This day will be a memorable one in the annals of the Empire ; the restoration of British rule in the East dates from the 20th September 1857.

IN THE ROYAL PALACE, DELHI, *September* 22*nd.*—I was quite

unable to write yesterday, having had a hard day's work. I was fortunate enough to capture the King and his favourite wife. To-day, more fortunate still, I have seized and destroyed the King's two sons and a grandson (the famous, or rather infamous, Abu Bukr), the villains who ordered the massacre of our women and children, and stood by and witnessed the foul barbarity; their bodies are now lying on the spot where those of the unfortunate ladies were exposed. I am very tired, but very much satisfied with my day's work, and so seem all hands. We were to have accompanied the movable column, but to-day it is counter-ordered, and we remain here.*

*September* 23*rd.*—When shall I have time to write really a letter? It seems as if I were each day doomed to fresh labour and worry, and I long to shake off the whole coil, and go where I can find repose and peace. Fortunately, my health stands the wear and tear, and as my success has been great I must not grumble. . . . I came to camp this morning to see after the march of a detachment of my regiment which is ordered, after half-a-dozen changes, to accompany a movable column which is ordered to proceed towards Agra to-morrow. I am to remain here, and to tell the truth, the business is so mismanaged that I have ceased to care whether I go or stay. I fancy they find me too useful here. We move down bodily to or near the town to-morrow, and everything is in confusion and bustle.

*September* 24*th.*—The true account of the cavalry "demonstration" is this:—On the morning on which the city and palace were finally evacuated (19th), the whole of the available cavalry (not

---

\* *Extract from the Despatches of* GENERAL WILSON *on the Fall of Delhi.*

"DELHI, *Sept.* 22*nd*, 1857.

"I beg also to bring very favourably to notice the officers of the Quartermaster-General's Department, . . . and Captain Hodson, who has performed such good and gallant service with his newly-raised regiment of Irregular Horse, and at the same time conducted the duties of the Intelligence Department under the orders of the Quartermaster-General with rare ability and success."

otherwise employed) moved out through the suburbs in the direction of, though not on the road to, the Kootub, but with strict orders not to go under fire! Well, we all marched out to the top of the hill on which stands the "Eedgah," and thence, from a safe and respectful distance, overlooked the camp of the Bareilly and Nusseerabad force, under "General" Bukt Khan, quondam Subadar of artillery. While minutely examining the camp through my glass (I was with Brigadier Hope Grant, to show the way), I perceived by unmistakable signs that it was being evacuated. Shortly after a loud explosion showed that they were blowing up their ammunition previous to a flight; these signs were on the moment confirmed by the arrival of my "Hurkaras" (messengers), and I immediately got leave to go and tell the General. I did so, galloping down along the front of the city to see if that was quite clear. I then asked leave to go down through the camp, and see what was really the state of the case; and Macdowell and I started with seventy-five men, and rode at a gallop right round the city to the Delhi gate, clearing the roads of plunderers and suspicious-looking objects as we went. We found the camp as I had been told, empty, and the Delhi gate open; we were there at 11 A.M. at latest, and it was not until 2 P.M. that the order was given for the cavalry to move out, and they were so long about it, that when at sunset Macdowell and I were returning (bringing away three guns left by the enemy, and having made arrangements and collected camels for bringing in the empty tents, &c.), we met the advance-guard coming slowly forward in grand array! We had been on to the jail and old fort, two or three miles beyond Delhi, and executed many a straggler. I brought in the mess plate of the 60th Native Infantry, their standards, drums, and other things. Macdowell and I had been for five hours inside the Delhi gate, hunting about, before a guard was sent to take charge of it.

The next day I got permission, after much argument and entreaty, to go and bring in the King, for which (though negotiations for his life had been entertained) no provision had been made and no steps taken, and his favourite wife also, and the young imp (her son) whom he had destined to succeed him on the throne. This was successfully accomplished, at the expense of vast fatigue and no trifling risk.* I then set to work to get hold of the villain princes. It was with the greatest difficulty that the General was persuaded to allow them to be interfered with, till even poor Nicholson roused himself to urge that the pursuit should be attempted. The General at length yielded a reluctant consent, adding, "But don't let me be bothered with them." I assured him it was nothing but his own order which "bothered" him with the King, as I would much rather have brought him into Delhi dead than living. Glad to have at length obtained even this consent, I prepared for my dangerous expedition. Macdowell accompanied me, and taking 100 picked men, I started early for the tomb of the Emperor Humayoon, where the villains had taken sanctuary. I laid my plans so as to cut off access to the tomb or escape from it, and then sent in one of the inferior scions of the royal family (purchased for the purpose by the promise of his life) and my one-eyed Moulvie Rujub Alee, to say that I had come to seize the Shahzadahs for punishment, and intended to do so, dead or alive. After two hours of wordy strife and very anxious suspense, they appeared, and asked if their lives had been promised by the Government, to which I answered "Most certainly not," and sent them away from the tomb towards the city, under a guard. I then went with the rest of the sowars to the tomb, and found it crowded with, I should think, some 6000 or 7000 of the servants, hangers-on, and scum of the palace and city, taking refuge in the cloisters which lined the walls of the tomb. I saw at a glance that there was nothing for it but determination and a bold front, so I demanded in a voice of authority the instant surrender of their arms, &c. They immediately obeyed, with an alacrity I scarcely dared to hope for, and in less than two hours they brought forth from innumerable hiding-places some 500 swords, and more than that number of firearms, besides horses, bullocks, and covered carts called "Ruths,"

* A more detailed account will be found afterwards.

used by the women and eunuchs of the palace. I then arranged the arms and animals in the centre, and left an armed guard with them, while I went to look after my prisoners, who, with their guard, had moved on towards Delhi. I came up *just in time*, as a large mob had collected, and were turning on the guard. I rode in among them at a gallop, and in a few words I appealed to the crowd, saying that these were the butchers who had murdered and brutally used helpless women and children, and that the Government had now sent their punishment: seizing a carbine from one of my men, I deliberately shot them one after another. I then ordered the bodies to be taken into the city, and thrown out on the "Chiboutra," in front of the Kotwalie,* where the blood of their innocent victims still could be distinctly traced. The bodies remained before the Kotwalie until this morning, when, for sanitary reasons, they were removed. In twenty-four hours, therefore, I disposed of the principal members of the house of Timur the Tartar. I am not cruel, but I confess I did rejoice at the opportunity of ridding the earth of these wretches. I intended to have had them hung, but when it came to a question of "they" or "us," I had no time for deliberation.

*September 24th.*—The picture drawn from the usually mendacious reports at Simla, is not even founded on fact. The women of the palace had all escaped before the troops entered.

The troops have behaved with singular moderation towards women and children, considering their provocation. I do not believe, and I have some means of knowing, that a single woman or child has been purposely injured by our troops, and the story on which your righteous indignation is grounded is quite false; the troops have been demoralised by drink, but nothing more.

---

* It was on this spot that the head of Gooroo Teg Bahadoor had been exposed by order of Aurungzebe, the Great Mogul, nearly 200 years before. The Sikhs considered that in attacking Delhi they were "paying off an old score." A prophecy had long been current among them, that by the help of the white man they should reconquer Delhi. After this they looked on Captain Hodson as the "avenger of their martyred Gooroo," and were even more ready than before to follow him anywhere.

*September* 25*th*.— . . . I miss Colonel Seaton terribly: we have lived in the same tent for months, and had become brothers in affection as well as in arms. I mourn deeply for poor Nicholson: with the single exceptions of my ever-revered Sir Henry Lawrence and Colonel Mackeson, I have never seen his equal in field or council; he was pre-eminently our "best and bravest," and his loss is not to be atoned for in these days. I cannot help being pleased with the warm congratulations I receive on all sides for my success in destroying the enemies of our race; the whole nation will rejoice, but I am pretty sure that however glad —— will be at their destruction, he will take exception to my having been the instrument, in God's hands, of their punishment. That will not signify, however; I am too conscious of the rectitude of my own motives to care what the few may say, while my own conscience and the voice of the many pronounce me right.

A fuller account of the capture of the King will be found in a letter addressed to me shortly afterwards, and published by me in the *Times*, which I now reprint:—

"I have before explained to you what your brother's (Captain Hodson's) position officially was—namely, that he was appointed Assistant-Quartermaster-General and Intelligence Officer on the Commander-in-Chief's own Staff. His reports were to be made to him direct, without the intervention of the Quartermaster-General or any other person.

"For this appointment, which was then a most responsible one, as intelligence of the enemy's movements and intentions was of the utmost importance, his long acquaintance with Sikhs and Affghans, and his having been similarly employed in the Punjab war, had peculiarly fitted him. Of course, there were always plenty of traitors in the enemy's camp ready to sell their own fathers for gain, or to avoid punishment, and he was invested with full power to promise reward or punishment, in proportion to the deserts of those who assisted him.

"On our taking possession of the city gate, reports came in

that thousands of the enemy were evacuating the city by the other gates, and that the King also had left his palace. We fought our way inch by inch to the palace walls, and then found truly enough that its vast arena was void. The very day after we took possession of the palace (the 20th), Captain Hodson received information that the King and his family had gone with a large force out of the Ajmere Cate to the Kootub. He immediately reported this to the General commanding, and asked whether he did not intend to send a detachment in pursuit, as with the King at liberty and heading so large a force, our victory was next to useless, and we might be besieged instead of besiegers. General Wilson replied that he could not spare a single European. He then volunteered to lead a party of the Irregulars, but this offer was also refused, though backed up by Neville Chamberlain.

"During this time messengers were coming in constantly, and among the rest one from Zeenat Mahal (the favourite Begum), with an offer to use her influence with the King to surrender on certain conditions. These conditions at first were ludicrous enough—viz., that the King and the whole of the males of his family should be restored to his palace and honours; that not only should his pension be continued, but the arrears since May be paid up, with several other equally modest demands. I need not say these were treated with contemptuous denial. Negotiations, however, were vigorously carried on, and care was taken to spread reports of an advance in force to the Kootub. Every report as it came in was taken to General Wilson, who at last gave orders to Captain Hodson to promise the King's life and freedom from personal indignity, and make what other terms he could. Captain Hodson then started with only fifty of his own men for Humayoon's Tomb, three miles from the Kootub, where the King had come during the day. The risk was such as no one can judge of, who has not seen the road,* amid the old ruins scattered about of what was once the real city of Delhi.

* "At a short distance, about a mile before reaching the tomb, the road passes under the Old Fort—a strong tower, commanding the road on two

"He concealed himself and men in some old buildings close by the gateway of the tomb, and sent in his two emissaries to Zeenat Mahal with the *ultimatum*—the King's life and that of her son and father (the latter has since died). After two hours passed by Captain Hodson in most trying suspense, such as (he says) he never spent before, while waiting the decision, his emissaries (one an old favourite of poor Sir Henry Lawrence) came out with the last offer—that the King would deliver himself up to Captain Hodson only, and on condition that he repeated with his own lips the promise of the Government for his safety.

"Captain Hodson then went out into the middle of the road in front of the gateway, and said that he was ready to receive his captives and renew the promise.

"You may picture to yourself the scene before that magnificent gateway, with the milk-white domes of the tomb towering up from within, one white man among a host of natives, yet determined to secure his prisoner or perish in the attempt.

"Soon a procession began to come slowly out, first Zeenat Mahal, in one of the close native conveyances used for women. Her name was announced as she passed by the Moulvie. Then came the King in a palkee, on which Captain Hodson rode forward and demanded his arms. Before giving them up, the King asked whether he was 'Hodson Bahadoor,' and if he would repeat the promise made by the herald? Captain Hodson answered that he would, and repeated that the Government had been graciously pleased to promise him his life, and that of Zeenat Mahal's son, on condition of his yielding himself prisoner quietly, adding very emphatically, that if any attempt was made at a rescue he would shoot the King down on the spot like a dog. The old man then gave up his arms, which Captain Hodson handed to his orderly, still keeping his own sword drawn in his hand. The sides, in which the King and his party first took refuge on their escape from Delhi. This was filled with his adherents, and it was a moment of no small danger to Hodson and his little troop; when passing under it on his way out to the tomb, any stray shot from the walls might have laid him low."—*Note by a friend.*

same ceremony was then gone through with the boy (Jumma Bukh); and the march towards the city began, the longest five miles, as Captain Hodson said, that he ever rode, for of course the palkees only went at a foot pace, with his handful of men around them, followed by thousands, any one of whom could have shot him down in a moment. His orderly told me that it was wonderful to see the influence which his calm and undaunted look had on the crowd. They seemed perfectly paralysed at the fact of one white man (for they thought nothing of his fifty black sowars) carrying off their King alone. Gradually as they approached the city the crowd slunk away, and very few followed up to the Lahore gate. Then Captain Hodson rode on a few paces and ordered the gate to be opened. The officer on duty asked simply as he passed what he had got in his palkees. 'Only the King of Delhi,' was the answer, on which the officer's enthusiastic exclamation was more emphatic than becomes ears polite. The guard were for turning out to greet him with a cheer, and could only be repressed on being told that the King would take the honour to himself. They passed up that magnificent deserted street to the palace gate, where Captain Hodson met the civil officer (Mr. Saunders), and formally delivered over his Royal prisoners to him. His remark was amusing, 'By Jove! Hodson, they ought to make you Commander-in-Chief for this.'

"On proceeding to the General's quarters to report his successful return, and hand over the Royal arms, he was received with the characteristic speech, 'Well, I'm glad you have got him, but I never expected to see either him or you again!' while the other officers in the room were loud in their congratulations and applause.

"On the following day, as you already know, he captured three of the Princes: but of this more hereafter. I am anxious now that you should fully understand that your brother was bound by orders from the General to spare the King's life, much against his own will; that the capture alone was on his own risk and responsibility, and not the pledge."

I am allowed to insert here a most graphic letter, written by Lieutenant Macdowell, second in command of Hodson's Horse:—

"On the morning of the 19th we formed up and saw the townspeople coming in thousands out of the Delhi gate (still in the enemy's possession), and passing through their camp, taking the high road to the Kootub. Too far off to do any damage, we waited (the ground a mass of hard rocks, impracticable for cavalry) till 9 A.M., and then retired. Hodson, my commanding officer, then went to the General, and at ten I received a note from him, 'Gallop down with fifty men and meet me at the Cashmere gate as sharp as possible.' Down I went, and he told me he had volunteered to ride through the enemy's camp and reconnoitre; that no one knew if they were there in force or not, and he asked me if I would accompany him. Of course I was only too glad, and off we went. They fired at us as we approached, from gardens and places all round, but I imagine they thought more men were coming, and bolted, we (only fifty of us) cutting up all their stragglers to the tune of some fifty or sixty. As we came back we intercepted a whole lot of townspeople escaping. Well, I must not linger on this. Having done our work (and it wasn't a bad thing to do, to gallop through their camp with fifty men, not knowing whether they were there or not), we cautiously approached the Delhi gate. It was open, but all was silent. Our troops had not as yet ventured so far. Afar off we heard the firing in the city in other quarters; leaving our men outside, with four sowars behind us with cocked carbines, we rode in, holding our revolvers ready for a row. Not a soul was there; all still as death. I looked round, and close to where I was sitting were two bottles of beer amidst a heap of plate, silver, clothes, &c. Perhaps I didn't jump off sharp! It was all right; real beer! madam. We uncorked, and drank the Queen's health at once. After a little time, as the firing approached, and we found all was right, we rode away, and reported what we had done. The General was very pleased.*

* For the remainder, see Introduction.

Some months later my brother wrote with reference to the capture of the King and Princes:—

CAMP, ON THE LEFT BANK OF THE GANGES, OPPOSITE CAWNPORE, *Feb.* 12*th*, 1858.

... I see that many people suppose that I had promised the old King his life *after* he was caught. Pray contradict this. The promise was given two days before, to induce him to leave the rebel troops, and return to the near neighbourhood of Delhi within reach. General Wilson refused to send troops in pursuit of him, and to avoid greater calamities I then, and not till then, asked and obtained permission to offer him his wretched life, on the ground, and solely on the ground, that there was no other way of getting him into our possession. The people were gathering round him. His name would have been a tocsin which would have raised the whole of Hindoostan, and the Rajas and Rajpootana in the south would have been forced to have joined in the rising, which would then have been universal. Was it not better to get rid of all this, and secure ourselves from further mischief, at the simple cost of sparing the life of an old man of ninety? It must be remembered, too, that we had no troops left to meet any further augmentation of our enemies. A small force under Colonel Greathed was with difficulty found, some days later, to go towards Agra; and it was clear to me then (as experience has since shown) that we had still months to wait for reinforcements from home. Here is February; the King was caught in September, and yet up to this present day the Commander-in-Chief has not been able to send a single soldier of all that have arrived from England up as far as Delhi; and all Rohilcund, all Oude, a great part of British India, all Bundelcund, and most of Behar, are still in the hands of the enemy. Would it have been wise to have given, in addition to all this, so strong an incentive to combination, to the warlike men of the north-west, as they would have had in the person of a sacred and "heaven-born" monarch, dethroned, wandering and homeless, but backed by a whole army in rebellion? I am blamed for it now; but knowing that there was no other way of getting him into our power, I am quite content to take the obloquy. It will hereafter be admitted that one of the greatest blows was struck at the root of the rebellion when the old king was led a captive into his own palace on the 21st of September 1857.* Strange, that some of those who are loudest against me for sparing the King, are also crying out at my destroying his sons. "Quousque tandem?" I may well exclaim. But, in point of fact, I am quite indifferent to clamour either way. I made up my mind at the time to be abused. I was convinced I was right, and when I prepared to run the great physical risk of the attempt, I was equally game for the moral risk of praise or blame. These have not been, and are not times when a man who would serve his country dare hesitate as to the personal consequences to himself of what he thinks his duty.

Those who, like Colonel Malleson and others, have attacked Captain Hodson for shooting the Shahzadahs, are forced to confess that the act was approved at the time by some of the best and wisest men in India. Why, then, is he to be branded as a murderer for doing that in an extraordinary emergency which good men, with their knowledge of the facts, in their calmer judgment applauded. Is this just or fair dealing?

I am indebted to Sir T. Seaton for an answer to inquiries addressed to my brother, which never reached him:—

"I see you are anxious to clear up the two 'vexed questions':—Why did he guarantee the life of the King? Why did

---

\* *From* MR. MONTGOMERY, *now* SIR ROBERT, K.C.B.

"*Sept.* 29*th.*

"MY DEAR HODSON,—All honour to you (and to your 'Horse') for *catching* the King and slaying his sons. I hope you will bag many more!—In haste, ever yours, R. MONTGOMERY."

he strip the Princes? He guaranteed the life of the King, because he was ordered to do so by General Wilson; and I think that, under the circumstances, it was wise and prudent (though highly distasteful to the General), for it enabled us to get hold of the nominal head of the great rebellion, and to secure the capture of those greater scoundrels, the Princes. No one ever thought out here of asking why he stripped the Princes, or rather why he made them take off their upper garments. It certainly was not as the French stupidly assert, 'pour ne pas gâter le butin,' for if the upper corresponded with the nether clothes in which the bodies were laid out, they would have been dear at a shilling the lot. He made them strip off their upper garments, to render their death and subsequent exposure at the Kotwàlla more impressive and terrible. Some people ask, 'Why did he shoot them himself?' To this I will reply by another question, 'What would have been the effect on that vast crowd of a single moment's hesitation or appearance of hesitation?'"

I may add, on the best authority, that whatever may have been the value of the upper garments, they were left on the spot.

Before this chapter closes, I will insert one or two anecdotes and descriptions of my brother, from letters written at this time by officers before Delhi, which have been kindly placed at my disposal. They will help to fill up the picture of him which may be drawn from his own diary.

One says:—

"The way Hodson used to work was quite miraculous. He was a slighter man and lighter weight than I am. Then he had that most valuable gift, of being able to get refreshing sleep on horseback. I have been out with him all night following and watching the enemy, when he has gone off dead asleep, waking up after an hour as fresh as a lark; whereas, if I went to sleep in the saddle, the odds were I fell off on my nose.

"He was the very perfection of a 'free-lance,' and such an

Intelligence Officer! He used to know what the rebels had for dinner in Delhi.

"In a fight he was glorious. If there was only a good hard scrimmage he was as happy as a king. A beautiful swordsman, he never failed to kill his man; and the way he used to play with the most brave and furious of these rebels was perfect. I fancy I see him now, smiling, laughing, parrying most fearful blows as calmly as if he were brushing off flies, calling out all the time, 'Why, try again, now,' 'What's that?' 'Do you call yourself a swordsman?' &c.

"The way that in a pursuit he used to manage his hog-spear was miraculous. It always seemed to me that he bore a charmed life, and so the enemy thought.

"His judgment was as great as his courage, and the heavier the fire or the greater the difficulty, the more calm and reflecting he became."

Another (Sir T. Seaton):—

"You know that, during the whole of the terrible siege of Delhi, we lived together in the same tent, and, excepting while on duty, we were never separate. It was there I saw, in all their splendour, his noble soldierly qualities; never fatigued, never downcast, always cool and calm, with a cheerful countenance and a word of encouragement for every one.

"I used often to say, 'Here, Hodson, is somebody else coming for comfort?'

"It was there I learned the depth and intensity of his affection for his wife; like the man, it was out of the common. You know how he nursed me when I was wounded. I am indebted for my rapid recovery, in a very great measure, to his care and forethought; and it was whilst lying helpless and feeble I saw that the brave and stern soldier had also the tenderness of a woman in his noble heart. His constant care was to prevent Mrs. Hodson from feeling any anxiety that he could save her; so that, whenever he went out on any expedition that would detain him beyond twenty-four hours, he invariably asked me, and I used to make it my duty, to write to Mrs. Hodson daily, accounting for his absence, and giving such details as I could of his doings.

"He was ever ready to carry out my wishes and aid me with his best knowledge, skill, and courage. He supported me with the devotion of a brother; never, never shall I see his like again."

Another says:—

"He has wonderful tact in getting information out of the natives, and divining the movements of the enemy. He is scarcely out of the saddle day or night, for not only has he to lead his regiment and keep the country clear, but being Intelligence Officer, he is always on the move to gain news of the progress of affairs, and acts and intentions of the enemy.

"Even when he might take rest he will not, but will go and help work at the batteries, and expose himself constantly, in order to relieve some fainting gunner or wounded man."

I have this anecdote from another:—

"In the camp at Delhi, when the incessant fatigue to which the soldiers were exposed forbade the strict enforcement of the continual salute, it was remarked that Hodson never passed down the lines without every man rendering to him that mark of respect. The soldiers loved him as their own. 'There goes that 'ere Hodson,' said a drunken soldier as he cantered down the lines; 'he's sure to be in everything: he'll get shot, I know he will, and I'd a deal rather be shot myself: we can't do without him.'"

I venture to quote from Mr. H. Greathed's Letters (published by his widow) some further notices of my brother:—

"Hodson keeps an Argus eye on the rear and left flank, and is always ready for an adventurous ride. I am not surprised at Gough liking him; he has a rare gift of brains as well as of pluck! The uniform of his men, 'khakee' tunics, with a scarlet sash and turban, is very picturesque. They were called Flamingoes.

"Hodson is certainly the most wide-awake soldier in camp.

"A charge of cavalry was turned by a few musket shots from a party under Hodson, who always turns up in moments of difficulty."

Again, speaking of him while absent at Rohtuck, August 19th:—

"We have no further intelligence from Hodson. He is employed on just the wild work he likes, and will be loth to return. The public still amuses itself with giving his regiment new names. 'The Aloobokharas' and 'Ringtailed Roarers,' are the last I have heard of.

". . . There was some alarm yesterday about Hodson's safety. I cannot say I shared the feeling, I have such confidence in his audacity and resource.

". . . Hodson is quite safe; he will now return to camp, and, after being in for an hour, he will be seen looking as fresh, clean-shaved, and spruce, as if he had never left it."

As another illustration of the enthusiastic admiration with which he was regarded by the common soldiers, I will record part of a conversation with an old Carbineer many years afterwards.

After mentioning the stories which the men of the 11th Hussars had to tell of his daring and cleverness in the Punjab, and the great anxiety of the men to get sight of him, he went on:—

"The first time I saw him myself was in December 1857. He had just come into camp, and the men did *just* stare at him. They were halting for food, and an officer named Russell said, 'Well, Hodson, why don't you sit down to eat?' 'I never sit down on these occasions,' was his answer, and in twenty minutes they were engaged again.

"Another time, as Hodson was starting off somewhere, an officer called after him 'Take care of yourself' (because he was always exposing himself to danger), and he looked back and said as bright as possible, 'Some one else takes care of me.' He was always so respectable (you understand me). He never forgot Almighty God. He *was* a gentleman.

"Other officers waited till they were told to do anything; but if he saw a thing that should be done, he did it at once without being told. And if he was speaking to the other officers, you might hear a handkerchief drop. They all listened so, and his men were devoted to him."

## CHAPTER IV.

OPERATIONS IN THE NEIGHBOURHOOD OF DELHI — SHOWER'S COLUMN—SEATON'S COLUMN—GUNGEREE —PUTIALEE—MYNPOOREE—RIDE TO COMMANDER-IN-CHIEF'S CAMP—JUNCTION OF FORCES—SHUMSHABAD.

CAMP, DELHI, *Sept. 26th.*

My letters are of necessity short and newsless, for I am scarcely ever able to sit down to write what can be properly called a letter. Anything so mismanaged as the prize property has been, or so wasted, I never saw; so much so, that I look upon the appointment of prize agents at all as a simple injustice to the army, *i.e.*, to the officers. We are not allowed to plunder, and shall get nothing from the agents. Colonel Seaton has given up the prize agency in disgust, and I refused it altogether; he is taking you a real trophy from Delhi, no less than the turquoise armlet and signet rings of the rascally princes whom I shot; not actually worth twenty shillings, but I know they will be prized by you and the dear ones at home. I have bought you such a nice carriage for a mere song. Tombs declares I shall get a C.B. for capturing the King, &c., and, between ourselves, I *ought* to have anything they can give me, for it was a fearful risk, and, I must say, the "General's" share in it was about as meritorious as his recognition of the service was gracious ! but you will see *he* will get the reward. But never mind, I did my duty, perhaps something more, and have got the reward of my own conscience, and certainly the voice of the army, as the hero of this " crowning mercy," as they call it.

We march to-morrow instead of on the 20th, as we ought to have done, to clear out some of the hordes at Humayoon's Tomb.

I disarmed them when I took the princes, and collected all the arms, &c., into one spot, leaving as large a guard as I could spare, and yet the "General" has actually never sent until to-day to relieve the one or secure the other, and now only at my urgent representation! We shall be back from our expedition in four or five days. Colonel Showers commands.

CAMP, HUMAYOON'S TOMB, *Sept.* 28*th.*—I have been out all day and at work, varied by divers summonses from the Brigadier, and by such *very* amusing duties as packing off the royal family's lower branches into Delhi.

Poor Greathed! he was, indeed, a loss to every one! With the column sent out here (to complete with 1500 men the work of which I had overcome all the difficulties with 100), a young civilian was sent to carry on political duties, and take charge of the different members and hangers-on of the Royal family. In an hour I got possession of the persons of seven of the remaining sons and grandsons of the King who were "wanted;" they were made over, according to orders, to this civilian, and, two hours afterwards, all had escaped! In consequence of this we are halted here, and parties sent out in all directions to recapture the fugitives.

I shall try to get down in the Oudh direction to join Napier and his chief.

I confess I am much gratified by the congratulations I receive on all sides regarding the capture of the King and the retribution on the Shahzadahs; but I expect no reward, perhaps not even thanks. The Government will be delighted at the fact, but will perhaps pretend a reluctance to the judgment having been effected, which they certainly do not feel, and will probably throw all the *onus* on me. To tell the truth (in spite of all the praises and prophecies of the army), I expect nothing by this campaign but my brevet majority, and that was due to me for the Punjab war.

The execution of the princes could be hardly called one of "unresisting" enemies, since they were surrounded by an armed host, *to whom we should have been most unquestionably sacrificed if*

*I had hesitated for an instant.* It was *they* or *we*, and I recommend those who might cavil at my choice to go and catch the next rebels themselves! The King was very old and infirm, and had long been a mere tool, a name, in the hands of the Shahzadahs, Mirza Mogul in particular; moreover, the orders I received were such that I did not dare to act on the dictates of my own judgment to the extent of killing him when he had given himself up; but had he attempted either a flight or a rescue, I should have shot him down like a dog; as it is, he is the lion without his claws, now his villainous heir-apparent is disposed of. I must be prepared to have all kinds of bad motives attributed to me, for no man ever yet went out of the beaten track without being wondered at and abused; and so marked a success will make me more enemies than friends, so be prepared for abuse rather than reward; for myself I do not care, and I am proud to say that those whose opinion I value most highly think I did well and boldly.

CAMP NEAR THE KOOTUB, *Sept. 29th.*—We got here so late to-day that, before our tents were pitched and washing and breakfast over, the time to close our dâk has arrived. Thanks for letters, which are balm to my wounded spirit, vexed as I am to find that even here, in the field, working as I have done and successful as I have been, I am not safe from the malignant influence of —— and his myrmidons. From the day that he put —— into power at Delhi I experienced a difficulty never found before in carrying on my duties, and a system of backbiting and insinuation which could never have existed if it had not been encouraged, if not engendered, by listening to. This meanness *et id genus omne* has commenced, and has decided me on the course you have so long urged, namely, to give up the Intelligence Department.

General Wilson advised me, as a friend, to do so, adding that otherwise —— would find an opportunity of smashing me.

I have done quite enough to establish my name in the army, and as much as one man can do. We return to Delhi, I hope, to-morrow, for we have done little enough by leaving it. The other column, which went out across the Jumna, has had an engagement with the enemy at Bolundshur, and thrashed them soundly. This will open the road to Cawnpore. I shall write to Napier to-day to see if he can get my regiment sent towards Oudh, or anywhere near him.

CAMP, DELHI, *Oct. 1st.*—I was quite unable to write yesterday, as we did not return here and get under cover till after dark. I have to march again to-morrow towards Rewarree with another column under Brigadier Showers; a most gentlemanly person and gallant soldier, but sadly prolix and formal in all his arrangements, thereby spinning out an ordinary march to the dimensions of a day's journey. I am sorry to say my unlucky ankle gives me more pain and annoyance than before, and the doctors tell me it will never be better until I give it *perfect rest;* and as this said rest is perfectly impossible, I must bear it as patiently as I can; but it is a sad drawback to my comfort and activity.

You will rejoice with me that the detachment (of Hodson's Horse) under Hugh Gough, who were sent with the column across the Jumna, behaved extremely well in that action at Bolundshur, and have been much praised. I am very glad, indeed, of this : it is a great thing for a new regiment to be successful at a cheap rate in its first few encounters; it gives a *prestige* which it is long in losing, and gives the men confidence in themselves and their leaders. In this affair our loss was trifling, though the cavalry were principally employed. Poor Sarel, 9th Lancers, wounded severely, I am sorry to say. I fancy *we* go to Goorgaon and Rewarree. Whether we see the enemy is doubtful, and it may be merely a "military promenade," to settle the minds of the inhabitants. I long to get down towards Outram, and Oudh, and Napier.

I am so glad you have written home, for I was out of the way when the "Overland mail" left, and we none of us knew of its being despatched. It was a sad fatality which attended the two last, both from and to England. England ! How the writing the very name even fills me with sweet home memories and home longings; and though, during the last five years and three quarters, my life has been more blessed than I ever dreamed it possible that life could be, still there are times, and they increase in frequency, when my heart yearns for all its dear earlier ties. Yes, we must get home next year somehow, even if we have to live on barley bannocks.

I, and most other people, considered that I and my party had a right to all we found on the King and princes; but the General, to whom I referred the question, thought otherwise: so I gave up all, with the exception of the King's shield and a few swords which I had given to the officers (those of the King I gave to the General). The swords which I retained are historically most valuable. One was worn by, and bears the name of, Jehangire, and the other is stamped with the seal of Nadir Shah! They are singular and interesting trophies, or rather relics, of the house of Timour the Tartar.

DELHI, *Oct. 2nd.*—I have remained behind the force for a day in order to settle the business and pay up and discharge my Intelligence Establishment. I am so busy that my letter will of necessity be a short one. My having been out at camp has prevented my getting at the people and officers, who are all in the city and palace. We, that is, the cavalry, artillery, and some infantry, are outside on the glacis of the city, and much pleasanter it is, I think; especially as I have good shelter under the roof of an old mosque in a serai, where we can all put up together without jostling. I feel quite a free man now. I have no work to do but my regiment; though, truth to tell, *that* is quite enough for one man, even with so able and willing an assistant as MacDowell. I do not reckon on much fighting where we are going, and the weather is now getting very tolerable. The country we are going into is also much healthier than Delhi, and I expect much benefit from the change of air and quiet marching. After our return I shall get away, if but for a week; and then my anxiety is to join Napier, wherever he may be.

DELHI DISTRICT, *Oct. 3rd.*—I was yesterday four coss from

Bullnagurh, and the Rajah actually came out in his carriage; yet I had strict orders not to interfere with him, so the force marched off in another direction this morning without striking a blow, though the place was full of the Rajah's armed retainers and fugitive Pandies from Delhi, and they ought all to have been exterminated. The consequence is, he will give us trouble hereafter.* To-day we struck off to the right to this place (marching at Brigadier Showers' favourite pace of six miles in five hours), and go on to-morrow through Goorgaon to a place called Rewaree, where one Toli Ram, a farmer of Government revenue in better times, but who now "affectionates" independent authority, has collected a force round his fortlet of some 4000 to 5000 men, and shows fight; but again I opine we shall have a tedious march for our pains. I grieve daily in all bitterness for poor Nicholson's death. He was a man such as one rarely sees; next to dear Sir Henry, our greatest loss.

CAMP, GOORGAON, *Oct. 4th.*—Even the camp before Delhi (so long our abode that I write it mechanically) was more favourable for letter-writing than our present more peaceful but more moving life. We started at three A.M. and arrived here about nine. I had then to go through the village or town with the Brigadier, and it was noon before we got a tent pitched and breakfast ready; before I had finished I was summoned by Showers to give him some information as to some "Moofsids," and now at two P.M., though I am still unwashed and unshorn, I am ordered to be ready at three with a party to proceed to punish some refractory villages a few miles off. I shall be back, I trust, at dark, to dinner and bed, for we march again at midnight. Tell —— the swords I have kept are beautiful, and historically most valuable. It was like parting with my teeth to give up those I did to the General: I should not have cared so much if he had done anything towards the winning them. It will be something hereafter to wear a sword taken from the last of the House of Timour, which

* So he did, but ultimately gave himself up, and was hanged by the authorities in Delhi.—*Ed.*

had been girt round the waists of the greatest of his predecessors: if I ever part with it, it shall be "in a present," as mine O. would say, to our good Queen! She ought to give me her own Cross for it; and that's a fact, though I say it.*

*Oct. 6th*, 3 A.M.—We got back last night at dark, from our visit of retribution to Dholkote, having "polished off" a goodly number of rebels from Irregular Cavalry Regiments, and others who came out armed to the teeth, and making great demonstration of attack, but turned of course when we charged. Had we not absurdly been sent out in the afternoon, instead of morning, so that it got too dark for work, we should have cleared the place entirely. I had a most kind letter of congratulation from ———— yesterday. He seems very ill, poor fellow! How thankful I am that my health stands work so well: not that I do not feel it; and it will *tell* more still some day. I question whether there is a single one of us, however strong or unwounded, whose constitution does not pay for the Siege of Delhi. The weather is getting very pleasant, except in the middle of the day; but what a contrast to the climate of the Punjab! I hear General Wilson has gone to Meerût, and General Penny come to Delhi in his stead.

PATHONDHEE, *Oct. 5th, noon.*—I add a few lines to my letter of this morning to say that all is safe and well. Nothing has occurred but a skirmish with our advanced guard and some sowars of Toli Ram's, who came, I honestly believe, in all good faith, to bring an offer of submission; but the business was bothered by mutual distrust, so they turned, fired at our advance, and bolted at speed, my men after them as hard as they could go. They brought back about a dozen horses whose riders they had disposed of; very acceptable they are too, for "mounting" my men is my greatest difficulty. General Penny reigns at Delhi.

There is no chance of my regiment being stationary this cold weather, I imagine, for the country is still in a very unsettled state, and will be so for a long time to come.

CAMP, REWARREE, *Oct. 6th.*—We arrived here, after a tediously

* They are now at Windsor Castle.

protracted march, at eleven this morning, only to find my prediction verified, that the birds would be flown and the nest empty. Mr. Toli Ram bolted yesterday, and left only an empty fort and his guns behind him; in good hands it would have given us considerable trouble, and he was evidently a clever fellow, and had adroitly and promptly contrived so as to be first in the field, should our power have ceased. We found extensive preparations, and large workshops for the completion of military equipments of all kinds, guns, gun-carriages, gunpowder, accoutrements, and material of all kinds. He had already done much, and in a couple of months his position would have been so strong as to have given him the command of all the surrounding country, as well as the rich town and entrepôt of Rewarree, close to the walls of his fort. Had our empire fallen, he would have mastered all the surrounding villages and districts, and probably extended his power on all sides, and founded a "Raj" like that of Puttiala or Jheend, to fall in its turn before the (then) newly aroused energies of the Sikhs. At the same time he was prepared, if we won the day, to profess that he had done all this solely in our interests and to preserve the district *for us* from the Goojur depredators. This is now his line of defence. Showers yesterday sent to tell him that if he would come in and give himself up, as well as his guns and arms, he should be treated on his merits. This he would not do, and has eventually sealed his fate by bolting. The extent of his warlike preparations is too obviously the result of his really hostile, rather than of his professedly friendly, intentions. I do not know where we go next; back to Delhi, I trust, when I hope to find General Penny willing to forward my wishes by sending me on to join the army. It will spoil my new regiment to keep it on mere police duty.

CAMP, REWAREE, *Oct. 7th.*—We have been all day in the saddle, wandering about distant villages, but we did not see an enemy, and the inhabitants seemed very glad to see us, for the runaway rebels had plundered every place they passed through. The whole body of horsemen who were here up to two days before, fled in all directions when they heard of our approach (though their numbers were immense, they say 7000 to 8000), and now, ride where we will, in any direction for fifteen miles round Rewarree, not an armed man is to be seen.

Only this morning we heard of the capture of Lucknow, dimmed by the death of General Neill. He is a loss indeed. I trust our dear friend has escaped. I looked tremblingly through the list, and rejoiced to find the name of Napier not there. And now for matters of the lower world. I have drawn no pay either for the A. Q. M. Generalship or my regiment, except an advance of £500 for current expenditure. I have as yet been able to get no pay abstracts passed; and indeed such is the confusion of all things, from the want of some central authority, that no one knows where, or by whom, we are to be paid; so I have to draw money for my men "on account," to be settled hereafter: as yet, however, I take care that it shall not exceed a third, or at utmost half their pay, to be safely within the mark. Men and horses cannot live on "nothing a day and find themselves," and any regular office-work is utterly impossible while we are kept so perpetually in the saddle. It is rather hard on a new regiment, "raised on service"—and a little hard on their commandant too —but all will come straight in the end, I doubt not. I thought I mentioned that when we went to the Kootub the first time with Colonel Showers, I found a lot of silver and money, worth, I should think, 20,000 or 30,000 rupees, and 20 or 30 elephants; all which goes to swell the prize money. We ought to have a good proportionate sum each, for there has been an immense deal of property taken altogether, I should think; but the want of care and management will lessen it considerably. As a specimen— when Seaton was prize agent (and they could not have found a better or more upright), a quantity of property of all descriptions was brought in and put on the "chiboutra" in front of the house he was in. He immediately sent to ask the General either to appoint a place to stow it in, or for a guard to put over it. The answer was in General Wilson's usually *brusque* style. " He had no guard to spare, and Colonel Seaton must secure the property as he could." Colonel Seaton's reply was to resign the prize agency. He could not well do otherwise after this and other specimens.

*Oct. 8th.*—I go on an expedition early to-morrow morning to some villages, and shall be too late back for writing.

*Oct. 11th.*—Only three words to say that I am safe and well. I cannot ascertain whether we go back direct to Delhi, or by Jhujjur, to annex the Nawâb's country. Everything is perfectly quiet here, and the weather is really cold in the mornings: we shall all improve by the change, though fever is very prevalent amongst the natives. The Europeans are gaining strength daily.

CAMP, JÂTOO SANA, *Oct. 13th.*—We shall be at Jhujjur, I believe, in a couple of days; where part of General Cortland's force and the Jummoo troops will meet us, and they will, I fancy, be left in occupation, and we return to Delhi, where I hear a force under General Penny is to be formed to go towards Rohilcund. It is more than probable that we shall accompany him. If I am allowed to go to a station to *form* my regiment, I shall certainly try for Umbâla. The bazaars at Meerut, Cawnpore, &c., are all destroyed, and I could get nothing I wanted. Here I am interrupted by an order to start on a "*dour*," which will keep us out till midnight, if not longer.

*Oct. 14th.*—My expectations of yesterday were fulfilled, and we did not return till midnight to dinner, having been in the saddle without a halt since 3 P.M.

CAMP, DADREE, *Oct. 16th.*—The Jhujjur Nawâb has, or will give himself up; so not a shot will be fired, for all the swarms of Irregular Cavalry have dispersed to their homes, or rather to the hills and jungles, for shelter and security. Colonel Greathed's column has reached Agra, and there had a fight; a regular surprise—our people being attacked while at breakfast! However, the enemy were thoroughly thrashed eventually, and lost camp and guns. Poor French, of the Lancers, is the only officer whose name I have heard as killed. A report has reached me from Simla that you have got some magnificent diamond rings, &c., taken at Delhi. This is rather good, considering the only rings I sent you were the princes', and not worth twenty rupees altogether, and the only "diamonds" were in that little brooch I bought from a sowar more than a month before Delhi was taken —so much for the veracity of your good-natured *friends* at Simla! It is too rich. I like Macdowell increasingly—he is so thoroughly honest and gentlemanly, and brave as a lion. In Wise, too, I am fortunate; and Wells is a fat, good-tempered, willing-to-work school-boy. We do very well indeed together, and I have profited by past experience (and perhaps the natural result of increased age and knowledge of the world), but things are very different *now* and *then*.

We were waked up at midnight, and got to our camping ground at 11 A.M., and there found neither tents nor breakfast. We march on to Jhujjur early to-morrow. The Nawâb has made his submission, and we have nothing to do but receive it and move on.

CAMP, KUNOUND, *Oct.* 19*th*.—We left Dadree at 1 A.M. yesterday, and marched ten miles to Jhujjur, found the force dispersed, and fled, and took possession of the (very nice) fort, with heaps of guns and ammunition. My men were out after the fugitives till half-past ten. At noon we marched again (the 6th Dragoon Guards and my regiment), under Colonel Custance, to Nahur, twenty-four miles, which we reached at sunset. At 3 A.M. this morning we came on here, seventeen miles, and took one of the strongest forts I have seen, with fourteen guns, some very heavy ones, and five lacs of rupees, which, alas! is to be considered Government, not prize property. I was only out of my saddle for one hour yesterday, from one in the morning till sunset, and then only to get some cold food under a tree! But I am quite well and strong, much better than I was at Delhi; and as Colonel Custance and his officers are remarkably agreeable gentlemanlike people, we have had the most really pleasant days since leaving Delhi. The worst of this raid is that it takes me from all chance of getting away for a few days until our return.

KUNOUND, *Oct.* 20*th.*—I have just had a very nice and welcome letter from Grant—dated Calcutta, 5th September. He had had a long talk about me with Mr. Talbot, who told him that General Anson's representations had done much good, and that it was admitted on all hands that my exculpation *in re* the Guides was complete, and that no higher or more flattering testimonials were ever seen; so that, please God, I shall be righted at last; and *justice* is all I want.

This is a very healthy country, but sandy, and no doubt at times fearfully hot; even to-day there is a hot wind blowing, and yet by midnight it will be freezing!

CAMP, KUNOUND, *Oct.* 21*st.*—Another long day without a dâk. I have "betwitted" Captain Trench, who has charge of the Post-office, for taking more care of himself than he does of us; but of course he denies the soft impeachment *in toto*. I begin to despair of getting back to Delhi, as we do not march hence till the 23rd, and even then it is uncertain in what direction we go. I am not sorry for the rest, for my men and horses were beginning to suffer. I had this morning thirty-eight men and forty-three horses sick! My ankle gives me so much pain that I have been forced to take to a small pony to ride even about camp, so as to avoid walking even for fifty yards. I believe it will be good for a sick certificate.

*Oct.* 22*nd.*—Khuda Bux brings me untold money and bullion which he digs up, and is very indignant because I insist on its being handed over as prize money.

The detached state of this regiment is enough to ruin it. Three troops are at Agra, or thereabouts, under Hugh Gough; the sick and depôt at Delhi, and portions of five troops here; but it seriously increases the difficulty of managing a totally new regiment, and it is hardly fair either to the men or to the commanding officer. I have remonstrated, but I suppose with very little effect, as I have had no answer. I trust indeed I may get all together and go towards Oudh.

*Oct.* 23*rd.*—To-day we still halt, and I hear a rumour that on our return we go on to Agra. My other troops are on their way to Cawnpore, so that I think there is every chance of my getting that way too. Tell —— he may unhesitatingly contradict the story about the rupees. It was born in Delhi, and was partly the cause of General Wilson's bad behaviour to me; the money, 10,000 rupees, was brought to me late one night by the men, who had been desired (as Colonel Seaton will corroborate) to secure prize property for him and the other agents. We marched at daybreak next morning, and I had only time to make it over to Macdowell to see it locked up in the regimental chest for safety before we started. When I returned, three or four days afterwards, a story had been circulated by the native who had disgorged the coin, that I had kept the money for myself! Of course the very day I returned it was, with heaps of other things, made over to the agents. And so stories go in this world. The amount of petty jealousy excited by what my friends call my "successes" is beyond belief. The capture of the King and his sons, however ultimately creditable, has caused me more envy and ill-will than you would believe possible, but I have had too much experience of humanity, during the last few years, to care for envy now; and conscious as I am of my own rectitude of purpose at least, however I may err in judgment, I go on my way rejoicing.

CAMP, PATHONDHEE, *Oct. 27th.*—I am indeed most humbly and earnestly grateful to the good God who has so mercifully spared * what was so infinitely more precious to me than life itself; and I do feel how entirely our hearts should be filled with gratitude to Him for the bountiful mercies which we mutually and individually have experienced at His hands during the past year:—the preservation of us both from *such* perils; my re-employment in an honourable position; my ability to do such good service to the country at such a crisis; the preservation of health in such a time of exposure; my complete, though tardy vindication from unjust charges; my almost assured freedom from debt;—all

---

* Referring to his wife's almost miraculous escape, when the horse on which she was riding fell over a precipice and was killed.—*Ed.*

these mercies are almost more than my full heart can bear. May God crown all other blessings by granting us a safe re-union.

GOORGAON, *Oct. 28th.*—I hope to be in Delhi to-morrow, and shall lose no time, you may be very sure, in getting leave to go to Umbâla. I fear there is little chance of rest for me in any one place during the cold weather. We must be prepared for many a long and tedious march, as the future is still full of difficulty and some danger; but when all the troops have arrived, we may consider that rest is near.

DELHI, *Oct. 29th.*—I arrived here at last to-day safe and well, but very tired. I have seen General Penny, and he has given me leave, and I hope to come the day after to-morrow.

DELHI, *Oct. 30th.*—The pen has not been out of my hand since I got up. There is much to do here, but I hope to get the regiment sent off to Meerut by the 2nd at latest. I feel quite in want of rest; I have been over-strained and over-laboured, and I want repose. When I get our prize-money I hope to realise R.40,000, and if so, I shall be able to pay all our debts, and a great burden will be off my heart. I shall feel quite free and young again in heart when all is clear.

It will be seen by the foregoing letters that Hodson's Horse had by this time acquired such proportions that they admitted of being divided. One detachment, under Lieutenant Hugh Gough, had been sent with Colonel Greathed's column towards Agra, and afterwards joined Sir Colin Campbell's force, and took part, with much distinction, in the final relief of Lucknow by Sir Colin and Sir James Outram.

The main body, with their commandant, accompanied Brigadier Showers, and were of great service in anticipating the movements and cutting off the retreat of the flying enemy, as well as in scouring the country and bringing in supplies. Their rapidity of movement and dashing courage made them a terror to the rebel forces, who had, on more than one occasion, painful experience of the keenness of their sabres.

In the course of the expedition, the forces of several rebel rajahs were defeated, their strongholds captured, with many guns, and treasure amounting to £70,000 taken, besides large quantities of cattle.

On one occasion upwards of 1500 head of cattle had been taken. When they were brought in, Brigadier Showers exclaimed, "Hang me! what in the world am I to do with them? It would take half my force to convoy them back to Delhi. I can't take them." On this Captain Hodson said, "Well, sir, will you sell them to me, and let me take my chance?" "Willingly," said the Brigadier; so the bargain was struck for two rupees four annas a head, and R.3491 were paid by Captain Hodson to the Prize Agent. Captain Hodson sent them off, under charge of their drivers, and two or three of his own sowars, to Delhi, where they arrived safely, and were of course sold at a large profit.

The speculation turned out a good one, but the chances were against it. No one else, probably, under the circumstances, would have run the risk, and the cattle would have been left behind.

I mention this anecdote as showing that in small things as well as great my brother refused to acknowledge difficulties, and deserved the character given him of being the most "wide-awake" man in the army. Shortly afterwards he invested part of the proceeds in a house at Umbâla which happened to be then put up for a forced sale at a great depreciation. This consequently went among his friends by the name of the "cow house." *

A short time before the return of the column to Delhi, he

---

\* This transaction, however, has been twisted into a matter of accusation against him. See Introduction, p. xxxvii.

applied for a few weeks' leave, in order to join his wife, who had come down from Simla to Umbâla.

On November 3rd he wrote to his sister from Umbâla:—

After nearly six months of separation, I was happy enough to get back here yesterday night, and find my wife well, and all but recovered from the effects of her frightful accident, the most wonderful escape, perhaps, from imminent peril ever recorded. I take the first holiday I have had since the 15th May to write a few lines to you, my dearest sister, to say what deep and real pleasure and comfort your letters bring to me, amidst danger and toil and fatigue; and how cheering it is to feel that, come what may, I am sure of your loving sympathy and constant affection. I received yesterday your letter of the 4th May, and could not but be most forcibly struck with the contrast between my circumstances individually, and those of the country, then and now. No one will rejoice more than yourself at the sudden change, and at the tolerable success which has been permitted to my labours . . . . .

*Nov.* 15*th.*—Here my pen was arrested by the news that the mail was gone. In these days all regularity is set at defiance, and again we have been startled by a notice to send our letters within half-an-hour, and that, too, in the midst of preparation for a hurried return to Delhi and Meerut, to rejoin my regiment. We march at once to join Sir Colin Campbell and the army assembling at Cawnpore for the re-conquest of Lucknow.

I am getting on famously with my regiment: men of good family and fighting repute are really flocking to my standard,* and

---

* A letter from Delhi, in October, says:—

"The corps raised by that very gallant officer, Captain Hodson, is composed more than anything we have hitherto had of the old sirdars and soldiers of Runjeet Singh's time, in consequence of which, and the skill of their commander, they are already an extremely efficient corps.

"I was talking this morning to a very independent-looking Resaldar, who seemed to be treated by his men much more as they do a European officer than is ever seen in our service, and who bore himself as the inferior of no before the end of the year I hope to have 1000 horsemen under my command.

I had a letter the other day from —— at Calcutta, from which I learn that at last the truth is beginning to dawn on the minds of men in power regarding me. They now say that my remonstrance will be placed on record for preservation, "not for justification, which it is fully admitted was not required," and that "no higher testimonials were ever produced."

How much I have to be thankful for, not only for restored position and means of future distinction, but for safety and preservation during this terrible war, and for my dear wife's escape.

Unfortunately, however, his death shortly after prevented any steps being taken for a public and formal vindication of his character.

On the 2d December, "Hodson's Horse" were ordered to join a movable column under Colonel Thomas Seaton, C.B., proceeding down the country towards Cawnpore, in charge of an immense convoy of supplies of all kinds for the Commander-in-Chief's army. The convoy was calculated to extend over fifteen miles of road—hackeries of grain, camels, elephants, horses—and but 1500 men and four guns to protect them all. At Allygurh, the forces marching respectively from Delhi and Meerut united on the 11th. On the following day Colonel Seaton, leaving the convoy under the protection of the guns of the fort, proceeded by forced marches to look after some large parties of the rebel army who were encamped in the Doâb.

On the 10th my brother wrote to his wife from

CAMP SOMNA, 14 *miles from Allygurh,*
*Dec.* 10*th.*

After four days of forced marches we joined the column this morning, and march on to Allygurh to-morrow. We have been one, and I found that he had been long a colonel of artillery in Runjeet Singh's service, and very openly went through the part he had taken against us in the revolt of 1849."

quite out of the way of letters, both going and coming, until to-day. The "enemy," who were supposed to have been in our front at Khasgunge, have all disappeared, and there seems to be no immediate prospect of our finding another. Alfred Light marched down with me from Meerut to this place, and now goes on with Colonel Seaton as orderly officer, I am glad to say. We have a frightful convoy and crowd, but I hope not for long. The headquarter people, Colonels Keith, Young, Becher, and Congreve, are with us. It is said that our friend Napier is to be Adjutant-General of the army—delightful, if true. I have only just got my tent up, and it is nearly dark, so I can only say that I am safe and well.

ALLYGURH, *Dec.* 11*th.*—We arrived here early this morning, and I found Major Eld commanding and Arthur Cocks doing Commissioner. Everything perfectly quiet in the neighbourhood, and no large gathering of Pandies anywhere near. There is a small party at Khasgunge, and I hope we may be lucky enough to find them, but I doubt their waiting for us. Meantime we are to march down the Trunk Road, halting here to-morrow. I cannot get over our parting, each separation seems a greater wrench than the last.

Of public news there is none, but one broad fact, that since the 12th ultimo no news have been received from Lucknow, and not a word even from Cawnpore since the 25th. This necessarily excites alarm, but still my impression is, that though our people may be surrounded with a close cordon of disaffected and rebellious men, who cut off all communication, yet that any serious harm can happen to a force of 8000 or 9000 Europeans I will not readily believe. I have 596 sabres with me now, 50 more coming from Delhi, besides the 140 with Gough—not so bad that.

*Dec.* 12*th.*—We hear to-day from Agra that the ladies and sick and wounded from Lucknow and Cawnpore have been sent down to Allahabad, and the Gwalior Contingent beaten. The Commander-in-Chief is at Cawnpore, and troops will be assembling there, enough to put down all opposition, and open the road to Calcutta. We march to-morrow morning from hence, leaving the "*impedimenta*" behind here until we can ascertain that the road is clear; when it is so, all will move on. We have fifteen guns, mostly 9-pounders, with our small but compact force. Major Eld joins us with a part of his garrison, and Colonel Farquhar brings 300 Beloochees, 200 Affghans, and two guns to our aid. We shall be 2500 fighting men, and the "fathers of rebels" will hardly stomach so much as that! Colonel Seaton is doing admirably, very firm and very wide awake; so all will, I doubt not, go well.

JULÂLEE, *Dec.* 13*th.*—Your letter enclosing our darling sister's found us lying in the dust, with a pea-soup atmosphere of fine sand all around, discussing hot tea and eggs, just as I had returned from a reconnaissance to the front in virtue of my being big eye and ear of the camp. . . . *Apropos* of the newspapers, Arthur Cocks tells me that the *Friend of India* has apologised for its strictures on my conduct *in re* the Shahzadahs; so let that satisfy you, for nothing I could write, or my friends for me, could ever be half so effectual as the *Friend's* voluntary *amende*. . . . I intended to have written much to-day, but I was waked at 3 A.M., marched soon after, and with the exception of the dusty breakfast (cheered by my letters), I was in the saddle till half-past 2 P.M. Then regimental business, washed and dressed, then threw myself on my bed for half an hour till dinner, after which we get to bed as soon as we can, and up again at 3 A.M., so there is not much time for what I want to do of private matters. There's a history of a day in camp.

CAMP, GUNGEREE, *Dec.* 14*th.*—I have only time to say that I am safe and well, though we have had a hard fight. The enemy's cavalry with three guns and some infantry came on from Bilram to meet us this morning after breakfast—about 800 horsemen and a mob of foot—but our guns soon stopped their progress, and then the Carbineers and Lancers charged straight down on them in the most magnificent style, capturing all three of their guns at a dash! I grieve to say, however, that they paid most dearly for their splendid courage. All their officers went down. Captain

Wardlaw, Mr. Hudson, and Mr. Vyse, all killed, and Head, of the Lancers, badly wounded. The infantry were not engaged at all. *We* attacked their flying cavalry, and footmen on the left, and made very short work of all we could catch. I lost a fine old Resaldar, our dear old friend Mohammed Reza Khan's brother. None of my officers hurt; but my horse (Rufus this time) got a cut.

---

*From Despatch from* COLONEL T. SEATON, C.B., *to* MAJOR-GENERAL PENNY, *Commanding at Delhi.*

"KHASGUNGE, *Dec.* 15*th*, 1857.

"The General will see by the list of casualties, that Captain Hodson's newly raised body of horse was not backward, and rendered excellent service. It could not do less under its distinguished commander, whom I beg particularly to mention to the Major-General, as having on every possible occasion rendered me the most efficient service, whether in gaining information, reconnoitring the country, or leading his regiment."

CAMP NEAR PUTTIALEE, 17*th*.—I have but time for one line again to say that "all's well." We have been on our horses for eleven hours! The enemy had the boldness to await our arrival here in great force and partly entrenched. We attacked them soon after 8 A.M., they firing aimlessly at us as we advanced, our guns coming into play with fine effect. I then dashed into their camp with my regiment, Bishop's troop of Horse Artillery actually charging with us like cavalry fairly into their camp! We drove them through camp and town, and through gardens, fields, and lanes, capturing every gun and all their ammunition and baggage. We pushed on for six or seven miles, and read them a terrible lesson. The Carbineers and my men alone must have killed some 500 or 600 at least, all sowars and fanatics. We wound up by killing the Nawâb, who led them on his elephant, after a long chase and an ingenious struggle, in which he was fairly pulled out of his howdah.  I am very tired, but delighted with our day's work on Seaton's account.  We have captured thirteen guns and entirely dispersed the enemy.  He ought to be made a K.C.B. for this.

PUTTIALEE, 19*th*.—I have just returned from a twenty-five miles' ride reconnoitring towards the ghâts of the Ganges, and breakfasted *al fresco* at 1¼ P.M. ; so I am not too fresh, as you may imagine, after the last few days of hard work and hard galloping. Colonel Seaton tells me that he wrote to you after our very successful action here.  He does all his work so well and pleasantly that it is a pleasure to work under him.  We have a very compact force and capital officers, so everything goes on smoothly and comfortably.  The remnant of the gentry we thrashed here seem never to have stopped running since.  Another party have, however, crossed over from Rohilcund, and are said to be coming our way.  I only wish they may.

*Dec.* 20*th.*—We march back to-morrow, and shall be at Etah on the Grand Trunk Road on the 24th, when the convoy will come on to rejoin us.  I have ascertained that the result of our affair here has been to drive the whole of the rebels out of the country between this and Futtehgurh.

From Etah we shall disperse the Mynpooree party, and then I think there will be no rebels left in the Doâb save at Futtehgurh, and those the Commander-in-Chief will dispose of.

---

*Extract from a Despatch from* LIEUTENANT-COLONEL T. SEATON, *dated*

"PUTTIALEE, *Dec.* 18*th*, 1857.

"After the action at Gungeree I specially mentioned Captain Hodson and his regiment.  I can but repeat what I then said, and beg that the Major-General will be good enough to bring this officer and his great and important services to the special notice of the Commander-in-Chief."

KHASGUNGE, 23*rd*.—The more we move in this direction, the more do we realise of the satisfactory results of our expedition and our fight of the 17th. It really was a very complete affair, and had it been done under the eyes of the Commander-in-Chief, I should have been made a colonel. However, I can but admit that every disposition exists here to give me (perhaps more than) my due. To-day we have for the first time heard of the Commander-in-Chief's movements. He comes up in two columns, *viâ* the Grand Trunk Road, and *viâ* the Jumna towards Mynpooree. We shall be at the latter place on Christmas day, I hope, and clear out the remainder of the rebels who may still be lurking about the roads and villages. We caught yesterday one of the rebel leaders, an old Resaldar, covered with honours, pension, and dignity by our Government! These rascals are as impervious to gratitude as they are ignorant of truth. The neighbourhood of Futtehgurh has brought vividly home to me the horrors committed, and the dreadful fate of poor Tudor Tucker, his wife, children, and the other victims, is ever before me: it often recals a sterner judgment when we feel inclined to *spare*.

ETAH, *Dec.* 24*th*.—We got here after an eighteen miles' march, and hear that the Chief was to leave Cawnpore "in a few days" from the 14th, and would move up the Grand Trunk Road with one column, sending another to skirt the Jumna. General Windham is said to be coming up to take the divisional command at Umbâla.

MULLOWN, *Christmas Ddy*.—There seems a fatality against our spending these anniversaries together; but my heart is full of deep and earnest prayer for you and all my loved ones, and I try to hope that our next Christmas may be spent *at home*.

We march to Kerowlee to-morrow, and shall be at Mynpooree on the 27th, there to halt for a few days until the convoy is collected, and we can hear from the Commander-in-Chief. We have just heard that Mayhew is the new Adjutant-General, and Norman Deputy. This last is a splendid thing, and shows Sir Colin's determination to put the right man in the right place, in spite of all the red tape and seniority systems in the world! I can hear nothing of our dear friend Napier, but I suppose he is with Sir James Outram.

MYNPOOREE, *December 27th.*—We have just returned from a sixteen miles' pursuit of the rebel force posted in front of this place. They only waited until the Horse Artillery guns opened on them, and then fled precipitately, so we had to ride hard to overtake them. They flung away their arms, and became simple villagers with astonishing rapidity; it would have done credit to the stage. No one hurt but two of my sowars. We have got all their guns (six in number), and the Doâb is clear now to Futtehgurh.

MYNPOOREE, *December 28th.*—The Commander-in-Chief had not left Cawnpore on the 16th, but was to do so very soon; we hope to hear of him. Please send the enclosed notes to the ladies to whom they are addressed, and if they like to enclose me any *miniature* replies, I will take care they are safely forwarded to their husbands.

MYNPOOREE, *December 29th.*—I *have* spoken about poor Wardlaw's effects, and Mrs. ——'s kind offer was accepted gladly; but a reference to Meerut was necessary, and I have not yet had a final answer. Poor fellow! never was a more gallant charge than the last he led, and I agree with his brother officers that "a kinder friend, a more gallant soldier, and a better comrade, never stepped than George Wardlaw." Both his death and that of his comrade, Mr. Hudson, were perhaps unnecessary—by which I mean that a better acquaintance with their enemy might have saved both. The former, after the charge, dashed single-handed —with a cheer—into a knot of matchlock-men waiting to receive him, and was shot dead instantly. Had he gathered together only half-a-dozen dragoons, he might have ridden over them. The other (Hudson) was shot by a wretched fugitive lying prostrate in a field. Not understanding their tactics, he rode up to him and halted, thus offering a fair mark for the villain's ready musket. He was a son of the ex-Railway King.

MYNPOOREE, *December 30th*, 6 A.M.—I am just starting for the

Chief's camp, which is at or near Goorsahaigunge, some forty miles from hence. I am taking despatches from Colonel Seaton, and to see that the road is clear. I hope to be back to dinner. Mac goes with me.

BEWAR, GRAND TRUNK ROAD, *December* 31*st.*—Yesterday, I rode with Mac to the Commander-in-Chief's camp. It was further off than I had been led to believe, and I had to go fifty-four miles to reach him. I found him wonderfully fresh and well, and met with a most cordial and hearty welcome from him, General Mansfield, and in fact, from all. Bruce and Mackinnon all fat and well. Hope Grant was most cordial. I was much pleased with all I heard and saw; the sight of the sailors and the Highlanders did my eyes and heart good. Such dear, wild-looking fellows as these Jack-tars are, but so respectful and proper in conduct and manner. Our dear Napier is wounded, I grieve to say, though, thank God, not badly, and is left behind at Cawnpore. So I am gazetted a *Captain* at last! All the letters, papers, and despatches relative to Delhi have been published, and I am again thanked in despatches by the Governor-General. . . . Sir Colin was very complimentary, and my men, under Gough, have won great distinction and universal praise. I rejoiced to see my old friend Norman in his proper place, the *de facto* Adjutant-General of the army; and Hope Grant has done everything admirably. We Punjabee cavalry folks are quite "the thing" just now. . . . We had a narrow escape yesterday from a party of the enemy crossing the road *en route* from the southward to Futtehgurh; they attacked my sowars after we (Mac and I) had ridden on, and killed one of them, and wounded several. Coming back at night, we passed quite close to the enemy's bivouac, hearing their voices distinctly; but by taking it quietly, and riding on soft ground, we got past unmolested and into Bewar (to which place Seaton moved up this morning) by 3 A.M., having dined with the Commander-in-Chief last evening. We had ridden ninety-four miles since six in the morning. I, seventy-two on one horse, my gallant Rufus. We astonished the head-quarter people not a little.

The following extract from a private letter of an artillery officer, describing the state of the roads, will give some notion of the danger of this ride :—

"MYNPOOREE, *December* 29*th*.

"Since the 20th of October, no letters have passed this road. The 'Kossids,' whose trade it is to carry letters through an enemy's country, would not, and could not do it, and no wonder. At one place we saw a poor brute who had gone from us with a letter to the Chief, and had been caught by the rebels. He was hanging by the heels, had his nose cut off, had been made a target of, and roasted alive.

"Pleasant fellows, these rebels, and worthy of all consideration."

I am again indebted to the pen of Lieutenant Macdowell for a fuller account of the hair-breadth escape which he and my brother had in the course of this ride, in which they so gallantly and successfully opened communication between the two forces.

"CAMP, BEWAR,*Jan.* 1*st*, 1858.

"You know we took Mynpooree on the 27th. We halted that day and the two following. On the night of the 29th, Hodson came into my tent, about nine o'clock, and told me a report had come in that the Commander-in-Chief had arrived with his forces at Goorsahaigunge, about thirty-eight miles from Mynpooree, and that he had volunteered to ride over to him with despatches, asking me at the same time if I would accompany him. Of course I consented at once, and was very much gratified by his selecting me as his companion. At 6 A.M. the next morning we started, with seventy-five sowars of our own regiment. I do not wish to enhance the danger of the undertaking, but shall merely tell you that since Brigadier Grant's column moved down this road towards Lucknow, it had been closed against all Europeans ; that we were not certain if the Commander-in-Chief's camp was at Goorsahaigunge (which uncertainty was verified, as you will see) ;

and that, to say the least of it, there was a chance of our falling in with roving bands of the enemy.

"We started at 6 A.M., and reached Bewar all safe, fourteen miles from our camp. Here we halted, and ate sandwiches, and then leaving fifty men to stay till our return, pushed on to Chibberamow, fourteen miles farther on. Here we made another halt, and then, leaving the remaining twenty-five men behind, we pushed on by ourselves, unaccompanied, for Goorsahaigunge, where we hoped to find the Commander-in-Chief. On arriving there (a fourteen miles' stage), we found the Commander-in-Chief was at Meerun-ke-Serai, fifteen miles farther on. This was very annoying; but there was no help for it, so we struck out for it as fast as we could, the more so as we heard that the enemy, 700 strong, with four guns, was within two miles of us. We arrived at Meerun-ke-Serai at 4 A.M., and found the camp there all right. We were received most cordially by all, and not a little surprised were they to hear where we had come from. Hodson was most warmly received by Sir Colin Campbell, and was closeted with him till dinner-time. Meanwhile, I sought out some old friends, and amused myself with looking at the novel sight of English sailors employed with heavy guns. I also went to see the Highlanders, and magnificent fellows they are, with their bonnets and kilts, looking as they could eat up all the Pandies in India. A summons to the Commander-in-Chief's table called me away, and off I went to dinner, when I found Hodson seated by Sir Colin, and carrying on a most animated conversation with him. We had a very pleasant dinner, and at 8 P.M. started on our long ride (fifty-four miles) back. We arrived at Goorsahaigunge all safe, and pushed on at once for the next stage, Chibberamow. When we had got half way, we were stopped by a native, who had been waiting in expectation of our return. God bless him! I say, and I am sure you will say so too when you have read all. He told us that a party of the enemy had attacked our twenty-five sowars at Chibberamow, cut up some, and beaten back the rest, and that there was a great probability some of them (the enemy) were lurking about the road to our front. This was pleasant news, was it not?—twenty miles from the Commander-in-Chief's camp, thirty from our own; time, midnight; scene, an open road; *dramatis personæ*, two officers armed with swords and revolvers, and a howling enemy supposed to be close at hand. We deliberated what we should do, and Hodson decided we should ride on at all risks. 'At the worst,' he said, 'we can gallop back; but we'll try and push through.' The native came with us, and we started. I have seen a few adventures in my time, but must confess this was the most trying one I had ever engaged in. It was a piercing cold night, with a bright moon and a wintry sky, and a cold wind every now and then sweeping by and chilling us to the very marrow. Taking our horses off the hard road on to the side where it was soft, so that the noise of their footfalls could be less distinctly heard, we went silently on our way, anxiously listening for every sound that fell upon our ears, and straining our sight to see if, behind the dark trees dotted along the road, we could discern the forms of the enemy waiting in ambush to seize us. It was indeed an anxious time. We proceeded till close to Chibberamow. "They are there," said our guide in a whisper, pointing to a garden in a clump of trees to our right front. Distinctly we heard a faint hum in the distance—whether it was the enemy, or whether our imagination conjured up the sound, I know not. We slowly and silently passed through the village, in the main street of which we saw the dead body of one of our men lying stark and stiff and ghastly in the moonlight; and on emerging from the other side, dismissed our faithful guide, with directions to come to our camp—and then, putting spurs to our horses, we galloped for our dear life to Bewar, breathing more freely as every stride bore us away from the danger now past. We reached Bewar at about two o'clock A.M., and found a party of our men sent out to look for us. Our troopers had ridden in to say they had been attacked and driven back, and that we had gone on alone, and all concluded we must fall into the hands of the enemy. We flung ourselves down on charpoys and slept till daylight, when our column marched in, and we received the hearty congratulations of all on our escape. What do you think of it? The man whose information gave us such timely warning, and thereby prevented our galloping on, by which we should certainly have excited the attention of the enemy, has been very handsomely rewarded, and obtained employment.

"It appears from the reports afterwards received, that the party that cut up our men were fugitives from Etawah, where a column of ours, under General Walpole, had arrived. They consisted of about 1500 men, with seven guns, and were proceeding to Futtypore. We rode in at one end of Chibberamow in the morning—they rode in at the other. They saw us, but we did not see them, as we were on unfavourable ground. Thinking we were the advanced guard of our column, they retired hastily to a village some two koss off. Meanwhile, Hodson and I, unconscious of their vicinity, rode on. They sent out scouts, and ascertained that only twenty-five of our sowars were in the village, upon which they resumed their march, sending a party to cut up our men, and, I suppose, to wait for our return. All Hodson said when we were at Bewar, and safe, was 'By George! Mac, I'd give a good deal for a cup of tea,' and immediately went to sleep. He is the coolest hand I have ever yet met. We rode ninety-four miles. Hodson rode seventy-two on one horse, the little dun, and I rode Alma seventy-two miles also."

Colonel Seaton, in a letter written shortly afterwards to Mrs. Hodson, thus describes the anxiety he felt:—

"MAHOMEDABAD, *Jan. 5th.*

"Oh! what a fright I was in the night before we marched from Mynpooree. Your husband knew that I was most anxious to communicate with the Commander-in-Chief, and volunteered to ride across, and as Mr. Cocks said that he had most positive information that the Commander-in-Chief was at Goorsahaigunge, I consented. He started at daybreak, taking a strong party of his own regiment.

"At sunset one of his men returned, saying that he and Macdowell had left a party at Chibberamow, and ridden forward; that the party had subsequently been surprised by the enemy and cut up.

"At first this seemed most alarming, yet I had the greatest faith in his consummate prudence and skill. I knew Macdowell was with him, and I said to myself, 'If those two are not sharp enough to dodge the black fellows, why the d —— is in it.' But still I could not help feeling most uneasy, and saying, 'Oh! dear, what should I say to his poor wife.' I did not sleep one wink all night. In the morning a sowar galloped in with a note from him. Oh! what a relief to my mind.

"The day before yesterday we rode over together to the Commander-in-Chief's camp at Goorsahaigunge, and found he had moved on four miles beyond the Kalee Nuddee. We followed, and came in for the tail of a fight, as there were still some dropping shots. I was received with great cordiality by the Commander-in-Chief, and warmly congratulated on our successes.

"Your gallant husband has now left me, and I find it most painful to part, for he is a warm friend and true soldier; always ready with his pen, his sword, or his counsel at my slightest wish; indeed, he often anticipated my wishes, as if he could divine what I wanted. I missed his cheerful manly face at my breakfast this morning, and am not in a good humour at all to-day."

In a letter to England of the same date, my brother says:—

At last, after twelve years' service, I am a Captain regimentally from the 14th September last; poor Major Jacobs' death after the assault having given me my promotion—dearly purchased by the death of such a man! I have much to be thankful for, not only for the most unhoped-for escapes from wounds and death, but for the position I now occupy, and for the appreciation my work has received from those in power. My new regiment has done good service, and got much κῦδος.

On January 1, 1858, he writes to his wife from

CAMP, BEWAR.—I must write a few lines on this *jour de l'an*, though they will be but few, as we start shortly for the Commander-in-Chief's camp at Goorsahaigunge, twenty-eight miles off—the " we " means Colonel Seaton, Light, and myself. I do hope it will then be decided when we are to join the Chief, which, for many reasons, I am most anxious to do. Macdowell wrote you a capital account of our expedition to Meerun-ke-Serai, which you will get before this reaches you. He is *game* to the backbone, but he has not the physical stamina for such an adventure as that. I am sorry to say I lost three of my men killed and four wounded, and my horse, saddle and bridle (English), were lost. I wish you could coax Captain Swinton out of that horse he got of General Anson's; life and more than life sometimes depends on being well mounted.

*January 3rd.*—We did not get back from Goorsahaigunge till two this morning, very weary and tired, and now comes an order, just as I am sitting down to write, for my regiment to march at once to join the Chief's camp near Futtehgurh: so I am again reduced to the mere announcement that I am safe and well. I have just heard that the rebels have bolted from Futtehgurh.

FUTTEHGURH, *4th January.*—A night march of twenty-five miles, tents up at 1 P.M., after which breakfast, and two interviews with the Chief and his staff, have not left me much daylight or time for the post. Futtehgurh was abandoned as I foretold, and our troops are all concentrating here, not a shot having been fired. We remain here a few days, but a few inglorious but needful burning expeditions will probably be all we shall have to do. Our dear friend Napier is recovered, or nearly so, from his wound. I hope he will join the Chief, who appreciates him as he deserves.

*January 5th.*—The anniversary of the most blessed event in my life again to be spent in absence. . . . I see no chance just yet of any vigorous action by which the war might be concluded, and we released from this toilsome campaign. The Commander-in-

Chief is tied by red tape, and obliged to wait the orders of Government as to where he is to go!

*6th.*—We march to-day with a brigade under Colonel Adrian Hope, on some punishing expeditions. I hope to return in three or four days, and where we go next is not known. Seaton has subsided for the present into the simple Colonel of Fusiliers, which seems hard enough after all he has done. I hope they will soon give him a brigade.

CAMP, SHUMSHABAD, *January 7th.*—Here we are on the move again! Colonel Hope's brigade, consisting of the 42d and 73d Highlanders, 2d Punjab Infantry, a Royal Artillery battery, two guns Bengal H.A., a squadron of Lancers, and half my men—a splendid little force with nothing to do I fear but pull down houses, the owners of which have all escaped. We are only a few miles from the place to which we pursued the enemy from Puttialee, and had Colonel Seaton been allowed to push on *then*, we should have caught and punished these rascals as they deserved. Brigadier Hope is a very fine fellow and a pleasant; about my age, or younger if anything, though, of course, longer in the army. When he knows more of India he will do very well indeed, I should think.

CAMP, KAIMGUNGE, *January 8th.*—We remain here to-morrow, and then return, I fancy, to head-quarters. I can bear up manfully against absence and separation when we are actually doing anything; but when I see nothing doing towards an end, I confess my heart sinks and my spirit hungers after rest. I should be very, very glad, if dear Maynard would make up her mind to join you. It would be a real comfort to me to think that we had been able to do anything towards contributing to her peace or comfort. Independently of my sincere regard for her, she is her father's daughter, and I owe him too much gratitude and reverence not to desire to show it in every way to all of the name and blood of Thomason.

KAIMGUNGE, *January 10th.*—Our time has been taken up with riding about the country after Whip-poor-Wills, which elude our search and grasp, the only consolation being fine exercise in a fine country.

CAMP, FUTTEHGURH, *January* 12*th*.—We returned from our brief expedition this morning, not having effected much, though we frightened many I have no doubt. I was just talking to Colonel Hope (himself an old 60th man) about my dear good friend Douglas, when I got your letter enclosing his most welcome one. How rejoiced I shall be if he returns to India with his battalion! I quite long to see him once more. Indeed, as time goes on, old ties of affection and friendship seem to unite themselves more intimately with newer and dearer ones, and my heart pines more and more for home, and all which nought but home can give.

FUTTEHGURH, *January* 14*th*.—I was unhappily so much delayed by a tedious review yesterday morning, and an interview with the Chief afterwards, that I did not get to my tent till after post time, though I am thankful to say I found some very precious missives —the dear girls' letters were a treat indeed, and gave me very real pleasure. I am beginning to hope that I shall have my previous services recognised; for although I do not know that any record of the promise of a majority was down in Leadenhall Street, still Lord Dalhousie's promise was distinct, and there is evidently every desire on our present Chief's part to do me justice. Nothing can be kinder or more cordial than the Commander-in-Chief and General Mansfield. We seem destined to halt here at present; half the day has been occupied in changing ground. So when one can't get one's tent pitched till 1 or 2 P.M., there is little time for writing for a post closing at 5, considering that business and eating and washing have to be performed. I must try and write more to-night. I am going to dine with the Chief.

CAMP ON THE RAMGUNGA, *January* 15*th*.—I left off my last letter with a promised intention of writing more last night, but the result of dining with the Chief was, that I was kept up so late and had to rise so early that I was fain to carry my weary limbs to bed at once. You will hear of me before this reaches you; General Grant and Majors Norman and Turner having taken wing to Umbâla for a few days. They have had no holiday since May, and heartily deserved one, though I must confess I did feel a little envious when I saw them off. What would not I give for home once more!

We are here to force a passage across the Ramgunga, a confluent of the Ganges on the road to Bareilly; but it does not follow that we shall go there when the passage is open. Brigadier Walpole commands, and we have enough troops to eat up Rohilcund; whether we (*i.e.*, my regiment) partake of the "finish" in Oude or not, no one can pretend to foretell.

Colonel Becher will be at Umbâla soon on his way home. You will be kind to him, I am sure, both because you like him personally, and because he has been most kind and considerate to me. It was very ungracious, as well as ungraceful, that his name was not mentioned in the Despatches as it ought to have been; but he is not the only one who has cause to complain of the "ungraciousness" of our Delhi General.

CAMP ON THE RAMGUNGA, *January 17th.*—We are still in the same undignified attitude of looking at nothing and doing as little; but the halt has been very useful to me in the way of getting through business, and I have hardly stirred from my table all day. The plundering propensities of some of my men have given me much occupation and annoyance, as I always feel that the ill-conduct of a regiment must more or less reflect on the officers. The rascals will not discriminate between an enemy's property, which is fair game, and that of the villagers and cultivators of the soil. I have several times been obliged to bring them up with a sharp hand to save myself from discredit. I sent three sowars to-day to the Brigadier with evidence and proof enough to hang them, but he begged me to dispose of the matter summarily myself; but as I did not choose to be judge, jury, and hangman all in one, they saved their lives at the expense of their backs, though I believe the punishment was greater to me than to them, for I abhor flogging, and never resort to it but in the extremest cases. Still I must be obeyed by these wild hordes *coute qui coute;* and when reason and argument fail, they must learn that I will not weakly refrain from sterner measures. I am happy to find Sir Colin ready to back me *à l'outrance,* so as to maintain discipline. Have you written to our dear friends Napier and Prendergast yet? The latter is in Calcutta with his bride long ago. Sir James Outram and Napier have given Mister Pandy a glorious thrashing at Alumbagh. Hurrah!*

*January* 19*th.*—I had to go over to see the Chief yesterday, and did not return till night. I also saw good Colonel Seaton and Becher, who (the last) starts in a day or two for home and England. I did know about Mr. Wemyss's good appointment, for Sir Colin good-naturedly gave me the letter to take to him. Wemyss is a lucky fellow, and will, I hope, do credit to his luck. I am working to get some pay as Assistant-Quartermaster-General, in addition to my pay as commandant, which the pay officer objects to, on the ground that one man cannot draw the pay of two officers. They should have had two men to do it then; for I worked like a slave, and the labourer is worthy of his hire. I saw and had a long talk with your "charming" Mr. Raikes yesterday.

*January* 22*nd.*—There has been no news of public importance for some days, so I am taking advantage of the halt and comparative idleness to work off arrears of business and papers, and to prepare rolls and pay abstracts for Captain Swinton's office. I have consequently not been half-a-mile from my tent these two days; moreover, I am resting my unlucky ankle, which has given me much pain and trouble lately. I am very glad Mr. Montgomery is at Umbâla. I am sure you would tell him how grateful I have ever felt for his assistance in raising my regiment; the two troops he sent me I shall call Montgomery's troops, and the men will like it too.

23*rd.*—Our friend Colonel Seaton is to have command of a

---

* I would recommend this letter to the consideration of those who have charged Hodson with want of all humane feelings or pity.—*Ed.*

district to be formed of Allygurh, Futtehgurh, Mynpooree and the post at Meerun-ke-Serai. It is a very honourable and important post; but he would prefer, and I for him, a more active command. I expect the rest of the force will move into Oudh soon, and I do trust to be at the ultimate capture of Lucknow.

24*th*.—They say we are to move soon, but no one knows for certain, as I have not been into head-quarters for some days; meantime my pen is busy, *very* busy, with six months' arrears to work off, but I am getting on at it famously.

FUTTEHGURH, 26*th*.—Late last night I was roused up by an order to march in here at dawn, so here, accordingly, we came; and now at 10 P.M. we are off again, on some expedition which will last us a few days. The Chief sent for me as soon as we came in, and was very communicative, and asked my opinion in most flattering terms. I gave it honestly, and only hope he will follow it, if we are to make an end of this business before another hot season sets in. I fancy the whole force will be in motion soon towards Oudh; but nothing is certainly known as yet, except that we go to our old place Shumshabad. Colonel Adrian Hope again commands the brigade; we start almost immediately, and shall, I hope, do something effective.

FORT FUTTEHGURH, *Jan*. 28*th*.
(*Written with the left hand, in pencil.*)

Though I sent you a telegram I must manage a few words by letter to tell you that there is not the very slightest cause for alarm on my account, for I am really quite well; only my right arm will be useless for some weeks, but I can do my duty, and intend to march with the Commander-in-Chief. What grieves me most is the loss of poor Mac; he was invaluable to me as a brilliant soldier, a true friend, and thorough gentleman—I mourn as for a brother.

In a letter to England of the same date, he says—

CAMP, FUTTEHGURH, *Jan.* 31*st*, 1858.
(*Written with left hand.*)

My usual fortune deserted me on the 27th, at Shumshabad, for I got two sabre cuts on my right arm, which have reduced me to this very sinister style of writing (*absit omen*). We had a very stiff fight of it, as we were far in advance of the rest of the troops, and had to charge a very superior body of the mutineer cavalry; but there was nothing for it but fighting, as, had we not attacked them, they would have got in amongst our guns. We were only three officers, and about 180 horsemen—my poor friend and second in command, Macdowell, having received a mortal wound a few minutes before we charged. It was a terrible *mêlée* for some time, and we were most wonderfully preserved. However, we gave them a very proper thrashing, and killed their leaders. Two out of the three of us were wounded, and five of my men killed and eleven wounded, besides eleven horses. My horse had three sabre-cuts, and I got two, which I consider a rather unfair share. The Commander-in-Chief is very well satisfied, I hear, with the day's work, and is profusely civil and kind to me. The force moves on to-morrow towards Cawnpore and Lucknow, which has at last to be conquered; for neither Outram, Havelock, nor the Commander-in-Chief were able to effect a footing in Lucknow. All they could do was to bring away the Residency garrison. All the lion's share of the work in the six weeks which intervened between the *soi-disant* relief of the Lucknow garrison by Havelock, and the real one by the Commander-in-Chief, was done by our friend Colonel Napier. He is the best man we have left, now that poor Sir Henry Lawrence and Nicholson are gone. The next is Major Tombs, or I am much mistaken. . . . I hope to return to Umbâla when this war is over, to be refitted and get my men trained and drilled, which is very necessary. I do hope to be able to get home and see your dear faces once more, as soon as our great task is accomplished. I want a change after twelve years of work, and I want to try what home and good treatment will do for my ankle, which is very bad; in fact, I am unable to walk a hundred yards without pain. Well, I think I have done pretty well with my left hand. They say I shall be well in six weeks. *I* say in ten days; I trust so.

---

*To his Wife.*

FUTTEHGURH, *Jan.* 30*th*.

Mr. Raikes tells me that he wrote to you immediately after the action at Shumshabad, lest you should be made unhappy by report. This was most kind and thoughtful of him; and I do hope therefore, that among so many kind friends, you will have been spared any unnecessary pain. Everybody is very complimentary; even men I never spoke to before. A flattering rascal told me he considered it an "honour (forsooth!) to shake even my left hand." I might become too proud with so much notice, but the memory of 1854-55 is ever before me. The Commander-in-Chief has been unable to move as yet for many reasons, but I fancy we shall march ere long. I am wonderfully well, and the big wound is actually closing already! is not that famous?

*January* 31*st.*—I have been busy until post time with looking over poor Mac's things, and taking an inventory of them for his mother. I am sure you will write to her as soon as we can ascertain her address. I cannot tell you how much I feel his loss. We march on towards Cawnpore to-morrow morning; it is a grief to me to be disabled ever so little just at this time, but in a very few days I shall be all right again.

*January* 31*st.*—The Chief won't let me go on just yet, though I really am perfectly able to do so. I am not a bit the worse for these wounds, beyond the temporary inconvenience and disgust at being *hors de combat* in such times as these. I look forward with the utmost pleasure to seeing our friend Napier at Lucknow;

I wish we could hear from him. Inglis's despatch is, as you say, most touching, and his conduct most admirable, as well as hers. I always thought her a fine character.

*February 1st and 2nd.*—I am really doing very well, and the wounds are healing wonderfully fast. In ten days I hope to use my arm; they threatened me with six weeks! I have indeed cause for gratitude, not only for my preservation from greater evil, but for this rapid recovery; happily I was in good health at the time, and these wounds depend almost entirely on the state of the blood. I shall remain here until the day after to-morrow, and then accompany Brigadier Walpole's brigade to join the Chief at Cawnpore. Colonel Burn drives me along in a buggy; for though I *can* ride, it is not advisable to run the risk of a shake. Every one is most kind; Sir Colin markedly so. We are to have prize money for Delhi after all; this will please as well as benefit the army, the soldiers not being over-well contented with the six months' batta, thinking that was all they were to get. It is hardly perhaps to be expected that the masses should be satisfied with the mere consciousness of having done their duty through such months of suffering as those before Delhi.

*February 3d.*—I am overwhelmed with letters of congratulation, which I can only acknowledge by a few lines in this sinister writing. Light has written very warmly, also Lord William; you must thank them both for me at present, as we march for Cawnpore early in the morning. So I shall be at the capture of Lucknow after all! and after that may God restore us to each other to part no more!

CAMP, JELLALABAD, ON THE GRAND TRUNK ROAD, *February 5th.*—We shall be at Cawnpore in four days more, I trust. Nothing can be more favourable than the state of my wounds, and I have felt scarcely any inconvenience from travelling. I am fortunate in having Colonel Burn for a travelling companion; pleasant, intelligent, and warm-hearted. He drives me in his buggy, and we breakfast together *al fresco.* Fancy the Carbineers of poor Captain Wardlaw's squadron sending a deputation, headed by a sergeant, to say on the part of the men how grieved they were that I was hurt, and to express their hope that I should soon be well and in the field again. I confess these things are more gratifying to me than any mention in despatches.

CAMP, MEERUN-KE-SERAI, *February 6th.*—We had a very trying march this morning, a gale of wind bringing up clouds of dust and grit, which cut one's face and eyes to pieces. I half wished I was a lady to wear a veil.

*February 8th.*—I go on into Cawnpore in the morning, making two marches in one; my arm has not been going on quite so well the last three days, owing, the doctor says, to the sharp wind. The wound on the thumb is nearly closed, and I shall be all right, I hope, after two or three days' quiet at Cawnpore. The getting up in the cold mornings is very trying, now that I am unable to ride or walk to get warm.

CAWNPORE, *February 10th.*—I got here in good time yesterday, but was kept constantly at work fomenting this tiresome arm, which had got somewhat inflamed from the effects of the journey. To-day we cross the river, and encamp a mile or two on the other side, and there I hope to halt for a few days. Our friend (Napier) is Chief Engineer with the force, and a Brigadier to boot. I hope to see him in a day or two.

CAMP ON THE LEFT BANK OF THE GANGES, *February 11th.*—I came across the river late in the evening, and am very glad I did so, as the air is much purer and there is no dust. My arm is already better for the rest, and I hope soon to be able to begin to use it. Do not buoy yourself up with hope of honours for me. I shall be a Brevet-Major, and nothing more, I expect. It seems the authorities here never sent home a list of men recommended for honours; and the home authorities have been waiting until they get one. "Hinc illæ lacrymæ!" And we shall all suffer by the delay in more ways than one. But we are certainly to have prize money, and this with the batta, will take us home this time next year if not sooner. My share of prize money will be 6000 rupees, and my batta 1100 more. Dear, dear home, sadly changed and contracted since I left it, but home still, and dearer than ever, since the dearest part of myself will accompany me. . . . All old home memories were so vividly revived yesterday by Charles Harland's visit, and an extract he read me from a letter from his brother, describing the enthusiasm of the old people at Colwich (his father's old parish), when the news arrived that the King of Delhi was our prisoner, and how they came to inquire whether it was really their "Master William" who had done it? Bless their innocent hearts, where was they riz? as —— would say. I am sadly at a loss for a second in command, and do not know whom to ask for, as officers are so scarce.

*February* 12*th.*—Here I am, you see, writing (such as it is), with my right hand once more. I am indeed wonderfully better, and hope to be on horseback in a few days. The scar on my arm is a very ugly one, and will mark me for life; but then, as I am not a lady to wear short sleeves, it does not signify. We march on towards Lucknow to-morrow. It will be some days yet before the whole force is collected at Alumbagh. Captain Peel has just gone by with his sailors and their enormous ship guns, 68-pounders! I have little doubt but that Lucknow will be in our hands before another month is over; and then I shall do my utmost to get my regiment sent back to Umbâla to be formed and drilled, which it wants badly. I only wonder it does as well as it is. I could hardly take any other appointment, or even go home, until I had completed this task; and I like my regiment, and what is even more to the purpose, the regiment likes me, and would follow me any and everywhere, I do believe.

CAMP, OONAO, *February* 13*th.*—Only a short letter to-day, as I have been writing a right-handed one to satisfy the dear anxious hearts at home. I am able to use my arm, but very gently, and shall ride to-morrow. Oh! the pleasure of feeling myself on the outside of a horse again.

*February* 14*th.*—Your telegram has been going the rounds of all the camps before it found me out. Indeed you must not be anxious on my account, or listen to the wild reports which are always rife. Be sure if anything were amiss, there are plenty of our friends here to send you the truth. I am going on wonderfully, and but for the attack of inflammation I spoke of, and which turned out to be erysipelas, I should have been quite well before this; and as it is, I am actually nearer to a total cure than the men (Sikhs even) who were wounded the same day. My abstinence from spirit-drinking has stood me in good stead.

*February* 15*th*.—No letters again to-day! I wish the Commander-in-Chief would come out from Cawnpore, and there would be some chance of better postal duty. He is said to be waiting until the convoy of ladies from Agra has passed down, lest anything should occur to disturb the road where he had crossed into Oude with the army—a not unlikely thing to happen.

OONAO, *February* 16*th*.—I have this morning succeeded in exhuming four letters from the bottom of about a hundredweight of correspondence addressed to all parts of the world; the bag was sent up here in the night for people to find their letters as they could. Mine have made me so happy. This has been a red-letter day too, for I have at last seen our friend Napier. He rode out here with Sir Colin, and I need not say how thoroughly delighted I was to see him once more. He is looking better but older than when we parted, but his charming, affectionate manner is as nice as ever. God bless him! I do love him dearly, as if he were indeed my born brother. A note from him arrived while he was here; it had been three days going ten miles! Sir Colin was most kind and cordial, and prophesies I shall soon be Lieut.-Colonel. I told him I feared there was small hope of that, unless my majority could be counted as for the Punjab campaign, as Lord Dalhousie promised, but that it had not been put on record. He immediately said, "Oh, I'll do that with the greatest pleasure; let me have a memorandum of your services, and I'll do all I can for you." They do say I shall have the Victoria Cross, but I do not believe it. My arm is going on admirably, and you may be quite satisfied about me now I am near our friend Napier : he will always do what is kind, that we may be quite sure of, and all that is best and tenderest too, where you or I are concerned. I shall try to get away immediately after Lucknow is taken, but I fear every man may be needed for some time, even after that much-desired event takes place.

CAMP, OONAO, *February* 17*th*.—I grieve deeply at your anxiety, and can scarcely understand your "terror at the very name of Cawnpore and Lucknow," except for what has passed. I am not nearly so much exposed to peril here as at Delhi; the place, too, and time of year are more healthy; so continue to "hope on," bravely now as ever, until the end, which must be very soon. . . . . I am going to spend to-morrow in Cawnpore with Napier, and have a big talk. The delay in the brevet is an accident, *not* owing to the home authorities. It has gone home now, and my name is in it, Sir Colin told me.

CAWNPORE, *February* 19*th*.—I shall ride back to Oonao early to-morrow morning : the temptation of Napier's society was irresistible ; it is such a pleasure to see him again. There will be no move hence until the 23rd, I think, though it is getting rapidly hot in this hateful place ; but on the other side the river it is cool, and Lucknow is even more so, I hear.

OONAO, *February* 20*th*.—I rode out from Cawnpore this morning; Colonels Napier and Lugard accompanying me for some miles —the latter only arrived yesterday ; he is to command a division as Brigadier-General, I am glad to say. Our friend is nicer than ever, and looking well. We are forty miles from the enemy and as quiet as in Cantonments.

*February* 21*st*.—As far as I can learn we (*i.e.*, my Horse) shall have but little to do with the actual capture or assault of Lucknow, and I fancy our duty will be protecting the flanks and rear of the army from incursions of the enemy's cavalry, &c. General Lugard came out this morning to take the command. I hope Napier will soon follow. I am very anxious to get on and get the affair over.

*February* 22*nd*.—There is not a particle of news of any kind. I had an attack of fever last night, but it is gone this morning, and I am all right again; the wound on my arm is quite closed, and the last bandage discarded; the thumb is still very stiff, and the joint much enlarged. My wounds have healed with unprecedented rapidity; and I cannot be sufficiently grateful that I am so soon enabled to return to my duty. God grant I may be able to get home soon: that is my great desire now.

*February* 23*rd.*—It is midnight, and we march for Alumbagh at 4 A.M.; so I write a line at once to say I am doing well, and will send a telegram if anything occurs, which I do not expect yet. There has been a big fight within a few miles of us between the force under General Hope Grant and the rebels, and there was a bigger on Sunday at Lucknow with Sir James Outram's force. I have got hold of a strip of newspaper this morning, with Brigadier Hope's Shumshabad despatch, in which I figure so prominently that I am inclined to indorse it " Hope told a flattering tale," and send it home to the dear girls. The convoy arrived this morning (*i.e.*, the ladies, &c.) from Agra, so I hope the Chief will move soon. I was out all the morning with General Lugard, and was surprised to find how hot the weather is getting (in the sun) even here; but I am quite well—quite.

In a letter of this date to the Chaplain of the Lawrence Asylum, he says:—

. . . I have only to add that in gratitude for the many and unspeakable mercies which I have received during the past year, and also as a token of most affectionate regret for Sir H. Lawrence, I shall thank you to note the increase of my subscription to the asylum to 100 rupees per annum.

## CONCLUDING CHAPTER.

*ALUMBAGH, LUCKNOW—THE BEGUM'S PALACE—BANKS' HOUSE—THE SOLDIER'S DEATH—NOTICES—CONCLUDING REMARKS.*

*To his Wife.*

CAMP, ALUMBAGH, NEAR LUCKNOW,
*February* 24*th.*

WE arrived here last night at dusk, after a terribly dusty march of thirty-six miles. To-day we had a bit of a fight. The Pandies, ignorant of the reinforcements which had arrived, had as usual come round one flank of the camp, so we moved out and caught them as they were trying to get back again, and took two of their guns. By "we," I mean, my own men, and the Military Train men from home. Young Charles Gough, my adjutant, was wounded, and had his horse shot. I was luckily in the way, or it would have gone worse with him;* my own horse too (pretty "Child of the Desert") was wounded, and I was obliged to mount a sowar's horse. Gough will be laid up for a month, I fear; it is a flesh wound in the thigh. I do not think Master Pandy will try the same trick again. We have been out so long that there is time for no more to-day than this assurance of my safety.

ALUMBAGH, *February* 25*th.*—I have been calling on Sir James Outram this morning, and had a most pleasant interview; the

---

* Lieutenant Gough says that my brother saved his life by cutting down a rebel trooper in the very act of spearing him. "The spear had actually pierced me at the moment when the man fell under a blow from Hodson, who himself had received a sword cut."

brave old warrior greeted me most cordially, professing his satisfaction at having *at last* met one of whom he had heard so much, &c., &c. The pleasure was certainly mutual, for I have long wished to meet *him*. He made many inquiries about you also, and asked whether you had not been in the hills during the panic and helped the refugees, &c. How proudly I could answer all his praise in the affirmative. Altogether this good old soldier's compliments were pleasing to me, particularly as he was not one of those who in my time of trouble passed me by on the other side.

The enemy is quite quiet to-day. I fancy we were too much for his philosophy yesterday. Fancy the Queen Regnant coming out on an elephant to meet us, to encourage her wavering followers! I wish the Chief would make haste and finish this business, it is getting cruelly hot already.

*27th.*—All quiet still with the enemy. A packet of letters has arrived, and brought me all the comfort I am capable of receiving in this torturing absence; would it were over! I hear the Chief has crossed the Ganges and is coming on here. I believe we had some $κῦδος$ for the affair of the 25th, though beyond being exposed to a very galling fire, I did not think much of it myself. Gough's wound is a serious misfortune to me just now; a gallant, go-a-head boy like him is not to be easily replaced, any more than poor Mac is. I myself am laid up with a sore leg. I would not nurse it at first, and now it is so painful I cannot mount my horse or even stand without pain, so I shall go into the next scrimmage on an elephant! Dr. Brougham, however, says it will be well in four or five days.

ALUMBAGH, 1*st March.*—Nothing of public importance is occurring. I am still unable to ride, so I do regimental work. I dined with Sir J. Outram last night. He would quite charm you, and were I not out of love with vanity, would spoil me; but I confess the respectful homage of the soldiers is pleasanter to my spirit than the praise of great men.

*March* 2*nd.*—The Commander-in-Chief arrived with a large part of the force this morning, marched straight through our camp, and *at* the enemy (who of course ran away) and occupied the Dilkoosha, a large garden-house and park near the city. My unfortunate leg prevented my sharing in the fray, I grieve to say, and I am actually in a fright lest he (the Chief) should take Lucknow before I am able to ride!

ALUMBAGH, *March* 5*th*.—I had time for but the merest line yesterday, written from Dilkoosha, where the Commander-in-Chief is encamped, and whither we were erroneously brought yesterday to return here to-day. I had a long talk with Sir Colin, who was even more than commonly kind and cordial. I am not very well, I am sorry to say; this leg troubles me, and is the effect of the erysipelas which attacked my arm in consequence of the wounds closing too quickly. The truth is, that I lost about a pound and a half of blood when I was wounded, and having had two slight bouts of fever since, I am not so strong as I would be; however, I am getting on, and am dosed with steel, quinine, and port wine *ad lib*. My arm is pretty well, but the wound opened again partially after the 25th, and I have been obliged to submit to bandages, &c.; still I hope three or four days will set me all right again, though I fear the arm will never be quite straight again, or the thumb quite flexible. I shall have to go home for rest to my body, if not for comfort to my heart. I have seen Osborn Wilkinson; he is as nice as possible; and he is now Deputy-Assistant-Quartermaster-General to the Cavalry Brigade, to which my Horse is attached, so I hope to see more of him than of late. I breakfasted yesterday at head-quarters with Napier, and grieved to see that he looked worn and troubled. I fear his health is very precarious.

CAMP, NEAR LUCKNOW, *March* 6*th*.— . . . I grieve that you should be anxious on my account; the same merciful Providence which has so wonderfully preserved us both through so many and great dangers, will, I earnestly pray, continue the same gracious guardianship, yet I strive to be prepared for all . . .

I had to march again this morning; a message from Sir Colin last night to the Brigadier having directed him to put me in charge of the line of communications with Jellalabad, the Alumbagh, and his camp. So I had to bring my men up here, half way between the two camps, and to make arrangements for insuring the safety of the roads, and protecting the convoys on which the existence of the army depends. The worst part of it is I cannot ride, and have had for the first time in my life to do outpost duty in a dog-cart! *driving* across country to post videttes and picquettes, &c. What with this continued movement and the rest which I am *compelled* to take recumbent, I have had no time for writing as I fain would do.

*March 8th.*—I went up myself to-day to the headquarters' camp, to look for letters and see our friend, but failed in both; but I breakfasted and had a long chat with that pleasantest of persons, Lugard, now Sir Edward, and while there I had a letter from Norman to say that Reginald had been appointed to do duty with my Horse. I can but think he is too young; but if he must see hard service so early, better with me than elsewhere. God grant it may be for his good. I am looking for the end with an eager longing for rest which I cannot control.

*March 9th.*—I grieve that report should cause you fear and anxiety whenever there has been a fight, particularly as the chances are against my being in it. You should remember that our force extends now round three sides nearly of Lucknow. The extreme right of our position, or rather camps, being at least nine miles from the left; so that engagements occur at one part which those at the other never perhaps hear of till next day! Indeed I have not been on horseback since the 25th, as I am forced to save myself for emergencies. If anything important occurs, be sure I will send a telegram somehow. I do hope Charles Gough will soon be well; I do ill without such a dashing fine fellow.

In the affair of the 25th we were leading, and took the guns—*i.e.*, we fairly captured one, and drove the enemy away from the other, and kept them at bay until the "train" came up and secured it. I was not altogether satisfied with my men in this part of the affair. They hesitated, and let me go ahead unsupported except by Nihal Singh; old Mahommed Reza Khan, and one or two others, with Gough, being near. The consequence was that the enemy concentrated their fire on our little party. However, the Europeans of the Military Train hesitated to do what I wanted *my* men to do, and they behaved very well immediately afterwards. There has been a great fuss about the matter; Sir Colin having taken great and very just offence at its being reported to him that the cavalry were "led" by Colonel ——, a staff officer. .... He got wounded, and then was officially reported to have "led the cavalry," whereas we had Brigadier Campbell (a capital officer), and Colonel Haggart, of the 7th Hussars, present, besides the officers commanding regiments, "quorum pars fui." Sir Colin denounced Colonel ——'s "leading" as "an insufferable impertinence," called me up, and asked me before them all, "Were you present with your regiment on the 25th?" and on my saying "Yes," he cried out, "Now, look here; look at my friend Hodson here, does *he* look like a man that needs 'leading'? Is that a man likely to want 'leading'? I should like to see the fellow who'd presume to talk of 'leading' *that* man!" pointing to me, and so forth. I nearly went into convulsions; it was *such* a scene. ....

The Martinière was taken to-day without loss, except Captain Peel, who, I grieve to say, is wounded.

*March* 10*th*.—The mail is come with my Majority. The brevet has given general dissatisfaction. Some of the double honours are marvellous; but it should be remembered that these promotions are given *sponte suâ* by the home authorities, no recommendations having gone from hence till lately. I am content myself, having no interest. It proves they perceive I have done something, or I should not have this beginning; and it is satisfactory to find that it is universally considered that I have been shabbily used. Better this by far than to have people lifting up their eyes and saying I had got too much! Inglis is justly rewarded, and some others. I daresay more will come with time. I hope devoutly that when Lucknow falls I shall be released. We shall know in a few days—for even while I write Lucknow seems to be "falling" fast. Immense progress was made yesterday, with not more loss than some eighteen or twenty wounded, and I hear to-day they are going ahead again. Pandy has quite given up fighting, except potshots under cover, and runs at the very sight of troops advancing. I stood on the top of the Dilkoosha palace yesterday, and watched the capture of as strong a position as men could wish for (which at Delhi would have cost us hundreds) without the enemy making a single struggle or firing a shot. At this rate Lucknow will soon be in our hands. We (of the cavalry) are kept on the *qui vive* watching the southern outlets from the town to prevent escape, and I expect to see Lucknow taken without being under fire again. Well, it must be confessed that I have had my share of the dangers of the war, and whether I receive honours or not, I have the testimony of my own conscience that I have done one man's work towards the restoration of our power in India. . . . . I have been occupied to-day in trying to get the Victoria Cross for the two Goughs. Hugh certainly ought to have it. (It was given.—ED.)

*March* 11*th.*—Just as I sit down to write comes an order to move our camp towards Alumbagh again; Jung Bahadoor having at last arrived with his army and taken up ground between me and the enemy. . . . If anything occurs, I will get Colonel Napier or Norman to send you a service telegram. . . .

This was the last letter which my brother wrote. Having given directions to his Adjutant, Lieutenant C. Gough, he said he would ride on and look out a nice spot for their new camping ground, and be back in time to march with them. On his way he heard firing, and riding forward, found that the Begum's Palace was to be attacked. He immediately rode to the Mortar Batteries, where his friend Brigadier Napier was directing the attack. The assaulting column was formed of the 93d Highlanders and 4th Punjab Rifles. They went at it with a rush and carried it. He entered the breach with General Napier and several others. In a few minutes they were separated in the *mêlée*, and General Napier saw nothing more of him till he was sent for to him "dangerously wounded." The surgeon of his regiment, Dr. Anderson, gives the following account:—

"We struck our tents and were saddled, waiting for him till it became so dark that we were forced to go without him, and reached our ground after sunset. I had gone to the post-office and was five minutes behind the regiment. When I came up, I found that Hodson's orderly had come in great haste, saying that his master had sent for me, but with no other message. He said that his master had been hit when advancing with the troops on the Begum's Kotee on foot.

"I mounted and rode off with him at once. From the darkness of the night and the difficulty of passing the Goorkah sentries, I did not get to Dilkoosha till 9 P.M. There no one knew where he was. I then went on to the artillery mess and learnt that he was in Banks' House, which I reached about 10 P.M. I found him in a dooly and Dr. Sutherland with him, whom I at once relieved, and learnt the following particulars from him and from the orderly who remained with Hodson, and who had been by his side when hit. He had arrived at Banks' House just as the party going to attack the Begum's Palace were starting, and fell in with them. The place had been taken before he was wounded. When the soldiers were searching for concealed Sepoys in the courtyard and buildings adjoining, he said to his orderly, 'I wonder if any of the rascals are in there.' He turned the angle of the passage; looked into a dark room, which was full of Sepoys; a shot was fired from inside. He staggered back some paces and then fell. A party of Highlanders, hearing who had been hit, rushed into the room and bayoneted every man there.

"The orderly, Nihal Singh, a large powerful Sikh, carried him in his arms out of danger, and got a dooly and brought him back to Banks' House, where his wound was looked to and dressed.

"He was shot through the right side of the chest, in the region of the liver, the ball entering in front and going out behind. There had been profuse bleeding, and I saw that the wound was most likely mortal.

"He was very glad to see me, and began talking of his wound, which he thought himself was mortal. I lay beside him on the ground all night, holding his hand, on account of the great pain he suffered. He was very weak when I arrived, but by means of stimulants rallied wonderfully, and slept for an hour or two during the night. At daylight he was much better, his hands were warm and his pulse good, and I had hopes that, if the bleeding, which had ceased, did not return, he might recover. He drank two cups of tea, and said he felt very well.

"About 9 A.M. I had the dooly lifted into a room, which I had had cleared out, where he was much quieter. At 10 A.M., however, bleeding came on again profusely, and he rapidly became worse. I told him that recovery was impossible. He then sent for General Napier, to whom he gave directions about his property and messages to his wife. After this he rapidly sank, though he remained sensible and was able to speak till a quarter past one, when he became too weak; and in ten minutes more the sad scene was over. He died most quietly without a struggle. He merely ceased to breathe.

"His orderly* actually cried over him, he was so attached to him.

"He was buried that evening by the Rev. Dr. Smith. The Commander-in-Chief and his staff were present."

Further particulars are given in a letter written to his widow by General Napier (Lord Napier of Magdala) :—

"On the morning of our taking a range of Palaces called the Begum Kotee, I was reconnoitring the breach whilst the guns were

---

\* This orderly, Nihal Singh, afterwards travelled to Simla at his own expense to see Mrs. Hodson, and beg to be taken into her service and go to England with her. The men of his regiment cried like children when they heard the news of his death.

making it practicable, and waiting for the moment when I could send the word for the troops to advance, when your husband suddenly stood beside me and said laughingly, 'I am come to take care of you.' The signal was given for the troops to advance, and we watched their progress and entry into the building. All serious opposition soon ceased, and we followed through the breach into the Palace. None of the enemy remained except a few parties shut up in houses, whom our troops were despatching. Your poor husband, Captain Taylor and I, were together then. I got separated from them in the crowd, and proceeded to push on our advantage. When I returned, General Lugard told me that both your husband and Taylor were wounded, and that he was earnestly asking for me.

"I went immediately to Banks' House, and found him in a dooly, not suffering much pain. His wound had been dressed, and he had all necessary attendance. I was obliged to leave him to go to the Commander-in-Chief, but then returned and remained with him till the approach of morning obliged me to return to my duties.

"As soon as I could possibly leave them I went to see him again, and found him much better, and the doctor then thought favourably of him.

"He constantly held my hand whilst I was with him, and would not be satisfied till he held it. He was quite sensible and composed. His mind was occupied with thoughts of you, and of his brothers and sisters. He said, 'If I do not recover, let Susie go to England as soon as possible. I leave everything to her.' I was obliged to leave him for a time, and when I returned he was in more pain. He said, 'I think I am dying. The doctor gave me hopes, but I do not believe in them. I should like to have seen the end of the campaign, and to have returned to England to see my friends, but it has not been permitted. I trust I have done my duty.' I could have no difficulty in answering this question, as the voice of every one in the country proclaims it. I had good hopes of him then, as his pulse was good and strong

I was grieved to leave him, but it was necessary for me to be at my post, and before I had time to return to him he had gone to his rest, calm and composed at his last hour as he was in the front of danger in battle. I took his ring, and Dr. Anderson cut off his hair.

"Amidst universal sorrow and regret he was laid in his grave near the Martinière. I am going to enclose it with a masonry wall and build a tomb over it immediately. I grieve deeply now that I did not object to his entering the Palace at all, but you know his forward spirit, and how impossible it was to keep him out of danger. It is God's will and we must bow submissively."*

Thus, on the 12th of March 1858, in his thirty-seventh year, closed the earthly career of one of the best and bravest of England's sons, one of her truest heroes, of whom it may be said—" Quanquam medio in spatio integræ ætatis ereptus, quantum ad gloriam longissimum ævum peregit."

Great and irreparable as was his loss to his family and his friends, as a husband, a brother, and a friend, I believe that, at the particular juncture at which he was taken away, it was still greater, as a soldier, to his country. It would be difficult to over-estimate the value of the services which he might have rendered, if spared, in the pacifying of Oude after the capture of Lucknow, or the influence which he might have had on the fortunes of the war. One of those best qualified to judge declared that "Hodson with his regiment would have been worth 10,000 men." His peculiar qualifications for Asiatic warfare would have found an appropriate field for their display.

It is unnecessary, however, for me to attempt to pronounce his eulogium. This has been done by those more capable of forming an estimate of his rare excellence as a soldier, and of doing it justice by their words.

* For another account, see Introduction, p. xl.

Sir Colin Campbell, in a letter of condolence to his widow, thus expressed himself:—

"MARTINIERE, *March* 13, 1858.

"MADAM,—It is with a sentiment of profound regret that I am compelled to address you, for the purpose of communicating the sad news that your gallant and distinguished husband, Major Hodson, received a mortal wound from a bullet on the 11th instant. He unfortunately accompanied his friend Brigadier Napier, commanding Engineers in the successful attack on the Begum's Palace. The whole army, which admired his talents, his bravery, and his military skill, deplores his loss, and sympathises with you in your irreparable bereavement. I attended your husband's funeral yesterday evening, in order to show what respect I could to the memory of one of the most brilliant officers under my command.

(Signed) "C. CAMPBELL,
*Com.-in-Chief in East Indies.*"

An officer who was present at the funeral says:—

"When the part of the service came where the body is lowered into the grave, all the old warrior's courage and self-possession could no longer control the tears—undeniable evidence of what he felt. 'I have lost one of the finest officers in the army,' was his remark."

Even Sir John Lawrence, no friendly judge, pronounced him in an official paper to be—

"One of the ablest, most active, and bravest soldiers who have fallen in the present war."

Sir R. Montgomery says:—

"I look round and can find no one like him. Many men are as brave, many possess as much talent, many are as cool and accurate in judgment, but not one combines all these qualifications as he did."

I shall best give an idea of the universal feeling of regret awakened at the tidings of his death by subjoining a few extracts from the public press at home and abroad, and from private letters. The Bombay correspondent of the *Times*, after detailing the assault on the Begum's Palace, wrote thus :—

"At this point fell mortally wounded Hodson of the 1st Bengal Fusiliers, Hodson of Hodson's Horse, Hodson the captor of the King of Delhi and the princes of his house. Few of the many losses that have occurred during the operations consequent upon the mutinies, have caused such universal regret throughout India as the death of this excellent officer; and among those in England who have read of and admired his exploits, not only his comrades of the Sikh battlefields, but many an old friend at Rugby or at Trinity, will mourn that his career has been thus early closed."

The *Times*, in a leading article, thus announced his death:—

"The country will receive with lively regret the news that the gallant Major Hodson, who has given his name to an invincible and almost ubiquitous body of cavalry, was killed in the attack on Lucknow. Major Hodson has been from the very beginning of this war fighting everywhere and against any odds with all the spirit of a Paladin of old. His most remarkable exploit, the capture of the King of Delhi and his two sons, astonished the world by its courage and coolness. Hodson was indeed a man who, from his romantic daring and his knowledge of the Asiatic character, was able to beat the natives at their own weapons. We could better have spared an older and more highly placed officer."

The following notice appeared in a Bombay paper :—

"From a Lucknow letter which we publish to-day our readers will learn, with sorrow and regret, that that most able and gallant officer, Captain Hodson, who has distinguished himself on so many occasions since the breaking out of the rebellion, and whose services have been of so brilliant and valuable a character, has been killed at Lucknow. As a leader of Irregular Horse, or indeed as a soldier of any of the non-scientific forces, Captain Hodson was almost without an equal. He was one of those squadron leaders which the Indian army can alone rear up. There are few men who would have managed the capture of the ex-King of Delhi as this departed hero. On that occasion his force was small compared to that he had to cope with; but the determined daring of the man made up for the disparity, and the old King came out of his fortification—for a strong fortification it was—and surrendered. So also with the capture of the King's sons, who also surrendered themselves, but whom Hodson found rescued when he reached them, after having completed the disarming of their band. That was a moment to test a man. But he of whom we write was equal to the emergency. The carts in which the princes were, were retaken immediately. Still the aspect of the armed Mohammedan crowd around—growing every moment more numerous—was dark and threatening. It was a situation which required prompt decision, and promptly did the British leader decide. He saw that it was necessary that his prisoners should die, and resolved himself to become their executioner: a wise resolve, for probably had he asked one of his own Mohammedan troopers to kill the sons of the Mogul, a refusal would have followed, and that refusal might have been acted up to by all. He adopted the wiser course, harangued his men, ordered the prisoners to take off their robes in the cart, and shot them with his own hand. Had the prisoners been allowed to leave the cart, their bodies would have been left behind; for to touch them would, by the troopers, have been considered defilement, and, left behind, they might have been fanatically paraded through the country as an incitement to a fresh rising. Besides, it was necessary that their remains should be exposed at the Kotwallie in Delhi with something of the indignity they themselves had caused to be inflicted on the murdered victims of the 11th of May."

The writer (in *Blackwood's Magazine*) of a series of papers on the 1st Fusiliers, says:—

"Then fell one of the bravest in the Indian army, an officer whose name has been brought too often before the public by those in high command to need my humble word in praise. There was not a man before Delhi who did not know Hodson; always active, always cheery, it did one's heart good to look at his face, when all felt how critical was our position. Ask any soldier who was the bravest man before Delhi, who most in the saddle, who foremost? and nine out of ten in the Infantry will tell you Hodson, in the Artillery as many will name Tombs.

"I once heard one of the Fusiliers say, 'Whenever I sees Captain Hodson go out, I always prays for him, for he is sure to be in danger.' Yet it was not only in the field that Hodson was to be valued, his head was as active as his hand was strong, and I feel sure, when we who knew him heard of his death, not one but felt that there was a vacancy indeed in our ranks."

The *Times'* Correspondent (Mr. Russell), in his letter of March 13th, writes:—

"When I returned to headquarters' camp this evening, I found that poor Hodson had died the previous day, and been buried the same evening.

"He was a zealous and accomplished officer, of great bravery, ability, and determination, an excellent judge of the native character, of a humane and clement disposition, but firm in the infliction of deserved punishment.

"The last time I saw him alive he expressed a decided opinion that Government must resort to an amnesty, or be prepared for a long continuance of disturbances."

From private letters of condolence, which would fill a volume, I select a few passages, in which the writers seem to have seized with great felicity upon some of the more remarkable features in my brother's character and actions.

"It is hard to lose one upon whom all eyes were fixed, and whose noble qualities seemed so certain of recognition, and of speedy advancement to such employments as his fine natural abilities well fitted him to discharge.

"The very presence of such a man in India was an element of power apart from all official rank, and he could ill be spared from among the very few who have learnt to impersonate in themselves the power of the English nation, and to let the natives of India feel the irresistible character of that power. You must have watched him so anxiously and so proudly that, though thousands of us have done the same, none can approach the measure of your sorrow or mourn as you that he can confer no more honour on your name, but that the opportunities of the future must be reaped by other and less capable hands.

"I cannot feel easy without expressing to you the great grief and consternation with which I read the account of your brother's death. Certainly it would have been little less than miraculous if, being what he was, he had lived out this war. And yet I, for one, had always cherished a hope that I might have seen once more with my own eyes so noble and gallant a soldier.

"There is, after all, something about skilful courage which draws the heart to itself more than eloquence, or learning, or anything else, and your brother seems to have been endued with this almost more than any living Englishman, brave as our countrymen are."

---

"Closely have I watched, during these last few sad months, the career of that brave brother of yours. I could estimate his bold and self-sacrificing courage, and knowing as I did the sort of people over whom he had acquired such perfect sway, I knew how much a clear and commanding intellect must have been called into exercise, to aid a strong and devoted heart. What victims has Lucknow offered up to the fiendish treachery of those ungrateful men —Lawrence! Havelock! and Hodson!

"My grief is not for him; he had done his work in that station of life in which God had placed him, nobly, heartily, and as in the sight of God (would that we did all our work in half such a Christian spirit); but for you all, who were looking forward to seeing him again, crowned with the honours he had so hardly won. Well, it has pleased God that this was not to be; but there is a good hope more than a hope, that a reward of a higher kind is his."

From one who had known him in India :—

"From the love and esteem I bore your brother, you will, I feel sure, allow me to write and express, however imperfectly words can do it, my deep and heartfelt sympathy with you and your sisters under this heavy blow. Our acquaintance was not of long standing, but had rapidly ripened into intimacy, and I look back to the days spent in his society as amongst my happiest in India. His very presence was sunshine.

"Of my admiration for his talents, and the service he rendered his country, it would be impertinent to speak—they are of public note; but of the tender sympathies, the ready advice, the forgetfulness of self and the ever-mindfulness of others, I may testify. His was indeed a rare and beautiful character, and the better he was known the more he could not fail to be appreciated."

I will add one more letter from General Johnstone, which will show that even to the last my brother was pursued by the same jealousy and malignity which had caused him so much suffering in former years. Nor has that malignity ceased. It has been lately shown that it is still active, and has pursued him beyond the grave :—

"He was too noble to pass through the world without detractors. The ambitious and brave envied him, because the brilliancy of his acts put theirs in the shade; I mean, those not possessed of the disinterestedness of Christians.

"The mean and despicable hated him because they quailed

before the eagle eye that could endure neither dishonesty nor cowardice. Their base slanders were in whispers during his life; now that his gallant spirit is gone they come forward in unblushing malignity. I heard the whispers only: my indignation at learning the baseness with which this true hero has been treated is beyond all my powers of expression."

Some of my readers may be interested in a description of Major Hodson's personal appearance and manner, given in a letter describing a visit which he paid the writer a few years previously at Calcutta:—

"He was remarkably well made, lithe, and agile; in height about five feet eleven inches. His hair had slightly receded from a high and most intellectual forehead, and was light and curly. His eyes were blue, but animated by a peculiarly determined, and sometimes even fierce look, which would change to one of mischievous merriment, for he was keenly susceptible of the ridiculous, in whatever shape it presented itself; but usually his look impressed me at once with that idea of his determination and firmness which have ever characterised his actions. His nose was inclining to the aquiline, and the curved, thin nostrils added a look of defiance in noways counteracted by the compressed lips, which seemed to denote many an inward struggle between duty and inclination. These are my impressions of Hodson as I last saw him; and if you add to this an open, frank manner, that, *bongré malgré*, impressed you favourably at first sight with the owner, you will have the charming *ensemble* that presides over my recollections of three as happy weeks as I ever passed."

As a pendant to this portrait I give another from a lady's pen, drawn more recently:—

"There was an indescribable charm of manner about him, combining all the gentle playfulness of the boy, the deep tenderness of the woman, and the vigorous decision of the soldier.

"His powers of attraction extended even to animals; and it was touching to see his large white Persian cat following him from room to room, escaping from the caresses of others to nestle by him. I have often watched the pretty creature as he threw himself exhausted with the day's work on an easy chair or sofa, rubbing himself against his master, whisking the long white tail against his fair moustache, and courting the endearments liberally bestowed. Restless with others, pussy was at rest if established by him.

"At Delhi there was a wild shy little kitten which fled from every one else, but mewed provokingly whenever he appeared—would jump on his knee with all the familiarity of an old friend.

"With his horses he had the same power of domestication. They yielded to the sound of his voice with the instinct that seemed to convey to all that in him they had found master and friend.

"Over the natives that influence seemed almost magic. When at Umbâla, on ten days' leave, in November last, the wounded and convalescent Guides (his old corps) were all day straying into the compound simply to 'salaam' the 'Sahib.' And if, when lingering on the steps, or in front of the study door, they were questioned what they wanted, their answer would be, 'Nothing; they liked to look at the Sahib.' And so they hung about his steps, and watched like so many faithful dogs. Especially there was an Affghan boy (he had once been a slave), whose very soul seemed bound up in the master who had rescued him from his degraded position, and for whom every service seemed light. He would watch his master's movements with a look of very worship, as if the ground were not good enough for him to tread.

"His joyousness of nature made him the most charming companion. There was a certain quaintness of expression which gave zest to all he said; and yet there was a reverence, too, so that, were subjects graver than usual introduced even by allusion, they at once commanded his earnest response."

It will doubtless excite surprise that one whom the Commander-in-Chief pronounced "one of the most brilliant soldiers under his command"—one whom all ranks of the army in India reckoned amongst their bravest and most skilful leaders—one whom the popular voice has already enrolled amongst the heroes of the nation—one whose name was "known, either in love or fear, by every native from Calcutta to Cabul,"—should have received during his life, with the exception of a brevet majority (to which he was entitled for services in 1849), no recognition of gallant services and deeds of daring, one-tenth part of which would have covered many of fortune's favourites with decorations.

That recognition, however, has been given in a more marked form by the spontaneous expression of the feelings of his brothers-in-arms. After his death, a committee, composed of officers of the highest eminence, was formed at Calcutta for the sake of recording, by some permanent memorial, their admiration of his gallantry and skill, and it was determined that it should take the form of a monument in Lichfield Cathedral, which has been erected from the designs of G. E. Street, Esq., R.A. On it he is represented receiving the sword of the King of Delhi.

Nor will his name be forgotten in India. The regiment which he raised was, by an order published in the *Gazette* of August 13th, constituted a brigade, consisting of the 1st, 2d, and 3d Regiments of "Hodson's Horse."

I do not know that his warmest friends could desire any more distinguished testimony to his services.

---

After these remarks were written, my brother's services received a still more public acknowledgment. On the occasion of the vote of thanks to the Indian Army, on 14th April 1859, both Lord Derby in the Upper, and Lord Stanley in the Lower House, mentioned his name in the most honourable manner.

Lord Stanley spoke as follows :—

"And now, Sir, having paid the tribute that is due to those who live, it is not fitting that we should pass away entirely from this subject without recognising the services of the dead. (Hear, hear.) Operations like those which have been carried on for the last eighteen months, could not be conducted without a great and lamentable loss of life, and their loss to the public service is not one which can be measured by any numerical test, because it is always the best and bravest officers who rush to the front,—who volunteer for every service of danger or difficulty, who expose themselves to every risk, and among whom, therefore, there is necessarily the greatest loss of life. There are two names which are especially distinguished. The first is that of Major Hodson, of the Guides—(hear, hear)—who, in his short but brilliant military career displayed every quality which an officer should possess. (Hear.) Nothing is more remarkable in glancing over the biography of Major Hodson that has just appeared than the variety of services in which he was engaged. At one time he displayed his great personal courage and skill as a swordsman in conflict with Sikh fanatics; he was then transferred to the civil service, in which he performed his duties as though he had passed his whole life at the desk, afterwards recruiting and commanding the corps of Guides, and, lastly, taking part in the operations before Delhi, volunteering for every enterprise in which life could be hazarded or glory could be won. He crowded into the brief space of eleven eventful years the services and adventures of a long life. He died when his reward was assured, obtaining only that reward which he most coveted—the consciousness of duty done, and the assurance of enduring military renown. The other name to which I shall refer is a name which will always be received with feelings of special and individual interest by this House. No words of mine can add to the glory attaching to the short but noble career of Sir W. Peel. (Cheers.) He bore a name which is inseparably connected with the Parliamentary history of this country, and it was with feelings of almost personal pride and of personal grief that a great number of the members of this House received the accounts of his glorious achievements and of his untimely end. (Hear, hear.) For his own reputation he had lived long enough; no future acts could have enhanced his fame. It is England, it is his country, that deplores his loss."

I have also much pleasure in stating that " in testimony of the high sense entertained of the gallant and distinguished services of the late Brevet-Major W. S. R. Hodson," the Secretary of State for India in Council granted a special pension to his widow, and that the Queen was graciously pleased to assign to her apartments in Hampton Court Palace.

THE END.

PRINTED BY BALLANTYNE, HANSON AND CO.
EDINBURGH AND LONDON.

A LIST OF

*KEGAN PAUL, TRENCH & CO.'S
PUBLICATIONS.*

7.83.

1, *Paternoster Square,*
*London.*

A LIST OF

# KEGAN PAUL, TRENCH & CO.'S PUBLICATIONS.

## CONTENTS.

| | PAGE | | PAGE |
|---|---|---|---|
| GENERAL LITERATURE. | 2 | MILITARY WORKS. | 33 |
| PARCHMENT LIBRARY. | 18 | POETRY. | 34 |
| PULPIT COMMENTARY. | 20 | NOVELS AND TALES. | 39 |
| INTERNATIONAL SCIENTIFIC SERIES. | 29 | BOOKS FOR THE YOUNG | 41 |

## GENERAL LITERATURE.

*AINSWORTH, W. F.*—A Personal Narrative of the Euphrates Expedition. With Map. 2 vols. Demy 8vo, 30s.

*A. K. H. B.*—From a Quiet Place. A Volume of Sermons. Crown 8vo, 5s.

*ALEXANDER, William, D.D., Bishop of Derry.*—The Great Question, and other Sermons. Crown 8vo, 6s.

*ALLIES, T. W., M.A.*—Per Crucem ad Lucem. The Result of a Life. 2 vols. Demy 8vo, 25s.

A Life's Decision. Crown 8vo, 7s. 6d.

*AMHERST, Rev. W. J.*—The History of Catholic Emancipation and the Progress of the Catholic Church in the British Isles (chiefly in England) from 1771-1820. 2 vols. Demy 8vo, 24s.

*AMOS, Professor Sheldon.*—The History and Principles of the Civil Law of Rome. An aid to the Study of Scientific and Comparative Jurisprudence. Demy 8vo, 16s.

Ancient and Modern Britons. A Retrospect. 2 vols. Demy 8vo, 24s.

Are Foreign Missions doing any Good? An Enquiry into their Social Effects. Crown 8vo, 1s.

*ARISTOTLE.*—The Nicomachean Ethics of Aristotle. Translated by F. H. Peters, M.A. Third Edition. Crown 8vo, 6s.

*AUBERTIN, J. J.*—A Flight to Mexico. With 7 full-page Illustrations and a Railway Map of Mexico. Crown 8vo, 7s. 6d.

Six Months in Cape Colony and Natal. With Illustrations and Map. Crown 8vo, 6s.

A Fight with Distances. Illustrations and Maps. Crown 8vo, 7s. 6d.

Aucassin and Nicolette. Edited in Old French and rendered in Modern English by F. W. BOURDILLON. Fcap 8vo, 7s. 6d.

*AZARIAS, Brother.*—Aristotle and the Christian Church. Small crown 8vo, 3s. 6d.

*BADGER, George Percy, D.C.L.*—An English-Arabic Lexicon. In which the equivalent for English Words and Idiomatic Sentences are rendered into literary and colloquial Arabic. Royal 4to, 80s.

*BAGEHOT, Walter.*—The English Constitution. Fourth Edition. Crown 8vo, 7s. 6d.

Lombard Street. A Description of the Money Market. Eighth Edition. Crown 8vo, 7s. 6d.

Essays on Parliamentary Reform. Crown 8vo, 5s.

Some Articles on the Depreciation of Silver, and Topics connected with it. Demy 8vo, 5s.

*BAGOT, Alan, C.E.*—Accidents in Mines: their Causes and Prevention. Crown 8vo, 6s.

The Principles of Colliery Ventilation. Second Edition, greatly enlarged. Crown 8vo, 5s.

The Principles of Civil Engineering as applied to Agriculture and Estate Management. Crown 8vo, 7s. 6d.

*BALDWIN, Capt. J. H.*—The Large and Small Game of Bengal and the North-Western Provinces of India. With 20 Illustrations. New and Cheaper Edition. Small 4to, 10s. 6d.

*BALL, John, F.R.S.*—Notes of a Naturalist in South America. With Map. Crown 8vo, 8s. 6d.

*BALLIN, Ada S. and F. L.*—A Hebrew Grammar. With Exercises selected from the Bible. Crown 8vo, 7s. 6d.

*BASU, K. P., M.A.*—Students' Mathematical Companion. Containing problems in Arithmetic, Algebra, Geometry, and Mensuration, for Students of the Indian Universities. Crown 8vo, 6s.

BAUR, *Ferdinand, Dr. Ph.*—A Philological Introduction to Greek and Latin for Students. Translated and adapted from the German, by C. KEGAN PAUL, M.A., and E. D. STONE, M.A. Third Edition. Crown 8vo, 6s.

BAYLY, *Capt. George.*—Sea Life Sixty Years Ago. A Record of Adventures which led up to the Discovery of the Relics of the long-missing Expedition commanded by the Comte de la Perouse. Crown 8vo, 3s. 6d.

BENSON, *A. C.*—William Laud, sometime Archbishop of Canterbury. A Study. With Portrait. Crown 8vo, 6s.

BLACKBURN, *Mrs. Hugh.*—Bible Beasts and Birds. 22 Illustrations of Scripture photographed from the Original. 4to, 42s.

BLOOMFIELD, *The Lady.*—Reminiscences of Court and Diplomatic Life. New and Cheaper Edition. With Frontispiece. Crown 8vo, 6s.

BLUNT, *The Ven. Archdeacon.*—The Divine Patriot, and other Sermons. Preached in Scarborough and in Cannes. New and Cheaper Edition. Crown 8vo, 4s. 6d.

BLUNT, *Wilfrid S.*—The Future of Islam. Crown 8vo, 6s.

Ideas about India. Crown 8vo. Cloth, 6s.

BOWEN, *H. C., M.A.*—Studies in English. For the use of Modern Schools. Ninth Thousand. Small crown 8vo, 1s. 6d.

English Grammar for Beginners. Fcap. 8vo, 1s.

Simple English Poems. English Literature for Junior Classes. In four parts. Parts I., II., and III., 6d. each. Part IV., 1s. Complete, 3s.

BRADLEY, *F. H.*—The Principles of Logic. Demy 8vo, 16s.

BRIDGETT, *Rev. T. E.*—History of the Holy Eucharist in Great Britain. 2 vols. Demy 8vo, 18s.

BROOKE, *Rev. Stopford A.*—The Fight of Faith. Sermons preached on various occasions. Fifth Edition. Crown 8vo, 7s. 6d.

The Spirit of the Christian Life. Third Edition. Crown 8vo, 5s.

Theology in the English Poets.—Cowper, Coleridge, Wordsworth, and Burns. Sixth Edition. Post 8vo, 5s.

Christ in Modern Life. Sixteenth Edition. Crown 8vo, 5s

Sermons. First Series. Thirteenth Edition. Crown 8vo, 5s.

Sermons. Second Series. Sixth Edition. Crown 8vo, 5s.

BROWN, *Horatio F.*—Life on the Lagoons. With 2 Illustrations and Map. Crown 8vo, 6s.

Venetian Studies. Crown 8vo, 7s. 6d.

BROWN, *Rev. J. Baldwin.*—The Higher Life. Its Reality, Experience, and Destiny. Sixth Edition. Crown 8vo, 5s.

Doctrine of Annihilation in the Light of the Gospel of Love. Five Discourses. Fourth Edition. Crown 8vo, 2s. 6d.

The Christian Policy of Life. A Book for Young Men of Business. Third Edition. Crown 8vo, 3s. 6d.

BURDETT, *Henry C.*—Help in Sickness—Where to Go and What to Do. Crown 8vo, 1s. 6d.

Helps to Health. The Habitation—The Nursery—The Schoolroom and—The Person. With a Chapter on Pleasure and Health Resorts. Crown 8vo, 1s. 6d.

BURKE, *Oliver J.*—South Isles of Aran (County Galway). Crown 8vo, 2s. 6d.

BURKE, *The Late Very Rev. T. N.*—His Life. By W. J. FITZPATRICK. 2 vols. With Portrait. Demy 8vo, 30s.

BURTON, *Lady.*—The Inner Life of Syria, Palestine, and the Holy Land. Post 8vo, 6s.

CANDLER, *C.*—The Prevention of Consumption. A Mode of Prevention founded on a New Theory of the Nature of the Tubercle-Bacillus. Demy 8vo, 10s. 6d.

CAPES, *J. M.*—The Church of the Apostles: an Historical Inquiry. Demy 8vo, 9s.

CARPENTER, *W. B.*—The Principles of Mental Physiology. With their Applications to the Training and Discipline of the Mind, and the Study of its Morbid Conditions. Illustrated. Sixth Edition. 8vo, 12s.

Nature and Man. With a Memorial Sketch by the Rev. J. ESTLIN CARPENTER. Portrait. Large crown 8vo, 8s. 6d.

Catholic Dictionary. Containing some Account of the Doctrine, Discipline, Rites, Ceremonies, Councils, and Religious Orders of the Catholic Church. By WILLIAM E. ADDIS and THOMAS ARNOLD, M.A. Third Edition. Demy 8vo, 21s.

Century Guild Hobby Horse. Vols. I. and II. Half parchment, 12s. 6d. each.

CHARLES, *Rev. R. H.*—Forgiveness, and other Sermons. Crown 8vo, 4s. 6d.

CHEYNE, *Canon.*—The Prophecies of Isaiah. Translated with Critical Notes and Dissertations. 2 vols. Fourth Edition. Demy 8vo, 25s.

Job and Solomon; or, the Wisdom of the Old Testament. Demy 8vo, 12s. 6d.

The Psalms; or, Book of The Praises of Israel. Translated with Commentary. Demy 8vo, 16s.

**Churgress, The.** By "THE PRIG." Fcap. 8vo, 3s. 6d.

*CLAIRAUT.*—**Elements of Geometry.** Translated by Dr. KAINES. With 145 Figures. Crown 8vo, 4s. 6d.

*CLAPPERTON, Jane Hume.*—**Scientific Meliorism and the Evolution of Happiness.** Large crown 8vo, 8s. 6d.

*CLARKE, Rev. Henry James, A.K.C.*—**The Fundamental Science.** Demy 8vo, 10s. 6d.

*CLODD, Edward, F.R.A.S.*—**The Childhood of the World : a Simple Account of Man in Early Times.** Eighth Edition. Crown 8vo, 3s.
  A Special Edition for Schools. 1s.

  **The Childhood of Religions.** Including a Simple Account of the Birth and Growth of Myths and Legends. Eighth Thousand. Crown 8vo, 5s.
  A Special Edition for Schools. 1s. 6d.

  **Jesus of Nazareth.** With a brief sketch of Jewish History to the Time of His Birth. Small crown 8vo, 6s.

*COGHLAN, J. Cole, D.D.*—**The Modern Pharisee and other Sermons.** Edited by the Very Rev. H. H. DICKINSON, D.D., Dean of Chapel Royal, Dublin. New and Cheaper Edition. Crown 8vo, 7s. 6d.

*COLERIDGE, Sara.*—**Memoir and Letters of Sara Coleridge.** Edited by her Daughter. With Index. Cheap Edition. With Portrait. 7s. 6d.

*COLERIDGE, The Hon. Stephen.*—**Demetrius.** Crown 8vo, 5s.

*CONNELL, A. K.*—**Discontent and Danger in India.** Small crown 8vo, 3s. 6d.

  **The Economic Revolution of India.** Crown 8vo, 4s. 6d.

*COOK, Keningale, LL.D.*—**The Fathers of Jesus.** A Study of the Lineage of the Christian Doctrine and Traditions. 2 vols. Demy 8vo, 28s.

*CORR, the late Rev. T. J., M.A.*—**Favilla;** Tales, Essays, and Poems. Crown 8vo, 5s.

*CORY, William.*—**A Guide to Modern English History.** Part I.—MDCCCXV.-MDCCCXXX. Demy 8vo, 9s. Part II.—MDCCCXXX.-MDCCCXXXV., 15s.

*COTTON, H. J. S.*—**New India, or India in Transition.** Third Edition. Crown 8vo, 4s. 6d.; Cheap Edition, paper covers, 1s.

*COWIE, Right Rev. W. G.*—**Our Last Year in New Zealand.** 1887. Crown 8vo, 7s. 6d.

*COX, Rev. Sir George W., M.A., Bart.*—**The Mythology of the Aryan Nations.** New Edition. Demy 8vo, 16s.

COX, *Rev. Sir George W., M.A., Bart.—continued.*
>Tales of Ancient Greece. New Edition. Small crown 8vo, 6s.
>A Manual of Mythology in the form of Question and Answer. New Edition. Fcap. 8vo, 3s.
>An Introduction to the Science of Comparative Mythology and Folk-Lore. Second Edition. Crown 8vo. 7s. 6d.

COX, *Rev. Sir G. W., M.A., Bart., and JONES, Eustace Hinton.—*
>Popular Romances of the Middle Ages. Third Edition, in 1 vol. Crown 8vo, 6s.

COX, *Rev. Samuel, D.D.*—A Commentary on the Book of Job. With a Translation. Second Edition. Demy 8vo, 15s.
>Salvator Mundi; or, Is Christ the Saviour of all Men? Tenth Edition. Crown 8vo, 5s.
>The Larger Hope. A Sequel to "Salvator Mundi." Second Edition. 16mo, 1s.
>The Genesis of Evil, and other Sermons, mainly expository. Third Edition. Crown 8vo, 6s.
>Balaam. An Exposition and a Study. Crown 8vo, 5s.
>Miracles. An Argument and a Challenge. Crown 8vo, 2s. 6d.

CRAVEN, *Mrs.*—A Year's Meditations. Crown 8vo, 6s.

CRAWFURD, *Oswald.*—Portugal, Old and New. With Illustrations and Maps. New and Cheaper Edition. Crown 8vo, 6s.

CRUISE, *Francis Richard, M.D.*—Thomas à Kempis. Notes of a Visit to the Scenes in which his Life was spent. With Portraits and Illustrations. Demy 8vo, 12s.

Dante: The Banquet (Il Comito). Translated by KATHARINE HILLARD. Crown 8vo.

DARMESTETER, *Arsene.*—The Life of Words as the Symbols of Ideas. Crown 8vo, 4s. 6d.

DAVIDSON, *Rev. Samuel, D.D., LL.D.*—Canon of the Bible: Its Formation, History, and Fluctuations. Third and Revised Edition. Small crown 8vo, 5s.
>The Doctrine of Last Things contained in the New Testament compared with the Notions of the Jews and the Statements of Church Creeds. Small crown 8vo, 3s. 6d.

DAWSON, *Geo., M.A.* Prayers, with a Discourse on Prayer. Edited by his Wife. First Series. Ninth Edition. Small Crown 8vo, 3s. 6d.
>Prayers, with a Discourse on Prayer. Edited by GEORGE ST. CLAIR, F.G.S. Second Series. Small Crown 8vo, 3s. 6d.
>Sermons on Disputed Points and Special Occasions. Edited by his Wife. Fourth Edition. Crown 8vo, 6s.

*DAWSON, Geo., M.A.—continued.*

    **Sermons on Daily Life and Duty.** Edited by his Wife. Fifth Edition. Small Crown 8vo, 3s. 6d.

    **The Authentic Gospel,** and other Sermons. Edited by GEORGE ST. CLAIR, F.G.S. Third Edition. Crown 8vo, 6s.

    **Every-day Counsels.** Edited by GEORGE ST. CLAIR, F.G.S. Crown 8vo, 6s.

    **Biographical Lectures.** Edited by GEORGE ST. CLAIR, F.G.S Third Edition. Large crown 8vo, 7s. 6d.

    **Shakespeare, and other Lectures.** Edited by GEORGE ST. CLAIR, F.G.S. Large crown 8vo, 7s. 6d.

*DE JONCOURT, Madame Marie.*—**Wholesome Cookery.** Fourth Edition. Crown 8vo, cloth, 1s. 6d; paper covers, 1s.

*DENT, H. C.*—**A Year in Brazil.** With Notes on Religion, Meteorology, Natural History, etc. Maps and Illustrations. Demy 8vo, 18s.

*DOWDEN, Edward, LL.D.*—**Shakspere:** a Critical Study of his Mind and Art. Eighth Edition. Post 8vo, 12s.

    **Studies in Literature, 1789-1877.** Fourth Edition. Large post 8vo, 6s.

    **Transcripts and Studies.** Large post 8vo. 12s.

**Dulce Domum.** Fcap. 8vo, 5s.

*DU MONCEL, Count.*—**The Telephone, the Microphone, and the Phonograph.** With 74 Illustrations. Third Edition. Small crown 8vo, 5s.

*DUNN, H. Percy.*—**Infant Health.** The Physiology and Hygiene of Early Life. Crown 8vo. 3s. 6d.

*DURUY, Victor.*—**History of Rome and the Roman People.** Edited by Prof. MAHAFFY. With nearly 3000 Illustrations. 4to. 6 vols. in 12 parts, 30s. each vol.

**Education Library.** Edited by Sir PHILIP MAGNUS:—

    **An Introduction to the History of Educational Theories.** By OSCAR BROWNING, M.A. Second Edition. 3s. 6d.

    **Old Greek Education.** By the Rev. Prof. MAHAFFY, M.A. Second Edition. 3s. 6d.

    **School Management.** Including a general view of the work of Education, Organization and Discipline. By JOSEPH LANDON. Sixth Edition. 6s.

*EDWARDES, Major-General Sir Herbert B.*—**Memorials of his Life and Letters.** By his Wife. With Portrait and Illustrations. 2 vols. Demy 8vo, 36s.

*ELSDALE, Henry.*—Studies in Tennyson's Idylls. Crown 8vo, 5*s.*

Eighteenth Century Essays. Selected and Edited by AUSTIN DOBSON. Cheap Edition. Cloth 1*s.* 6*d.*

Emerson's (Ralph Waldo) Life. By OLIVER WENDELL HOLMES. English Copyright Edition. With Portrait. Crown 8vo, 6*s.*

Five o'clock Tea. Containing Receipts for Cakes, Savoury Sandwiches, etc. Fcap. 8vo, cloth, 1*s.* 6*d.* ; paper covers, 1*s.*

*FLINN, D. Edgar.*—Ireland: its Health-Resorts and Watering-Places. With Frontispiece and Maps. Demy 8vo, 5*s.*

Forbes, Bishop: A Memoir. By the Rev. DONALD J. MACKAY. With Portrait and Map. Crown 8vo, 7*s.* 6*d.*

*FORDYCE, J.*—The New Social Order. Crown 8vo, 3*s.* 6*d.*

*FOTHERINGHAM, James.*—Studies in the Poetry of Robert Browning. Second Edition. Crown 8vo, 6*s.*

Franklin (Benjamin) as a Man of Letters. By J. B. MACMASTER. Crown 8vo, 5*s.*

*FREWEN, MORETON.*—The Economic Crisis. Crown 8vo, 4*s.* 6*d.*

From World to Cloister; or, My Novitiate. By BERNARD. Crown 8vo, 5*s.*

*GARDINER, Samuel R., and J. BASS MULLINGER, M.A.*—Introduction to the Study of English History. Second Edition. Large crown 8vo, 9*s.*

Genesis in Advance of Present Science. A Critical Investigation of Chapters I.-IX. By a Septuagenarian Beneficed Presbyter. Demy 8vo, 10*s.* 6*d.*

*GEORGE, Henry.*—Progress and Poverty: An Inquiry into the Causes of Industrial Depressions, and of Increase of Want with Increase of Wealth. The Remedy. Fifth Library Edition. Post 8vo, 7*s.* 6*d.* Cabinet Edition. Crown 8vo, 2*s.* 6*d.* Also a Cheap Edition. Limp cloth, 1*s.* 6*d.*; paper covers, 1*s.*

Protection, or Free Trade. An Examination of the Tariff Question, with especial regard to the Interests of Labour. Second Edition. Crown 8vo, 5*s.*

Social Problems. Fourth Thousand. Crown 8vo, 5*s.* Cheap Edition, paper covers, 1*s.*; cloth 1*s.* 6*d.*

*GILBERT, Mrs.*—Autobiography, and other Memorials. Edited by JOSIAH GILBERT. Fifth Edition. Crown 8vo, 7*s.* 6*d.*

*GILLMORE, Parker.*—Days and Nights by the Desert. Illustrated. Demy 8vo, 10*s.* 6*d.*

*GLANVILL, Joseph.*—Scepsis Scientifica; or, Confest Ignorance, the Way to Science; in an Essay of the Vanity of Dogmatizing and Confident Opinion. Edited, with Introductory Essay, by JOHN OWEN. Elzevir 8vo, printed on hand-made paper, 6*s.*

*GLASS, H. A.*—**The Story of the Psalters.** A History of the Metrical Versions from 1549 to 1885. Crown 8vo, 5*s.*

**Glossary of Terms and Phrases.** Edited by the Rev. H. PERCY SMITH and others. Second and Cheaper Edition. Medium 8vo, 7*s.* 6*d.*

*GLOVER, F., M.A.*—**Exempla Latina.** A First Construing Book, with Short Notes, Lexicon, and an Introduction to the Analysis of Sentences. Second Edition. Fcap. 8vo, 2*s.*

*GOODENOUGH, Commodore J. G.*—**Memoir of,** with Extracts from his Letters and Journals. Edited by his Widow. With Steel Engraved Portrait. Third Edition. Crown 8vo, 5*s.*

*GORDON, Major-General C. G.*—**His Journals at Kartoum.** Printed from the original MS. With Introduction and Notes by A. EGMONT HAKE. Portrait, 2 Maps, and 30 Illustrations. Two vols., demy 8vo, 21*s.* Also a Cheap Edition in 1 vol., 6*s.*

**Gordon's (General) Last Journal.** A Facsimile of the last Journal received in England from GENERAL GORDON. Reproduced by Photo-lithography. Imperial 4to, £3 3*s.*

**Events in his Life.** From the Day of his Birth to the Day of his Death. By Sir H. W. GORDON. With Maps and Illustrations. Second Edition. Demy 8vo, 7*s.* 6*d.*

*GOSSE, Edmund.*—**Seventeenth Century Studies.** A Contribution to the History of English Poetry. Demy 8vo, 10*s.* 6*d.*

*GOULD, Rev. S. Baring, M.A.*—**Germany, Present and Past.** New and Cheaper Edition. Large crown 8vo, 7*s.* 6*d.*

**The Vicar of Morwenstow.** A Life of Robert Stephen Hawker. Crown 8vo, 5*s.*

*GOWAN, Major Walter E.*—**A. Ivanoff's Russian Grammar.** (16th Edition.) Translated, enlarged, and arranged for use of Students of the Russian Language. Demy 8vo, 6*s.*

*GOWER, Lord Ronald.* **My Reminiscences.** MINIATURE EDITION, printed on hand-made paper, limp parchment antique, 10*s.* 6*d.*

**Bric-à-Brac.** Being some Photoprints illustrating art objects at Gower Lodge, Windsor. With descriptions. Super royal 8vo. 15*s.*; extra binding, 21*s.*

**Last Days of Mary Antoinette.** An Historical Sketch. With Portrait and Facsimiles. Fcap. 4to, 10*s.* 6*d.*

**Notes of a Tour from Brindisi to Yokohama, 1883-1884.** Fcap. 8vo, 2*s.* 6*d.*

*GRAHAM, William, M.A.*—**The Creed of Science,** Religious, Moral, and Social. Second Edition, Revised. Crown 8vo, 6*s.*

**The Social Problem, in its Economic, Moral, and Political Aspects.** Demy 8vo, 14*s.*

GRIMLEY, *Rev. H. N., M.A.*—Tremadoc Sermons, chiefly on the Spiritual Body, the Unseen World, and the Divine Humanity. Fourth Edition. Crown 8vo, 6s.

The Temple of Humanity, and other Sermons. Crown 8vo, 6s.

HADDON, *Caroline.*—The Larger Life, Studies in Hinton's Ethics. Crown 8vo, 5s.

HAECKEL, *Prof. Ernst.*—The History of Creation. Translation revised by Professor E. RAY LANKESTER, M.A., F.R.S. With Coloured Plates and Genealogical Trees of the various groups of both Plants and Animals. 2 vols. Third Edition. Post 8vo, 32s.

The History of the Evolution of Man. With numerous Illustrations. 2 vols. Post 8vo, 32s.

A Visit to Ceylon. Post 8vo, 7s. 6d.

Freedom in Science and Teaching. With a Prefatory Note by T. H. HUXLEY, F.R.S. Crown 8vo, 5s.

HALCOMBE, *J. J.*—Gospel Difficulties due to a Displaced Section of St. Luke. Second Edition. Crown 8vo, 6s.

Hamilton, Memoirs of Arthur, B.A., of Trinity College, Cambridge. Crown 8vo, 6s.

Handbook of Home Rule, being Articles on the Irish Question by Various Writers. Edited by JAMES BRYCE, M.P. Second Edition. Crown 8vo, 1s. sewed, or 1s. 6d. cloth.

HAWEIS, *Rev. H. R., M.A.*—Current Coin. Materialism—The Devil—Crime—Drunkenness—Pauperism—Emotion—Recreation—The Sabbath. Fifth Edition. Crown 8vo, 5s.

Arrows in the Air. Fifth Edition. Crown 8vo, 5s.

Speech in Season. Fifth Edition. Crown 8vo, 5s.

Thoughts for the Times. Fourteenth Edition. Crown 8vo, 5s.

Unsectarian Family Prayers. New Edition. Fcap. 8vo, 1s. 6d.

HAWTHORNE, *Nathaniel.*—Works. Complete in Twelve Volumes. Large post 8vo, 7s. 6d. each volume.

HEATH, *Francis George.*—Autumnal Leaves. Third and cheaper Edition. Large crown 8vo, 6s.

Sylvan Winter. With 70 Illustrations. Large crown 8vo, 14s.

HEIDENHAIN, *Rudolph, M.D.*—Hypnotism, or Animal Magnetism. With Preface by G. J. ROMANES. Second Edition. Small crown 8vo, 2s. 6d.

HINTON, *J.*—Life and Letters. With an Introduction by Sir W. W. GULL, Bart., and Portrait engraved on Steel by C. H. Jeens. Fifth Edition. Crown 8vo, 8s. 6d.

HINTON, J.—*continued.*

    Philosophy and Religion. Selections from the Manuscripts of the late James Hinton. Edited by CAROLINE HADDON. Second Edition. Crown 8vo, 5s.

    The Law Breaker, and The Coming of the Law. Edited by MARGARET HINTON. Crown 8vo, 6s.

    The Mystery of Pain. New Edition. Fcap. 8vo, 1s.

Homer's Iliad. Greek text, with a Translation by J. G. CORDERY. 2 vols. Demy 8vo, 24s.

HOOPER, *Mary.*—Little Dinners: How to Serve them with Elegance and Economy. Twentieth Edition. Crown 8vo, 2s. 6d.

    Cookery for Invalids, Persons of Delicate Digestion, and Children. Fifth Edition. Crown 8vo, 2s. 6d.

    Every-day Meals. Being Economical and Wholesome Recipes for Breakfast, Luncheon, and Supper. Seventh Edition. Crown 8vo, 2s. 6d.

HOPKINS, *Ellice.*—Work amongst Working Men. Sixth Edition. Crown 8vo, 3s. 6d.

HORNADAY, W. T.—Two Years in a Jungle. With Illustrations. Demy 8vo, 21s.

HOSPITALIER, E.—The Modern Applications of Electricity. Translated and Enlarged by JULIUS MAIER, Ph.D. 2 vols. Second Edition, Revised, with many additions and numerous Illustrations. Demy 8vo, 25s.

HOWARD, *Robert, M.A.*—The Church of England and other Religious Communions. A course of Lectures delivered in the Parish Church of Clapham. Crown 8vo, 7s. 6d.

How to Make a Saint; or, The Process of Canonization in the Church of England. By "THE PRIG." Fcap 8vo, 3s. 6d.

HYNDMAN, H. M.—The Historical Basis of Socialism in England. Large crown 8vo, 8s. 6d.

IDDESLEIGH, *Earl of.*—The Pleasures, Dangers, and Uses of Desultory Reading. Fcap. 8vo, in Whatman paper cover, 1s.

IM THURN, *Everard F.*—Among the Indians of Guiana. Being Sketches, chiefly anthropologic, from the Interior of British Guiana. With 53 Illustrations and a Map. Demy 8vo, 18s.

Ixora: A Mystery. Crown 8vo, 6s.

Jaunt in a Junk: A Ten Days' Cruise in Indian Seas. Large crown 8vo, 7s. 6d.

JENKINS, *E., and* RAYMOND, *J.*—The Architect's Legal Handbook. Third Edition, revised. Crown 8vo, 6s.

*JENKINS, Rev. Canon R. C.*—**Heraldry: English and Foreign.** With a Dictionary of Heraldic Terms and 156 Illustrations. Small crown 8vo, 3s. 6d.

Jerome, St., Life. By M. J. MARTIN. Large crown 8vo, 6s.

*JOEL, L.*—**A Consul's Manual and Shipowner's and Shipmaster's Practical Guide in their Transactions Abroad.** With Definitions of Nautical, Mercantile, and Legal Terms; a Glossary of Mercantile Terms in English, French, German, Italian, and Spanish; Tables of the Money, Weights, and Measures of the Principal Commercial Nations and their Equivalents in British Standards; and Forms of Consular and Notarial Acts. Demy 8vo, 12s.

*JOHNSTON, H. H., F.Z.S.*—**The Kilima-njaro Expedition.** A Record of Scientific Exploration in Eastern Equatorial Africa, and a General Description of the Natural History, Languages, and Commerce of the Kilima-njaro District. With 6 Maps, and over 80 Illustrations by the Author. Demy 8vo, 21s.

*JORDAN, Furneaux, F.R.C.S.*—**Anatomy and Physiology in Character.** Crown 8vo, 5s.

*KAUFMANN, Rev. M., M.A.*—**Socialism: its Nature, its Dangers, and its Remedies considered.** Crown 8vo, 7s. 6d.

**Utopias; or, Schemes of Social Improvement, from Sir Thomas More to Karl Marx.** Crown 8vo, 5s.

**Christian Socialism.** Crown 8vo, 4s. 6d.

*KAY, David, F.R.G.S.*—**Education and Educators.** Crown 8vo, 7s. 6d.

**Memory: what it is and how to improve it.** Crown 8vo, 6s.

*KAY, Joseph.*—**Free Trade in Land.** Edited by his Widow. With Preface by the Right Hon. JOHN BRIGHT, M.P. Seventh Edition. Crown 8vo, 5s.

\*\*\* Also a cheaper edition, without the Appendix, but with a Review of Recent Changes in the Land Laws of England, by the RIGHT HON. G. OSBORNE MORGAN, Q.C., M.P. Cloth, 1s. 6d.; paper covers, 1s.

*KELKE, W. H. H.*—**An Epitome of English Grammar for the Use of Students.** Adapted to the London Matriculation Course and Similar Examinations. Crown 8vo, 4s. 6d.

*KEMPIS, Thomas à.*—**Of the Imitation of Christ.** Parchment Library Edition.—Parchment or cloth, 6s.; vellum, 7s. 6d. The Red Line Edition, fcap. 8vo, cloth extra, 2s. 6d. The Cabinet Edition, small 8vo, cloth limp, 1s.; cloth boards, 1s. 6d. The Miniature Edition, cloth limp, 32mo, 1s.; or with red lines, 1s. 6d.

\*\*\* All the above Editions may be had in various extra bindings.

KEMPIS, *Thomas à—continued.*
>Notes of a Visit to the Scenes in which his Life was spent. With numerous Illustrations. By F. R. CRUISE, M.D. Demy 8vo, 12s.

KENDALL, *Henry.*—The Kinship of Men. An argument from Pedigrees, or Genealogy viewed as a Science. With Diagrams. Crown 8vo, 5s.

KENNARD, *Rev. R. B.*—A Manual of Confirmation. 18mo. Sewed, 3d.; cloth, 1s.

KIDD, *Joseph, M.D.*—The Laws of Therapeutics; or, the Science and Art of Medicine. Second Edition. Crown 8vo, 6s.

KINGSFORD, *Anna, M.D.*—The Perfect Way in Diet. A Treatise advocating a Return to the Natural and Ancient Food of our Race. Third Edition. Small crown 8vo, 2s.

KINGSLEY, *Charles, M.A.*—Letters and Memories of his Life. Edited by his Wife. With two Steel Engraved Portraits, and Vignettes on Wood. Sixteenth Cabinet Edition. 2 vols. Crown 8vo, 12s.

>\*\*\* Also a People's Edition, in one volume. With Portrait. Crown 8vo, 6s.

>All Saints' Day, and other Sermons. Edited by the Rev. W. HARRISON. Third Edition. Crown 8vo, 7s. 6d.

>True Words for Brave Men. A Book for Soldiers' and Sailors' Libraries. Sixteenth Thousand. Crown 8vo, 2s. 6d.

KNOX, *Alexander A.*—The New Playground; or, Wanderings in Algeria. New and Cheaper Edition. Large crown 8vo, 6s.

Land Concentration and Irresponsibility of Political Power, as causing the Anomaly of a Widespread State of Want by the Side of the Vast Supplies of Nature. Crown 8vo, 5s.

LANDON, *Joseph.*—School Management; Including a General View of the Work of Education, Organization, and Discipline. Sixth Edition. Crown 8vo, 6s.

LAURIE, *S. S.*—The Rise and Early Constitution of Universities. With a Survey of Mediæval Education. Crown 8vo, 6s.

LEFEVRE, *Right Hon. G. Shaw.*—Peel and O'Connell. Demy 8vo, 10s. 6d.

>Incidents of Coercion. A Journal of two visits to Loughrea. Crown 8vo.

Letters from an Unknown Friend. By the Author of "Charles Lowder." With a Preface by the Rev. W. H. CLEAVER. Fcap. 8vo, 1s.

Life of a Prig. By ONE. Third Edition. Fcap. 8vo, 3s. 6d.

LILLIE, *Arthur, M.R.A.S.*—The Popular Life of Buddha. Containing an Answer to the Hibbert Lectures of 1881. With Illustrations. Crown 8vo, 6s.

LILLIE, *Arthur, M.R.A.S.—continued.*
    **Buddhism in Christendom;** or, Jesus the Essene. With Illustrations. Demy 8vo, 15*s.*

LOCHER, *Carl.*—**An Explanation of Organ Stops**, with Hints for Effective Combinations. Demy 8vo, 5*s.*

LONGFELLOW, *H. Wadsworth.*—**Life.** By his Brother, SAMUEL LONGFELLOW. With Portraits and Illustrations. 3 vols. Demy 8vo, 42*s.*

LONSDALE, *Margaret.*—**Sister Dora:** a Biography. With Portrait. Twenty-ninth Edition. Small crown 8vo, 2*s.* 6*d.*

    **George Eliot: Thoughts upon her Life, her Books, and Herself.** Second Edition. Small crown 8vo, 1*s.* 6*d.*

LOUNSBURY, *Thomas R.*—**James Fenimore Cooper.** With Portrait. Crown 8vo, 5*s.*

LOWDER, *Charles.*—**A Biography.** By the Author of "St. Teresa." Twelfth Edition. Crown 8vo. With Portrait. 3*s.* 6*d.*

LÜCKES, *Eva C. E.*—**Lectures on General Nursing**, delivered to the Probationers of the London Hospital Training School for Nurses. Second Edition. Crown 8vo, 2*s.* 6*d.*

LYTTON, *Edward Bulwer, Lord.*—**Life, Letters and Literary Remains.** By his Son, the EARL OF LYTTON. With Portraits, Illustrations and Facsimiles. Demy 8vo. Vols. I. and II., 32*s.*

MACHIAVELLI, *Niccolò.*—**Life and Times.** By Prof. VILLARI. Translated by LINDA VILLARI. 4 vols. Large post 8vo, 48*s.*

    **Discourses on the First Decade of Titus Livius.** Translated from the Italian by NINIAN HILL THOMSON, M.A. Large crown 8vo, 12*s.*

    **The Prince.** Translated from the Italian by N. H. T. Small crown 8vo, printed on hand-made paper, bevelled boards, 6*s.*

MACNEILL, *J. G. Swift.*—**How the Union was carried.** Crown 8vo, cloth, 1*s.* 6*d.*; paper covers, 1*s.*

MAGNUS, *Lady.*—**About the Jews since Bible Times.** From the Babylonian Exile till the English Exodus. Small crown 8vo, 6*s.*

**Maintenon, Madame de.** By EMILY BOWLES. With Portrait. Large crown 8vo, 7*s.* 6*d.*

**Many Voices.** A volume of Extracts from the Religious Writers of Christendom from the First to the Sixteenth Century. With Biographical Sketches. Crown 8vo, cloth extra, red edges, 6*s.*

MARKHAM, *Capt. Albert Hastings, R.N.*—**The Great Frozen Sea:** A Personal Narrative of the Voyage of the *Alert* during the Arctic Expedition of 1875-6. With 6 full-page Illustrations, 2 Maps, and 27 Woodcuts. Sixth and Cheaper Edition. Crown 8vo, 6*s.*

MARTINEAU, Gertrude.—Outline Lessons on Morals. Small crown 8vo, 3s. 6d.

MASON, Charlotte M.—Home Education; a Course of Lectures to Ladies. Crown 8vo, 3s. 6d.

Matter and Energy: An Examination of the Fundamental Conceptions of Physical Force. By B. L. L. Small crown 8vo, 2s.

MATUCE, H. Ogram. A Wanderer. Crown 8vo, 5s.

MAUDSLEY, H., M.D.—Body and Will. Being an Essay concerning Will, in its Metaphysical, Physiological, and Pathological Aspects. 8vo, 12s.

Natural Causes and Supernatural Seemings. Second Edition. Crown 8vo, 6s.

McGRATH, Terence.—Pictures from Ireland. New and Cheaper Edition. Crown 8vo, 2s.

McKINNEY, S. B. G.—Science and Art of Religion. Crown 8vo, 8s. 6d.

MEREDITH, M.A.—Theotokos, the Example for Woman. Dedicated, by permission, to Lady Agnes Wood. Revised by the Venerable Archdeacon DENISON. 32mo, limp cloth, 1s. 6d.

MILLER, Edward.—The History and Doctrines of Irvingism; or, The so-called Catholic and Apostolic Church. 2 vols. Large post 8vo, 15s.

The Church in Relation to the State. Large crown 8vo, 4s.

MILLS, Herbert.—Poverty and the State; or, Work for the Unemployed. An Inquiry into the Causes and Extent of Enforced Idleness, with a Statement of a Remedy. Crown 8vo, 6s.

Mitchel, John, Life. By WILLIAM DILLON. 2 vols. 8vo. With Portrait. 21s.

MITCHELL, Lucy M.—A History of Ancient Sculpture. With numerous Illustrations, including 6 Plates in Phototype. Super-royal 8vo, 42s.

MOCKLER, E.—A Grammar of the Baloochee Language, as it is spoken in Makran (Ancient Gedrosia), in the Persia-Arabic and Roman characters. Fcap. 8vo, 5s.

MOHL, Julius and Mary.—Letters and Recollections of. By M. C. M. SIMPSON. With Portraits and Two Illustrations. Demy 8vo, 15s.

MOLESWORTH, Rev. W. Nassau, M.A.—History of the Church of England from 1660. Large crown 8vo, 7s. 6d.

MORELL, J. R.—Euclid Simplified in Method and Language. Being a Manual of Geometry. Compiled from the most important French Works, approved by the University of Paris and the Minister of Public Instruction. Fcap. 8vo, 2s. 6d.

*MORISON, J. Cotter.*—The Service of Man: an Essay towards the Religion of the Future. Crown 8vo, 5s.

*MORSE, E. S., Ph.D.*—First Book of Zoology. With numerous Illustrations. New and Cheaper Edition. Crown 8vo, 2s. 6d.

My Lawyer: A Concise Abridgment of the Laws of England. By a Barrister-at-Law. Crown 8vo, 6s. 6d.

*NELSON, J. H., M.A.*—A Prospectus of the Scientific Study of the Hindû Law. Demy 8vo, 9s.

Indian Usage and Judge-made Law in Madras. Demy 8vo, 12s.

*NEWMAN, Cardinal.*—Characteristics from the Writings of. Being Selections from his various Works. Arranged with the Author's personal Approval. Seventh Edition. With Portrait. Crown 8vo, 6s.

*⁂* A Portrait of Cardinal Newman, mounted for framing, can be had, 2s. 6d.

*NEWMAN, Francis William.*—Essays on Diet. Small crown 8vo, cloth limp, 2s.

Miscellanies. Vol. II. Essays, Tracts, and Addresses, Moral and Religious. Demy 8vo, 12s.

Reminiscences of Two Exiles and Two Wars. Crown 8vo.

New Social Teachings. By POLITICUS. Small crown 8vo, 5s.

*NICOLS, Arthur, F.G.S., F.R.G.S.*—Chapters from the Physical History of the Earth: an Introduction to Geology and Palæontology. With numerous Illustrations. Crown 8vo, 5s.

*NIHILL, Rev. H. D.*—The Sisters of St. Mary at the Cross: Sisters of the Poor and their Work. Crown 8vo, 2s. 6d.

*NOEL, The Hon. Roden.*—Essays on Poetry and Poets. Demy 8vo, 12s.

*NOPS, Marianne.*—Class Lessons on Euclid. Part I. containing the First Two Books of the Elements. Crown 8vo, 2s. 6d.

Nuces: EXERCISES ON THE SYNTAX OF THE PUBLIC SCHOOL LATIN PRIMER. New Edition in Three Parts. Crown 8vo, each 1s.

*⁂* The Three Parts can also be had bound together, 3s.

*OATES, Frank, F.R.G.S.*—Matabele Land and the Victoria Falls. A Naturalist's Wanderings in the Interior of South Africa. Edited by C. G. OATES, B.A. With numerous Illustrations and 4 Maps. Demy 8vo, 21s.

*O'BRIEN, R. Barry.*—Irish Wrongs and English Remedies, with other Essays. Crown 8vo, 5s.

C

OLIVER, *Robert.*—Unnoticed Analogies. A Talk on the Irish Question. Crown 8vo.

O'MEARA, *Kathleen.*—Henri Perreyve and his Counsels to the Sick. Small crown 8vo, 5*s*.

One and a Half in Norway. A Chronicle of Small Beer. By Either and Both. Small crown 8vo, 3*s*. 6*d*.

O'NEIL, *the late Rev. Lord.*—Sermons. With Memoir and Portrait. Crown 8vo, 6*s*.

    Essays and Addresses. Crown 8vo, 5*s*.

OTTLEY, *H. Bickersteth.*—The Great Dilemma. Christ His Own Witness or His Own Accuser. Six Lectures. Second Edition. Crown 8vo, 3*s*. 6*d*.

Our Priests and their Tithes. By a Priest of the Province of Canterbury. Crown 8vo, 5*s*.

Our Public Schools—Eton, Harrow, Winchester, Rugby, Westminster, Marlborough, The Charterhouse. Crown 8vo, 6*s*.

PALMER, *the late William.*—Notes of a Visit to Russia in 1840-1841. Selected and arranged by JOHN H. CARDINAL NEWMAN, with Portrait. Crown 8vo, 8*s*. 6*d*.

    Early Christian Symbolism. A Series of Compositions from Fresco Paintings, Glasses, and Sculptured Sarcophagi. Edited by the Rev. Provost NORTHCOTE, D.D., and the Rev. Canon BROWNLOW, M.A. With Coloured Plates, folio, 42*s*., or with Plain Plates, folio, 25*s*.

Parchment Library. Choicely Printed on hand-made paper, limp parchment antique or cloth, 6*s*. ; vellum, 7*s*. 6*d*. each volume.

    Sartor Resartus. By THOMAS CARLYLE.

    The Poetical Works of John Milton. 2 vols.

    Chaucer's Canterbury Tales. Edited by A. W. POLLARD. 2 vols.

    Letters and Journals of Jonathan Swift. Selected and edited, with a Commentary and Notes, by STANLEY LANE POOLE.

    De Quincey's Confessions of an English Opium Eater. Reprinted from the First Edition. Edited by RICHARD GARNETT.

    The Gospel according to Matthew, Mark, and Luke.

    Selections from the Prose Writings of Jonathan Swift. With a Preface and Notes by STANLEY LANE-POOLE and Portrait.

    English Sacred Lyrics.

    Sir Joshua Reynolds's Discourses. Edited by EDMUND GOSSE.

Parchment Library—*continued*.

    Selections from Milton's Prose Writings. Edited by ERNEST MYERS.

    The Book of Psalms. Translated by the Rev. Canon T. K. CHEYNE, M.A., D.D.

    The Vicar of Wakefield. With Preface and Notes by AUSTIN DOBSON.

    English Comic Dramatists. Edited by OSWALD CRAWFURD.

    English Lyrics.

    The Sonnets of John Milton. Edited by MARK PATTISON. With Portrait after Vertue.

    French Lyrics. Selected and Annotated by GEORGE SAINTSBURY. With a Miniature Frontispiece designed and etched by H. G. Glindoni.

    Fables by Mr. John Gay. With Memoir by AUSTIN DOBSON, and an Etched Portrait from an unfinished Oil Sketch by Sir Godfrey Kneller.

    Select Letters of Percy Bysshe Shelley. Edited, with an Introduction, by RICHARD GARNETT.

    The Christian Year. Thoughts in Verse for the Sundays and Holy Days throughout the Year. With Miniature Portrait of the Rev. J. Keble, after a Drawing by G. Richmond, R.A.

    Shakspere's Works. Complete in Twelve Volumes.

    Eighteenth Century Essays. Selected and Edited by AUSTIN DOBSON. With a Miniature Frontispiece by R. Caldecott.

    Q. Horati Flacci Opera. Edited by F. A. CORNISH, Assistant Master at Eton. With a Frontispiece after a design by L. Alma Tadema, etched by Leopold Lowenstam.

    Edgar Allan Poe's Poems. With an Essay on his Poetry by ANDREW LANG, and a Frontispiece by Linley Sambourne.

    Shakspere's Sonnets. Edited by EDWARD DOWDEN. With a Frontispiece etched by Leopold Lowenstam, after the Death Mask.

    English Odes. Selected by EDMUND GOSSE. With Frontispiece on India paper by Hamo Thornycroft, A.R.A.

    Of the Imitation of Christ. By THOMAS À KEMPIS. A revised Translation. With Frontispiece on India paper, from a Design by W. B. Richmond.

    Poems: Selected from PERCY BYSSHE SHELLEY. Dedicated to Lady Shelley. With a Preface by RICHARD GARNETT and a Miniature Frontispiece.

*PARSLOE, Joseph.*—**Our Railways.** Sketches, Historical and Descriptive. With Practical Information as to Fares and Rates, etc., and a Chapter on Railway Reform. Crown 8vo, 6s.

*PASCAL, Blaise.*—**The Thoughts of.** Translated from the Text of Auguste Molinier, by C. KEGAN PAUL. Large crown 8vo, with Frontispiece, printed on hand-made paper, parchment antique, or cloth, 12s.; vellum, 15s. New Edition. Crown 8vo, 6s.

*PATON, W. A.*—**Down the Islands.** A Voyage to the Caribbees. With Illustration. Medium 8vo, 16s.

*PAUL, C. Kegan.*—**Biographical Sketches.** Printed on hand-made paper, bound in buckram. Second Edition. Crown 8vo, 7s. 6d.

*PEARSON, Rev. S.*—**Week-day Living.** A Book for Young Men and Women. Second Edition. Crown 8vo, 5s.

*PENRICE, Major J.*—**Arabic and English Dictionary of the Koran.** 4to, 21s.

*PESCHEL, Dr. Oscar.*—**The Races of Man and their Geographical Distribution.** Second Edition. Large crown 8vo, 9s.

*PIDGEON, D.*—**An Engineer's Holiday;** or, Notes of a Round Trip from Long. 0° to 0°. New and Cheaper Edition. Large crown 8vo, 7s. 6d.

**Old World Questions and New World Answers.** Second Edition. Large crown 8vo, 7s. 6d.

Plain **Thoughts for Men.** Eight Lectures delivered at Forester's Hall, Clerkenwell, during the London Mission, 1884. Crown 8vo, cloth, 1s. 6d; paper covers, 1s.

*PLOWRIGHT, C. B.*—**The British Uredineæ and Ustilagineæ.** With Illustrations. Demy 8vo, 10s. 6d.

*PRICE, Prof. Bonamy.*—**Chapters on Practical Political Economy.** Being the Substance of Lectures delivered before the University of Oxford. New and Cheaper Edition. Crown 8vo, 5s.

**Prig's Bede:** the Venerable Bede, Expurgated, Expounded, and Exposed. By "THE PRIG." Second Edition. Fcap. 8vo, 3s. 6d.

**Pulpit Commentary, The.** (*Old Testament Series.*) Edited by the Rev. J. S. EXELL, M.A., and the Very Rev. Dean H. D. M. SPENCE, M.A., D.D.

Genesis. By the Rev. T. WHITELAW, D.D. With Homilies by the Very Rev. J. F. MONTGOMERY, D.D., Rev. Prof. R. A. REDFORD, M.A., LL.B., Rev. F. HASTINGS, Rev. W. ROBERTS, M.A. An Introduction to the Study of the Old Testament by the Venerable Archdeacon FARRAR, D.D., F.R.S.; and Introductions to the Pentateuch by the Right Rev. H. COTTERILL, D.D., and Rev. T. WHITELAW, M.A. Eighth Edition. 1 vol., 15s.

**Pulpit Commentary, The**—*continued.*

**Exodus.** By the Rev. Canon RAWLINSON. With Homilies by Rev. J. ORR, D.D., Rev. D. YOUNG, B.A., Rev. C. A. GOODHART, Rev. J. URQUHART, and the Rev. H. T. ROBJOHNS. Fourth Edition. 2 vols., 9s. each.

**Leviticus.** By the Rev. Prebendary MEYRICK, M.A. With Introductions by the Rev. R. COLLINS, Rev. Professor A. CAVE, and Homilies by Rev. Prof. REDFORD, LL.B., Rev. J. A. MACDONALD, Rev. W. CLARKSON, B.A., Rev. S. R. ALDRIDGE, LL.B., and Rev. MCCHEYNE EDGAR. Fourth Edition. 15s.

**Numbers.** By the Rev. R. WINTERBOTHAM, LL.B. With Homilies by the Rev. Professor W. BINNIE, D.D., Rev. E. S. PROUT, M.A., Rev. D. YOUNG, Rev. J. WAITE, and an Introduction by the Rev. THOMAS WHITELAW, M.A. Fifth Edition. 15s.

**Deuteronomy.** By the Rev. W. L. ALEXANDER, D.D. With Homilies by Rev. C. CLEMANCE, D.D., Rev. J. ORR, D.D., Rev. R. M. EDGAR, M.A., Rev. D. DAVIES, M.A. Fourth edition. 15s.

**Joshua.** By Rev. J. J. LIAS, M.A. With Homilies by Rev. S. R. ALDRIDGE, LL.B., Rev. R. GLOVER, REV. E. DE PRESSENSÉ, D.D., Rev. J. WAITE, B.A., Rev. W. F. ADENEY, M.A.; and an Introduction by the Rev. A. PLUMMER, M.A. Fifth Edition. 12s. 6d.

**Judges and Ruth.** By the Bishop of BATH and WELLS, and Rev. J. MORISON, D.D. With Homilies by Rev. A. F. MUIR, M.A., Rev. W. F. ADENEY, M.A., Rev. W. M. STATHAM, and Rev. Professor J. THOMSON, M.A. Fifth Edition. 10s. 6d.

**1 Samuel.** By the Very Rev. R. P. SMITH, D.D. With Homilies by Rev. DONALD FRASER, D.D., Rev. Prof. CHAPMAN, and Rev. B. DALE. Sixth Edition. 15s.

**1 Kings.** By the Rev. JOSEPH HAMMOND, LL.B. With Homilies by the Rev. E. DE PRESSENSÉ, D.D., Rev. J. WAITE, B.A., Rev. A. ROWLAND, LL.B., Rev. J. A. MACDONALD, and Rev. J. URQUHART. Fifth Edition. 15s.

**1 Chronicles.** By the Rev. Prof. P. C. BARKER, M.A., LL.B. With Homilies by Rev. Prof. J. R. THOMSON, M.A., Rev. R. TUCK, B.A., Rev. W. CLARKSON, B.A., Rev. F. WHITFIELD, M.A., and Rev. RICHARD GLOVER. 15s.

**Ezra, Nehemiah, and Esther.** By Rev. Canon G. RAWLINSON, M.A. With Homilies by Rev. Prof. J. R. THOMSON, M.A., Rev. Prof. R. A. REDFORD, LL.B., M.A., Rev. W. S. LEWIS, M.A., Rev. J. A. MACDONALD, Rev. A. MACKENNAL, B.A., Rev. W. CLARKSON, B.A., Rev. F. HASTINGS, Rev. W. DINWIDDIE, LL.B., Rev. Prof. ROWLANDS, B.A., Rev. G. WOOD, B.A., Rev. Prof. P. C. BARKER, M.A., LL.B., and the Rev. J. S. EXELL, M.A. Sixth Edition. 1 vol., 12s. 6d.

**Pulpit Commentary, The**—*continued.*

**Isaiah.** By the Rev. Canon G. RAWLINSON, M.A. With Homilies by Rev. Prof. E. JOHNSON, M.A., Rev. W. CLARKSON, B.A., Rev. W. M. STATHAM, and Rev. R. TUCK, B.A. Second Edition. 2 vols., 15s. each.

**Jeremiah.** (Vol. I.) By the Rev. Canon T. K. CHEYNE, D.D. With Homilies by the Rev. W. F. ADENEY, M.A., Rev. A. F. MUIR, M.A., Rev. S. CONWAY, B.A., Rev. J. WAITE, B.A., and Rev. D. YOUNG, B.A. Third Edition. 15s.

**Jeremiah (Vol. II.) and Lamentations.** By Rev. Canon T. K. CHEYNE, D.D. With Homilies by Rev. Prof. J. R. THOMSON, M.A., Rev. W. F. ADENEY, M.A., Rev. A. F. MUIR, M.A., Rev. S. CONWAY, B.A., Rev. D. YOUNG, B.A. 15s.

**Hosea and Joel.** By the Rev. Prof. J. J. GIVEN, Ph.D., D.D. With Homilies by the Rev. Prof. J. R. THOMSON, M.A., Rev. A. ROWLAND, B.A., LL.B., Rev. C. JERDAN, M.A., LL.B., Rev. J. ORR, D.D., and Rev. D. THOMAS, D.D. 15s.

**Pulpit Commentary, The.** (*New Testament Series.*)

**St. Mark.** By Very Rev. E. BICKERSTETH, D.D., Dean of Lichfield. With Homilies by Rev. Prof. THOMSON, M.A., Rev. Prof. J. J. GIVEN, Ph.D., D.D., Rev. Prof. JOHNSON, M.A., Rev. A. ROWLAND, B.A., LL.B., Rev. A. MUIR, and Rev. R. GREEN. Fifth Edition. 2 vols., 10s. 6d. each.

**St. John.** By Rev. Prof. H. R. REYNOLDS, D.D. With Homilies by Rev. Prof. T. CROSKERY, D.D., Rev. Prof J. R. THOMSON, M.A., Rev. D. YOUNG, B.A., Rev. B. THOMAS, Rev. G. BROWN. Second Edition. 2 vols. 15s. each.

**The Acts of the Apostles.** By the Bishop of BATH and WELLS. With Homilies by Rev. Prof. P. C. BARKER, M.A., LL.B., Rev. Prof. E. JOHNSON, M.A., Rev. Prof. R. A. REDFORD, LL.B., Rev. R. TUCK, B.A., Rev. W. CLARKSON, B.A. Fourth Edition. 2 vols., 10s. 6d. each.

**1 Corinthians.** By the Ven. Archdeacon FARRAR, D.D. With Homilies by Rev. Ex-Chancellor LIPSCOMB, LL.D., Rev. DAVID THOMAS, D.D., Rev. D. FRASER, D.D., Rev. Prof. J. R. THOMSON, M.A., Rev. J. WAITE, B.A., Rev. R. TUCK, B.A., Rev. E. HURNDALL, M.A., and Rev. H. BREMNER, B.D. Fourth Edition. 15s.

**2 Corinthians and Galatians.** By the Ven. Archdeacon FARRAR, D.D., and Rev. Prebendary E. HUXTABLE. With Homilies by Rev. Ex-Chancellor LIPSCOMB, LL.D., Rev. DAVID THOMAS, D.D., Rev. DONALD FRASER, D.D., Rev. R. TUCK, B.A., Rev. E. HURNDALL, M.A., Rev. Prof. J. R. THOMSON, M.A., Rev. R. FINLAYSON, B.A., Rev. W. F. ADENEY, M.A., Rev. R. M. EDGAR, M.A., and Rev. T. CROSKERY, D.D. Second Edition. 21s.

**Pulpit Commentary, The.**—*continued*.

 **Ephesians, Philippians, and Colossians.** By the Rev. Prof. W. G. BLAIKIE, D.D., Rev. B. C. CAFFIN, M.A., and Rev. G. G. FINDLAY, B.A. With Homilies by Rev. D. THOMAS, D.D., Rev. R. M. EDGAR, M.A., Rev. R. FINLAYSON, B.A., Rev. W. F. ADENEY, M.A., Rev. Prof. T. CROSKERY, D.D., Rev. E. S. PROUT, M.A., Rev. Canon VERNON HUTTON, and Rev. U. R. THOMAS, D.D. Second Edition. 21s.

 **Thessalonians, Timothy, Titus, and Philemon.** By the Bishop of Bath and Wells, Rev. Dr. GLOAG and Rev. Dr. EALES. With Homilies by the Rev. B. C. CAFFIN, M.A., Rev. R. FINLAYSON, B.A., Rev. Prof. T. CROSKERY, D.D., Rev. W. F. ADENEY, M.A., Rev. W. M. STATHAM, and Rev. D. THOMAS, D.D. 15s.

 **Hebrews and James.** By the Rev. J. BARMBY, D.D., and Rev Prebendary E. C. S. GIBSON, M.A. With Homiletics by the Rev. C. JERDAN, M.A., LL.B., and Rev. Prebendary E. C. S. GIBSON. And Homilies by the Rev. W. JONES, Rev. C. NEW, Rev. D. YOUNG, B.A., Rev. J. S. BRIGHT, Rev. T. F. LOCKYER, B.A., and Rev. C. JERDAN, M.A., LL.B. Second Edition. 15s.

*PUSEY, Dr.*—**Sermons for the Church's Seasons from Advent to Trinity.** Selected from the Published Sermons of the late EDWARD BOUVERIE PUSEY, D.D. Crown 8vo, 5s.

*QUEKETT, Rev. W.*—**My Sayings and Doings.** With Reminiscences of my Life. With Illustrations. Demy 8vo, 18s.

*RANKE, Leopold von.*—**Universal History.** The oldest Historical Group of Nations and the Greeks. Edited by G. W. PROTHERO. Demy 8vo, 16s.

*RENDELL, J. M.*—**Concise Handbook of the Island of Madeira.** With Plan of Funchal and Map of the Island. Fcap. 8vo, 1s. 6d.

*REVELL, W. F.*—**Ethical Forecasts.** Crown 8vo, 3s. 6d.

*REYNOLDS, Rev. J. W.*—**The Supernatural in Nature.** A Verification by Free Use of Science. Third Edition, Revised and Enlarged. Demy 8vo, 14s.

 **The Mystery of Miracles.** Third and Enlarged Edition. Crown 8vo, 6s.

 **The Mystery of the Universe our Common Faith.** Demy 8vo, 14s.

 **The World to Come:** Immortality a Physical Fact. Crown 8vo, 6s.

*RIBOT, Prof. Th.*—**Heredity:** A Psychological Study of its Phenomena, its Laws, its Causes, and its Consequences. Second Edition. Large crown 8vo, 9s.

*RIVINGTON, Luke.*—**Authority, or a Plain Reason for joining the Church of Rome.** Crown 8vo., 3*s.* 6*d.*

*ROBERTSON, The late Rev. F. W., M.A.*—**Life and Letters of.** Edited by the Rev. STOPFORD BROOKE, M.A.
    I. Two vols., uniform with the Sermons. With Steel Portrait. Crown 8vo, 7*s.* 6*d.*
    II. Library Edition, in Demy 8vo, with Portrait. 12*s.*
    III. A Popular Edition, in 1 vol. Crown 8vo, 6*s.*

**Sermons.** Four Series. Small crown 8vo, 3*s.* 6*d.* each.

**The Human Race,** and other Sermons. Preached at Cheltenham, Oxford, and Brighton. New and Cheaper Edition. Small crown 8vo, 3*s.* 6*d.*

**Notes on Genesis.** New and Cheaper Edition. Small crown 8vo, 3*s.* 6*d.*

**Expository Lectures on St. Paul's Epistles to the Corinthians.** A New Edition. Small crown 8vo, 5*s.*

**Lectures and Addresses,** with other Literary Remains. A New Edition. Small crown 8vo, 5*s.*

**An Analysis of Tennyson's "In Memoriam."** (Dedicated by Permission to the Poet-Laureate.) Fcap. 8vo, 2*s.*

**The Education of the Human Race.** Translated from the German of GOTTHOLD EPHRAIM LESSING. Fcap. 8vo, 2*s.* 6*d.*

The above Works can also be had, bound in half-morocco.

*\*\*\** A Portrait of the late Rev. F. W. Robertson, mounted for framing, can be had, 2*s.* 6*d.*

*ROGERS, William.*—**Reminiscences.** Compiled by R. H. HADDEN. With Portrait. Crown 8vo, 6*s.*

*ROMANES, G. J.*—**Mental Evolution in Animals.** With a Posthumous Essay on Instinct by CHARLES DARWIN, F.R.S. Demy 8vo, 12*s.*

*ROSMINI SERBATI, Antonio.*—**Life.** By the REV. W. LOCKHART. Second Edition. 2 vols. With Portraits. Crown 8vo, 12*s.*

*ROSS, Janet.*—**Italian Sketches.** With 14 full-page Illustrations. Crown 8vo, 7*s.* 6*d.*

*RULE, Martin, M.A.*—**The Life and Times of St. Anselm, Archbishop of Canterbury and Primate of the Britains.** 2 vols. Demy 8vo, 32*s.*

*SAVERY, C. E.*—**The Church of England; an Historical Sketch.** Crown 8vo.

*SAYCE, Rev. Archibald Henry.*—**Introduction to the Science of Language.** 2 vols. Second Edition. Large post 8vo, 21*s.*

*SCOONES, W. Baptiste.*—**Four Centuries of English Letters:** A Selection of 350 Letters by 150 Writers, from the Period of the Paston Letters to the Present Time. Third Edition. Large crown 8vo, 6*s.*

SEYMOUR, W. Digby, Q.C.,—Home Rule and State Supremacy. Crown 8vo, 3s 6d.

Shakspere's Works. The Avon Edition, 12 vols., fcap. 8vo, cloth, 18s.; in cloth box, 21s.; bound in 6 vols., cloth, 15s.

Shakspere's Works, an Index to. By EVANGELINE O'CONNOR. Crown 8vo, 5s.

SHELLEY, Percy Bysshe.—Life. By EDWARD DOWDEN, LL.D. 2 vols. With Portraits. Demy 8vo, 36s.

SHILLITO, Rev. Joseph.—Womanhood: its Duties, Temptations and Privileges. A Book for Young Women. Third Edition. Crown 8vo, 3s. 6d.

Shooting, Practical Hints on. Being a Treatise on the Shot Gun and its Management. By "20 Bore." With 55 Illustrations. Demy 8vo, 12s.

Sister Augustine, Superior of the Sisters of Charity at the St. Johannis Hospital at Bonn. Authorized Translation by HANS THARAU, from the German "Memorials of AMALIE VON LASAULX." Cheap Edition. Large crown 8vo, 4s. 6d.

SKINNER, James.—A Memoir. By the Author of "Charles Lowder." With a Preface by the Rev. Canon CARTER, and Portrait. Large crown, 7s. 6d.
  \*\*\* Also a cheap Edition. With Portrait. Fourth Edition. Crown 8vo, 3s. 6d.

SMEATON, D. Mackenzie.—The Loyal Karens of Burma. Crown 8vo, 4s. 6d.

SMITH, Edward, M.D., LL.B., F.R.S.—Tubercular Consumption in its Early and Remediable Stages. Second Edition. Crown 8vo, 6s.

SMITH, L, A.—The Music of the Waters: Sailor's Chanties and Working Songs of the Sea. Demy 8vo.

Spanish Mystics. By the Editor of "Many Voices." Crown 8vo, 5s.

Specimens of English Prose Style from Malory to Macaulay. Selected and Annotated, with an Introductory Essay, by GEORGE SAINTSBURY. Large crown 8vo, printed on hand-made paper, parchment antique or cloth, 12s.; vellum, 15s.

Stray Papers on Education, and Scenes from School Life. By B. H. Second Edition. Small crown 8vo, 3s. 6d.

STREATFEILD, Rev. G. S., M.A.—Lincolnshire and the Danes. Large crown 8vo, 7s. 6d.

STRECKER-WISLICENUS.—Organic Chemistry. Translated and Edited, with Extensive Additions, by W. R. HODGKINSON, Ph.D., and A. J. GREENAWAY, F.I.C. Second and cheaper Edition. Demy 8vo, 12s. 6d.

Suakin, 1885; being a Sketch of the Campaign of this year. By an Officer who was there. Second Edition. Crown 8vo, 2s. 6d.

SULLY, *James*, *M.A.*—Pessimism: a History and a Criticism. Second Edition. Demy 8vo, 14s.

SWANWICK, *Anna.*—An Utopian Dream, and how it may be Realized. Fcap. 8vo, 1s.

SWEDENBORG, *Eman.*—De Cultu et Amore Dei ubi Agitur de Telluris ortu, Paradiso et Vivario, tum de Primogeniti Seu Adami Nativitate Infantia, et Amore. Crown 8vo, 6s.

    On the Worship and Love of God. Treating of the Birth of the Earth, Paradise, and the Abode of Living Creatures. Translated from the original Latin. Crown 8vo, 7s. 6d.

    Prodromus Philosophiæ Ratiocinantis de Infinito, et Causa Finali Creationis: deque Mechanismo Operationis Animæ et Corporis. Edidit THOMAS MURRAY GORMAN, M.A. Crown 8vo, 7s. 6d.

TACITUS.—The Agricola. A Translation. Small crown 8vo, 2s. 6d.

TARRING, *C. J.*—A Practical Elementary Turkish Grammar. Crown 8vo, 6s.

TAYLOR, *Hugh.*—The Morality of Nations. A Study in the Evolution of Ethics. Crown 8vo, 6s.

TAYLOR, *Rev. Canon Isaac, LL.D.*—The Alphabet. An Account of the Origin and Development of Letters. With numerous Tables and Facsimiles. 2 vols. Demy 8vo, 36s.

    Leaves from an Egyptian Note-book. Crown 8vo.

TAYLOR, *Jeremy.*—The Marriage Ring. With Preface, Notes, and Appendices. Edited by FRANCIS BURDETT MONEY COUTTS. Small crown 8vo, 2s. 6d.

TAYLOR, *Reynell, C.B., C.S.I.* A Biography. By E. GAMBIER PARRY. With Portait and Map. Demy 8vo, 14s.

TAYLOR, *Sedley.*—Profit Sharing between Capital and Labour. To which is added a Memorandum on the Industrial Partnership at the Whitwood Collieries, by ARCHIBALD and HENRY BRIGGS, with remarks by SEDLEY TAYLOR. Crown 8vo, 2s. 6d.

THOM, *J. Hamilton.*—Laws of Life after the Mind of Christ. Two Series. Crown 8vo, 7s. 6d. each.

THOMPSON, *Sir H.*—Diet in Relation to Age and Activity. Fcap. 8vo, cloth, 1s. 6d.; paper covers, 1s.

TIDMAN, *Paul F.*—Money and Labour. 1s. 6d.

TODHUNTER, *Dr. J.*—A Study of Shelley. Crown 8vo, 7s.

TOLSTOI, *Count Leo.*—Christ's Christianity. Translated from the Russian. Large crown 8vo, 7*s.* 6*d.*

TRANT, *William.*—Trade Unions: Their Origin, Objects, and Efficacy. Small crown 8vo, 1*s.* 6*d.*; paper covers, 1*s.*

TRENCH, *The late R. C., Archbishop.*—Letters and Memorials. By the Author of "Charles Lowder." With two Portraits. 2 vols. 8vo, 21*s.*

Notes on the Parables of Our Lord. Fourteenth Edition. 8vo, 12*s.* Cheap Edition, 7*s.* 6*d.*

Notes on the Miracles of Our Lord. Twelfth Edition. 8vo, 12*s.* Cheap Edition, 7*s.* 6*d.*

Studies in the Gospels. Fifth Edition, Revised. 8vo, 10*s.* 6*d.*

Brief Thoughts and Meditations on Some Passages in Holy Scripture. Third Edition. Crown 8vo, 3*s.* 6*d.*

Synonyms of the New Testament. Tenth Edition, Enlarged. 8vo, 12*s.*

Sermons New and Old. Crown 8vo, 6*s.*

Westminster and other Sermons. Crown 8vo, 6*s.*

On the Authorized Version of the New Testament. Second Edition. 8vo, 7*s.*

Commentary on the Epistles to the Seven Churches in Asia. Fourth Edition, Revised. 8vo, 8*s.* 6*d.*

The Sermon on the Mount. An Exposition drawn from the Writings of St. Augustine, with an Essay on his Merits as an Interpreter of Holy Scripture. Fourth Edition, Enlarged. 8vo, 10*s.* 6*d.*

Shipwrecks of Faith. Three Sermons preached before the University of Cambridge in May, 1867. Fcap. 8vo, 2*s.* 6*d.*

Lectures on Mediæval Church History. Being the Substance of Lectures delivered at Queen's College, London. Second Edition. 8vo, 12*s.*

English, Past and Present. Thirteenth Edition, Revised and Improved. Fcap. 8vo, 5*s.*

On the Study of Words. Twentieth Edition, Revised. Fcap. 8vo, 5*s.*

Select Glossary of English Words Used Formerly in Senses Different from the Present. Sixth Edition, Revised and Enlarged. Fcap. 8vo, 5*s.*

Proverbs and Their Lessons. Seventh Edition, Enlarged. Fcap. 8vo, 4*s.*

Poems. Collected and Arranged anew. Ninth Edition. Fcap. 8vo, 7*s* 6*d.*

TRENCH, The late R. C., Archbishop.—continued.

    Poems. Library Edition. 2 vols. Small crown 8vo, 10s.

    Sacred Latin Poetry. Chiefly Lyrical, Selected and Arranged for Use. Third Edition, Corrected and Improved. Fcap. 8vo, 7s.

    A Household Book of English Poetry. Selected and Arranged, with Notes. Fourth Edition, Revised. Extra fcap. 8vo, 5s. 6d.

    An Essay on the Life and Genius of Calderon. With Translations from his "Life's a Dream" and "Great Theatre of the World." Second Edition, Revised and Improved. Extra fcap. 8vo, 5s. 6d.

    Gustavus Adolphus in Germany, and other Lectures on the Thirty Years' War. Third Edition, Enlarged. Fcap. 8vo, 4s.

    Plutarch: his Life, his Lives, and his Morals. Second Edition, Enlarged. Fcap. 8vo, 3s. 6d.

    Remains of the late Mrs. Richard Trench. Being Selections from her Journals, Letters, and other Papers. New and Cheaper Issue. With Portrait. 8vo, 6s.

TUTHILL, C. A. H.—Origin and Development of Christian Dogma. Crown 8vo.

TWINING, Louisa.—Workhouse Visiting and Management during Twenty-Five Years. Small crown 8vo, 2s.

Two Centuries of Irish History. By various Writers. Edited by Prof. J. BRYCE. Demy 8vo.

VAL d'EREMAO, Rev. J. P.—The Serpent of Eden. A Philological and Critical Essay. Crown 8vo, 4s. 6d.

VICARY, J. Fulford.—Saga Time. With Illustrations. Crown 8vo, 7s. 6d.

VOLCKXSOM, E. W. v.—Catechism of Elementary Modern Chemistry. Small crown 8vo, 3s.

WALPOLE, Chas. George.—A Short History of Ireland from the Earliest Times to the Union with Great Britain. With 5 Maps and Appendices. Third Edition. Crown 8vo, 6s.

Words of Jesus Christ taken from the Gospels. Small crown 8vo, 2s. 6d.

WARD, Wilfrid.—The Wish to Believe. A Discussion Concerning the Temper of Mind in which a reasonable Man should undertake Religious Inquiry. Small crown 8vo, 5s.

WARD, William George, Ph.D.—Essays on the Philosophy of Theism. Edited, with an Introduction, by WILFRID WARD. 2 vols. Demy 8vo, 21s.

WARTER, J. W.—An Old Shropshire Oak. 2 vols. Demy 8vo, 28s.

WEDMORE, Frederick.—The Masters of Genre Painting. With Sixteen Illustrations. Post 8vo, 7s. 6d.

WHITMAN, Sidney.—Conventional Cant: its Results and Remedy. Crown 8vo, 6s.

WHITNEY, Prof. William Dwight.—Essentials of English Grammar, for the Use of Schools. Second Edition. Crown 8vo, 3s. 6d.

WHITWORTH, George Clifford.—An Anglo-Indian Dictionary: a Glossary of Indian Terms used in English, and of such English or other Non-Indian Terms as have obtained special meanings in India. Demy 8vo, cloth, 12s.

WILSON, Mrs. R. F.—The Christian Brothers. Their Origin and Work. With a Sketch of the Life of their Founder, the Ven. JEAN BAPTISTE, de la Salle. Crown 8vo, 6s.

WOLTMANN, Dr. Alfred, and WOERMANN, Dr. Karl.—History of Painting. With numerous Illustrations. Medium 8vo. Vol. I. Painting in Antiquity and the Middle Ages. 28s.; bevelled boards, gilt leaves, 30s. Vol. II. The Painting of the Renascence. 42s.; bevelled boards, gilt leaves, 45s.

YOUMANS, Edward L., M.D.—A Class Book of Chemistry, on the Basis of the New System. With 200 Illustrations. Crown 8vo, 5s.

YOUMANS, Eliza A.—First Book of Botany. Designed to Cultivate the Observing Powers of Children. With 300 Engravings. New and Cheaper Edition. Crown 8vo, 2s. 6d.

## THE INTERNATIONAL SCIENTIFIC SERIES.

I. Forms of Water in Clouds and Rivers, Ice and Glaciers. By J. Tyndall, LL.D., F.R.S. With 25 Illustrations. Ninth Edition. 5s.

II. Physics and Politics; or, Thoughts on the Application of the Principles of "Natural Selection" and "Inheritance" to Political Society. By Walter Bagehot. Eighth Edition. 5s.

III. Foods. By Edward Smith, M.D., LL.B., F.R.S. With numerous Illustrations. Ninth Edition. 5s.

IV. Mind and Body: the Theories of their Relation. By Alexander Bain, LL.D. With Four Illustrations. Eighth Edition. 5s.

V. The Study of Sociology. By Herbert Spencer. Thirteenth Edition. 5s.

VI. **The Conservation of Energy.** By Balfour Stewart, M.A., LL.D., F.R.S. With 14 Illustrations. Seventh Edition. 5s.

VII. **Animal Locomotion;** or Walking, Swimming, and Flying. By J. B. Pettigrew, M.D., F.R.S., etc. With 130 Illustrations. Third Edition. 5s.

VIII. **Responsibility in Mental Disease.** By Henry Maudsley, M.D. Fourth Edition. 5s.

IX. **The New Chemistry.** By Professor J. P. Cooke. With 31 Illustrations. Ninth Edition. 5s.

X. **The Science of Law.** By Professor Sheldon Amos. Sixth Edition. 5s.

XI. **Animal Mechanism:** a Treatise on Terrestrial and Aerial Locomotion. By Professor E. J. Marey. With 117 Illustrations. Third Edition. 5s.

XII. **The Doctrine of Descent and Darwinism.** By Professor Oscar Schmidt. With 26 Illustrations. Seventh Edition. 5s.

XIII. **The History of the Conflict between Religion and Science.** By J. W. Draper, M.D., LL.D. Twentieth Edition. 5s.

XIV. **Fungi:** their Nature, Influences, and Uses. By M. C. Cooke, M.A., LL.D. Edited by the Rev. M. J. Berkeley, M.A., F.L.S. With numerous Illustrations. Fourth Edition. 5s.

XV. **The Chemistry of Light and Photography.** By Dr. Hermann Vogel. With 100 Illustrations. Fifth Edition. 5s.

XVI. **The Life and Growth of Language.** By Professor William Dwight Whitney. Fifth Edition. 5s.

XVII. **Money and the Mechanism of Exchange.** By W. Stanley Jevons, M.A., F.R.S. Eighth Edition. 5s.

XVIII. **The Nature of Light.** With a General Account of Physical Optics. By Dr. Eugene Lommel. With 188 Illustrations and a Table of Spectra in Chromo-lithography. Fourth Edition. 5s.

XIX. **Animal Parasites and Messmates.** By P. J. Van Beneden. With 83 Illustrations. Third Edition. 5s.

XX. **On Fermentation.** By Professor Schützenberger. With 28 Illustrations. Fourth Edition. 5s.

XXI. **The Five Senses of Man.** By Professor Bernstein. With 91 Illustrations. Fifth Edition. 5s.

XXII. **The Theory of Sound in its Relation to Music.** By Professor Pietro Blaserna. With numerous Illustrations. Third Edition. 5s.

XXIII. **Studies in Spectrum Analysis.** By J. Norman Lockyer, F.R.S. With six photographic Illustrations of Spectra, and numerous engravings on Wood. Fourth Edition. 6s. 6d.

XXIV. **A History of the Growth of the Steam Engine.** By Professor R. H. Thurston. With numerous Illustrations. Fourth Edition. 5s.

XXV. **Education as a Science.** By Alexander Bain, LL.D. Sixth Edition. 5s.

XXVI. **The Human Species.** By Professor A. de Quatrefages. Fourth Edition. 5s.

XXVII. **Modern Chromatics.** With Applications to Art and Industry. By Ogden N. Rood. With 130 original Illustrations. Second Edition. 5s.

XXVIII. **The Crayfish:** an Introduction to the Study of Zoology. By Professor T. H. Huxley. With 82 Illustrations. Fourth Edition. 5s.

XXIX. **The Brain as an Organ of Mind.** By H. Charlton Bastian, M.D. With numerous Illustrations. Third Edition. 5s.

XXX. **The Atomic Theory.** By Prof. Wurtz. Translated by E. Cleminshaw, F.C.S. Fifth Edition. 5s.

XXXI. **The Natural Conditions of Existence as they affect Animal Life.** By Karl Semper. With 2 Maps and 106 Woodcuts. Third Edition. 5s.

XXXII. **General Physiology of Muscles and Nerves.** By Prof. J. Rosenthal. Third Edition. With 75 Illustrations. 5s.

XXXIII. **Sight:** an Exposition of the Principles of Monocular and Binocular Vision. By Joseph le Conte, LL.D. Second Edition. With 132 Illustrations. 5s.

XXXIV. **Illusions:** a Psychological Study. By James Sully. Third Edition. 5s.

XXXV. **Volcanoes: what they are and what they teach.** By Professor J. W. Judd, F.R.S. With 96 Illustrations on Wood. Fourth Edition. 5s.

XXXVI. **Suicide:** an Essay on Comparative Moral Statistics. By Prof. H. Morselli. Second Edition. With Diagrams. 5s.

XXXVII. **The Brain and its Functions.** By J. Luys. With Illustrations. Second Edition. 5s.

XXXVIII. **Myth and Science:** an Essay. By Tito Vignoli. Third Edition. With Supplementary Note. 5s.

XXXIX. **The Sun.** By Professor Young. With Illustrations. Third Edition. 5s.

XL. **Ants, Bees, and Wasps:** a Record of Observations on the Habits of the Social Hymenoptera. By Sir John Lubbock, Bart., M.P. With 5 Chromo-lithographic Illustrations. Eighth Edition. 5s.

XLI. **Animal Intelligence.** By G. J. Romanes, LL.D., F.R.S. Fourth Edition. 5*s*.

XLII. **The Concepts and Theories of Modern Physics.** By J. B. Stallo. Third Edition. 5*s*.

XLIII. **Diseases of Memory**; An Essay in the Positive Psychology. By Prof. Th. Ribot. Third Edition. 5*s*.

XLIV. **Man before Metals.** By N. Joly, with 148 Illustrations. Fourth Edition. 5*s*.

XLV. **The Science of Politics.** By Prof. Sheldon Amos. Third Edition. 5*s*.

XLVI. **Elementary Meteorology.** By Robert H. Scott. Fourth Edition. With Numerous Illustrations. 5*s*.

XLVII. **The Organs of Speech and their Application in the Formation of Articulate Sounds.** By Georg Hermann Von Meyer. With 47 Woodcuts. 5*s*.

XLVIII. **Fallacies.** A View of Logic from the Practical Side. By Alfred Sidgwick. Second Edition. 5*s*.

XLIX. **Origin of Cultivated Plants.** By Alphonse de Candolle. Second Edition. 5*s*.

L. **Jelly-Fish, Star-Fish, and Sea-Urchins.** Being a Research on Primitive Nervous Systems. By G. J. Romanes. With Illustrations. 5*s*.

LI. **The Common Sense of the Exact Sciences.** By the late William Kingdon Clifford. Second Edition. With 100 Figures. 5*s*.

LII. **Physical Expression:** Its Modes and Principles. By Francis Warner, M.D., F.R.C.P., Hunterian Professor of Comparative Anatomy and Physiology, R.C.S.E. With 50 Illustrations. 5*s*.

LIII. **Anthropoid Apes.** By Robert Hartmann. With 63 Illustrations. 5*s*.

LIV. **The Mammalia in their Relation to Primeval Times.** By Oscar Schmidt. With 51 Woodcuts. 5*s*.

LV. **Comparative Literature.** By H. Macaulay Posnett, LL.D. 5*s*.

LVI. **Earthquakes and other Earth Movements.** By Prof. John Milne. With 38 Figures. Second Edition. 5*s*.

LVII. **Microbes, Ferments, and Moulds.** By E. L. Trouessart. With 107 Illustrations. 5*s*.

LVIII. **Geographical and Geological Distribution of Animals.** By Professor A. Heilprin. With Frontispiece. 5*s*.

LIX. **Weather.** A Popular Exposition of the Nature of Weather Changes from Day to Day. By the Hon. Ralph Abercromby. Second Edition. With 96 Illustrations. 5*s*.

LX. **Animal Magnetism.** By Alfred Binet and Charles Féré. 5s.

LXI. **Manual of British Discomycetes,** with descriptions of all the Species of Fungi hitherto found in Britain included in the Family, and Illustrations of the Genera. By William Phillips, F.L.S. 5s.

LXII. **International Law.** With Materials for a Code of International Law. By Professor Leone Levi. 5s.

LXIII. **The Geological History of Plants.** By Sir J. William Dawson. With 80 Figures. 5s.

LXIV. **The Origin of Floral Structures through Insect and other Agencies.** By Rev. Prof. G. Henslow. With 88 Illustrations. 5s.

LXV. **On the Senses, Instincts, and Intelligence of Animals.** With special Reference to Insects. By Sir John Lubbock, Bart., M.P. 100 Illustrations. 5s.

## MILITARY WORKS.

*BRACKENBURY, Col. C. B., R.A.*—Military Handbooks for Regimental Officers.

   I. **Military Sketching and Reconnaissance.** By Col. F. J. Hutchison and Major H. G. MacGregor. Fifth Edition. With 16 Plates. Small crown 8vo, 4s.

   II. **The Elements of Modern Tactics Practically applied to English Formations.** By Lieut.-Col. Wilkinson Shaw. Sixth Edition. With 25 Plates and Maps. Small crown 8vo, 9s.

   III. **Field Artillery.** Its Equipment, Organization and Tactics. By Major Sisson C. Pratt, R.A. With 12 Plates. Third Edition. Small crown 8vo, 6s.

   IV. **The Elements of Military Administration.** First Part: Permanent System of Administration. By Major J. W. Buxton. Small crown 8vo, 7s. 6d.

   V. **Military Law:** Its Procedure and Practice. By Major Sisson C. Pratt, R.A. Third Edition. Revised. Small crown 8vo, 4s. 6d.

   VI. **Cavalry in Modern War.** By Major-General F. Chenevix Trench. Small crown 8vo, 6s.

   VII. **Field Works.** Their Technical Construction and Tactical Application. By the Editor, Col. C. B. Brackenbury, R.A. Small crown 8vo.

*BROOKE, Major, C. K.*—**A System of Field Training.** Small crown 8vo, cloth limp, 2s.

D

Campaign of Fredericksburg, November—December, 1862. A Study for Officers of Volunteers. By a Line Officer. With 5 Maps and Plans. Second Edition. Crown 8vo, 5*s*.

CLERY, *C. Francis, Col.*—Minor Tactics. With 26 Maps and Plans. Seventh Edition, Revised. Crown 8vo, 9*s*.

COLVILE, *Lieut.-Col. C. F.*—Military Tribunals. Sewed, 2*s*. 6*d*.

CRAUFURD, *Capt. H. J.*—Suggestions for the Military Training of a Company of Infantry. Crown 8vo, 1*s*. 6*d*.

HAMILTON, *Capt. Ian, A.D.C.*—The Fighting of the Future. 1*s*.

HARRISON, *Col. R.*—The Officer's Memorandum Book for Peace and War. Fourth Edition, Revised throughout. Oblong 32mo, red basil, with pencil, 3*s*. 6*d*.

Notes on Cavalry Tactics, Organisation, etc. By a Cavalry Officer. With Diagrams. Demy 8vo, 12*s*.

PARR, *Col. H. Hallam, C.M.G.*—The Dress, Horses, and Equipment of Infantry and Staff Officers. Crown 8vo, 1*s*.

Further Training and Equipment of Mounted Infantry. Crown 8vo, 1*s*.

SCHAW, *Col. H.*—The Defence and Attack of Positions and Localities. Third Edition, Revised and Corrected. Crown 8vo, 3*s*. 6*d*.

STONE, *Capt. F. Gleadowe, R.A.*—Tactical Studies from the Franco-German War of 1870-71. With 22 Lithographic Sketches and Maps. Demy 8vo, 10*s*. 6*d*.

WILKINSON, *H. Spenser, Capt. 20th Lancashire R.V.*—Citizen Soldiers. Essays towards the Improvement of the Volunteer Force. Crown 8vo, 2*s*. 6*d*.

## POETRY.

ADAM OF ST. VICTOR.—The Liturgical Poetry of Adam of St. Victor. From the text of GAUTIER. With Translations into English in the Original Metres, and Short Explanatory Notes, by DIGBY S. WRANGHAM, M.A. 3 vols. Crown 8vo, printed on hand-made paper, boards, 21*s*.

ALEXANDER, *William, D.D., Bishop of Derry.*—St. Augustine's Holiday, and other Poems. Crown 8vo, 6*s*.

AUCHMUTY, *A. C.*—Poems of English Heroism : From Brunanburh to Lucknow ; from Athelstan to Albert. Small crown 8vo, 1*s*. 6*d*.

*BARNES, William.*—**Poems of Rural Life, in the Dorset Dialect.** New Edition, complete in one vol. Crown 8vo, 6s.

*BAYNES, Rev. Canon H. R.*—**Home Songs for Quiet Hours.** Fourth and Cheaper Edition. Fcap. 8vo, cloth, 2s. 6d.

*BEVINGTON, L. S.*—**Key Notes.** Small crown 8vo, 5s.

*BLUNT, Wilfrid Scawen.*—**The Wind and the Whirlwind.** Demy 8vo, 1s. 6d.

**The Love Sonnets of Proteus.** Fifth Edition, 18mo. Cloth extra, gilt top, 5s.

**Book of Verse, A.** By J. R. W. Small crown 8vo, 2s. 6d.

*BOWEN, H. C., M.A.*—**Simple English Poems.** English Literature for Junior Classes. In Four Parts. Parts I., II., and III., 6d. each, and Part IV., 1s. Complete, 3s.

*BRYANT, W. C.*—**Poems.** Cheap Edition, with Frontispiece. Small crown 8vo, 3s. 6d.

**Calderon's Dramas:** the Wonder-Working Magician—Life is a Dream—the Purgatory of St. Patrick. Translated by DENIS FLORENCE MACCARTHY. Post 8vo, 10s.

**Camoens' Lusiads.**—Portuguese Text, with Translation by J. J. AUBERTIN. Second Edition. 2 vols. Crown 8vo, 12s.

*CAMPBELL, Lewis.*—**Sophocles.** The Seven Plays in English Verse. Crown 8vo, 7s. 6d.

*CHRISTIE, Albany J.*—**The End of Man.** Fourth Edition. Fcap. 8vo, 2s. 6d.

*COXHEAD, Ethel.*—**Birds and Babies.** With 33 Illustrations. Imp. 16mo, 1s.

**Dante's Divina Commedia.** Translated in the *Terza Rima* of Original, by F. K. H. HASELFOOT. Demy 8vo, 16s.

*DENNIS, J.*—**English Sonnets.** Collected and Arranged by. Small crown 8vo, 2s. 6d.

*DE VERE, Aubrey.*—**Poetical Works.**
   I. THE SEARCH AFTER PROSERPINE, etc. 6s.
   II. THE LEGENDS OF ST. PATRICK, etc. 6s.
   III. ALEXANDER THE GREAT, etc. 6s.

**The Foray of Queen Meave,** and other Legends of Ireland's Heroic Age. Small crown 8vo, 5s.

**Legends of the Saxon Saints.** Small crown 8vo, 6s.

**Legends and Records of the Church and the Empire.** Small crown 8vo, 6s.

*DOBSON, Austin.*—Old World Idylls and other Verses. Eighth Edition. Elzevir 8vo, gilt top, 6s.

At the Sign of the Lyre. Fifth Edition. Elzevir 8vo, gilt top, 6s.

Dorica. By E. D. S. Small crown 8vo, 5s.

*DOWDEN, Edward, LL.D.*—Shakspere's Sonnets. With Introduction and Notes. Large post 8vo, 7s. 6d.

*DUTT, Toru.*—A Sheaf Gleaned in French Fields. New Edition. Demy 8vo, 10s. 6d.

Ancient Ballads and Legends of Hindustan. With an Introductory Memoir by EDMUND GOSSE. Second Edition, 18mo. Cloth extra, gilt top, 5s.

*ELLIOTT, Ebenezer, The Corn Law Rhymer.*—Poems. Edited by his son, the Rev. EDWIN ELLIOTT, of St. John's, Antigua. 2 vols. Crown 8vo, 18s.

English Verse. Edited by W. J. LINTON and R. H. STODDARD. 5 vols. Crown 8vo, cloth, 5s. each.
 I. CHAUCER TO BURNS.
 II. TRANSLATIONS.
 III. LYRICS OF THE NINETEENTH CENTURY.
 IV. DRAMATIC SCENES AND CHARACTERS.
 V. BALLADS AND ROMANCES.

*GOSSE, Edmund.*—New Poems. Crown 8vo, 7s. 6d.

Firdausi in Exile, and other Poems. Second Edition. Elzevir 8vo, gilt top, 6s.

*GURNEY, Rev. Alfred.*—The Vision of the Eucharist, and other Poems. Crown 8vo, 5s.

A Christmas Faggot. Small crown 8vo, 5s.

*HAMILTON, Ian.*—The Ballad of Hadji, and other Poems. With Frontispiece and Vignettes. Elzevir 8vo, 3s. 6d.

*HARRISON, Clifford.*—In Hours of Leisure. Second Edition. Crown 8vo, 5s.

*HEYWOOD, J. C.*—Herodias, a Dramatic Poem. New Edition, Revised. Small crown 8vo, 5s.

Antonius. A Dramatic Poem. New Edition, Revised. Small crown 8vo, 5s.

Salome. A Dramatic Poem. Small crown 8vo, 5s.

*HICKEY, E. H.*—A Sculptor, and other Poems. Small crown 8vo, 5s.

*KEATS, John.*—Poetical Works. Edited by W. T. ARNOLD. Large crown 8vo, choicely printed on hand-made paper, with Portrait in *eau-forte*. Parchment or cloth, 12s.; vellum, 15s. New Edition, crown 8vo, cloth, 3s. 6d.

*KING, Mrs. Hamilton.*—**The Disciples.** Ninth Edition. Small crown 8vo, 5*s.* ; Elzevir Edition, cloth extra, 6*s.*

**A Book of Dreams.** Third Edition. Crown 8vo, 3*s.* 6*d.*

**The Sermon in the Hospital** (From " The Dimples "). Fcap. 8vo, 1*s.* Cheap Edition for distribution 3*d.*, or 20*s.* per 100.

*LANG, A.*—**XXXII. Ballades in Blue China.** Elzevir 8vo, 5*s.*

**Rhymes à la Mode.** With Frontispiece by E. A. Abbey. Second Edition. Elzevir 8vo, cloth extra, gilt top, 5*s.*

*LAWSON, Right Hon. Mr. Justice.*—**Hymni Usitati Latine Redditi**: with other Verses. Small 8vo, parchment, 5*s.*

**Living English Poets MDCCCLXXXII.** With Frontispiece by Walter Crane. Second Edition. Large crown 8vo. Printed on hand-made paper. Parchment or cloth, 12*s.* ; vellum, 15*s.*

*LOCKER, F.*—**London Lyrics.** Tenth Edition. With Portrait, Elzevir 8vo. Cloth extra, gilt top, 5*s.*

**Love in Idleness.** A Volume of Poems. With an Etching by W. B. Scott. Small crown 8vo, 5*s.*

*MAGNUSSON, Eirikr, M.A., and PALMER, E. H., M.A.*—**Johan Ludvig Runeberg's Lyrical Songs, Idylls, and Epigrams.** Fcap. 8vo, 5*s.*

**Matin Songs.** Small crown 8vo, 2*s.*

*MEREDITH, Owen [The Earl of Lytton].*—**Lucile.** New Edition. With 32 Illustrations. 16mo, 3*s.* 6*d.* Cloth extra, gilt edges, 4*s.* 6*d.*

*MORRIS, Lewis.*—**Poetical Works of.** New and Cheaper Editions, with Portrait. Complete in 3 vols., 5*s.* each.
Vol. I. contains "Songs of Two Worlds." Twelfth Edition.
Vol. II. contains " The Epic of Hades." Twenty-second Edition.
Vol. III. contains "Gwen" and "The Ode of Life." Seventh Edition.
Vol. IV. contains " Songs Unsung " and " Gycia." Fifth Edition.

**Songs of Britain.** Third Edition. Fcap. 8vo, 5*s.*

**The Epic of Hades.** With 16 Autotype Illustrations, after the Drawings of the late George R. Chapman. 4to, cloth extra, gilt leaves, 21*s.*

**The Epic of Hades.** Presentation Edition. 4to, cloth extra, gilt leaves, 10*s.* 6*d.*

**The Lewis Morris Birthday Book.** Edited by S. S. COPEMAN, with Frontispiece after a Design by the late George R. Chapman. 32mo, cloth extra, gilt edges, 2*s.* ; cloth limp, 1*s.* 6*d.*

*MORSHEAD, E. D. A.*—**The House of Atreus.** Being the Agamemnon, Libation-Bearers, and Furies of Æschylus. Translated into English Verse. Crown 8vo, 7*s.*

*MORSHEAD, E. D. A.—continued.*

    The Suppliant Maidens of Æschylus. Crown 8vo, 3s. 6d.

*MULHOLLAND, Rosa.*—Vagrant Verses. Small crown 8vo, 5s.

*NADEN, Constance C. W.*—A Modern Apostle, and other Poems. Small crown 8vo, 5s.

*NOEL, The Hon. Roden.*—A Little Child's Monument. Third Edition. Small crown 8vo, 3s. 6d.

    The House of Ravensburg. New Edition. Small crown 8vo, 6s.

    The Red Flag, and other Poems. New Edition. Small crown 8vo, 6s.

    Songs of the Heights and Deeps. Crown 8vo, 6s.

*O'HAGAN, John.*—The Song of Roland. Translated into English Verse. New and Cheaper Edition. Crown 8vo, 5s.

*PFEIFFER, Emily.*—The Rhyme of the Lady of the Rock, and How it Grew. Second Edition. Small crown 8vo, 3s. 6d.

    Gerard's Monument, and other Poems. Second Edition. Crown 8vo, 6s.

    Under the Aspens: Lyrical and Dramatic. With Portrait. Crown 8vo, 6s.

**Rare Poems of the 16th and 17th Centuries.** Edited by W. J. LINTON. Crown 8vo, 5s.

*RHOADES, James.*—The Georgics of Virgil. Translated into English Verse. Small crown 8vo, 5s.

    Poems. Small crown 8vo, 4s. 6d.

    Dux Redux. A Forest Tangle. Small crown 8vo, 3s. 6d.

*ROBINSON, A. Mary F.*—A Handful of Honeysuckle. Fcap. 8vo, 3s. 6d.

    The Crowned Hippolytus. Translated from Euripides. With New Poems. Small crown 8vo, 5s.

*SCOTT, Fredk. George.*—The Soul's Quest. Small crown 8vo.

*SHARP, Isaac.*—Saul of Tarsus, and other Poems. Small crown 8vo, 2s. 6d.

*SMITH, J. W. Gilbart.*—The Loves of Vandyck. A Tale of Genoa. Small crown 8vo, 2s. 6d.

    The Log o' the "Norseman." Small crown 8vo, 5s.

    Serbelloni. Small crown 8vo, 5s.

**Sophocles: The Seven Plays in English Verse.** Translated by LEWIS CAMPBELL. Crown 8vo, 7s. 6d.

*SYMONDS, John Addington.*—Vagabunduli Libellus. Crown 8vo, 6s.

Tasso's Jerusalem Delivered. Translated by Sir JOHN KINGSTON JAMES, Bart. Two Volumes. Printed on hand-made paper, parchment, bevelled boards. Large crown 8vo, 21s.

*TAYLOR, Sir H.*—Works. Complete in Five Volumes. Crown 8vo, 30s.

   Philip Van Artevelde. Fcap. 8vo, 3s. 6d.

   The Virgin Widow, etc. Fcap. 8vo, 3s. 6d.

*TODHUNTER, Dr. J.*—Laurella, and other Poems. Crown 8vo, 6s. 6d.

   Forest Songs. Small crown 8vo, 3s. 6d.

   The True Tragedy of Rienzi: a Drama. 3s. 6d.

   Alcestis: a Dramatic Poem. Extra fcap. 8vo, 5s.

   Helena in Troas. Small crown 8vo, 2s. 6d.

   The Banshee, and other Poems. Small crown 8vo, 3s. 6d.

*TYNAN, Katherine.*—Louise de la Valliere, and other Poems. Small crown 8vo, 3s. 6d.

   Shamrocks. Small crown 8vo, 5s.

*TYRER, C. E.*—Fifty Sonnets. Small crown 8vo, 1s. 6d.

Victorian Hymns: English Sacred Songs of Fifty Years. Dedicated to the Queen. Large post 8vo, 10s. 6d.

*WILLIS, E. Cooper, Q.C.*—Tales and Legends in Verse. Small crown 8vo, 3s. 6d.

Wordsworth Birthday Book, The. Edited by ADELAIDE and VIOLET WORDSWORTH. 32mo, limp cloth, 1s. 6d.; cloth extra, 2s.

## NOVELS AND TALES.

*BANKS, Mrs. G. L.*—God's Providence House. Crown 8vo, 6s.

*CHICHELE, Mary.*—Doing and Undoing. A Story. Crown 8vo. 4s. 6d.

*CRAWFURD, Oswald.*—Sylvia Arden. With Frontispiece. Crown 8vo, 6s.

*GARDINER, Linda.*—His Heritage. With Frontispiece. Crown 8vo, 6s.

*GRAY, Maxwell.*—The Silence of Dean Maitland. Fifteenth thousand. With Frontispiece. Crown 8vo, 6s.

*GREY, Rowland.*—In Sunny Switzerland. A Tale of Six Weeks. Second Edition. Small crown 8vo, 5s.

GREY, *Rowland.—continued.*
    Lindenblumen and other Stories. Small crown 8vo, 5s.
    By Virtue of his Office. Crown 8vo, 6s.

*HUNTER, Hay.*—The Crime of Christmas Day. A Tale of the Latin Quarter. By the Author of "My Ducats and my Daughter." 1s.

*HUNTER, Hay, and WHYTE, Walter.*—My Ducats and My Daughter. With Frontispiece. Crown 8vo, 6s.

*INGELOW, Jean.*—Off the Skelligs: a Novel. With Frontispiece. Crown 8vo, 6s.

*JENKINS, Edward.*—A Secret of Two Lives. Crown 8vo, 2s. 6d.

*KIELLAND, Alexander L.*—Garman and Worse. A Norwegian Novel. Authorized Translation, by W. W. Kettlewell. Crown 8vo, 6s.

*LANG, Andrew.*—In the Wrong Paradise, and other Stories. Crown 8vo, 6s.

*MACDONALD, G.*—Donal Grant. A Novel. With Frontispiece. Crown 8vo, 6s.

    Home Again. With Frontispiece. Crown 8vo, 6s.

    Castle Warlock. A Novel. With Frontispiece. Crown 8vo, 6s.

    Malcolm. With Portrait of the Author engraved on Steel. Crown 8vo, 6s.

    The Marquis of Lossie. With Frontispiece. Crown 8vo, 6s.

    St. George and St. Michael. With Frontispiece. Crown 8vo, 6s.

    What's Mine's Mine. With Frontispiece. Crown 8vo, 6s.

    Annals of a Quiet Neighbourhood. With Frontispiece. Crown 8vo, 6s.

    The Seaboard Parish: a Sequel to "Annals of a Quiet Neighbourhood." With Frontispiece. Crown 8vo, 6s.

    Wilfred Cumbermede. An Autobiographical Story. With Frontispiece. Crown 8vo, 6s.

    Thomas Wingfold, Curate. With Frontispiece. Crown 8vo, 6s.

    Paul Faber, Surgeon. With Frontispiece. Crown 8vo, 6s.

    The Elect Lady. With Frontispiece. Crown 8vo, 6s.

*MALET, Lucas.*—Colonel Enderby's Wife. A Novel. With Frontispiece. Crown 8vo, 6s.

    A Counsel of Perfection. With Frontispiece. Crown 8vo, 6s.

*MULHOLLAND, Rosa.*—Marcella Grace. An Irish Novel. Crown 8vo. 6s.

*OGLE, Anna C.*—A Lost Love. Small crown 8vo, 2s. 6d.

*PALGRAVE, W. Gifford.*—Hermann Agha: an Eastern Narrative. Crown 8vo, 6s.

Romance of the Recusants. By the Author of "Life of a Prig." Crown 8vo, 5s.

*SEVERNE, Florence.*—The Pillar House. With Frontispiece. Crown 8vo, 6s.

*SHAW, Flora L.*—Castle Blair: a Story of Youthful Days. Crown 8vo, 3s. 6d.

*STRETTON, Hesba.*—Through a Needle's Eye: a Story. With Frontispiece. Crown 8vo, 6s.

*TAYLOR, Col. Meadows, C.S.I., M.R.I.A.*—Seeta: a Novel. With Frontispiece. Crown 8vo, 6s.

    Tippoo Sultaun: a Tale of the Mysore War. With Frontispiece. Crown 8vo, 6s.

    Ralph Darnell. With Frontispiece. Crown 8vo, 6s.

    A Noble Queen. With Frontispiece. Crown 8vo, 6s.

    The Confessions of a Thug. With Frontispiece. Crown 8vo, 6s.

    Tara: a Mahratta Tale. With Frontispiece. Crown 8vo, 6s.

Within Sound of the Sea. With Frontispiece. Crown 8vo, 6s.

## BOOKS FOR THE YOUNG.

Brave Men's Footsteps. A Book of Example and Anecdote for Young People. By the Editor of "Men who have Risen." With 4 Illustrations by C. Doyle. Ninth Edition. Crown 8vo, 2s. 6d.

*COXHEAD, Ethel.*—Birds and Babies. With 33 Illustrations. Second Edition. Imp. 16mo, cloth, 1s.

*DAVIES, G. Christopher.*—Rambles and Adventures of our School Field Club. With 4 Illustrations. New and Cheaper Edition. Crown 8vo, 3s. 6d.

*EDMONDS, Herbert.*—Well Spent Lives: a Series of Modern Biographies. New and Cheaper Edition. Crown 8vo, 3s. 6d.

*EVANS, Mark.*—The Story of our Father's Love, told to Children. Sixth and Cheaper Edition of Theology for Children. With 4 Illustrations. Fcap. 8vo, 1s. 6d.

*MAC KENNA, S. J.*—Plucky Fellows. A Book for Boys. With 6 Illustrations. Fifth Edition. Crown 8vo, 3s. 6d.

*MALET, Lucas.*—**Little Peter.** A Christmas Morality for Children of any Age. With numerous Illustrations. Fourth thousand. 5*s.*

*REANEY, Mrs. G. S.*—**Waking and Working**; or, From Girlhood to Womanhood. New and Cheaper Edition. With a Frontispiece. Crown 8vo, 3*s.* 6*d.*

**Blessing and Blessed**: a Sketch of Girl Life. New and Cheaper Edition. Crown 8vo, 3*s.* 6*d.*

**Rose Gurney's Discovery.** A Story for Girls. Dedicated to their Mothers. Crown 8vo, 3*s.* 6*d.*

**English Girls**: Their Place and Power. With Preface by the Rev. R. W. Dale. Fifth Edition. Fcap. 8vo, 2*s.* 6*d.*

**Just Anyone,** and other Stories. Three Illustrations. Royal 16mo, 1*s.* 6*d.*

**Sunbeam Willie,** and other Stories. Three Illustrations. Royal 16mo, 1*s.* 6*d.*

**Sunshine Jenny,** and other Stories. Three Illustrations. Royal 16mo, 1*s.* 6*d.*

*STORR, Francis, and TURNER, Hawes.*—**Canterbury Chimes**; or, Chaucer Tales re-told to Children. With 6 Illustrations from the Ellesmere Manuscript. Third Edition. Fcap. 8vo, 3*s.* 6*d.*

*STRETTON, Hesba.*—**David Lloyd's Last Will.** With 4 Illustrations. New Edition. Royal 16mo, 2*s.* 6*d.*

*WHITAKER, Florence.*—**Christy's Inheritance.** A London Story, Illustrated. Royal 16mo, 1*s.* 6*d.*

MESSRS.

# KEGAN PAUL, TRENCH & CO.'S

EDITIONS OF

# SHAKSPERE'S WORKS.

*THE PARCHMENT LIBRARY EDITION.*

*THE AVON EDITION.*

*The Text of these Editions is mainly that of Delius. Wherever a variant reading is adopted, some good and recognized Shaksperian Critic has been followed. In no case is a new rendering of the text proposed; nor has it been thought necessary to distract the reader's attention by notes or comments.*

1, PATERNOSTER SQUARE.

[P. T. O.

# SHAKSPERE'S WORKS.

## THE PARCHMENT LIBRARY EDITION.

In 12 volumes Elzevir 8vo., choicely printed on hand-made paper, and bound in parchment or cloth, price £3 12s., or in vellum, price £4 10s.

The set of 12 volumes may also be had in a strong cloth box, price £3 17s., or with an oak hanging shelf, £3 18s.

### SOME PRESS NOTICES.

". . . There is, perhaps, no edition in which the works of Shakspere can be read in such luxury of type and quiet distinction of form as this, and we warmly recommend it."—*Pall Mall Gazette.*

"For elegance of form and beauty of typography, no edition of Shakspere hitherto published has excelled the 'Parchment Library Edition.' . . . They are in the strictest sense pocket volumes, yet the type is bold, and, being on fine white hand-made paper, can hardly tax the weakest of sight. The print is judiciously confined to the text, notes being more appropriate to library editions. The whole will be comprised in the cream-coloured parchment which gives the name to the series."—*Daily News.*

"The Parchment Library Edition of Shakspere needs no further praise."—*Saturday Review.*

---

*Just published. Price* 5s.

## AN INDEX TO THE WORKS OF SHAKSPERE.

Applicable to all editions of Shakspere, and giving reference, by topics, to notable passages and significant expressions; brief histories of the plays; geographical names and historic incidents; mention of all characters and sketches of important ones; together with explanations of allusions and obscure and obsolete words and phrases.

### By EVANGELINE M. O'CONNOR.

---

LONDON: KEGAN PAUL, TRENCH & CO., 1, PATERNOSTER SQUARE.

# SHAKSPERE'S WORKS.

## *THE AVON EDITION.*

Printed on thin opaque paper, and forming 12 handy volumes, cloth, 18s., or bound in 6 volumes, 15s.

The set of 12 volumes may also be had in a cloth box, price 21s., or bound in Roan, Persian, Crushed Persian Levant, Calf, or Morocco, and enclosed in an attractive leather box at prices from 31s. 6d. upwards.

## SOME PRESS NOTICES.

"This edition will be useful to those who want a good text, well and clearly printed, in convenient little volumes that will slip easily into an overcoat pocket or a travelling-bag."—*St. James's Gazette.*

"We know no prettier edition of Shakspere for the price."—*Academy.*

"It is refreshing to meet with an edition of Shakspere of convenient size and low price, without either notes or introductions of any sort to distract the attention of the reader."—*Saturday Review.*

"It is exquisite. Each volume is handy, is beautifully printed, and in every way lends itself to the taste of the cultivated student of Shakspere."—*Scotsman.*

---

LONDON: KEGAN PAUL, TRENCH & CO., 1, PATERNOSTER SQUARE.

# SHAKSPERE'S WORKS.

## SPECIMEN OF TYPE.

4        *THE MERCHANT OF VENICE*     Act 1

*Salar.*            My wind, cooling my broth,
Would blow me to an ague, when I thought
What harm a wind too great might do at sea.
I should not see the sandy hour-glass run
But I should think of shallows and of flats,
And see my wealthy Andrew, dock'd in sand,
Vailing her high-top lower than her ribs
To kiss her burial. Should I go to church
And see the holy edifice of stone,
And not bethink me straight of dangerous rocks,
Which touching but my gentle vessel's side,
Would scatter all her spices on the stream,
Enrobe the roaring waters with my silks,
And, in a word, but even now worth this,
And now worth nothing? Shall I have the thought
To think on this, and shall I lack the thought
That such a thing bechanc'd would make me sad?
But tell not me: I know Antonio
Is sad to think upon his merchandise.
   *Ant.* Believe me, no: I thank my fortune for it,
My ventures are not in one bottom trusted,
Nor to one place; nor is my whole estate
Upon the fortune of this present year:
Therefore my merchandise makes me not sad.
   *Salar.* Why, then you are in love.
   *Ant.*                      Fie, fie!
   *Salar.* Not in love neither? Then let us say you
      are sad,
Because you are not merry; and 'twere as easy
For you to laugh, and leap, and say you are merry,
Because you are not sad. Now, by two-headed
      Janus,
Nature hath fram'd strange fellows in her time:
Some that will evermore peep through their eyes
And laugh like parrots at a bag-piper;
And other of such vinegar aspect

LONDON: KEGAN PAUL, TRENCH & CO., 1, PATERNOSTER SQUARE.

www.ingramcontent.com/pod-product-compliance
Lightning Source LLC
Chambersburg PA
CBHW022109290426
**44112CB00008B/609**